AMERICAN JESUITS
AND THE WORLD

Princeton University Press
PRINCETON AND OXFORD

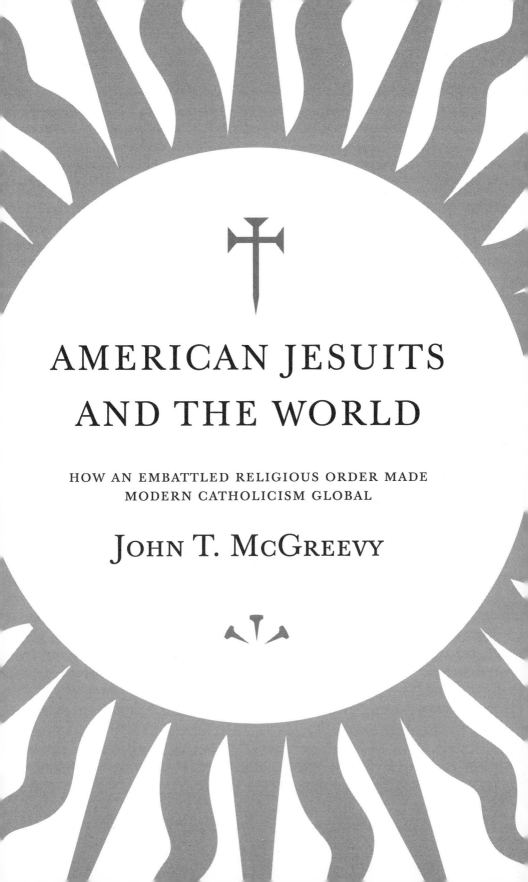

AMERICAN JESUITS
AND THE WORLD

HOW AN EMBATTLED RELIGIOUS ORDER MADE
MODERN CATHOLICISM GLOBAL

JOHN T. MCGREEVY

Requests for permission to reproduce material
from this work should be sent to Permissions,
Princeton University Press

Published by Princeton University Press,
41 William Street, Princeton, New Jersey 08540

In the United Kingdom: Princeton University Press,
6 Oxford Street, Woodstock, Oxfordshire OX20 1TW

press.princeton.edu

Jacket art: 1799 Map of the World, courtesy of World Trade Press:
Copyright © 2015 World Trade Press.

ISBN 978-0-691-17162-3

Library of Congress Cataloging-in-Publication Data

Names: McGreevy, John T., author.
Title: American Jesuits and the world : how an embattled religious order made
    modern Catholicism global / John T. McGreevy.
Description: Princeton, NJ : Princeton University Press, 2016. | Includes
    bibliographical references and index.
Identifiers: LCCN 2016013493 | ISBN 9780691171623 (hardcover : alk. paper)
Subjects: LCSH: Jesuits—United States—History. | Jesuits. | Globalization—
    Religious aspects—Catholic Church.
Classification: LCC BX3708 .M34 2016 | DDC 271/.5302—dc23 LC record available
    at http://lccn.loc.gov/2016013493

British Library Cataloging-in-Publication Data is available

This book has been composed in Baskerville 10 Pro

Printed on acid-free paper. ∞

Printed in the United States of America

10 9 8 7 6 5 4 3 2 1

CONTENTS

ILLUSTRATIONS

AMERICAN JESUITS
AND THE WORLD

INTRODUCTION

I do not like the late Resurrection of the Jesuits. They have a General, now in Russia, in correspondence with the Jesuits in the U.S. who are more numerous than every body knows. Shall we not have Swarms of them here? . . . If ever any Congregation of Men could merit, eternal Perdition on Earth and in Hell . . . it is this Company of Loiola. Our System however of Religious Liberty must afford them an Asylum. But if they do not put the Purity of our Elections to a severe Tryal, it will be a Wonder.

—JOHN ADAMS TO THOMAS JEFFERSON, MAY 6, 1816

I dislike, with you, their restoration; because it marks a retrograde step from light toward darkness.

—THOMAS JEFFERSON TO JOHN ADAMS, AUGUST 1, 1816

This Society has been a greater Calamity to Mankind than the French Revolution or Napoleon's Despotism or Ideology. It has obstructed the Progress of Reformation and the Improvement of the human mind in society much longer and more fatally.

—JOHN ADAMS TO THOMAS JEFFERSON, NOVEMBER 4, 1816

I

The suppression of the Jesuits (or Society of Jesus) in 1773 by Pope Clement XIV does not appear in US history textbooks. It is a puzzling event, with Catholic monarchs pressuring the pope to abolish a religious order perceived as excessively loyal to the papacy. Forty-one years later another pope, Pius VII, reversed course and restored the Jesuits, provoking an anxious exchange between two provincial Enlightenment intellectuals (and former US presidents). John Adams was sufficiently exercised about the

Jesuit restoration to compose two essays on the topic, lamenting the "surprise, deception and violence" employed by the Society.[1]

American Jesuits and the World begins where Adams and Thomas Jefferson end. It tracks some of the roughly one thousand Jesuits who left Europe for the United States over the course of the nineteenth century as well as American Jesuits who left for mission territories in the early twentieth century.

The significance of the Jesuits to either the history of modern Catholicism or the history of the United States was not predictable—certainly not at the moment of the Jesuit restoration in 1814. Then the Society counted only six hundred aged members; a century later the Jesuits numbered close to seventeen thousand men.[2] These Jesuits had become allies and admirers of Pope Pius IX (1846–78). They had become even more influential during the papacy of Leo XIII (1878–1903), whose closest advisers included a brother who was a Jesuit. Other priests, nuns, laypeople, and bishops of course led the burst of missionary activity and institution building that historians now term the nineteenth-century Catholic revival.[3] But no other group possessed the Jesuit reach, from the Roman Curia to hundreds of schools and colleges and far-flung mission stations.[4]

These Jesuits desired not just the expansion of Catholicism but its uniformity. Their orientation toward Rome as the focal point of a global Catholic community made daily Catholic life across the world more similar in 1914 than in 1814. Eighteenth-century Catholics, especially in majority Protestant or non-Catholic societies, worshipped discreetly and quietly catechized their young. Nineteenth-century Catholics, often led by Jesuits, disdained other religious traditions and cultivated Catholic distinctiveness. When an exiled Swiss Jesuit organized a youth group for boys in Boston in 1858 he and the boys proudly identified themselves as "communing" with counterparts in Rome.[5]

These same Jesuits became central to the nationalist imagination. The emergence of the modern nation-state in the nineteenth century is a conventional textbook story, with Italy, Germany, Mexico, France, the United States, and other countries developing stronger national governments, funding systems of education, and cultivating identification with a nation's history and culture, as opposed to the history and culture of a particular region.[6] A Catholicism centered in Rome and unaccountable to national leaders, and the Jesuits as an international religious order managing independent colleges and schools, threatened nationalist projects. Politicians and intellectuals around the world worried that the Jesuits would, in the words of one Mexico City editor, "detain the course of the century."[7]

These worries prompted government officials to expel the Jesuits, often multiple times, from Switzerland, various parts of modern-day Italy (including Rome, Piedmont, and Naples), Colombia, Uruguay, Ecuador, El Salvador, Costa Rica, Peru, Austria, Spain, Germany, Guatemala, France, and Nicaragua. In Mexico, a liberal government expelled "foreign-born" Jesuits.[8] The Jesuits were not expelled from Canada, Britain, and Australia, but leading politicians and prominent writers in all of these countries denounced them. Or as one Maryland legislator (and future US senator) explained, "The Jesuits have been successfully expelled from nearly every Catholic kingdom in Europe because they would meddle in political intrigues. We have no reason to wonder that they have not neglected so tempting a field as our free institutions open to their arts."[9]

This hostility prompted Jesuits and their allies to accelerate the building of a dense Catholic subculture of parishes, schools, associations, colleges, and magazines, all constructed in a reciprocal relationship with a particular devotional culture and communal sensibility. This social imaginary, to use the language of philosopher Charles Taylor, endured through the 1960s and profoundly shaped how Catholics understood the world around them.[10] And in part for this reason Catholics and Protestants in majority Protestant countries such as the United States, Germany, and the Netherlands as well as Catholics and anticlericals in France, Italy, and much of Latin America became more segregated from each other over the course of the nineteenth century, not less. Even Chinese Catholics, a tiny minority among a sea of non-Christians, developed closer ties to Rome. What in the eighteenth century remained local disputes, between Catholics and non-Catholics, or among Catholics themselves, became measured against heightened Roman standards of orthodoxy and parallel disputes across the globe. The polemics that resulted from a more tightly defined religious identity typically did not lead to violence—a welcome restraint when compared to the Reformation era. But religious divisions structured a new confessional age.[11]

This more confessional age was also more global. If Jesuits journeying to Manila, Havana, and Lima soon after the Society's founding by Ignatius of Loyola in 1540 made Catholicism the first world religion, the nineteenth century marked another leap forward in global range.[12] In the 1830s and 1840s alone, the Society established new missions in Syria (1831), Calcutta (1834), Argentina (1836), Madurai (1837), Nanking (1841), Canada (1842), Madagascar (1844), Algeria (1848), and Australia (1848).[13] Tiny Luxembourg sent Jesuit missionaries to Africa, South Asia, China, North America, and South America.[14]

This book uses European Jesuits emigrating to the United States and some American Jesuits working beyond American borders to examine how Catholic globalization worked. The US focus stems from accessibility to archives and my own linguistic capacities. But since the United States was such an important site for Jesuit work, drawing more Jesuits from around the world than any other place in the nineteenth century, the choice is less idiosyncratic than it might appear. The Jesuit protagonists of this book are "American" in that they all lived and worked in the United States. Yet they all lived and worked outside the United States for long periods too.

In fact, more than most of their contemporaries, more than almost any of ours, these Jesuits lived in nation-states, including the United States, but were not entirely of them. The Jesuit Father General or leader, Jan Roothaan, grew up in the Netherlands before sojourns in Saint Petersburg, Switzerland, and Turin. By then he had "stopped being a Hollander." In fact, "I have been since then a Pole or a Russian, then a Swiss, or a German, or a Frenchman, according to needs, and now I am an Italian."[15] At various moments in the nineteenth century, up to half of German Jesuits worked outside Germany; a third of French Jesuits worked outside France. In 1902, a full 26 percent of Jesuits worked in foreign missions.[16] Jesuits from particular European houses saw themselves and their friends sent to utterly distant locales based on the exigencies of expulsion and the needs of the Society at a particular moment: Madagascar or Beirut, Cleveland or Quito.

Every Jesuit expulsion led to a scattering of Jesuits, with men expelled from Austria in 1848 landing in Australia, men expelled from Spain in 1868 heading to Colombia and the Philippines, and men expelled from Germany in 1871 journeying to England and Ecuador. The most significant migration of Jesuits to the United States occurred after the 1848 revolutions as Father General Roothaan struggled to place Jesuits expelled from Europe. By the 1870s, Jesuits from Turin worked in San Francisco and among the Blackfeet Indians in the Rocky Mountains; Jesuits from Naples worked in New Mexico and as professors at the theologate for advanced Jesuit seminarians in Maryland; Jesuits from Paris worked in New York City along with the Yukon and Klondike regions in Alaska; Jesuits from Belgium worked in central Missouri and the Pacific Northwest; Jesuits from Lyon worked in New Orleans, Tampa, and El Paso; Jesuits from Germany worked on Indian reservations in the Dakota territory as well as Saint Louis, Milwaukee, Chicago, and Buffalo; Jesuits from Switzerland worked up and down the East Coast, on Indian reservations in Kansas and the Dakota territory, and in Saint Louis, Cincinnati, and Boston. A handful of Jesuits from Poland eventually came to Nebraska and various cities on the East Coast, and a few Jesuits came from Portugal to New England fishing towns. A group of Jesuits expelled from Mexico spent a decade working in Texas.

The intensity of the connections between these Jesuits and colleagues in Rome and their countries of origin distinguishes them from their sixteenth- and seventeenth-century predecessors. All of the world's great religious traditions became more self-conscious about doctrine and uniform practice in the nineteenth century, as speedier travel and new communication technologies permitted more frequent contact with coreligionists. Jesuits in Saint Louis, for example, pleaded with their Roman colleagues to use the telegraph,

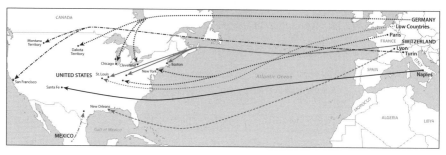

MAP 1. Jesuit Migration to the United States, 1820s–80s

not the slower postal service, to alert them to developments at the First Vatican Council.[17]

Here historians of Catholicism can make a distinctive contribution. Certainly Protestant revivalists crisscrossed not only Europe and North America but also once-remote locales such as Australia and South Africa. Certainly, too, Muslim scholars created new communities reaching from Istanbul to Cairo to Calcutta.[18]

In contrast to Protestantism or Islam, however, modern Catholicism included not just transient networks of individuals moving across the globe but an increasingly powerful central institution. The Jesuit Father General lived in Rome, when not in exile, surrounded by Jesuit assistants from varied national backgrounds monitoring, advising, and at times ordering colleagues across the world. Similarly, the bureaucratic and symbolic reach of the papacy expanded, in part as a reaction to expanded governmental authority in nation-states. More vigorous Roman offices for doctrine, canon law, and missionary work emerged, along with a diplomatic corps staffed by ambassadors (termed envoys or nuncios). If the papacy was an abstraction to most eighteenth-century Catholics, Jesuits and their allies made the embattled nineteenth-century popes known across the Catholic world. The Coeur D'Alene Indians, dwelling in the most remote section of what is now Montana and Idaho, organized themselves in 1871, with the aid of an exiled Italian Jesuit, to declare their willingness to "spill their blood and give their lives for our good Father

Pius IX." The allure of studying a corporate body such as the Jesuits is to do history in multiple registers, moving from local religious experience to the modern nation-state to the world's most multicultural and multilingual institution.[19]

Chapter 1 surveys the history of the nineteenth-century Jesuits and that of their critics. Each subsequent chapter tells the story of a revealing event. The events include the tarring and feathering of a Swiss Jesuit in Maine, an accusation of treason made against a Belgian Jesuit in civil-war Missouri, a woman claiming a miraculous healing in rural Louisiana and the promotion of that miracle by French Jesuits, the construction of one of Philadelphia's largest churches and a Jesuit college by a Swiss Jesuit, and finally, the educational efforts of American and Spanish Jesuits in early twentieth-century Manila. The conclusion sketches the global history of the Jesuits until Pope Francis, elected in 2013 as not only the first Jesuit Pope but also the first modern pope from outside Europe.

Once told in Jesuit rectories and periodicals, these stories are now largely forgotten.[20] But they merit more than parochial concern. Some of the issues confronted by these Jesuits, notably the meaning of religious liberty in a pluralist age, bedevil us still. And the sheer presence of Jesuits in the United States alerts us to ideas and institutions in tension with a "liberal tradition" once thought all encompassing. Oddly enough, then, the Latin textbooks, miracle accounts, scholarly articles, sermons, travelogues, devotions to the Sacred Heart, educational treatises, and baroque churches of the Jesuits may help place the history of the United States into a more global frame.[21]

NINETEENTH-CENTURY
JESUITS AND THEIR CRITICS

I

Hostility toward the Jesuits first reached British North America in the seventeenth century as an extension of European political and religious conflicts. The leaders of the Massachusetts Bay Colony, taking into account the "the great warrs & combustions which are this day in Europe" and blaming this discord "on the secret practices of those of the Jesuiticall order," prohibited Jesuits from entering the colony in 1647, with town officials in Salem describing them as the "terror of the Protestant world." In Virginia, colonists worried about Jesuits fomenting rebellion among local Indians. In Massachusetts and New York, colonists banned the Jesuits, with New York authorities deeming them "disturber[s] of the public peace" meriting "perpetual imprisonment."[1]

These fears were abstract. At the time of the suppression, thousands of Jesuits ran many of the most important educational institutions in Europe and Latin America. North America was different. Only twenty-five Jesuits lived in the British North American colonies in the 1760s, with perhaps an equal number in French Louisiana, on the Illinois prairie, and in Spanish California. Because of legal restrictions on their public activities, Jesuits in the British colonies kept a low profile, evading unwanted attention by wearing standard gentlemen's dress instead of clerical robes, addressing one another as "Mr." and not "Fr.," and building their churches on side streets. Philadelphia's most prominent resident, Benjamin Franklin, working in Paris, negotiated directly with anxious papal representatives to name the first American bishop, ex-Jesuit John Carroll. But even in Franklin's Philadelphia, Jesuits bemoaned the limited freedom "enjoyed by us."[2]

In 1805, ex-Jesuits living in the United States quietly affiliated themselves with Jesuits living in Russia, where Catherine the Great was disinclined to obey papal edicts and permitted Jesuits to maintain their colleges and residences. In 1814, Bishop Carroll, who had personally witnessed the "catastrophe" of the Jesuit suppression in 1773 while training for the priesthood in Bruges, expressed "joy and thanksgiving" at the restoration of the Society by Pope Pius VII.[3]

Still, Jesuit influence within the new United States remained modest. That changed when in one of the great migrations of modern history sixty million Europeans left the continent in the nineteenth and early twentieth centuries. The Catholic portion of the migration was immense—probably over half—and was led in sequence by immigrants from Ireland, Germany, Italy, and Poland.[4]

The single-largest group of migrants made their way to the United States. Just 3 percent of the American population in 1830, Catholics numbered 18 percent of the population by 1900. This "continual inpouring of Catholic immigrants from almost all of the countries of Europe," in the words of one Jesuit observer, transformed the tiny Catholic Church in the United States into the nation's single-largest religious organization.[5] By the 1840s, Father General Roothaan found himself continually appealing to European Catholic monarchs and missionary societies for funds to support Jesuits willing to work with Catholic immigrants in the United States.[6]

Some Jesuits volunteered for missionary service. A larger number were pushed. The first wave of expulsions began in Russia and the Netherlands, and was followed by expulsions from Spain, Naples, France, and Portugal. These initial expulsions were the lingering aftershocks of the eighteenth-century controversies between

Jesuits and their theological opponents that had resulted in the 1773 suppression. Often, the Jesuits became pawns in a contest between the papacy and Catholic monarchs. The expulsions were frequently brief, quickly followed by negotiations for the Jesuits' return.

Liberal nationalists sparked the second wave of Jesuit expulsions, beginning in the 1840s, with politicians, ministers, and popular novelists drawing on older anti-Jesuit tropes and texts, but now also portraying the Jesuits as conspirators against national unity and the ideal of progress that so captivated educated men and women.[7] An initial trigger for this second wave of Jesuit expulsions was Eugène Sue's 1844 novel, *Le Juif Errant*, first serialized in leading French newspapers, and one of the century's best sellers not simply in France but also across the globe. Despite the title—"The Wandering Jew"—the plot revolved less around Jews than crafty Jesuits uniting from all corners of the globe to maneuver a vast fortune away from an honorable but needy French Protestant family. In Colombia, legislators referenced the novel in an ultimately successful campaign to expel the Jesuits. In Belgium, where leading newspapers also serialized *Le Juif Errant*, crowds inspired by the novel vandalized Jesuit residences and schools, and chanted anti-Jesuit slogans. In Santiago, Montevideo, Buenos Aires, and Vienna, the "avid" consumption of *Le Juif Errant* and other novels of a similar style astonished and worried prominent Jesuits.[8] In Britain, the novel appeared in three English translations within a year of its publication.[9]

Two leading French intellectuals, Jules Michelet and Edgar Quinet, simultaneously offered a course on the Jesuits at the Collège de France, with their lectures immediately printed to great acclaim. Their conclusion that "Jesuitism" and "ultramontanism" (a term denoting Catholics sympathetic to the nineteenth-century revival and Roman authority) menaced new nation-states became a commonplace. That England, Prussia, and the United States were more prosperous than Ireland, Poland, and Spain only underlined the enervating "decadence" of a theological system incapable of cultivating either individual initiative or national loyalty. The choice was stark: either "Jesuitism must abolish the spirit of France," Quinet explained, "or France must abolish the spirit of Jesuitism."[10] The Jesuit was a "machine" and a "Christian automaton."[11] Julio Arboleda, a Colombian statesman, drew on Michelet and Quinet to express his fear that a Jesuit's "patria" would always be the Society of Jesus, not Colombia or any single nation-state.[12]

Leaders of almost all the European revolutions of 1847–48 (and their Latin American admirers) expressed animosity toward the Jesuits. In Switzerland, attacks on the Jesuit role in the educational system spurred a civil war, and after the victory of the Protestant cantons over the Catholic cantons, the Jesuits were immediately expelled. Some of the leading figures in the Frankfurt Parliament, where reformers gathered in spring 1848 in an effort to unify Germany and create a democratic republic, published anti-Jesuit texts. In Prague, major Czech literary figures and nationalists did the same. Public demonstrations against the Jesuits stretched the length of the Italian peninsula, from Turin to Naples. These events culminated in the Roman revolution of 1848–49, when the revolutionary government forced the Jesuits to abandon the city a short time before the pope himself.[13]

Most anti-Jesuit rhetoric came from Protestants, liberal Jews, and anticlericals, but some Catholics also criticized the Jesuits for thwarting the union of Catholicism and modern nationalism, and bolstering antimodern factions within the episcopacy and in Rome. A German Catholic priest, Johannes Ronge, appalled by the enthusiasm for miraculous cures among some Catholics, founded a breakaway church and also led attacks on the Jesuits.[14] A handful of leading Catholics, not just Protestants, advocated banning the Jesuits from Prussia during the heady days of the 1848 revolution.[15] One of the key figures of Italian nationalism, Vincenzo Gioberti, an Italian priest influenced by Michelet and Quinet, published an influential attack on the Jesuits titled *Il Gesuito Moderno*. He defined the Jesuits as the "enemies of nationalities" and "allies of despots." In Spanish translation, Gioberti's writings inspired anti-Jesuit oratory across Latin America.[16] In

Naples, crowds chanted "Long live Italy, long live Gioberti; death to the traditions, away with the Jesuits, death to the Jesuits."[17]

II

Nineteenth-century Jesuits occasionally dismissed "ignominious stories" about the Society as a regrettable consequence of the "unbridled license of writing and reading in our times."[18] They wryly contrasted mobs in Vienna and Rome chanting against the Jesuits in the name of "progress" with the "good manners and cordiality" of putatively uncivilized Blackfeet and Flathead Indians meeting Jesuits in the western United States.[19] And they noted the incongruity of anti-Jesuit fervor given the small numbers of Jesuits—1200 in France in 1848, 650 in Germany in 1872—in any given country at any given time.

Still, all Jesuits recognized that they stood in an uneasy relationship with new understandings of individual freedom and national identity. The initial trauma was the suppression, beginning in Portugal in 1759 and culminating with a 1773 papal decree. The decree forced twenty-three thousand Jesuits to abandon the Society along with its hundreds of churches and schools. Major Jesuit communities in Italy, France, and Poland dissolved almost overnight, as did small Jesuit houses all over the world, from the Mariana Islands to French Guyana to New Orleans. Nineteenth century Jesuits came to blame the suppression on an alliance of corrupt monarchs and anti-Catholic Enlightenment intellectuals, who together forced the hand of a reluctant Pope Clement XIV.[20]

The second trauma, shared by many Catholics, not just Jesuits or ex-Jesuits, was the French Revolution and Napoleonic Wars, with thousands of churches desecrated, priests and nuns persecuted, and libraries and schools destroyed. The formal restoration of the Jesuits in 1814 ameliorated some of the damage caused by the suppression, even if nineteenth-century Jesuits never shook a feeling of vulnerability to papal whim. But the French Revolution remained a backdrop for Catholic life well into the twentieth century. Tales of priests, nuns, and families fleeing Catholic Europe after the revolution, sustaining the faith despite persecution, became set pieces, reminders of modern Catholicism's founding drama. Even after the 1814 restoration, the training of young Jesuits often occurred in secret because of hostility from monarchs and politicians, and Jesuit leaders found themselves making (frequently unsuccessful) pleas for the repatriation of confiscated churches and facilities.

The surge of anti-Jesuit agitation in the 1840s, then, reactivated latent Jesuit anxieties about nationalism and democratic reforms associated with the Enlightenment and the French Revolution. One Italian Jesuit writing to an American Jesuit in 1848 termed the explusions sweeping Europe a "great catastrophe" and "modern dispersion" more cruel than the 1773 suppression.[21] When a few Italian Jesuits tentatively proposed joining forces with other Catholic nationalists in the 1840s, Father General Roothaan was dismissive. In Roothaan's view, contemporary nationalist leaders willing to expel Jesuits replicated the horrors of the "grand revolution in France."[22]

The notion that the Jesuits stood athwart modernity, not in it, became for reformers conventional wisdom. François Guizot, professor of modern history at the Sorbonne, and later French prime minister, lamented persistent Jesuit opposition to "the development of modern civilization" and "freedom of the human mind."[23] Or as Roothaan explained, "The Jesuits are [viewed] as an expression of Catholicism" and those who wish to "modernize" society must "destroy" them.[24]

Jesuits themselves disparaged the modern world with enough frequency to confirm Guizot's stereotype. Still, distance from old arguments permits a more measured assessment. Jesuit opposition to modernity was selective, not wholesale. It included hostility to new notions of nonsectarian education, religious freedom, and the idea that science and the miraculous were incompatible. It valued the community over the individual. It drove the construction of a dense network of Catholic institutions to shelter the faithful from potentially hostile influences. But the very construction and maintenance of those institutions required engagement with host societies. Over time, Jesuits and other Catholics crafted a distinctive version of modernity, askew to dominant currents but immersed in the same river carrying their opponents.[25]

This Jesuit path toward a Catholic modernity began with an act of historical retrieval, an effort to skip the bewildering history of the eighteenth century and the suppression, and reestablish the Society on foundations laid by Ignatius of Loyola.[26] This process started with a reassessment of Jesuit spiritual life. Roothaan insisted on an almost-literal reading of Saint Ignatius's *Spiritual Exercises*, the key document for spiritual formation within the order, and personally translated a new edition from the original text.[27]

Exactly how nineteenth-century Jesuits understood the *Exercises*—in daily meditations, annual retreats of eight days, and a thirty-day retreat at some point during their training—is difficult to recapture. But the focus was clearly on the Lord's passion and suffering, notably the regret of one Jesuit that Jesus desired to "suffer more, while I am occupied only in trying to suffer less." The stress was on humility, "mortification and abnegation." The "terrible enemy" of authentic Jesuit work, explained one pastor in New York, was "selfishness." Its remedy: "obedience."[28]

That a leading Jesuit taking the thirty-day retreat in 1853 identified "inordinate self-love" as his "principal fault" only confirmed the sense among anticlericals that Jesuit spirituality was "an assault on individuality and selfhood." That Roothaan's notes on the *Spiritual Exercises* stress "the obedience of the Child Jesus" as a spiritual model highlighted the vast gulf between Jesuit piety and the simultaneous effort by Americans such as Ralph Waldo Emerson to promote self-reliance.[29]

In an era marked by fierce competition between Protestants and Catholics, and Catholics and anticlericals, Jesuit spirituality took on martial overtones. Many aspiring Jesuits wavered between careers as a soldier or priest, and they habitually used military metaphors to describe evangelization efforts. In Maryland, Jesuit instructors pledged to train "young warriors with fresh courage and with weapons of proof, who will fear no danger and dread no defeat."[30]

Alongside a set of reenergized spiritual practices came a revitalized missionary ethos. Roothaan viewed evangelization as the Society's highest priority and worked carefully with like-minded bishops to send Jesuits to the far-flung corners of the world. Roothaan specifically noted in an 1833 plea that the "burden of every letter" from Jesuits already in the United States was a request for more missionaries to combat "ministers of error" (i.e., Protestant clergy) also "sent from Europe."[31] He worried that European Catholic immigrants, moving to "faraway countries, their numbers rising," might "go into Protestant churches to hear the *word* of God, and to even celebrate Easter."[32] Or as one Belgian Jesuit later wrote to European colleagues, invoking the great sixteenth-century Jesuit missionary to India and Japan, "Where are the [Saint Francis] Xaviers . . . of the nineteenth century?"[33]

The appropriation of the sixteenth century shaped Jesuit educational practice as well. Roothaan made a detailed study of the original 1599 Ratio Studiorum, or plan of studies, for Jesuit schools and required in the early 1830s that it again become operative as the restored Society took over new educational establishments. A group of Jesuits working in the United States who authored a report on the Ratio Studiorum in 1889 triumphantly concluded that "the Method of the old [1599] and the new Ratio [1832] is the same."[34]

This effort to recast Jesuit intellectual life extended beyond the classroom. Eighteenth-century Catholic reformers often disparaged the Jesuits as leaders of a backward, reactionary Catholicism. These intra-Catholic disputes help explain the willingness of some European Catholic monarchs and bishops to support the Jesuit suppression.[35]

Still, even the most determined opponents of the Jesuits in the eighteenth century recognized the centrality of the Society to the era's scientific investigations, theatrical productions, and publishing ventures. What historians term the "Republic of Letters" rested in its Catholic variant on the learned labors of Jesuits scattered from Vienna to Macao.[36]

Nineteenth-century Jesuits sustained some strands of eighteenth-century Jesuit intellectual life, notably a passion for astronomy.[37] But the dominant impulse was to again return to the sixteenth and seventeenth centuries, when a philosophical tradition, Scholasticism, derived from Saint Thomas Aquinas, dominated the intellectual life of the Society. One Irish Jesuit serving in the United States scanned the room at a gathering of the world's Jesuits in 1829 and admitted that "the Society can no longer boast of so many brilliant men as she had in the age when Scholasticism flourished." He nonetheless insisted that Scholasticism "has always been the Theology of the Society and the weapon with which our forefathers conquered the enemies of the Catholic Truth."[38] At the same meeting, the assembled Jesuits cautioned each other "against the dangers of novelty, especially in any matters that in some way touch on religion."[39]

Over the course of the nineteenth century this scholastic revival, led by German and Italian Jesuits, triumphed over its intellectual foes through a combination of intellectual firepower and papal patronage. In 1879, Pope Leo XIII mandated primacy of place for Scholastic philosophy in all Catholic seminaries and universities. A generation later, the Jesuit Father General could look back with pride on the central role played by nineteenth-century Jesuits in rescuing Aquinas from the "effrontery" of misguided Catholics unwilling to recognize his enduring wisdom.[40]

Within the church, Jesuits prevented any repeat of conflicts with the papacy. In contrast to the seventeenth and eighteenth centuries, when Jesuits occasionally aligned themselves with local bishops and monarchs in disputes with papal officials, nineteenth-century Jesuits were papal loyalists.[41] After initial tension between Pope Pius IX and the Jesuits during the tumultuous events of the late 1840s, when Pius IX was mistakenly hailed as a "liberal," he became more tightly tied to the Society. During his two-year exile after the 1848 revolution in Rome, the pope urged the Jesuits to publish a journal of opinion, and immediately on its founding in 1850, *Civiltà Cattolica* became the most influential publication in the Catholic world. (Meeting with *Civiltà* editors every two weeks, the pope took an active hand in editorial decisions.) The Italian Jesuit editors explicitly saw their task as battling "heterodox" ideas popularized in contemporary newspapers and journals, and in the United States, Jesuits from New Mexico to Maryland subscribed to *Civiltà* and contributed to its foreign news section.[42]

In turn, Jesuits played pivotal roles in support of the controversial declaration in 1854 of the Immaculate Conception of Mary—a signal event in the consolidation of papal authority and a decision isolating Catholicism from other Christian churches. They helped draft and defend Pope Pius IX's notorious 1864 Syllabus of Errors, with its denial that Catholicism should reconcile itself with "progress, liberalism and modern civilization."[43] They emphatically supported (and again helped draft) the even more controversial declaration of papal infallibility in 1870, and defended the declaration against Catholics who judged it imprudent and non-Catholics for whom it confirmed Catholic authoritarianism. When Leo XIII met privately with Jesuit leaders from around the world in 1896, he emphasized that the Society's mission was to "defend the Church and the Roman Pontificate." That "we are living in evil times" where our "enemies are many" heightened the need for "greater devotedness."[44]

At times, even loyal Catholics worried that the Jesuits had cornered themselves into an ideological cul-de-sac. English convert to Catholicism and future cardinal John Henry Newman regretted that the Jesuits were considered "the enemies of all improvements and advances," and "identified with the anti-national party."[45] Wilhelm Ketteler, a prominent German bishop, expressed admiration for the pastoral work of Jesuits, but judged their sympathy for a union of church and state and fierce support of papal infallibility "pernicious."[46]

Attempts by Catholics to reconcile faith with contemporary ideas provoked a harsh Jesuit response. *Civiltà Cattolica* bluntly described the idea of a liberal Catholicism as "bizarre and monstrous," and one American Jesuit—who spent much of his career working in Rome—complained of Catholic "enemies described as friends."[47] In 1883, the Jesuits formally resolved as a body to "repudiate by name" the "doctrine known as Catholic liberalism."[48]

Outside the church, the Jesuits similarly disparaged the Enlightenment ideals so powerful in the aftermath of the American, French, and Latin American revolutions and consequential within Catholicism as well. Instead, Jesuits helped sustain an oppositional ethos that spread outward from Europe into the Americas.[49] Some even became enthusiasts for the early nineteenth-century polemicist Joseph de Maistre, whom they admired for his rejection of the focus on individual autonomy so appealing to nineteeth-century intellectuals. Roothaan himself served as the confessor to de Maistre's daughter, and lectured on the "pseudo-philosophy" of French Enlightenment heroes such as Voltaire and Jean-Baptiste d'Alembert. He dismissed efforts to describe the popes of the eighteenth century as in any way sympathetic to Enlightenment "philosophes."[50]

To most Jesuits, the new emphasis on the rights of the individual in the nineteenth century threatened the foundations of society. Freedom of the press—permitting the publication of an "obscene" book with no more restriction than on the printing of a religious book—seemed a worrisome novelty. Freedom of religion had its benefits, as Jesuits scarred by persecution appreciated. But freedom of religion as a first principle, with any and all religious groups able to worship in public, educate their young, and proselytize, meant condoning religious error. Or as a French Jesuit based in Rome wrote, religious liberty could not be supported "in general and without distinction. It is evident that this liberty is an evil against which Christianity has struggled since its origin."[51]

Jesuits across the world also promoted the work of the Catalan priest Jaime Balmes, whose *Protestantism and Catholicity Compared* became a touchstone for nineteenth-century Catholics. Balmes's claim—that Protestant-inspired liberty inevitably turned into lawlessness, and that Catholicism better fostered the mix of freedom and order necessary for an advanced civilization—appealed to Catholics wishing to dismantle an assumed connection between Protestantism and progress. Jesuits recommended the book frequently, in part because in even the most remote villages they met Protestant ministers and traders who accused them of impeding the "progress of civilization."[52] Other Jesuits joined Balmes in developing a Catholic counternarrative, with the Reformation, in the Catholic view, as the precursor to absolutist monarchies, not constitutional democracy. The era of "kings and princes" might now be ending, and many Jesuits readily admitted the abuses associated with monarchical governments, but they also desired a more harmonious balance between authority and liberty than on display in the democracies of the nineteenth century.[53]

The willingness of nominally freedom-loving European and Latin American politicians to expel the Jesuits in the 1840s seemed conclusive proof of liberal intolerance, demonstrating the need for "another kind of language of liberty."[54] As one Jesuit forced out of Switzerland explained to a friend in Paris, "In the name of freedom [the Swiss liberals have] driven [us] out of their country[,] looted our house[,] disgraced our churches, desecrated the graves of our brothers."[55] When an American-born Jesuit living in the United States attempted to reassure the readers of the *New York Herald* in 1848 by identifying the Jesuits as "unqualified defenders of human liberty," his European-born superiors regretted such "imprudent" rhetoric.[56]

Roothaan visited many European Jesuit houses during his exile from Rome between 1848 and 1850, where he recounted the dramatic tale of the public attacks on the Jesuits, the mobs of "red republicans" chanting outside Jesuit residences, and his flight from Rome in disguise.[57] Writing from Marseilles, occasionally in code to evade government censors, he noted to one American Jesuit the "violent aggression" in Rome that made exile inevitable.[58]

Memories of exile and persecution saturated Jesuit life, with one Jesuit in the United States (but originally from Belgium) handing out holy cards comparing the "humiliations of the manger [for Mary and Joseph]" with "the exhaustion of exile." Roothaan integrated reflections on Matthew 5:10—"Blessed are the persecuted"—into retreats for Jesuits across Europe and along with each of his successors composed dolorous letters— cumulatively a Jesuit jeremiad—sent to Jesuits around the world.[59] Roothaan's immediate successor as Father General, Belgian Peter Beckx, thought it "most true [that] we are despised, persecuted, condemned to exile, deprived of the common rights of citizens and men."[60] Beckx's successor, German Anthony Anderledy, expelled from Switzerland (and sent for a time to Green

Bay, Wisconsin) and writing from Fiesole, Italy, because an anticlerical Italian government had again ejected the Jesuits from their headquarters in Rome, complained of the "injustice of the times, and the bitter harassing of evil-minded men whom we see raging against the Church of God, and raging against the Society of Jesus."[61] Anderledy's successor, Spaniard Luis Martín, bemoaned the "pitiless persecution" of the Jesuits by political leaders "tainted and captivated with those principles which are absurdly called 'liberal.' "[62]

III

American leaders, too, forged a more unified nation-state during the middle decades of the nineteenth century, with the US Civil War as the pivotal episode. Even more than in a Europe where the leaders of new nation-states built on a legacy of shared customs, Americans in one of the most immigrant of nations labored to form citizens through civic rituals and public schools.

American participation in the global surge of opposition to the Jesuits and Catholicism, then, is unsurprising. Fear of Catholicism had eased for a brief time in the early nineteenth century, with surprisingly cordial relations between Catholics and Protestants in both the cities on the Atlantic coast and on the frontier. One 1813 Harvard lecturer calmly informed his audience that "we may . . . abate much of that abhorrence of papists which our fathers felt themselves obliged to maintain and inculcate." Another Harvard lecturer remarked that the "thunders of the Vatican have long since spent their rage."[63]

These assessments proved overly sanguine. With the exception of slavery, nineteenth-century American ministers and editors may have written more on Catholicism than any single topic, and anti-Catholic tracts such as *Maria Monk's Awful Disclosures of the Hotel Dieu Nunnery of Montreal* (1835) were among the century's best-selling texts.[64]

As in Europe and Latin America, the Jesuits were the most reviled actors—the "quintessence" in the words of one opponent—of a resurgent Catholicism.[65] As Jesuits trickled out of Europe in the

1820s and 1830s, archetypes of the Jesuit as a threat to republican government took on new salience. Noah Webster's *American Dictionary of the English Language*, exactly like dictionaries in other European languages, defined the Jesuits as "remarkable for their cunning in propagating their principles." "Jesuitism" meant "deceit; strategem; artifice."[66] American minister Lyman Beecher's description of the Jesuits as a "silent, systematized, unwatched" threat reached a wide audience, as did Samuel Morse's accusation that the Jesuits were "hostile [to] the very nature [of] republican liberty."[67]

Anti-Jesuit agitation in the United States, again as in Europe and Latin America, swelled in the 1840s, and continued with ebbs and flows into the 1880s. Leading American ministers and editors, like their European and Latin American counterparts, devoured Sue's anti-Jesuit novel, *Le Juif Errant*.[68] One English traveler, the geologist Charles Lyell, found talk in the United States of *Le Juif Errant* so inescapable that "in the course of my journey I began to read it in self-defense." The book's American publisher, James Harper, also the publisher of many other anti-Catholic publications, told Lyell that the book had sold eighty thousand copies immediately on publication.[69]

Americans also read Michelet and Quinet's anti-Jesuit texts, and worried that "civilized countries" in Europe exported the Jesuit problem across the Atlantic.[70] The American translator of Michelet's *Des Jesuites* explained that he felt compelled to demonstrate to Americans "how the [anti-Jesuit] Reformers of France and Europe were working."[71]

The self-image of the United States as a country of self-governing free laborers made Jesuit vows of obedience troubling. Harriet Beecher Stowe worried about Jesuits trained to "unhesitatingly obey," and Yale professor Noah Porter feared that the Jesuit stress on "obedience and dependence" corroded the "individual self." He contrasted this dependency with the "freedom and independence" underlying American society.[72]

The anti-Jesuit dimensions of the European revolutions did not escape notice in the United States, and Margaret Fuller, the most prominent American supporter of the 1848 effort by

Romans to overthrow the papal government, denounced the Jesuits as "against the free progress of humanity."[73] (By contrast, an American Jesuit based in Rome informed his colleagues in the United States that "the revolution in Rome is a phenomenon of the very worst character.")[74] One Milwaukee editor observing Jesuits migrate from Germany and Switzerland to Wisconsin worried that "these indefatigable enemies of democracy and enlightenment, who have stood by despotism everywhere in Europe," would now "poison" the state's fledgling democracy.[75] A generation later, the editor of *Harper's Weekly* bemoaned Jesuit influence in the United States and across Europe, hidden beneath "the guise" of adherence to democratic principles.[76]

Some Catholics in the United States also joined the anti-Jesuit chorus. In Philadelphia, the attempt by the local bishop to transfer the deed of a German Catholic parish owned by a board of lay trustees to the Jesuits prompted fierce attacks from parishioners. They alleged that Jesuits "from foreign countries" desired "universal despotism in ecclesiastical affairs." Jesuits were said to be "illiberal in the extreme, the result of their secluded and bigoted education. These are the men who crush to earth the secular [or diocesan] priests, and oppose public education, and 'hate with perfect hatred' republican institutions." Restrictions on the Jesuits (and other religious orders) did not inhibit the "free exercise" of religion.[77] In San Jose, California, a local priest influenced by *Le Juif Errant* unsuccessfully petitioned the town council to prevent exiled Italian Jesuits from establishing a Catholic college.[78] A New York diocesan priest endorsed Gioberti's critique of the Jesuits, and described local Jesuits, mostly French émigrés, as desiring to "fossilize us with the habits of the middle ages."[79]

By the early 1850s, discussion of the threat posed by the Jesuits and Catholicism to American society saturated the pages of both the religious and secular press, occupied theologians in the learned journals, and provoked fiery exchanges in Congress. Mobs destroyed a dozen Catholic churches across the North in the early 1850s, and anti-Catholic preachers and orators toured the country to large audiences. The anti-Catholic Know-Nothing order claimed ten thousand lodges and over one million members by January 1855, and its political wing, the American Party, elected mayors in Boston, Philadelphia, and Chicago, eight governors, over one hundred congressmen, and thousands of local officials.[80] In 1855, Jefferson Davis, then secretary of war, forwarded to a Jesuit leader a query from an acquaintance as to whether Jesuits took an oath to subvert "all Republican institutions and bring them under subjection to the Pope." On the floor of the House of Representatives, one New York congressman worried that "the Jesuit mind, ever alive to schemes for the temporal aggrandizement of Rome, had seized eagerly the occasion to obtain a strong foothold in America."[81]

IV

Compared to European turmoil—one Swiss Jesuit described "Rome in revolution, Italy upside-down, France aflame, Belgium threatened, Germany in a storm"—the United States in 1848 seemed a refuge. A Jesuit expelled from Turin and landed in San Francisco predicted a "magnificent role" for the Society. "Blessings on American soil" would compensate for the loss of Jesuit houses and schools in Europe.[82]

The contrast between European nationalists—some Catholic—eager to expel Jesuits and a Protestant-dominated United States willing to welcome them did not escape notice. Fr. Roothaan contrasted the "liberty" to "exercise our ministry" in the United States with the "despotism" evident in Europe, and urged expelled Jesuits to direct their "eyes and mind" to America. One French Jesuit who had spent time in the United States told a group of French municipal officials that he now held "republican notions from America," and thought the church and modern democracy could live in "perfect accord."[83] Another prominent French Jesuit advocated the "total independence" of the church in the United States as a worthy model.[84]

Hesitations about the United States only became evident when this initial gratitude faded. Roothaan worried about an informality in Jesuit residences in the United States, with unpredictable mealtimes, women housekeepers (theoretically impermissible so as to avoid scandal), and irregular retreat schedules. He disliked Jesuits in the United States sending letters to Rome in English, not Latin, the "usual tongue of the Society and the Church."[85]

The helter-skelter character of Jesuit institutions in the United States, with every available man lobbed into service even if their twelve-year training was incomplete, also troubled Roothaan. He agreed with an American Jesuit who complained that his "own studies were abridged and confined to what was strictly necessary in order that we might the sooner be employed in teaching."[86]

This organizational disarray prompted reflections from European Jesuits on a more general "spirit of liberty and independence" and "an inordinate emphasis on personal freedom" in the United States.[87] One Fourth of July sermon by a Maryland Jesuit praised "liberty" as a "great gift," but regretted that "so many to their great injury abuse it."[88]

Jesuits also found themselves forced to acknowledge growing anti-Jesuit and anti-Catholic hostility, even in the United States. One Belgian Jesuit traced the movement against the Jesuits to its first stirrings in Switzerland in the early 1840s, where it had been "crowned with success." He thought it had then skipped to Austria, Bavaria, Belgium, and France before crossing the Atlantic. All this had been amplified by texts such as Sue's *Le Juif Errant* and Gioberti's *Gesuita Moderno*.[89] Another Jesuit worried that under the "pretense of 'liberty,' 'progress,' [and] 'enlightenment,'" radicals in the United States might reenact the "bloody deeds of the Red Republicans of France and Italy, and the Radicals of Switzerland."[90]

The first permanent Jesuit theologate for advanced seminarians, named Woodstock after a neighboring Maryland village, might as well have been located in rural France. At the theologate's founding, European exiles constituted almost the entire faculty, with almost all of them teaching from (or composing) the Latin texts incubating the Thomistic revival on the continent. One Italian Jesuit informed European colleagues that "revolutionary tempests" in Europe had given Woodstock the "best Jesuit faculty in the world."[91]

These European-trained Jesuits were concerned that their American-born students might absorb false principles—including an overemphasis on democracy and the separation of church and state—in an atmosphere where "the protestant and infidel element predominates immensely."[92] At least initially, they decided, Americans should not serve as instructors, since Europeans were more reliable "as far as doctrines are concerned."[93]

This oppositional stance on display in the Maryland woods has its own history, and over time, and in the final chapters of this book, Jesuits come to see themselves as at home in modern nation-states, including the United States. They also come to understand their goal as more complicated than barricading themselves, their students, and their parishioners against a destructive modernity.

But let's move to the barricades. One Jesuit faculty member at Woodstock, Benedict Sestini, an Italian astronomer who fled Rome in 1848 and spent most of his career managing Georgetown University's observatory, might seem the prototype of the modern academic. Except that Sestini awoke at 3:00 a.m. each morning for most of his adult life to edit a journal promoting devotion to the Sacred Heart, repeatedly denouncing the "tendencies to paganism" he observed in the contemporary world. On trips to Italy, he purchased relics, shipping his finds back to the United States for installation in Jesuit churches.[94] Only by probing the complicated and sometimes surprising world of Sestini and his contemporaries can we assess what one Saint Louis Jesuit termed the battle against "heathenish progress."[95]

ELLSWORTH, MAINE: EDUCATION

AND RELIGIOUS LIBERTY

I

In spring 1854, Fr. John Bapst, a Jesuit priest, petitioned the Ellsworth, Maine, school committee to prohibit requiring Catholic schoolchildren to read from the King James Bible. When his petition was denied, he encouraged Catholic children to withdraw from the town's two public schools and arranged for the opening of a Catholic school enrolling eighty students.

That summer, vandals repeatedly broke the windows of Bapst's residence, and on one June evening someone lit a crude explosive—gunpowder loaded into a canister—and blew up the chapel Bapst used as a classroom.[1] Continued harassment in Ellsworth prompted Bapst's bishop, Boston's John Fitzpatrick, to move Bapst twenty miles west to Bangor. After he left, a town meeting resolved that should Bapst return to Ellsworth, his "kindly interference with our free schools" would merit "an entire suit of new clothes; such as cannot be found at the shop of any taylor [*sic*] and that when thus appareled he be presented with a free ticket to leave Ellsworth upon the first rail road operation that may go into effect."[2]

On October 15, Bapst stopped in Ellsworth en route to a sick call in nearby Cherryfield and heard confessions for much of the day. Near midnight that evening, a mob of one hundred men carrying lanterns and torches surrounded the modest home of

FIGURE 1. John Bapst, S.J. BC.2000.005, John J. Burns Library, Boston College.

a Mr. Kent, where Bapst was known to be staying. Kent at first denied that Bapst was inside. "We know he is, and we must have him," yelled the mob.[3] Bapst crept into the cellar of the home, closing a trapdoor behind him. Kent invited the mob to look in the windows. The mob would not relent. "If you don't produce him we will burn down your house and roast him alive."

Bapst emerged from the cellar to spare an attack on Kent's home. According to one witness, he still hoped that the "instincts of humanity" would prevail, but the mob rushed on him, dragged him one mile down the hill toward the Union River, and tied him to a rail. Some in the mob advocated burning Bapst alive. The consensus was to tar and feather him—that is, strip him naked, cover his body with tar, and attach feathers to the tar. This the mob did, after taking his watch and emptying his wallet. Following this ordeal, Bapst staggered back toward the Kent home during what one resident later recalled as the "stormiest night I ever saw." One eyewitness recalled plucking feathers from Bapst's body after a search party had found him, and then shaving off the priest's hair and eyebrows to remove remaining bits of tar.[4]

The next day Bapst said Mass in Ellsworth. Fearful that "the mob would gather again," he took refuge in the home of Charles Jarvis, "one of the leading Protestants of the town." Jarvis hustled Bapst out of Ellsworth and rode with him to Bangor, as accounts of the attack began filtering out from Maine into the far corners of the world.[5]

II

Bapst was born in 1815 in La Roche, a small Swiss village. Desiring always to be a priest, he recalled in his old age building little altars as a boy and preaching to imaginary congregations. He joined the Jesuits at the age of twenty, and spent the next decade studying and teaching at the Jesuit boarding school and college in Fribourg, Switzerland. Soon after the Jesuit restoration in 1814, city leaders had arranged for the Jesuits to return to Fribourg, where the Jesuits had been forced after their 1773 suppression to abandon one of their oldest colleges.

In Fribourg, Bapst absorbed the central messages of the Catholic revival, including the conviction that the destruction wrought by modern philosophy and the French Revolution had placed Catholics and modern liberals on opposite sides of an unbridgeable chasm. French students studying in Fribourg would later become among the leading opponents of the secular republic, and one Jesuit instructor at Fribourg continually contrasted the "horror" of the modern world with previous "centuries of faith."[6] Another Jesuit, whose texts shaped history instruction at the college, compared the spirit of the church with that of modern philosophy: "the one of submission, the other independence; the one of peace, the other of discord; the one of life, the other of death."[7]

That the student body and faculty at Fribourg came from over a dozen countries occasioned a series of attacks on the Jesuits by Swiss nationalists in the 1830s and 1840s. Precisely because the Jesuits prized loyalty to the pope, these nationalists charged, they could not inculcate loyalty to the Swiss nation. The leading Swiss novelist of the era, Gottfried Keller, decried the Jesuits in fiction and verse, and as in much of Europe and North America the influence in Switzerland of Eugène Sue's *Le Juif Errant* was enormous.[8] One commentator summarized the liberal view: "[The] Jesuits are a body of conspirators who overspread the Roman Catholic world; men who have no national ties, whose interests are not Swiss."[9]

The Jesuits composed a textbook on Swiss history to demonstrate their patriotic bona fides, but such gestures did not ease liberal fears, perhaps because even in their textbook the Jesuits could not refrain from jabs at John Calvin and other Swiss heroes of the Protestant Reformation.[10] And in fact, the atmosphere in Fribourg tilted sharply toward the countercultural side in the debate over how the church should resist or accommodate the modern world, with adulatory reports on the school's activities printed in Louis Veuillot's *Univers*, an ultramontane Parisian journal whose influence extended across the Catholic world.[11] The tendency of French monarchist families to enroll their sons in Fribourg also provoked comment. As the most prominent French historian of the nineteenth century, Jules Michelet, put it, "If you have a Jesuit heart, pass that way, that is to the side of Fribourg; if you are upright and straightforward come here, this is France." Even leading French Catholics such as Charles Montalembert (a defender of the Jesuits' right to operate their own schools) privately thought the Jesuit view of the modern world "false, narrow and unfortunate."[12]

The role of the Jesuits in the educational system, more than any other single issue, divided Swiss Catholic from Swiss Protestant cantons. When the Catholic canton of Lucerne invited the Jesuits to administer a local college and seminary, liberal politicians and editors reacted with horror. Eventually this dispute spread from Lucerne and escalated into a civil war, the first of the revolutions that erupted in Europe in 1847 and 1848, and that in Switzerland culminated in a Catholic defeat in November 1847.

As the armies of the Catholic cantons surrendered, Bapst fled Fribourg with fellow priests and students, disguised and divided into groups of four or five men. For Bapst and his Jesuit contemporaries, this forced exile made an enduring impression. As Swiss liberals denounced the Jesuits, and mobs looted Jesuit residences, defaced church walls, and destroyed Jesuit libraries, Jesuits found their suspicions of modernity confirmed. One of Bapst's Jesuit contemporaries in Fribourg, exiled to Georgetown University in Washington, DC, bemoaned the hypocrisy of Swiss liberals, evicting Jesuits on one day and proclaiming their belief in freedom during the next.[13]

Bapst eventually made his way from Fribourg to the Jesuit residence in Notre Dame d'Ay in France. He still anticipated a career as a university instructor. But one night he reported a "singular dream." He saw "a people who were not fashioned as other peoples," with skin coloring neither black nor white. "At the same time," he related, "a voice told me distinctly that on the morrow I should set out to go and live among these strange men." The next day—despite his "repugnance for the foreign missions"—a letter arrived from his provincial ordering him to the United States. When he finally arrived in New York City, the local Jesuit superior sent him to Indian Island, just across the Penobscot River from Oldtown, Maine.

When Bapst arrived in Oldtown by canoe on August 7, 1848, nine months after fleeing Fribourg, he recognized in the five hundred Penobscot Indians living there the "very men who I had seen in my dream." The assembled Indians led him to the Catholic Church, accompanied by the ringing of "long silent" church bells. Bapst ventured a short address in French, but then realized that "no one understood me." After these opening ceremonies, the Indians left him "alone on that wild island, three thousand leagues from my country," and Bapst "realized the full import of the sacrifice I had made."[14]

Bapst's dream was not so singular. Roothaan's 1833 plea for missionaries specifically requested men to work with North American Indians, "banished from their homes by new settlers, and driven into the western wilds."[15] And in fact many Jesuits, and other Catholic priests and nuns, devoted their lives to working with Indians in some of the most remote sections of North America, including Maine, the Kansas plains, the Great Lakes region (in both the United States and Canada), the Dakota territory, and the Pacific Northwest.

The letters of Belgian Jesuit Pierre-Jean De Smet describing his work among the Nez Perce and Flathead Indians became one of the best sellers of Catholic Europe, with his tales of missionary adventure doubling as a fund-raising tool. De Smet carried with him a history of the Jesuit missions in South America, and early in his career naively hoped to establish a Jesuit republic among the Flathead Indians in Montana paralleling the one established by Jesuits in Paraguay among the Guarani Indians in the seventeenth century.[16]

When nineteenth-century Jesuits arrived in the United States, they also made a point of venerating their predecessors. The most notable of these predecessors was the sixteenth-century Jesuit missionary Francis Xavier, and Bapst and other Jesuits in Maine often invoked Xavier's epic journeys in India and Japan when describing their own work. But Bapst naturally saw himself as the figurative descendant of one particular French Jesuit, Sebastian Râle. Râle had founded the Oldtown mission in the late seventeenth century. He worked in the settlements around Oldtown from 1694 until his death in 1724, killed by New England militia members who viewed Râle as the instigator of attacks on Puritan settlements. One American textbook even named these skirmishes between Puritans and Penobscots "the Jesuit's or [Râle's] war."[17]

Râle's death made him one of the final casualties of the wars between Protestants and Catholics convulsing much of Europe after the Reformation, and whose bloody reverberations extended across the Atlantic. After slaughtering Râle and taking his scalp for display in Boston, the Massachusetts militia, in an iconoclastic gesture redolent of the Calvinist Reformation, ripped down the crucifixes marking "false religion" in Râle's humble chapel.[18] Or in Bapst's telling, in a letter reprinted in *Civiltà Cattolica*, "After [Râle] had converted the Indians of Maine, and had devoted himself to their service during more than twenty years, at the cost of immense sacrifices and privations, he was at last butchered by the Protestants at the foot of a cross which he himself had erected."[19]

Râle's memory endured among New England's Catholics, just as the memory of other martyred Jesuits endured on the Canadian side of the border, and bishops in both Montreal and New England saw the return of the Jesuits in the mid-nineteenth century as a chance to reignite missionary fervor in the region. One early Boston bishop, Benedict Fenwick, himself a Jesuit, traveled to the spot where Râle was slain to dedicate a monument in Râle's name. As Fenwick privately explained, Râle's murder by "the Bostonians" was an act of "shocking barbarity." Even worse, in Fenwick's view, were accusations of Jesuit conspiracies made in the region's history books. Indeed, "not satisfied with waylaying and murdering this truly great and good Jesuit missionary, [New Englanders] must go and infamously calumniate him and try to cover his memory even with infamy." Anti-Catholic vandals, presumably, destroyed the monument three years after Fenwick led its dedication.[20]

A determined Fenwick also tried, unsuccessfully, to interest French Jesuits just then returning to Canada to move to Maine.[21] Only the expulsions of Jesuits from Europe in the late 1840s and subsequent enhanced Jesuit manpower in the United States allowed the Jesuits to reclaim Maine as mission territory. In his first extant letter from Maine, Bapst remarked that the "numerous priests who came to and left this mission" in the 124 years since Râle's death had left virtually no records.[22]

Bapst adopted a serene tone in his first letters back to Jesuits in Europe, despite comparing himself to Jonah, "here in complete isolation."[23] He compiled ethnographic details of Penobscot life—from table manners to religious beliefs—in the manner of the *Lettres édifiantes et Curieuse*, a collection of letters from missionary Jesuits around the world, and *The Jesuit Relations*, a collection of letters specifically sent by Jesuits, including Râle, from North America. Avidly read by European Jesuits and indeed by an educated audience eager for details of the New World, both collections were republished multiple times in the nineteenth century.

Like Râle, who had composed the first dictionary of a local Indian language, Bapst immediately devoted himself to learning the language of the Penobscots, the "hardest in all the world."[24] (Nineteenth-century Jesuits, like their seventeenth-century predecessors, immersed themselves in indigenous languages. They composed the first dictionaries and grammars in languages as diverse as Albanian and Salish.)[25] Bapst thought the language had "no analogy of any living tongue," but perhaps "derived from Hebrew."[26]

From the beginning of his Oldtown sojourn, Bapst also found himself drawn into the world of Maine's Euro-American Catholic immigrants. In fact, after cataloging his frustrations with the Penobscots, unwilling to unite behind his leadership and prone to drunkenness, a disillusioned Bapst hastened to add that "the white population on the contrary give grounds for the fairest hopes." Extant baptism and marriage records kept (in French) by Bapst list a mixture of Irish, French, and Penobscot surnames in his first years at Oldtown, but more Irish and French names as he began to travel widely in Maine.[27]

Bapst's assigned territory was vast: everything north from Bangor to the Canadian border and east to the Atlantic coast. When not in Oldtown, he primarily ministered to Irish Catholics, often-bedraggled refugees from the 1847 Irish famine, or pockets of French Canadian Catholics. As Bapst bluntly explained, "All of the Catholics are immigrants, with the exception of the Indians and some American converts, and they are generally poor."[28]

The pace was punishing. Each of his thirty-three missions, he told one European correspondent mischievously, "would form in Switzerland a very pretty parish. (What do you say to that?) So you may be sure no one can complain of not having enough to do." A typical month lists Bapst conducting two baptisms in Bucksport on January 4, 1852, a wedding ceremony, forty miles away, in Rockland on January 20, and a wedding in Ellsworth, sixty-five miles away, a week later.[29] Despite these distances, traveled on horseback in rugged country, parishioners complained of being "forgotten" if Bapst failed to visit in a given month. A fellow priest visiting Bapst in that year worriedly wrote to his provincial of Bapst's "fatigue" and need of "encouragement."[30]

Bapst's efforts in Maine paralleled those of other nineteenth-century Jesuits. In Europe as well as the United States, the Jesuits generally shied away from public disputations, often relying on glib dismissals of Protestants and "heretics" as terminally inconsistent.[31] Their theological and philosophical training remained gauged to another era. In fact Bapst worried that young Jesuits—because their doctrinal knowledge came entirely from European Latin textbooks—could "triumphantly" refute ancient heresies such as Arianism more competently than they could answer Protestant questions about devotion to Mary and the saints (as opposed to Jesus), or why Catholics recognized the leadership of the pope.[32]

As a result, Jesuits across the globe found greater success in catalyzing the faith and practice of nominally Catholic populations—from small groups of Chinese Catholics in Shanghai to large Catholic populations in Italy and Ireland—than in converting Protestants or non-Christians.[33] The key was to instill basic doctrinal knowledge. Bapst judged Maine's Irish and French Canadians, like the Catholic Oldtown Indians, as effectively pagans, so distant were they from Catholic practice. Absent a priest for years, sometimes decades, there was "no longer reason for them for Mass, nor confession, nor communion, nor marriage, nor fasting, nor abstinence, nor feast, nor Sunday."[34] He worried about the "pathetic state" of their catechesis, the "shameful ignorance in which the burgeoning generation stagnates." Bapst "announced publicly that not one child will receive his first communion" without knowledge of the catechism and "we will refuse the future absolution to the parents who neglect the religious instruction of their children."[35]

Next was the parish mission, a sequence of liturgies, exhortations, and prayer, pioneered by Jesuits and Redemptorist priests in eighteenth-century Europe, and revitalized by members of the same orders, including Jan Roothaan, in the early nineteenth century. (Roothaan preached extensive missions in Switzerland in the 1820s, and Bapst might have attended such a mission as a boy.) After arriving in a town, Bapst typically organized a mission lasting three or four days, and including long hours (for Bapst) in the confessional.[36]

Mission psychology pivoted between two poles: a doctrinal severity centered on the horror of sin and everlasting damnation, and a practical, even generous piety aimed at persuading Catholics to view the sacraments (especially confession) and church as their best shield in a bewildering world. The severity is evident in Bapst's correspondence. He viewed missions as "spiritual weapons" for "reclaiming a very large number of bad Catholics" and converting the occasional "Protestant or heretic." "Hardened sinners" must understand that eternal life depended on reconciliation with the church. Bapst admiringly noted how his Jesuit partner, Fr. Force, after "not a single" Catholic attended his first lecture, eventually recruited an audience and "gave free reign to the torrents of his heart's holy rage; he let ring in their ears the dreadful bursts of vengeful thunderbolts ready to strike apostates; he let glisten in their eyes the dismal glow of the eternal flames of Hell."[37] (Local Protestants of a more liberal bent shocked Bapst by claiming that "there is no hell, or if there is, it is not for men, as Christ ransomed us all.")[38]

At the same time, Bapst and other mission preachers reassured their listeners, "who seemed lost without hope," that their sins could be forgiven in the confessional. To some eighteenth-century Catholics, the idea that a lifetime of sins could be forgiven with one confession seemed unworthy of a dignified faith.[39] But Bapst and his fellow Jesuits had no doubts. "Few weeks go by," Bapst explained, "that I do not have to deal with penitents who have not confessed for twenty or thirty years or more." "Such penitents," he added, "have consciences heavily laden with sin."[40] Another Jesuit on the mission trail wrote of the joy of those Catholics brought back into the church, after staying away "because of some vague fear instilled in them through the severity of the priests."[41]

Catholic solidarity seemed especially important since Maine's Catholics lived in what Bapst accurately described as a "nearly exclusively Protestant" milieu. Bapst conceded that many Protestants seemed "generally well disposed toward the Catholic religion," but this superficial acceptance made self-conscious markers of Catholic identity the more vital.[42]

Leading non-Catholic citizens often endorsed Bapst's work, in part because he inveighed against drunkenness at every opportunity in a state that would soon pass the nation's strictest temperance law. (Bapst probably did not support laws banning the sale of alcohol—as opposed to voluntary abstinence. Fr. Roothaan thought the church had "never preached total abstinence" and should beware a movement supported by heretics.)[43]

Within weeks of arriving in Oldtown, Bapst formed a temperance society and decreed that any Indian who became intoxicated would offer a public apology. After "numerous equivocations, threats, and incredible reluctance," Bapst reported, "I saw these proud children of nature move toward the middle of the church, and there on their knees, the humiliation evident on their faces, ask pardon from all the faithful gathered there."[44] The same drunkenness marred the lives of Irish and French Canadian Catholics, and Bapst insisted on the same remedies. The Waterville, Maine, newspaper editorialized that "benevolent" and "liberal-minded" men should support Bapst's efforts to build a chapel because of his insistence on sobriety.[45] (Four years earlier, the town licensing board had resolved, with apparently little effect, that "no liquor should be sold to foreigner[s] or persons not naturalized.")[46] As Catholic use of liquor in Waterville declined, Bapst boasted, "the Protestant magistrates themselves, witnesses of this change, regard me with great favor."[47]

Bapst moved to Ellsworth, a town of just over just over four thousand residents, in January 1853, but he had been visiting Ellsworth regularly for two years. During one of his first visits he had organized a successful mission—"only three people did not participate"—preaching each morning and working each day in the confessional. He also encouraged the closing of six of the town's seven "grog-shops," and as had become his pattern, established a temperance association enrolling seventy-five members. "Drunkenness," he prematurely claimed, "disappeared from Ellsworth." As a result, the Americans—"by this I mean Protestants"—praised him "to the sky and wish to have a resident priest in Ellsworth among the Catholics for Temperance."[48]

Bapst also established a Sunday school since the town's Catholic children knew "neither prayer nor catechism," and indeed a large portion of Ellsworth's Irish-born population was illiterate.[49] He also launched a lecture series on Catholic doctrine. It resulted in the conversion of a number of Protestants, including twelve young women, some of whose families resented Bapst, in his words, for "reducing free-born Americans to Rome's galling yoke."[50] (One of the converts, Mary Agnes Tincker, became the first teacher in the Catholic school that Bapst founded, and later wrote a thinly veiled novel, *The House of Yorke*, describing these events. In the novel, Bapst is conspicuously named Rasle, a variation on Râle.)[51]

The affection held for Bapst by Ellsworth's Catholics seems genuine. His impoverished parishioners impetuously resolved to build a new church during Bapst's first visit.[52] Even Ellsworth Catholics off to California to try their luck in the gold rush cobbled together funds in support.[53]

In 1852, St. Joseph's Catholic Church was completed. And on the Fourth of July of that year, the usual town celebration culminated with a procession up the main street to the church door. Inside, town notables read the Declaration of Independence, the town's most prominent minister, Congregationalist Sewell Tenney, offered a blessing, and a local lawyer gave the day's main address, which included an expression of sympathy for "oppressed Ireland. Her only crime is proximity to England."[54]

III

The unraveling of this harmonious tableau—Catholics and Protestants amicably celebrating the nation's independence inside a

Catholic church—began in the local schoolhouse. Across Europe and in North and South America, Jesuits thrust themselves into mid-nineteenth-century debates on education—a pivotal issue in every nation-state developing systems of mass education and determined to produce loyal citizens. In predominantly Catholic nations, Jesuits favored the integration of Catholicism and public education, with priests and nuns teaching in publicly funded schools, and religious ceremonies linked to the school calendar. In nations with a Protestant majority, as one German Jesuit put it, "the fight for liberty of education" meant agitation for independent Catholic schools, ideally supported with public funds.[55]

Bapst became aware of the importance that New Englanders placed on public education soon after his arrival in Maine when he maneuvered himself into disputes between two rival Penobscot factions. He claimed early in his tenure at Oldtown to have effected a "beautiful reconciliation" between the feuding parties, erecting a cross to replace the two poles marking each faction's section of the village.[56] Within another year, however, both factions had become enmeshed in an acrimonious dispute over education, sparked by Bapst's application for funds from the state to support a Catholic teacher for the Oldtown school.[57]

Initially, the Maine authorities seemed likely to grant Bapst funding. His opponents then persuaded the authorities to funnel the funds through an Indian agent paid by the government. This arrangement eventually led to public funding for a formally nonsectarian but (in Bapst's eyes) effectively Protestant school. Bapst then "declared to them [the Indians] that I could no longer stay among them," and in an extended discussion conducted on the significant date of July 4 persuaded the Penobscots to reverse this decision. "The School," he informed Boston's Bishop Fitzpatrick, "was declared Catholic and put under the surveillance of the priest."[58]

Even Bapst, however, admitted that the victory might be temporary, since any instructor "must be a good Catholic" as well as an "American, or at least able to pass for one," because of the prejudice against foreigners and the need for English-language competency. A few months later, his opponents declared the Catholic teacher selected by Bapst unacceptable on religious grounds, and Bapst, in a revealing phrase, complained about an emerging "war of religion."[59] Bapst lost this fight, and a putatively nonsectarian school opened in Oldtown using public funds. One report described students in the public school studying the King James Bible, and writers for Maine's religious press, even years later, delighted in recounting the defeat of "the priest."[60]

Bapst's last letter on the subject, just before he moved away from Oldtown, portrayed his opponents as the "radical party," the exact term used to describe the opponents of the Jesuits in Switzerland.[61] Members of the "radical party"—again as in Switzerland—did not hesitate to lambaste what seemed to them Jesuit authoritarianism. Bapst's goal, explained a correspondent for the *Independent*, the nation's most influential religious weekly, was to keep the Indians "ground down in ignorance and vice." Bapst "tells them," the correspondent added, that "if they do not stop at once in the course they are now pursuing, they will all go to hell. They now heed not his impotent anathemas."[62] When Henry David Thoreau ventured into the Maine woods several years later, his Indian guide relished recounting his struggles with Bapst.[63]

The story was much the same in Ellsworth. In the phrasing of a local onlooker, Bapst "conceived it his duty or right, to prohibit among [his] people the reading of the Protestant Bible (the version in common use) and instructed the Catholic youth in our schools to decline reading the Bible when it was required in company with the other scholars to do so." Bapst, by contrast, blamed the problem on a "town-school teacher, out of bigotry, being the son of a parson," who had obstinately required that Catholic schoolchildren read the King James Bible.[64]

Regardless of whether Bapst or the local schoolteacher began the dispute, Bapst organized a petition to protest the use of the King James Bible, or what his Jesuit colleagues termed a "mauvaise" or "bad" Bible.[65] To Jesuits such as Bapst, the King James

Bible's version of the Ten Commandments, with its caution in the second commandment against the false worship of graven images, seemed anti-Catholic. Bapst allowed that Protestant schoolchildren might in the abstract benefit from reading some parts of the King James Bible, but asked that Catholic children "should be allowed to read the Catholic Bible, or at least, to be excused from reading a version essentially against their conscience."[66]

Ellsworth residents accustomed to reading the King James Bible in their school and at public ceremonies thought this claim outrageous. (And indeed, from the moment of Bapst's arrival rumors circulated that he hoped to burn King James Bibles, not simply prohibit their use in public schools.)[67] The Ellsworth school committee rejected Bapst's petition, and reports spread that Bapst had described the King James Bible as the "counterfeit word of God."[68] Bapst arranged the withdrawal of the Catholic schoolchildren from the public schools, as accusations flew that some of the students stamped their feet during the reading of the Bible, or even broke into the empty schoolhouse after hours to destroy copies of the New Testament. (Town authorities sentenced one young Irish Catholic, not a student, to thirty-six hours in jail for this offense.)[69] Bapst alternated between hope that "public opinion & the press are turning against the School Committee," and recognition that the "whole town was in the greatest excitement on account of the bible and schools, [and] the most brutal abuses & threatenings were spread against me as the author of the troubles."[70]

Bapst's calm demeanor impressed his opponents, but his poor English—six years after arriving in Maine he remained "very deficient in the English language"—did not facilitate communication across religious lines.[71] He denied accusations that he had threatened Ellsworth's Irish Catholics with damnation if they did not support his stance on the Bible question, or that he had claimed "my opinion is theirs."[72]

Even so, one Boston Jesuit, monitoring events from afar, assessed Bapst's tactics as "not seasoned by prudence."[73] Bapst thought prudence beside the point. Because American public officials refused to contemplate subsidizing Catholic schools with tax dollars, Bapst assessed American rhetoric about religious liberty as hollow when measured against the reality of Catholic schoolchildren forced to read the King James Bible and sing Protestant hymns in schoolhouses where a Protestant minister often doubled as instructor. When Bapst lost his battle to establish a Catholic school in Oldtown, he blamed a local Protestant minister for rallying opposition even while " 'spouting' much about the blessing of liberty of conscience and religion."[74] Other Jesuits reported prohibitions on Catholic priests (and more mandatory King James Bible reading) in poorhouses, hospitals, orphanages, and jails.[75]

Bapst rejoiced after Ellsworth's Catholics rallied to his plea to found a parochial school. He thought the support "a great blessing for the Catholics and a bitter mortification & a great disappointment for the bigots who thought already that our children were going to turn protestants en masse sooner than to leave the town school."[76] Or as he explained, "To save the cath. religion here, we may say what we please, there is only one way, it is to establish catholic schools everywhere under the control of the Priests."[77]

IV

As European Jesuits such as Bapst destabilized the religious equilibrium of Ellsworth, a wave of street orators, European exiles, and prominent American ministers mobilized local Protestants. Lecturing throughout New England and writing widely distributed columns and books, they preached a surprisingly consistent message: that Catholicism—especially "Jesuitism"—was "associated with religious and social evils," and was the "enemy of true liberty."[78]

In Ellsworth the key figure was William Chaney, the editor of the *Ellsworth Herald*. After purchasing the paper in 1853, Chaney turned the *Herald* into one of the state's anti-Catholic newspapers, filling it with anti-Catholic attacks, short stories, and even the occasional painstakingly wrought cartoon.[79] He also used his position as town clerk to call numerous meetings to discuss the Catholic threat, and encouraged the formation of Know-Nothing militias or street gangs. As Bapst wearily noted, "The Bigots of Ellsworth and among others the editor of the *Ellsworth Herald* indulge in all kind of abuses, outrages, slanders & abominations against the church, the priest, the Catholics & chiefly the converts."[80]

Chaney's slashing, crude style—jabs at "Jack Catholics" (Protestants unwilling to support Chaney's anti-Catholic campaign) and unsubstantiated hints that Bapst fathered illegitimate children in Oldtown—did not endear him to Ellsworth's leading citizens. But even pillars of the community became worried about Catholicism's influence.[81] Shipbuilder Seth Tisdale, the town's leading employer and president of its first bank, served on the local school committee that refused Bapst's request and became a member of the nativist American Party. The Reverend Sewall Tenney, pastor of the town's Congregational Church, regretted Chaney's "indiscretion and violence," but he too addressed one town meeting in spring 1854 "at some length upon the subject of Papal interference with our school, and was listened to with marked attention."[82] J. P. French, the town's Methodist minister, preached that "Catholicism is an old worn-out institution, it is behind the age," and complained that "for fifty years the various Catholic countries of Europe have been annually disgorging upon our shores, her tens and hundreds of thousands of paupers and criminals."[83] Charles Lowell, local attorney and essayist, denounced Chaney's "ruthless, inflammatory course," yet also worried that Catholicism remained incompatible with the "freedom of thought, and personal responsibility, necessary to the support of republican institutions."[84]

By this time, a string of anti-Catholic European exiles had begun to crisscross New England and even Maine. They included the most notorious street orator of the era, the white-bearded John Orr, self-identified as the Angel Gabriel, who began preaching against Catholicism in England in the 1830s, but drew more attention as he traveled through Scotland, Ireland, Quebec, and the United States in the early 1850s.[85] Wearing a long white robe and carrying a six-foot staff topped by British and American flags, Orr announced his arrival in a given town with blasts on his silver trumpet and then hectored local crowds on the Catholic menace, often leaving in his wake a brawl between his supporters and local Catholics. Orr drew large crowds to the Boston Common for several days in April 1854, and a May 8 address in nearby Chelsea preceded the tearing of the cross down from the local Catholic Church.[86] In Maine, Orr appeared on Saint Croix Island, just across the river from New Brunswick, and then spent two days in Portland less than a month before the attack on Bapst. His tirades were later said to have motivated Ellsworth residents. (Another anti-Catholic street preacher attacking the Jesuits had already inspired the citizens of Bath, Maine, to burn down a building used as a church by its Catholics.)[87]

Orr's antics embarrassed respectable Protestants—one editor observed that Orr's "trumpet has less brass and more sense than his head"—but they also resisted attempts to arrest Orr, since "if the Romanists are allowed to triumph at this time, and to put down the Protestants, the victory will be a bloody one thereafter."[88] A surviving handbill authored by Orr issued the following warning to Americans: "In this blessed land but in the dark, his Jesuits now are at their work." He continued: "When Romanists as one combine, Then Protestants to each should join. Ye sons of freedom be awake, Your rights these despots seek to take."[89]

Continental European exiles had even more impact. Or as Chaney later explained, "Father GAVAZZI appeared in our midst, and the whole scene was changed."[90] A onetime Italian priest who had played a leading role in the 1848 Italian revolution against papal rule, and who had then left Italy with the aid of the American consul after the suppression of the revolution by French troops, Alessandro Gavazzi delivered widely publicized lectures attacking Pius IX and the Jesuits in London in 1851 and Dublin in 1852. The enthusiastic response resulted in lecture tours of England and Scotland, where he attracted enormous crowds.[91] Gavazzi then came to North America, where he again created a sensation, lecturing across the United States

FIGURE 2. Alessandro Gavazzi, an Italian ex-priest and leader in the Roman revolution of 1848. Gavazzi was one of the most prominent of the anti-Catholic lecturers who traveled across Europe and North America in the 1850s. Courtesy of the National Gallery in London.

and Canada. Wearing the black robe of a monk with an open Bible sewn on the chest, Gavazzi dazzled his audiences despite his halting English. Henry Longfellow thought him "a fine orator, after the Italian model," and Boston ministers quickly began inserting Gavazzi's insights into their own sermons on the papal threat.[92]

Gavazzi never spoke in Ellsworth, but his lectures in New York and Boston were reprinted in major newspapers, with Ellsworth readers prompting requests for their local papers to follow suit. Chaney's predecessor as editor of the *Herald* declined, since the "*Herald* does not wish to wage war with any of the religious sects of the day, whether Protestant or Catholic." And Thomas White, the town's sole Catholic attorney, fumed in a letter to the editor against Gavazzi's "putrid, foul-mouthed calumnies against us and our creed." When Chaney purchased the *Ellsworth Herald*, he reversed editorial course and reprinted a Gavazzi address, explaining that "the thunders of Gavazzi still reverberate along our shores, and each echo startles into action some slumbering Protestant. Even Ellsworth caught the sound."[93]

Gavazzi's reception reflects the ease with which American Protestants and European anticlericals could unite around what Gavazzi termed the "religione antipapale."[94] Gavazzi became aware of American anti-Catholic agitation through contacts in New York's Italian exile community. (Indeed, leading American Protestants bankrolled publications begun by these Italian exiles.)[95] Gavazzi devoted considerable attention in his lectures to the school issue, concluding that "it was the Bible, and the Bible alone, which made your freedom." Jesuits newly arrived in the United States, from Italy, Germany, and the "Jesuitical college at Fribourg," seemed to Gavazzi an obvious threat to American liberty, and he advised Americans that they should follow the lead of so many European contemporaries and expel the Jesuits.[96]

Also alert to the importance of European exiles was Boston's Theodore Parker, one of the most prominent liberal Protestant ministers in the United States. Parker lectured to Bangor residents for two consecutive evenings in spring 1854. Persona non grata among American evangelicals because of his dismissal of biblical miracle accounts and the idea of literal truth in scripture, Parker, like many liberals in the early 1840s, shrugged off Reformation-style anti-Catholicism as an anachronism. When he first visited Rome in 1844, he thought Catholicism better able to cultivate "the feelings of reverence, of faith, of gentleness" than orthodox Protestantism, and he enjoyed conversing with a bishop and cardinal "perfectly free from cant." In the first months of his pontificate, Pius IX seemed to Parker "noble and manly," and worthy of comparison with Martin Luther.[97]

Pius IX's acquiescence in the crushing of the Roman revolution by French troops and the simultaneous mass migration of

Irish Catholics to New England quashed nascent Parker's ecumenical impulses. Parker was also influenced by his friendship with Boston's Margaret Fuller, an opponent of papal rule in Rome, and his admiration for Johannes Ronge, a German Catholic priest who broke away from Rome in 1844 to found the German Catholic movement, ultimately a free-church organization resembling Parker's brand of Unitarianism.[98]

By the time he spoke in Bangor, Parker's onetime admiration for Catholicism was a distant memory. Now he meditated in his public addresses on the incompatibility of "a priest [standing] betwixt the nation and its God." He frequently contrasted public education in New England with the "small and mean buildings" devoted to public education in Rome, "where the priesthood is mighty and the people are subjects of the Church." A few weeks after his Bangor lectures, Parker was more blunt. "Jesuits," he warned, "come in abundance, some are known, others stealthily prowl about the land, all the more dangerous in their disguise." He added: "The Catholic Church opposes everything which favors democracy and the natural rights of man. It hates our free churches, free press and, above all, our free schools."[99]

Rev. George Cheever differed from Parker on most theological questions. Where Parker disparaged the Calvinism of his ancestors, Cheever defended the "fire and brimstone" of preacher Jonathan Edwards against the sneers of sophisticated moderns. A Maine native, Cheever became one of the country's best-known Congregationalist ministers, opposing Unitarianism ("infidelity disguised"), Andrew Jackson's Indian removal campaign, and alcohol consumption.[100]

Despite their theological differences, Cheever shared Parker's fear of Catholic aggression. Cheever's offhanded remarks about Catholicism in the early 1830s included a warning against the "powerful machinations" of the Jesuits, but conveyed little urgency.[101] Two trips to Europe opened his eyes. On his first trip, the "ignorance" of "true religion" among even educated Spaniards seemed "quite astonishing." Clearly "the genius of Popery has crushed alike the genius and patriotic spirit of the nation." He came to worry that "the Catholics [in the United States] are not native Americans, but foreigners, and for the most part, of the most inveterate and superstitious class."[102]

During Cheever's second European trip, Switzerland offered especially vivid contrasts between prosperous, Protestant Genevans and the "lean, poor and ignorant" Catholics living in the adjoining Swiss Catholic cantons.[103] When visiting Fribourg in 1844, Cheever bumped into a group of Jesuit priests and students on a stroll. Even this innocent encounter elicited from him a disquisition on the "pitiless axes and instruments of torture" condoned by the Jesuits, and their affinity for the "bondage of ignorance and superstition."[104]

Both trips allowed Cheever to cultivate an international network of English, Scottish, and Swiss evangelical colleagues, notably the Scottish Presbyterian leader Thomas Chalmers along with the Swiss historian and minister Jean-Henri Merle d'Aubigne. Like Cheever, these European evangelicals felt themselves pinned between a growing rationalism—which Cheever compared to Unitarianism in the United States—and a resurgent Catholicism visible in the Irish and Italian immigrants pouring into Manchester, Glasgow, and Geneva as well as Boston and New York City. (Or as Cheever put it, "Romanism increases in Geneva, as it does in our own country, by emigration.") The need to return to Protestant principles seemed imperative, and Cheever thrilled to d'Aubigne's influential four-volume history of the Reformation, which painted Luther, Calvin, and other reformers in heroic colors.[105]

After returning to the United States, Cheever took leadership roles in the cluster of anti-Catholic Protestant societies founded in the 1840s. These societies enrolled many of the most prominent ministers in the North, and developed close ties with parallel organizations in Protestant Europe as part of their common effort to "diffuse and promote the principles of Religious Liberty, and a pure and Evangelical Christianity, both at home and abroad, wherever a corrupted Christianity exists." Dozens of lecturers funded by the groups toured the United States and Europe.[106]

Cheever also helped arrange for Gavazzi's 1853 North American tour. He thought Gavazzi the most "eloquent man I have ever heard" and continued to praise Gavazzi in his private correspondence thirty years later.[107] He also promoted the cause of Rosa and Francesco Madiai, a couple imprisoned by Tuscan authorities for distributing (or some said just reading) an Italian translation of the Bible supplied by American and British Protestant missionaries.[108]

Cheever and his ministerial colleagues organized mass meetings in New York City, Boston, Baltimore, and other cities in support of the Madiai, and ignored Catholic counterclaims that the Madiai used religious meetings as a cover to plot against the state. They linked resistance to Protestant missionaries in Italy to the "violence that is now made by Roman Catholics in all sections of the United States against our Common School system."[109] After England's Lord Shaftesbury led a diplomatic initiative, the king of Tuscany freed the Madiai, but not before members of the American and Foreign Christian Union, with Cheever in the lead, had persuaded the state legislature of New York to remonstrate against the "cruel and flagrant oppressions" tolerated by the papacy. (P. T. Barnum also inquired as to whether the Madiai would tour the United States as an attraction for his circus.)[110] In the US Senate, Michigan's Lewis Cass thought the episode "one of the most flagrant violations of the rights of conscience recorded in the long chapter of religious intolerance."[111]

Despite the anti-Catholic invective in which these street orators, ministers, and politicians indulged themselves, defending the rights of Protestant missionaries abroad and occasionally other religious minorities such as Jews drew many Americans into a more principled defense of religious liberty—a humanitarian campaign with parallels to the international effort to abolish slavery.[112] This development was unpredictable. In the 1850s, most European leaders, whether monarchical or republican, Protestant, Catholic, or Orthodox, assumed that civil order depended on religious foundations, including the state support of a particular church. Only the First Amendment to the US Constitution developed an alternative model with no established church in the United States, although taxpayers supported

Congregational churches in Connecticut until 1818 and Massachusetts until 1832.

The migration of large numbers of Catholics to once-Protestant nations made practical questions of religious freedom more pressing. When complaining of the imprisonment of the Madiai, Senator Cass explained that his understanding of religious freedom included Catholics, Protestants, and Jews. Indeed, he defended the "inalienable right of worshipping God agreeably to the dictates of [one's] own conscience." Cass denied that the Constitution provided for a "mere temporary arrangement," but instead led to the "ever-enduring establishment of a great principle."[113]

A remarkable speech by Cheever's fellow Congregationalist minister, Leonard Bacon, at the annual meeting of the American and Foreign Christian Union in 1853, conveys the drift of informed Protestant opinion. Bacon defined religious liberty as the "great question of our present age" and defined "absolute religious liberty as a doctrine for the world." As the history of the United States demonstrated, "religious liberty, wherever it is established, brings in its train all other sorts of reasonable and real liberty."[114]

This emphasis on religious liberty—the right of an individual to choose and publicly advocate one's religious beliefs—meshed with a growing nineteenth-century conviction about the importance of the freely acting self. In such disparate venues as marriage (now viewed as a contract between two independent partners), civic life (where restrictions on suffrage diminished over the course of the century), and the marketplace (where economic actors made or lost their own fortunes), the individual was presumed sovereign. One of the most frequently made accusations against Jesuits (in Maine and elsewhere) was that a Jesuit "loses his individuality" through vows of obedience to his order and to the Pope.[115]

Harassment of itinerant preachers and Protestant converts by Catholic authorities in Tuscany and the papal states seemed to many Protestants (and some Catholics) an assault on individual conscience. Similarly, when Pope Pius IX and leading papal officials condoned the 1858 abduction of a Jewish child, Edgardo

Mortara, because he had been secretly baptized as a Catholic, leading Protestants joined Jews and more secular liberals in condemning a pope who, they believed, had declared war on the "rights and liberties of humanity."[116] When the US government contemplated annexing Cuba in the late 1850s, New Hampshire senator John Hale, a favorite of Maine's Republican Party press, argued against the venture, pointing to Cuba's Catholicism as an insuperable barrier, since the "history of modern times, the history of civil liberty, is the history of Protestant liberty."[117]

Eventually, the logic of this Protestant campaign for religious liberty, precisely because it focused on autonomy and the sanctity of the individual conscience, propelled Americans toward a greater willingness to separate church from state. This notion in turn undermined efforts to keep the King James Bible in the public schools. A few Protestant ministers and newspaper editors had already made this conceptual leap in the 1850s, much to Cheever's dismay. Joseph Thompson, one of Cheever's closest colleagues in the campaign against Catholic influence in American society, ventured the opinion in 1854 that "the principle of religious liberty forbids that in [a public] school, to which all have an equal right, there should be any distinctive religious teaching against the conscientious protest of any who have that legal right."[118]

This view had little purchase in Ellsworth in 1854, where the town's leading ministers and faculty at the nearby Bangor Theological Seminary still defended the mandatory use of the King James Bible in the schools, and where the *Ellsworth Herald* editorialized that free schools with the King James Bible were the only way to ensure that immigrants "become Republicanized." Under Bapst's leadership, the *Herald* warned, "the [Catholic] laity is fast retrograding into the follies and superstitions of the dark ages."[119] Repeating a rumor that spread throughout the country in the mid-1850s, even reaching the floor of Congress, Ellsworth residents told each other that the Marquis de Lafayette, a potent symbol of republican liberty, had warned on his deathbed that "if the liberties of the Republic are ever destroyed, it will be through the machinations of Romish Priests." Some accounts claimed Lafayette specified "Jesuits."[120]

Bapst further inflamed the situation in Ellsworth by pursuing justice in the courts. In concert with attorney Thomas White, Bapst orchestrated a test case, in which fifteen-year-old Bridget Donahoe claimed the public school violated her "constitutional right of liberty of conscience" by forcing her "to take part in a religious exercise."

The lawsuit forced disgruntled Ellsworth leaders to dip into the town treasury to fund the school committee's legal defense. They hired one of the country's most famous attorneys, Boston's Richard Henry Dana Jr. On behalf of the town, Dana denied that general readings from the King James Bible were a sectarian or religious exercise. Instead, he affirmed conventional Ellsworth wisdom, describing the King James Bible and the common school as "the best means of acquaintance and sympathy with the nature of our institutions." And he darkly warned that the Donahoe family was surely not "acting on their own convictions" but rather under the "influence of men [i.e., Bapst] whose office gives them great power to lead." The Maine Supreme Court, in a ruling important for church–state jurisprudence over the next century, agreed with Dana, finding that "mere citizenship" could not assimilate Maine's "large masses of foreign population." Requiring the reading of the King James Bible in public schools was not an "infringement upon religious freedom." Catholics must instead "imbibe the liberal spirit of our laws and institutions [so as to] become citizens in fact as well as in name."[121]

Cheever made similar claims during extended lecture tours of Maine, in his widely read columns in the *Independent*, frequently quoted in the *Ellsworth Herald* and Maine religious press, and in his 1854 *The Bible in the Public Schools*.[122] "The ridiculous pretension of conscience" made by Catholics annoyed Cheever because he understood the Bible as "neither Protestant nor Romish" but simply the indispensable text for a "Christian commonwealth." Laws prohibiting commerce on the Sabbath or polygamy also offended individual consciences, Cheever added, but "true religion" could not be banned from the schools, certainly not in a country where many never "attend any church, or any other schools than the free schools." He warned his readers that "at the instigation of the sect of Roman Catholics, a powerful effort has been made, and is still making, to divide and break up our system of free common schools. The effort is to be continued and urged with all the energy, authority, and perseverance of the papal power in our country."[123]

V

As figures as diverse as the Angel Gabriel, Gavazzi, Parker, and Cheever knitted together individual liberty, Protestantism, and republican government, Catholics found themselves torn. Initially, Bapst and his fellow Jesuits thought the United States a refreshing contrast to an often anticlerical Europe. They admired how American bishops and religious orders owned property, held meetings, and appointed priests without "the menace of government interference," in contrast to a Europe where monarchs, state officials, and, as the Jesuits knew, mobs exercised control over church affairs.[124] Or as Bapst explained to a European Jesuit in 1850:

> The United States is the freest country in the world. You believe yourselves free in France and in Belgium; but be assured that you possess but the shadow of the liberty which we enjoy in America. I can establish here as many schools as I can wish, and no one will interfere with them. What is more, I could preach the doctrines of the Catholic religion in the most Protestant town, before an audience composed entirely of Protestants, and I feel sure that I would not suffer a single interruption.[125]

Appreciation for religious liberty (in practice) did not mean appreciation for religious individualism. To Jesuits, Protestant tributes to the "the Bible alone" or "private judgment" seemed naive—the direct cause of the endless variations on doctrine and church organization found within the United States. Accordingly, Bapst and Jesuit contemporaries received much instruction on the primacy of Peter, moving from Matthew 16:18—"you are Peter and upon this rock I will build my Church"—to the inability of "the sects" (i.e., Protestants) to grasp "the most obvious and natural sense" of scripture on the topic of church authority.[126] Only "religious individualism," explained one German Jesuit, could produce exotica such as Mormons and spiritualists.[127]

The gap between a Catholicism built on the church and a Protestantism built on individual interpretation of the Bible even became clear in Ellsworth. In one chance encounter on Ellsworth's main street, Bapst attempted to persuade the town's leading minister, Rev. Sewell Tenney of the Congregational Church, of the inadequacy of the Bible "without the aid of tradition." After reflecting with a European colleague on the discussion, Bapst concluded that "between Protestants of good faith and ourselves, everything might be reduced to this point—the proof of the insufficiency of private interpretation and the infallibility of the Church."[128]

When after his tarring and feathering a group of Bangor businessman presented Bapst with a gold watch and expressed their dismay at the incident, he politely accepted the gift, speculating that the "outcome of this incident will be extremely useful for the cause of the Church in Maine."[129] But he privately described public schools as designed by "extremely cunning men" to "corrupt and destroy the souls of Catholics." Catholic schools were the only response, although funding such schools without state support would lead to "countless difficulties."[130]

The popularity of anti-Catholic speakers such as Gavazzi and the surge in anti-Catholic violence in the 1850s also tempered Jesuit notions of the United States as a haven from European anti-Catholicism.[131] Details of Bapst's tarring and feathering quickly made their way back to Europe, via an Italian translation of articles in the Maine press made for the Jesuit Father General and titled "On Torture Endured by Fr. Bapst," letters to Irish Cardinal Paul Cullen, and an article in the London *Tablet*, which noted that "republican hands have perpetrated an outrage on

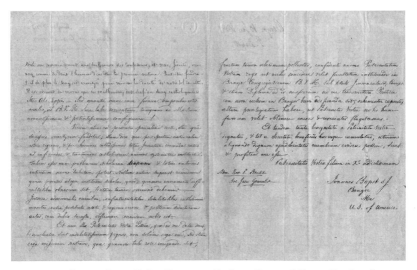

FIGURE 3. Letter from John Bapst to Father General Peter Beckx, January 10, 1855, discussing the attack on Bapst in Ellsworth, Maine. Courtesy of Archivum Romanum Societatis Iesu.

an amiable Priest which makes us thank God we are not republicans."[132] Fr. De Smet thought the attack on Bapst a sobering comment on "American liberty and tolerance, so highly boasted, [which exists] less in the Great Republic than in the most oppressed country of Europe."[133] Louisville bishop Martin Spalding described the "savage mob at Ellsworth" as imitators of the "radical republicans of Europe."[134]

To Bapst's Jesuit superiors, his suffering evoked martyrdom and the militancy necessary to preserve the faith in a hostile environment. The Jesuit Father General congratulated Bapst on his courage, asking him to "accept the multitude of your crosses, good father, in order that you might confirm your station through your crucifixion."[135] After detailing how Bapst refused to leave Ellsworth until after he had celebrated Mass, his immediate superior in Maryland proudly noted that "the warrior of Christ scorned their threats."[136] Bapst took pride in his identity as "the Jesuit who was insulted by the Protestants of Ellsworth" and later expressed gratitude for the opportunity to "suffer something for God's glory."[137] This suffering, he explained, made him recognize the "great honor" in following one's "conscience."[138]

That Ellsworth residents did not repent of their actions only further disillusioned Catholics. In a town meeting after Bapst's tarring and feathering, townspeople, led by Chaney, continued to decry "this designing Jesuit."[139] A jury convened in Ellsworth refused to issue any indictments against the perpetrators. Ellsworth residents made a point of presenting a King James Bible to a Bangor schoolteacher, Miss Thayer, for her insistence on reading the King James Bible in Bangor schools. (In Bangor, city authorities had attempted to defuse the issue by allowing reading from the Catholic or Douay translation.)[140]

Vandals destroyed the now-unused St. Joseph's Catholic Church in Ellsworth. "The triumph of the rowdies," Bapst grimly concluded, "is complete." Even four years later Bapst had "nothing good" to say about Ellsworth.[141] Bapst became a US citizen in 1856, indicating a resolve to remain in the country. But in contrast to his ebullient assessment of the United States soon after his arrival, he now emphasized the "reverse side of the medal," warning Catholics in Europe that "this infidel country" was making "extraordinary efforts to tempt Catholics, or crush them."[142]

VI

At precisely the moment when arguments over religion in the public schools exploded in Ellsworth, the national debate over slavery took a pivotal turn. Already the Fugitive Slave Act of 1850 and celebrated cases of escaped slaves captured in the North had shifted northern public opinion in an antislavery direction. Stephen A. Douglas's introduction of the Kansas–Nebraska Act into Congress in February 1854 sparked more controversy than any piece of legislation in American history and solidified among many white northerners the fear of an aggressive slave power.

The same principles structuring discussion of the Jesuits, Catholicism, and religious liberty—notably a heightened sense of the importance of individual autonomy—infused the slavery debate. British evangelical Hugh McNeile wrote of the "perfect consistency" involved in advocating the suppression of "slavery and popery." The Chilean nationalist Francisco Bilbao fulminated against the Jesuits and slavery with equal vehemence. Richard D. Webb, an Irish (but Quaker) antislavery agitator, compared the "rampant audacious, insolent Ultramontanism of the Romish clergy" with the "kindred system of chattel slavery."[143]

The most extended meditations on the links between Catholicism and slavery came in the United States. When over three thousand Protestant ministers signed a petition attacking the Kansas–Nebraska Act, but not a single Catholic priest did, antislavery activists in Maine and elsewhere pounced on this fact. As Parker noted in Bangor, "But do you know a single Catholic priest that is opposed to slavery? I wish I did. . . . I wish I could hear of a single Catholic priest of any eminence who ever cared anything for the freedom of the most oppressed men that are here in America."[144]

Parker glided from Catholic opposition to "liberty of mind or conscience" to the claim that

> the Catholic clergy are on the side of slavery. They find it is the dominant power, and pay court thereto that they may rise by its help. They love slavery itself; it is an institution thoroughly congenial to them, consistent with the first principles of their Church. Their Jesuit leaders think it is "an ulcer which will eat of the Republic," and so stimulate and foster it for the ruin of democracy, the deadliest foe of the Roman hierarchy.[145]

And Parker was not unusual. In one Fourth of July oration, Anson Burlingame, soon to be elected to Congress from Massachusetts, jumped from "that terrible order of Jesuits" to the Madiai case to the fact that "no catholic priest signed the protest against the Nebraska bill."[146] Eden Foster, a minister from Lowell, Massachusetts, thought "slavery and Romanism a two-edged dagger with which to stab liberty to the heart."[147]

Even the Angel Gabriel, according to one source, "railed at the Catholics, at Slavery, [and] at the Fugitive Slave Law" during his tour of New York, Massachusetts, and Maine in spring 1854. (The Angel Gabriel later migrated to British Guyana, where his attacks on both Catholicism and the treatment of Africans prompted the governor to ban all public meetings and imprison him.)[148] As one New York congressman argued, "Protestantism results in civil enfranchisement; Jesuitism, on the contrary, affiliates with and tends to political despotism. As in the empires of the Old World Jesuitism allies itself with 'kingcraft,' so in the New, it strikes hands with slavery."[149]

The opportunistic *Ellsworth Herald* editor Chaney avoided comment on slavery for most of 1854, but he swung behind an antislavery, anti-Catholic platform in 1855. "In vain," he concluded, "may croaking politicians preach sympathy for the papists as an evidence of Christian charity; or the extension of human slavery as evidence of philanthropy." Meeting in Ellsworth, the Hancock County American Party resolved in August 1855 to be "true in our opposition to the aggressions of Popery, but also true to the instincts of Liberty [which] will require the concentration of the whole Anti-Nebraska strength."[150]

The absorption of voters from the American Party into the new Republican Party, noticeable throughout the North, proved unusually smooth in Ellsworth. By 1856, the Republicans controlled every major state office, and in the presidential election that year Republican John Fremont won 66 percent of the vote in Ellsworth, where just a year earlier the American Party had triumphed.[151] A number of Ellsworth American Party stalwarts moved into leadership positions in the local Republican Party, and hosted lectures by nationally prominent antislavery Republicans such as Congressman Joshua Giddings and Senator Benjamin Wade. That J. C. Pitrat, author of *Americans Warned of Jesuitism, or, the Jesuits Unveiled*, and an ex-priest from France, followed Giddings on the Ellsworth lecture circuit again suggests the overlap between antislavery and anti-Catholic agitation.[152]

If Maine's Democrats understood religious liberty to mean protection from government interference, Maine's Republicans understood religious liberty as threatened by an aggressive Catholicism. One leading Republican activist and editor, Bangor's John Sawyer, explained that "my experience and observation in political affairs had taught me that the ascendancy of the so-called Democratic party had been maintained by bidding successfully for the votes of foreigners and slaveholders. So long continued and systematic had this course become, that Popery and American slavery seemed united in the effort to sustain and strengthen each other."[153] A year later, the *Ellsworth American* editorialized that Maine now contained two political parties, "one [Republican] in favor of freedom, political, social and religious, and the other [Democratic] in favor of slavery to the blacks and submission to Romish influences, for the sake of Catholic votes on the part of the whites."[154]

In both the United States and Europe, Catholics did not defend slavery as a positive good in the manner of some white southerners, but they typically viewed immediate emancipation as a misguided liberalism, especially when measured against the disruption slavery's abolition would entail.[155] In Rome, the Jesuit editors of *Civiltà Cattolica* stressed the church's efforts to mitigate the excesses of slavery, but still thought "slavery in a restrained sense is not absolutely contrary to the law of nature."[156] Jesuits owned slaves in Maryland until 1838, and not a single prominent Catholic took a leading role in an abolitionist organization.[157]

Bapst left no record of his own opinion on slavery, although in one 1855 letter he noted that a slave as housekeeper would not do "in our abolitionist state."[158] Other Jesuits, such as Bapst's fellow Swiss exile Bernardin Wiget, thought slaves "a happy lot of people compared to the poor Irish in Boston" and later rejected the abolitionist arguments of a liberal French bishop, explaining that "our Savior and St. Paul never preached universal emancipation, and that is a forced conclusion to derive such doctrine from the text, 'Do unto others etc.'"[159]

Local Democrats allied themselves with Bapst and Ellsworth's Catholics. Bapst reported that the most prominent Democrat in

Ellsworth, Charles Jarvis, agreed that the school committee had "violated the Constitution by compelling our children to read the protestant Bible, or otherwise by turning them out of school."[160] Jarvis sheltered Bapst the night after his tarring and feathering, and later became a target of abuse in the Ellsworth press for his support of the Kansas–Nebraska Act.[161] In the congressional election of 1856, the Democratic candidate appealed to Catholic voters by linking "the Republican party of Hancock [County], and particularly its intelligent and prominent members in Ellsworth," to "the persons who mobbed Mr. Bapst, burnt down the church and caused other outrages."[162]

If many white northerners linked opposition to the King James Bible with support of slavery, viewing both as symptomatic of Catholic antagonism to liberty, Catholics connected mob violence against Catholics with abolitionist refusal to obey unjust laws. That the Ellsworth perpetrators escaped punishment only proved the "heinousness" of appeals by Parker and others to resist the Fugitive Slave Act. As one Catholic editor explained, the "spirit of intolerance towards the Catholic religion and those who profess it" naturally supported a "fanaticism" aimed against the "rights of property guaranteed by the constitution to the South."[163] Another Catholic editor decried "desperate fanatics" willing at once to attack Bapst and "destroy the Union of North and South."[164]

VII

Bapst moved to Bangor after the attack in Ellsworth. He initially complained of health problems—"I feel that I am exhausted and worn out, & I have in my chest a pain of long standing"—but recovered within a year.[165] He had much success as a Bangor pastor. When he led a successful fund-raising campaign for a new church, grateful parishioners placed in the cornerstone a piece of Bapst's clothing from the night of his attack in Ellsworth, smeared with tar and feathers, and saved by his housekeeper as a relic.[166] When a rumor reached parishioners that he might be transferred away from Maine—in yet another marker of the global character of the Society, the Father General contemplated sending him to Bombay—the "female members of the Catholic Congregation of Bangor" pleaded with Jesuit leaders to keep Bapst in place. Prior to the arrival of Bapst, these women explained, "Our youth grew up without a proper knowledge of their Faith and consequently many of them were Catholics only in name, though sufficiently identified with the Church to furnish her enemies with a pretext to attribute to her teaching the vices learned of themselves."[167]

Bapst did leave Maine, but just for Boston, where he became the first president of Boston College. There he renewed his friendship with Nathaniel Shurtleff Jr., a Harvard student appalled by Gavazzi's anti-Catholic lectures who had entered the church under Bapst's tutelage. Shurtleff explained to his Harvard classmates that he served a greater purpose by forfeiting his "liberty, position, [and] the ties of family and friendship" so that he might become a "humble priest of the Catholic Church, in the Society of Jesus."[168]

Shurtleff joined the Union army immediately after the start of the war and was killed on the battlefield on September 16, 1862. He left specific instructions for his funeral service: his dead hands must hold rosary beads, masons must chisel the words Ave Maria into his coffin, no Protestant minister should take part in the service, and a cross must be placed on his tombstone, a few careful steps away from the official family vault. Bapst eulogized Shurtleff at the funeral Mass, where, as one Boston Jesuit informed his superior, "the Church was never so well packed" with most of the city's "respectable citizens," including "several parsons." In honor of this fallen war hero, the flag at the Massachusetts State House flew at half-mast.[169]

The harmony between Protestants and Catholics evident at Shurtleff's funeral did not endure. If in 1861 Bapst still thought that the "designs of Providence" had exiled Jesuits from an "old" Europe with its "fading" faith to the United States, he would worry in 1873 that "in the United States, this sanctuary of liberty . . . we commence to experience the moral, political and religious misery of Europe."[170]

Initial scholarly assessments of the Bapst episode reflected this gap between Catholics and their critics. Two New England historians blamed the Ellsworth attack on "the determined efforts of the Romanists to obtain the control of the common school system." The authors hoped the "stringent proceedings" of the tarring and feathering had "awed the Romanists into good behavior."[171] By contrast, John Gilmary Shea, the first prominent historian of Catholicism in the United States, contacted Bapst within days of the attack to get a firsthand report. Shea placed Bapst directly in the line of Catholic martyrs, terming Bapst an "illustrious sufferer" at the hands of citizens "more savage than the original [Indian] occupants of the soil."[172]

Unlike Fr. Râle, Bapst did not die a martyr, even if one of his admirers later described him as a "martyr at Ellsworth in desire."[173] And in fact Bapst wished he could visit Rome and see the "places blessed & hallowed by the blood and triumphs of so many martyrs, & visiting the Shrines, where their relics are preserved and venerated, & where so many miracles have been wrought by their instrumentality."[174] But just as Râle entered Catholic textbooks as a murdered victim of Protestant intolerance, Bapst came to symbolize for Jesuits their own participation in the Catholic story of the nineteenth century: a tale of persecution, exile, and reconstruction. When American Jesuits ate their communal meals in silence, listening to readings from the lives of famous missionaries or martyrs, they now occasionally heard, along with readings from the letters of Saint Francis Xavier, recitations of Bapst's initial letters from Maine.[175]

Bapst continued to work as an administrator and parish priest in cities on the Eastern Seaboard.[176] When asked about the night in Ellsworth, Bapst spoke "pleasantly about it" and displayed the gold watch given to him by the "respectable citizens of Maine."[177] He grew a long white beard fit for "a holy old patriarch," and accounts circulated of his ability to heal the sick through his prayers or even predict the future. Admirers boasted of his "childlike, unquestioning, absolute great love for the church."[178]

Eventually, his memory became unpredictable. As he admitted in one of his last letters, "I can read very little, write very little, do no work, my memory has almost gone; in a word, God in His Goodness has deprived me of almost everything, leaving me only the power of praying."[179] He struggled to distinguish "between dream and reality," occasionally waking up in horror as his mind replayed that night in Ellsworth so long ago.[180]

3

WESTPHALIA, MISSOURI: NATION

I

Missouri residents experienced the savagery of the US Civil War with unusual force. From the beginning of the war, regions, towns, and even families split between affiliation with the Union or the Confederacy, and armies and guerrilla bands roamed across the state for the full four years of the conflict. One Belgian Jesuit, Ferdinand Helias, found himself in the middle of the maelstrom. While working as a pastor in Taos, Missouri, a few months after the start of the war, Helias was accused by a group of local men—he later identified them as "free-thinkers" and the "choir leaders of Protestantism"—of sympathizing with the Confederacy, and even harboring ammunition and concealing spies in his rectory.[1]

Helias insisted that he remained loyal to the Union and viewed Confederate secession as a "flagrant violation of the original pact, a sacred contract." Still, unnerved by this incident, Helias fled from Taos to a parish where he had also served as pastor, St. Joseph Catholic Church in Westphalia, Missouri, nine miles to the east across the Osage River. (Union militia members took the opportunity afforded by his absence to ransack the abandoned rectory in Taos.) In Westphalia, Helias tried to remain hidden but word leaked out of his presence. Again there were accusations of disloyalty. Again Helias fled, this time to the house of a friend in the country. Word reached Jesuits in Saint Louis that "Fr. Helias was not well received at Westphalia and was even compelled to leave the house at night."[2]

FIGURE 4. Ferdinand Helias, S.J. Courtesy of Jesuit Archives of the Central United States.

Helias then composed a letter to his accusers. "The founder of the Mission of Central Missouri," he explained in the third person, "has not failed to employ every means in his power to maintain the people in submission to the law." Military authorities eventually assured him that there would be no repetition of the harassment, and Helias returned to his rectory in Taos. But two years later, he still complained of both the "vexations" and "depredations" that marked this "calamitous civil war" and continual abuse directed by Unionists at the Jesuits.[3]

In October 1864, a Confederate army swept through the region and Helias fled his rectory for a third time, retreating to Saint Louis to avoid the fighting.[4] Now sixty-six, he took the opportunity to work on his memoir—a pastiche, initially written in Latin, French, and English, of old letters, reports, and recollections. (In a disarming preface, he apologized for the "impudence, the lack of order, the length and confusion of content, the bad writing [and] the shortcoming of style.")

His sympathies also became clear. He titled his survey of the 1850s—with its anti-Catholic nativism and antislavery agitation—a period of "troubles and religious persecution." He blamed the war on the "mad ravings of puritan fanaticism" as exemplified by William Lloyd Garrison, a man willing to term the Constitution "a covenant with death" and "league with Hell." Garrison and his followers propagated their views in "pamphlets, periodicals and books, in conversation from the school and lecture room and the pulpits."

At the war's onset, Helias explained, "peaceful, law-abiding" Missouri had effectively been invaded by militant easterners. Kansas, he thought, had been settled by "puritan fanatics sent from the East." Cole County, where he resided in Taos, and which had been one of the only Missouri counties to offer significant electoral support to Abraham Lincoln in 1860, seemed to him a center of "puritan corruption."[5] Indeed, American nationalism had become worrisome in its fervor. "Each country," he explained, "has advantages and disadvantages, and everywhere we find the good and the bad." Unfortunately, Americans seemed convinced that theirs was the "Nation of Nations."[6]

In the months after the war, Missouri Jesuit colleagues of Helias would become embroiled in a series of controversies, with one reaching the US Supreme Court, on the nature of religious liberty and limits of national authority. These disputes prompted one of Helias's colleagues to wonder if American nationalists would destroy, for Catholics, the benefits of the "land of liberty."[7]

II

Helias's story, like so many nineteenth-century Catholic stories, began with the French Revolution. Born in Ghent in 1796 along with a twin brother, Helias was baptized just before French revolutionary armies occupying the Austrian Netherlands (modern Belgium) closed his parish church as part of an antireligious campaign—with priests forced into exile, church bells silenced, and the persecution of men's and women's religious orders—as severe as any in Europe since the seventeenth century.[8] Helias later recalled, in a self-dramatizing flourish, that "at the same hour when the enemies of religion believed that they had buried [Catholicism] under a mass of ruins, it was already reborn in the person of that child."[9]

Helias's father, Emmanuel, a magistrate, had long resisted the efforts of Hapsburg emperor Joseph II to minimize Roman influence on Catholicism—an attitude toward church–state matters often termed "Josephinism." Even late in life, Helias regretted Joseph II's desire to align Catholicism with his "philosophical views." "The protection of a Catholic prince," he observed, "has very often degenerated into oppression."[10]

Joseph II's immediate successors were less suspicious of Rome, but revolutionary French armies conquered the region in the 1790s. Arrested by French soldiers a year after the birth of his twin sons, Emmanuel Helias spent two years in a Parisian jail. Later, his son Emmanuel, Ferdinand's twin brother, served his own Parisian jail term for defending the bishop of their hometown against the "godless plans" of Napoleon.[11]

Ferdinand entered the Jesuits in 1817, a fateful choice given the hostility toward the order promoted by King William I, a Dutch Calvinist then ruling what is now the Netherlands and Belgium.[12] In fact, the Jesuits were prohibited from public work for most of the period from the 1773 suppression until Belgian independence in 1830.[13] Helias would later bemoan "protestant intolerance" and recall a willingness to "persecute" Catholic subjects.[14]

The hazy legal status of the Jesuits mandated secrecy. Helias's father offered his residence as a covert site for young men, including Ferdinand, training to be Jesuits. But the prohibition on public activities forced aspiring Jesuits to move to Switzerland, and nurtured in young Helias, as for so many Jesuits, a sense of the "ingratitude of the present century" toward Catholicism.[15] He studied in Switzerland for over a decade, and like Bapst, observed Jesuit mission campaigns, some led by Roothaan. (Years later, he recalled crowds "full of faith" around the confessional.")[16] An initial trip to Rome with visits to St. Peter's and the Jesuit home church of the Gesù, made an enduring impression.[17] He eventually stayed in Rome for a year assisting Roothaan, now Father

General, with his correspondence and compiling his own collection of relics.[18]

Even in these early days of the restored Society, Belgian Jesuits proved unusually willing to join the foreign missions, and over the course of the century hundreds of Belgian Jesuits would serve in missions as diverse as Sri Lanka and the Congo. The first Belgian mission enterprise, however, was in the United States. In 1833, Helias himself left Belgium, and after brief stops at Georgetown University and Conewago, Pennsylvania, moved to Saint Louis. There Fr. Roothaan thought Helias might work—as Bapst would a decade later—for the "salvation of the Indians."[19]

Instead, Helias taught a variety of subjects at Jesuit-run Saint Louis University. In 1838, Helias left Saint Louis for an assignment on the thinly settled frontier of central Missouri, with responsibility for a six-hundred-square-mile swath of land, composing parts of eleven counties on both sides of the Missouri River. The impetus behind his departure was the presence of a group of roughly eighty Catholic immigrants from Westphalia. The surnames of these settlers—Dohmen, Messerschmidt, Kunermann, Zellerhoff, Huber, and Höcker—convey their Germanic origins, as does the name they chose for their village, New Westphalia. (Confusingly, residents dropped the "New" soon after the town's founding.)

Helias used Westphalia as his base for ceaseless rounds of horseback journeys to twenty-four missions, counting roughly three thousand Catholics as parishioners.[20] He visited missions near Westphalia at least once a month. More distant missions, often blocked by swollen rivers, received two or three visits a year. The conditions were raw. One Jesuit who worked briefly with Helias noted in a letter to the Father General in Rome that the "poverty of my parishioners" explained why Helias lived in a "miserable building in the woods."[21] When the bishop of Saint Louis met with Helias in Jefferson City, Missouri, he observed that Helias celebrated Mass "in the dining room of a public tavern, the proprietor of which is a Catholic."[22]

Helias built seven churches in his first years in central Missouri—a reckless building campaign that worried his superiors

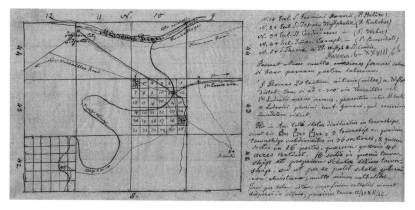

FIGURE 5. Map of Jesuit missions in central Missouri, drawn by Andreas Ehrensberger, S.J., in 1851. Courtesy of Archivum Romanum Societatis Iesu.

and taxed his small congregations. His priorities mirrored those of Bapst: to pull Catholic immigrants toward the institutional church and its sacraments, and create Catholic enclaves within a potentially hostile American society. When Helias purchased land for the church in Westphalia, for example, he insisted that Catholic families occupy the lots surrounding the church. As he explained, "The building of new churches was necessary and desirable, so that the new settlers who arrived daily would not disperse themselves but settle near a church and so build a village."[23] Again like Bapst, Helias lamented the catechetical ignorance of many Catholics even as he rejoiced in their occasional return to the "Roman Catholic faith of their ancestors."[24]

Helias also made a conscious effort to reproduce the material trappings of Catholic Europe. He made multiple requests to European Catholic missionary societies for funds, explaining that his parishioners did not own "even candles or decent receptacles for the worthy celebration of the [Mass]," and his Roman superiors were cajoled into echoing his requests.[25] He importuned wealthy Belgian relatives to support his work, and squabbled with Jesuit leaders in Belgium, Rome, and Missouri over whether he or his religious superiors controlled donated funds. When his

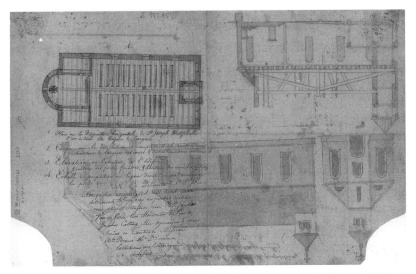

FIGURE 6. Plans for St. Joseph Catholic Church in Westphalia, ca. 1848, probably drawn by Ferdinand Helias, S.J. Courtesy of the Jesuit Archives of the Central United States.

mother died, her will provided monies to furnish one of Helias's churches.[26]

In a first memoir composed in the 1840s, Helias dwelled on his decorating scheme for the interior and exterior of St. Joseph in Westphalia. He crammed into the church six columns "splendidly sculpted in the likeness of candlesticks," a tapestry of Joseph, Jesus, and Mary, crafted by a "master's hand," pictures of the scene at Calvary and the Annunciation, fourteen stations of the cross, paintings of "those mourning the suffering Jesus being tortured," smaller tapestries of prominent Jesuits, a tabernacle "displayed on a truly elegant throne of flowers completely surrounded by lighted candles," and a linen canopy above the altar bearing a portrait of the Immaculate Heart of the Virgin. Hanging above the church was a ninety-six-pound bronze bell that "convenes the townsfolk" for liturgies and special occasions. The bell also reminded town dwellers "to greet the mother of God" when rung each day. Displayed near the altar were relics of

Saint Francis Xavier and other Jesuit saints, purchased by Helias when in Rome, the city he termed the "capital of the world."[27]

Outside the church were solid wood trellises, "elegant in their craftsmanship," which enclosed the cemetery. In the middle of the cemetery rested a tall crucifix, which could "be seen far and wide by travelers." When Helias traveled, he distributed rosaries and holy pictures "as well as pamphlets and tracts." He ordered church decorations from Catholic suppliers in Münster, and when a ship carrying books, priestly vestments, and "ornamentations of every type" sank outside Saint Louis, he was disconsolate.[28]

In all this Helias reproduced the familiar, appealing to Catholic immigrants with the memories of their youth. But this reliance on sight (candles, tapestries, stained glass, and paintings), sound (bells and music), and smell (incense) served a confessional purpose, distinguishing Catholic from Protestant in the same way that Bapst distinguished the Protestant King James Bible from the Catholic Douay version. If anything, Catholics such as Helias placed even greater emphasis on the sensory dimensions of Catholicism than their predecessors, precisely to heighten denominational contrasts. Helias compared the lush "ornamentation of the sanctuary" in his church in Westphalia "with the gloomy abodes of the Methodists, Anabaptists and other sects in this area." "It is no wonder," he concluded in self-congratulatory fashion, that "these preachers of false doctrine . . . keep their own people away from the holy chapels of the Catholics." Given this Catholic visual and aural spectacle, the efforts of "fanatic" preachers relying on scripture alone could not prevail. Or as Helias put it, "When they [Protestants] admire the attractively decorated altars, the pomp of the rituals, and the pleasant harmony of music, and on the other hand, in their own places of assembly they see all things naked and unkempt and vile in their squalor, they are moved and they begin to doubt their own dogmas."[29]

In tiny Taos, Helias even provided a direct link to the Italian baroque. There Helias's acquaintance with Father General Roothaan and financial support from his mother allowed him to purchase three paintings done by an artist in the school of Guido

Reni, a Bolognese painter favored by popes and Catholic patrons in the early seventeenth century, and a favorite of ultramontane nineteenth-century Catholics as well.

Helias installed the paintings—Saint Francis Xavier, Saint Francis of Assisi, and the flagellation of Christ—near the main altar. Francis Xavier especially appealed to Jesuits because of his determination to bring Christianity to distant lands, and in 1833, as Helias knew, Roothaan had recounted Xavier's career in a letter read out loud within every Jesuit residence and aimed at inspiring Jesuits to join the missions. A decade later, Helias named the Taos church St. Francis Xavier, and frequently compared his own sufferings on the Missouri frontier along with his willingness to travel with few possessions and only one set of clothes to trials endured by Xavier in his mission to India and Japan.

III

Assessing Helias's efforts during his first decade in central Missouri means probing the beliefs of the Catholics he presumed to lead. His own account stressed the "rejoicing spirit" he encountered when arriving in a new village.[30] He baptized infants, absolved men and women in the confessional of their "chronic sins," and lured lapsed Catholics away from "negligence and fickleness." He delighted in the "incredible eagerness and reverent feeling" exhibited toward confession and the Mass as well as the sight of immigrants striding to Mass across the fields on the sound of the church bell. When cholera swept through the region in 1843 and 1844, grimly evident in his annual tabulation of burials, Helias journeyed from house to house comforting the sick and administering last rites.[31]

Hints of conflict, though, also dot the archival record. Helias became "exceedingly angry" when parishioners disagreed among themselves or with him, and as early as 1842 one Jesuit superior wished "that this good man would learn discretion in his words."[32] In 1855, another superior termed him *sui generis*, "respected among his own" but also "fiery and disorderly" and "often foolish."[33]

More than Helias's temperament was at issue. Helias ministered to small groups of French Creoles, Bavarians, Belgians, and
Irish Catholics as well as the Germans at Westphalia, occasionally preaching in French, English, and German during the same
liturgy. Like many missionary priests, he evaluated these immigrants on a devotional scale. The Irish, saturated in the ethos of
the nineteenth-century Catholic revival, received uniform praise,
from Helias and other Jesuit missionaries. One Philadelphia Jesuit described them as "not rich" but extraordinarily "generous."[34]
At the opposite end of the scale were French-speaking Creoles—
"infidels living out in the woods."[35]

German Catholics received a mixed verdict. Helias and other
missionary priests frequently lauded German Catholics for their
"spirit of faith," and eagerness to build schools and churches.[36]
Still, Jesuit missionaries working among German Catholics in
Missouri recognized the same tensions then shaping Catholic life
in Germany. Middle-class Catholic Germans, in particular, often
resented the firm lines drawn by clergy between Catholic and
non-Catholic, disliked Catholic opposition to state-sponsored
schools, and questioned the new emphasis on specific devotions
and miracle accounts.[37]

These tensions crossed the Atlantic, with some German diocesan priests uneasy about the goals of the Jesuits, and some Jesuits concerned about a "liberalism" surfacing in German Catholic
parishes.[38] One of the most bitter Catholic disputes of the nineteenth century occurred in Buffalo, New York, in the 1850s when
the local bishop attempted to end lay control of a largely Al-
satian and middle-class parish. Defying the bishop's excommu-
nications, these Buffalo parishioners denounced not only the
exiled Jesuit asked by the bishop to negotiate with them but all
"Jesuits inimical to our republican institutions." They pleaded
their case with New York state legislators, who in turn urged the
passage of laws restricting corporate ownership of church property, since Catholic priests were "generally foreigners, educated
in the most absolute doctrines of Papal Supremacy, who have no
faith in human progress, who regard the doctrine of individual
independence as heresy."[39]

In Westphalia, Helias complained of "savage wolves" who refused to acknowledge his authority. He regretted that the "chief laity" urged him to "consult the parishioners" in a manner "contrary to the canons of the Baltimore Provincial Council and the will of the Pope," and complained to his family of the "perfidy" of his congregation in contrast to the "eminently Catholic" atmosphere of Belgium.[40]

In 1842, Helias stalked away from Westphalia to St. Francis Xavier parish in Taos. Helias's superior explained to the Father General in Rome that "the people of the congregation did not stand by their pastor as they should have done." Before departing, Helias attached to the church door the following Latin tag:

Ardua qui quaerit, rubros cur currit ad Indos
Westphalian veniat, ardua cuncta dabunt.

Why should the man who wishes hardship go to the
   Indies?
Let him come to Westphalia and he will find hardships
   aplenty.[41]

Helias's most prominent opponent in this Westphalia dispute was Bernhard Bruns, who had emigrated from Germany in 1836. A physician and farmer, Bruns built the first log house in Westphalia, opened the first store, and served as the town postmaster.[42] Delighted to live just "500 paces from the church," Bruns became a lay leader of the Catholic community.[43] He jokingly referred to himself as a "Latin farmer," a term then used to describe educated German immigrants unprepared for the daily agricultural grind.[44]

In 1838, Helias met Bruns for the first time, describing him as a "learned doctor of medicine."[45] But relations between the two men soured. Remarkably, a cache of letters survives from Bruns and his wife, Henriette (or Jette), to relatives in Germany. These letters offer a rare glimpse of life in the pews for devout yet disaffected Catholics. "One can never go to church without finding some objection to his [Helias's] sermons," Jette complained in

May 1841. "He exaggerates horribly and turns everybody against him. Most of them are determined not to contribute any more to his subsistence."⁴⁶ She added, "He has insulted [Bernard] Bruns several times, but we keep quiet. If only his removal could take place without further friction." After Helias's stormy departure, Jette explained that "[Helias] has completely lost the confidence of the community, he threatens and scolds as usual."⁴⁷

Helias's efforts "to enlighten the blind minds" of the recalcitrant congregation did not ease the tense situation. Neither did his depiction of them—in a phrase he considered a compliment but that also suggests his pastoral approach—as a "single-minded and simple people."⁴⁸

Jette, by contrast, identified herself as an "educated German" and resented the fact that "our congregation is more numerous than any other, but we have few divine services." Helias, she continued, lives "on the other side of the Osage with his favorite people." In 1846, an argument over property rights between Helias and those he termed "evildoers" degenerated into a lawsuit. Helias enlisted the bishop in his defense, and when the bishop visited the region to administer confirmation he duly denounced any "attempt at schism" and "troublesome men" unwilling to "submit to your lawful pastors."⁴⁹ Three years later Helias belatedly acknowledged that any priest in central Missouri must be "discreet, prudent, [and] moderate" to avoid offending "the notables of the place."⁵⁰

When Helias arranged for a prominent Jesuit preacher to offer a parish mission, the visiting Jesuit noted some initial resistance in the congregation—"Hell is hot enough, it is said; why does one need mission sermons additionally!"—although he applauded the piety of the local Bavarians and their "respect" for their pastor.⁵¹ Jette was less enthusiastic about "narrow-minded" Jesuits:

> The good man preached for nine days, he gave instructions, he heard confessions, etc., etc., and promoted brotherhood. On the third day my husband ran off, and his poor wife then had to decide for herself what to do. So every day I went to

church and suffered humbly when he heckled the sinners who were not ready to confess, and I tried to carry home at least something that was good. But it was so repulsive to me, and in my innermost soul there was a voice that whispered, "You have not been cast out even if your service to God is of a different kind." And the Mother of God looked down on me so quietly and so peaceably as if she agreed with me and did not approve of all this commotion.[52]

IV

The European revolutions that sent Bapst from Switzerland to Maine also reshaped Catholic life in Missouri. The most immediate impact was enhanced Jesuit manpower. Thirty-eight Jesuits exiled from Switzerland made their way to Saint Louis. At the time, as one of the Jesuits later recounted, the United States seemed "destined by God to become the asylum of liberty and of religion in place of a Europe already grown old and decayed."[53]

Even as exiled Jesuits scattered across the Midwest, however, the experience of the 1840s, with Jesuits expelled from many European and Latin American nations, had already altered their understandings of the modern nation-state. In the first decades of the nineteenth century, many Jesuits had sympathized with popular nationalism. In Mexico and Peru, a reform-minded Catholicism and nationalist desires to break from Spain reinforced each other, with some ex-Jesuits (after the suppression) leading the effort to build new nation-states.[54] The sufferings of Catholic Poland at the hands of imperial Russia and Catholic Ireland at the hands of imperial Britain drew sympathetic attention, with one Polish Jesuit insisting that "patriotic citizens of a free and independent country" such as the United States should empathize with the plight of all "persecuted" nations.[55]

Helias, too, thought early nineteenth-century nationalism compatible with Catholicism. He pointed to his native Belgium, where an 1831 constitution drafted largely by Catholic politicians guaranteed freedom of the press and religion, disproving accusations that Catholicism could not coexist with fundamental civil liberties.[56] In Belgium, Helias boasted, the Catholic Church had "perfect independence."[57]

The American constitutional system, never tainted by the patronage systems of Europe's "old monarchies" (with kings and queens often exercising veto power over episcopal appointments), seemed to Helias even more promising. That the "leading orator of the republic," New Hampshire senator Daniel Webster, would speak to an appreciative audience at Jesuit-run Saint Louis University in 1837, seemed to Helias remarkable, as did a Fourth of July custom of students and professors marching into the campus church for speeches and a reading of the Bill of Rights.[58] One of Helias's Jesuit colleagues, observing such a celebration, wrote of "persons of every sect treating us in a very friendly manner."[59]

Attacks on the Jesuits in the 1840s prompted a reassessment for Helias and his Jesuit contemporaries. Criticism of the Jesuits as unpatriotic and rootless instilled in them a jaundiced perspective on nationalist rhetoric even as the globe's most educated citizens became more attached to nation-states. "Where is the unity of the nation," Roothaan sardonically asked after he had been expelled from Rome, "in Italy, in Germany?" Efforts to forge a nation out of diverse regions and linguistic communities "produced precisely the opposite, disunion." He thought the "fantasy of nationality directly in opposition to the spirit of the Gospels and Catholicism."[60]

These Jesuits took pride in their ability to rise above national jealousies. When early in the nineteenth century a handful of Jesuits in the United States resisted the idea of a superior trained in Europe, the response from Jesuit leaders in Rome was swift. "Nationality has taken possession of the spirit of Ours," Father General Tadeusz Brzozowski complained. "The native born [American] Jesuits cannot put up with either an Italian or German or a Belgian superior." In response, he vowed to "stamp out and eradicate this spirit."[61]

Luigi Taparelli d'Azeglio, one of the most influential Italian Jesuits, scrutinized modern nationalism in an 1849 pamphlet and the first issues of *Civiltà Cattolica*. Taparelli conceded the signif-

icance of national loyalties, but he thought nationalist sentiments should emerge organically from more fundamental ties of
church, family, and local community. Premature efforts to forge
national unity—characteristic, in Taparelli's view, of nationalists
influenced by Protestantism—required state coercion. And the regions coerced by the leaders of Prussia, France, and Italy—Silesia,
Brittany, Alsace, and Calabria—were among the most Catholic
in Europe. This "conquest" seemed to Taparelli and other Jesuits
a high price for the false "idol" of national unity.[62] In Spain, the
diocesan priest, Jaime Balmes, much admired by Jesuits, came
to similar conclusions, insisting that a proper nationalism developed only when church and state were linked, and when the
aspirations of the nation were built on a stronger religious foundation than an individualist notion of citizenship.[63]

The light even dimmed on the Belgian example. Helias and
other Saint Louis Jesuits possessed direct reports of heightened
Belgian anticlericalism in the 1840s—a few Missouri Jesuits visiting Europe witnessed mobs chanting against the Jesuits in Brussels during the turbulence of 1848—and viewed this as a declension
from the high ideals of the country's founding.[64] Roothaan, similarly, conceded that "much good" had come from the Belgian
Constitution, but now dismissed the "so-called liberty" evident in
a Belgium bereft of "public spirit" and good government. Roman
Jesuits had once assessed the freedom of religion guaranteed by
the Belgian Constitution as "less bad" than available alternatives,
yet they now took a gloomier view. The Belgian Constitution
seemed "essentially anti-Catholic" because it placed Catholicism
and other belief systems on an equal footing. Such compromises
might be necessary "for the time being," but they tarnished the
Catholic ideal of church–state unity.[65]

V

Differing vantage points on modern nationalism became evident in Missouri in the early 1850s. Anti-Jesuit and anti-Catholic
feeling had long percolated in Saint Louis, although French Catholicism's significance for the city's heritage muted its public

expression. As in New England, some antislavery activists decried Catholic influence. Elijah Lovejoy, the region's most famous antislavery activist, alternated between attacks on slavery and "Jesuitism" before an antiabolitionist mob murdered him in 1837.[66]

A new group of Saint Louis residents revived and amplified these religious tensions. If Jesuits left Europe in 1847 and 1848 because of the initial success of the European revolutions, several thousand disappointed revolutionaries left German-speaking Europe because of their eventual failure.[67] The most notable of these exiles was Carl Schurz—an important figure in the 1848 revolutions in Germany, and later a Union army general, ambassador to Spain, and US senator—who worked to make the Republican Party accepting of foreign-born citizens even as he combatted the "seed of superstition" sown by the "intrigues of the Roman hierarchy."[68]

Other failed German revolutionaries had more radical views. They supplemented Protestant anti-Catholicism in the United States with a European anticlericalism that dismissed orthodox Christianity and Judaism as delusory, with special contempt for the Jesuits. Saint Louis became a major center of influence for these exiles, in part because such a high percentage of the city's residents were German speaking. One radical German, Franz Schmidt—again, a leading figure in the 1848 revolts—arrived in Saint Louis in 1849 and became the editor of the strongly anti-Jesuit *Freie Blätter*.[69] That same year, Friedrich Hecker, the leader of the revolution in the German state of Baden, and the most celebrated German revolutionary to move to the United States, settled in Belleville, Illinois, just outside Saint Louis. Hecker favored a strict separation of church and state along the American model, and admired Johannes Ronge, the onetime Catholic priest who had led a major dissident church movement in Germany. He thought Ronge's movement "in the grand tradition of liberty."[70]

The key Saint Louis figure was Heinrich Börnstein, the editor during the 1850s of the city's most important German-language newspaper, the *Anzeiger des Westens*, whose readership may have exceeded any of the city's English-language newspapers. An

Austrian, Börnstein devoted himself to radical politics in Vienna and Paris during the 1840s. A newspaper he founded in Paris, *Vorwärts!* counted as contributors and fellow editors the young Karl Marx, Friedrich Engels, and Heinrich Heine.[71] Börnstein lauded French revolutionaries of 1848 for American readers as a correspondent for the *New York Tribune*, but he left Paris after the failure of those revolutions and arrived in Saint Louis in 1849. There he quickly immersed himself in the German exile community, becoming the editor of the *Anzeiger des Westens* in 1850.[72]

The *Anzeiger des Westens* displayed Börnstein's interests in politics, theater, and international affairs, but no theme comes through more consistently than his anti-Catholicism and suspicion of the Jesuits. By 1851, his attacks on "religious fanaticism" included repeated warnings about Jesuit "machinations."[73] "Germans of other nations," he explained, are depending on us to resist "Jesuit encroachment" in the United States, "that last bulwark of freedom."[74] Engels informed one friend in 1852 that "Schmidt of Lowenberg is waging crusades against the Jesuits in the area of St. Louis, and in this enterprise he has allied himself . . . with Mr. Bornstein of Paris memory."[75]

Frequent reports from Europe—where Börnstein highlighted attacks by European liberals on Catholic bishops, Pius IX, and the Jesuits—reinforced the point, and Börnstein worried that gains by the "ultra-Catholic party in Europe" would result in gains for the same Catholic party in the United States.[76] With Börnstein's encouragement, the editors of the *Revue de l'Ouest*, a French-language paper with offices in the same building as the *Anzeiger des Westens*, followed the same anticlerical and anti-Jesuit line.[77] In an 1851 article titled "The Holy Alliance, of Jesuitism with Despotism," Börnstein glossed recent correspondence from Germany to conclude that "at this very moment in Europe, despotism, in order to shackle the people completely and eternally has made a close alliance with Jesuitism and the Roman priesthood." He warned that "the same danger also menaces our own Republic in the not too distant future."[78]

Börnstein also printed allegations—which he later admitted to be false—that the Jesuits had imprisoned a man at their residence in the nearby town of Florissant and public authorities had to prevent a mob from marching to Florissant on a rescue mission. (Alerted by friends, the Florissant Jesuits spent an anxious evening wondering whether they would need to defend themselves from violent attack.)[79]

That same year Börnstein increased circulation at the *Anzeiger des Westens* by serializing his own novel, and then publishing it in German, English, French, and Czech editions.[80] Titled *Die Geheimnisse von St. Louis*, or *The Mysteries of St. Louis: The Jesuits on the Prairie De Noyers: A Western Tale*, the novel's form drew inspiration from two novels published by his Parisian friend Eugène Sue: *Le Juif Errant* and *The Mysteries of Paris*.[81] It was not unusual. At least a dozen anti-Catholic novels, many inspired by Sue, including some of the best-selling texts of the era, were published in the United States and Britain during this period, and many more in France, Spain, central Europe, and Italy.[82]

The conventions of the genre rarely varied. Writers portrayed the Jesuit as a sinister, Machiavellian figure, eager to trade moral integrity for material gain. Often, too, the Jesuit sexually exploited young women in the confessional, occasionally locking them in convents, or turned married women against their husbands through extended counseling sessions. Periodic rumors of real-life women imprisoned in convents fueled the sales of such novels, and just months before the attack on Bapst a false rumor swept through New England, even reaching Ellsworth, that a young Irish woman had been imprisoned in a Catholic convent and taken to a Jesuit church in Philadelphia.[83]

Börnstein's *The Mysteries of St. Louis* fits this pattern. It traces the travails of a German immigrant family, the Böttchers, hoping to establish a modest home in Saint Louis. The Böttchers are earnest deists, immune to the hypocrisy endemic to conventional religion.

The Jesuits, by contrast, are scheming villains. Jesuits at Saint Louis University cultivate wealthy donors through lavish dinners, each place setting marked by a bottle of expensive champagne. Jesuits also insinuate themselves into family life and obtain bequests as they feign to comfort the dying. The Jesuits lure one naive Frenchwoman into a convent, where she is locked up until she agrees to remain, and loses her freedom, money, and beauty. Jesuits also gather for a midnight meeting to plot the detachment of the South from the Union and its alliance with "European Catholic powers." "Already," one Jesuit concludes, in a conspiratorial tone, "we have adherents and friends in all places; in the administration, in Congress, faithful lay brothers are at work."[84]

Börnstein also reprinted the most popular German novel of the nineteenth century, Gustav Freytag's *Soll und Haben* (Debit and Credit), immediately on its publication. Just as Americans worried about the destabilizing effect of Catholic immigration on republican institutions, Freytag, too, noted the worrisome role of ignorant, corrupt Catholics in a Prussia built on literacy and "free labor." He specifically compared backward Polish Catholics in eastern Prussia with the disruptive effect of Irish Catholics on another "modern" society—the United States.[85]

Lajos (Louis) Kossuth's visit to Saint Louis also energized both German radicals and native-born Protestants. The leader of the failed 1848–49 Hungarian Revolution—a revolt against the Vienna-based Catholic monarchy of the Austro-Hungarian Empire—toured the United States in 1851 and 1852 as the most celebrated foreign visitor since Lafayette, addressing both houses of Congress, visiting the White House, and drawing spectacular crowds in Boston, Pittsburgh, Cincinnati, and other cities. Kossuth's American sojourn is a familiar set piece for scholars, with the standard—and accurate—conclusion that over the course of his visit, Kossuth alienated some abolitionists by avoiding the topic of slavery, even as most white southerners never overcame their suspicion of someone so clearly allied with northern liberals. White southerners and Catholics together made the most vigorous attacks on Kossuth for his unqualified support of the 1848 revolutions.[86]

Kossuth—like Alessandro Gavazzi, another anticlerical European refugee—often spoke on the issue of religious liberty. A then-obscure Illinois lawyer, Abraham Lincoln, in fact organized a committee that praised Kossuth as a "worthy and distinguished representative of the cause of civil and religious liberty on the continent of Europe." Other tributes to Kossuth's support of religious liberty frequently morphed into attacks on Catholicism. In Lowell, Massachusetts, one minister thought "the Jesuits of Rome and Vienna" would naturally oppose Kossuth, as "defenders of despotism, civil and religious."[87]

Several weeks of buildup in the pages of the *Anzeiger des Westens* preceded Kossuth's Saint Louis visit.[88] He did not disappoint. In his most publicized Saint Louis address, given in German and following an introduction by Börnstein, Kossuth described himself as opposed to "intolerance and to sectarianism," and devoted to religious freedom for both Protestants and Catholics. Clutching a copy of the Jesuit directory, he urged Missouri's citizens to beware European Jesuits now residing in Saint Louis. Many Hungarian Catholics, he advised, had been on the opposite side of the Jesuits in 1848. Given "the terrible history of that order," he wondered if the "Reverend Father Jesuits" would prove "good citizens" or "traitors to your republic." He worried about the "hypocritical tactics of men imported from Austria to advance the noble cause of Russo-Austrian despotism in America and chiefly in your city here."[89]

Börnstein also welcomed the 1854 Louisville Platform, drafted by German exiles, and widely circulated in both the German- and English-language press. This statement of "free Germans" began by condemning slavery—"a political and moral cancer"— as incompatible with the principles of the 1848 German revolutions and American Declaration of Independence.

The statement then moved to the "entirely private" topic of religion. Laws limiting Sunday commerce, prayers in Congress, and the presence of the Bible in "free schools" all seemed an "open violation of human rights." The platform alluded to Pius IX as the "murderer of the Roman Republic" and thought the obedience professed by Catholic priests to the pope nothing less than treason. "The order of the Jesuits" must be treated "as a declared enemy of the republic."[90]

The implausibility of the Louisville Platform as the basis for a national political movement—including its demand for women's suffrage and higher taxes to eliminate "unproductive monies or [a] land aristocracy"—should not disguise the important political role played by the radical German exiles and their followers. When German radicals attacked "slavery and Jesuitism," they linked themselves to reformers across the North. And indeed Börnstein reprinted articles from antislavery Boston papers, arguing that German immigrants must choose between "the side of the Jesuits" and "the side of America's free institutions."[91]

Börnstein also had local allies. William Greenleaf Eliot, a Boston native, the most prominent minister in Saint Louis during the 1840s and 1850s and later the founder of Washington University, became a leading Republican Party supporter. Worried about Catholic efforts to subvert the public schools, Eliot managed to eliminate "sectarianism" in the public schools by ending Bible reading, although he also knew that Catholics were unhappy with any educational system "wherein loyal native-born children are trained to be republican, and 'nothing else.'"[92] He hired teachers from Massachusetts to staff the new public school system, even as the local Catholic bishop recruited priests, brothers, and nuns from Europe. (In 1850, Catholic schools enrolled as many Saint Louis pupils as did the public schools—a reflection of the long institutional heritage of Catholicism in Saint Louis and the feeble beginnings of public education in Missouri.)[93] A disheartening trip to Rome in 1852 confirmed Eliot's suspicion of Catholicism's incompatibility with progress.[94]

Another New England migrant and Saint Louis pastor, Truman Post, was also concerned about a resurgent Catholicism. He lectured frequently on the 1848 revolutions, lamenting the "ghostly despotism" enveloping Italy.[95] Catholicism naturally "anathematizes the free press and free speech and free schools." It thrives only by the "repression of the thought and utterance of mankind." Only the "spiritual liberty" of Protestantism could combat a Catholic despotism symbolized most powerfully by the "all pervading" and "immoral" Jesuits.[96]

This alliance of German radicals and native-born Protestant reformers had its complications, notably the enthusiasm of Protestant reformers for temperance and restrictions on Sunday commerce. (Sundays without beer gardens appalled the Germans.)[97] But the uncertainty of the political moment created new possibilities. Both German radicals and Protestant reformers emphasized the importance of individual autonomy, free trade, and free speech. And in Missouri as throughout the North, the 1854 Kansas–Nebraska Act and its elimination of geographic restrictions on slavery convinced antislavery Missourians that the Democratic Party was no longer an acceptable political home. After the Kansas–Nebraska Act, these Germans and native-born Protestants combined to form the state's branch of the new Republican Party.[98]

VI

As Missouri's German radicals and Protestant reformers united, in part around a common antipathy to Catholicism, Missouri's Catholics rejected what they understood as a dangerous liberalism. This distaste for reform led to strong Irish Catholic support for the Democratic Party, and significant majorities of German Catholics also voted Democratic during this period, although the exact percentages varied from state to state.[99] During Lincoln's 1858 US Senate race, one adviser suggested that Lincoln keep his distance from 1848 German radical and exile Hecker, since "among the Catholics and even orthodox protestants [Hecker] is considered as the very anti-Christ."[100]

If some Jesuits dismissed the "insults and slanders" offered by the "Radicals," and even brushed aside Kossuth's description of the Jesuits as "the fiercest haters of free institutions," others voiced their unease.[101] "It is hard times," explained Fr. De Smet in a letter to Fr. Helias. "Never before, has there been in St. Louis a greater excitement (both religious and political) against the Catholics in general and against the Jesuits, in particular. This fuss is chiefly owing to infidel and radical germans, who are daily pouring out their hatred against us."[102]

As in New England, anti-Catholic agitation in Missouri in 1854 and 1855 proved disillusioning. Ordered to avoid public partisanship, most Jesuits still agreed that the Democrats would win the loyalty of Catholic voters, and one Catholic journal in Saint Louis became an official organ of the party.[103] De Smet predicted that Know-Nothing agitation would push many white southern Democrats away from ancestral anti-Catholicism. Instead, he speculated, "they will become hostile to Protestantism in general."[104]

De Smet also complained to French Catholic readers that "the anti-Catholic spirit" was now cultivated by "German and Swiss radicals, red-refugees from France, Italy and Hungary [and] infidels of all varieties."[105] He informed Jesuit Father General Peter Beckx that "we fear a great persecution will occur before long."[106] De Smet juxtaposed American boasts about "unbounded liberalism and liberty" with scenes of Catholics facing persecution.[107] A deadly Election Day riot in November 1854, with mobs marching on Saint Louis University, heightened Jesuit anxieties. Our enemies, explained one Jesuit in a report to Rome, call us the "pest of all free institutions, and as something to be expelled completely from this glorious asylum of liberty."[108]

Another exiled Jesuit, the Austrian Francis Weninger, played an important role in the Catholic response to nativism. Like Helias, Weninger had grown up under Hapsburg rule, although in Austria, not Belgium. Like Helias, he recoiled against the "Josephinism" or state control of the church favored by the Hapsburg monarchs. Ordained a diocesan priest, he later chose to become a Jesuit, along with his brother, because the order was an "impregnable fortress" and "sure refuge" for "able and zealous champions of the church."[109] When the revolutions of 1848 reached Vienna, and his Austrian Jesuit colleagues fled to Brazil and Australia, Weninger moved to Paris and then the United States.

Soon after his arrival, Weninger demanded that German Catholics cancel their subscriptions to the *Anzeiger des Westens*, and along with another Austrian Jesuit relocated to Saint Louis, where he began a Catholic library to "offset the bad books" in the public library as well as a German Catholic paper to counter Börnstein's invective.[110] In Saint Louis and its environs, Weninger repeatedly clashed with anti-Jesuit agitators and endured taunts from Börnstein in the *Anzeiger*.[111] In Belleville, Illinois, across the Mississippi River, he found "a bad crowd of non-Catholics here, some of these recent arrivals from Europe." The town's Catholics feared irritating non-Catholics by holding a mission, but Weninger insisted they proceed. German exiles responded by disparaging Weninger's "theatrical show and mummery." Indeed, the "intelligent citizens" of Belleville protested "the intolerant denunciations of the Jesuit fathers of other religions."[112]

In New Bremen, Missouri, after Weninger planted the mission cross in front of the church at the conclusion of the mission and shot off the town cannon, one radical complained that it "sounded as if St. Louis were being besieged."[113] In Hermann, Missouri, a local center of German radicalism, where one resident referred to Jesuits as the "devil's black police," Weninger discovered "torpor in the practice of religion" and "godless" German revolutionaries. Only five days before his arrival, town leaders had shot off their town cannon in honor of the "notorious Kossuth." At the conclusion of his mission, Weninger again arranged for the erection of a forty-foot cross. In response, echoing anticlerical responses to parish missions in Europe, a "freethinker" sawed it down in front of a raucous crowd. Offended Catholics then rushed to kiss the fallen cross.[114]

Weninger also urged Catholics in the United States to resist the allure of modern nationalism. The "machinations" of anti-Catholic nativists seemed to him the logical consequence of an excessive American patriotism.[115] In 1855, at the height of the nativist furor, the most prominent American Catholic writer, the convert Orestes Brownson, insisted to his fellow Catholics that "in America on American soil, the American nationality is the nationality, if any, that has the right to predominate."[116] Weninger disagreed, chiding Brownson for a nationalism that can "hardly be called Catholic." After all, "the whole human race is one nation."[117]

A similar dynamic developed in central Missouri. In Taos, Helias labored under orders not to involve himself in political affairs. As one superior informed him, "Politics are not our portion & particularly now, should be avoided."[118] But Helias had opinions. After the 1848 revolutions, he now feared that an "anti-Catholic liberalism" had resurfaced on both sides of the Atlantic.[119]

He traced this anti-Catholicism in the United States to three sources: the "demagogues" of 1848, among whom he included German radicals and Gavazzi, "intolerant and jealous Protestants," and the new "Republican party."

Or as he put it,

We are on the eve of grave difficulties. The Anti-Catholic spirit increases from day to day. All of the enemies of our holy religion are leagued against us. As in time of persecution, they seek to excite the people by falsehoods and atrocious slanders. Lately three Catholic churches have been destroyed and each newspaper tells us of some new outbreak. The demagogues come from Europe, work with all of their strength to cause their maxims of intolerance and persecution prevail on the free soil of America.[120]

Helias supported the Democrats and claimed in his memoirs to have made the "leading men of the Democratic party" more sympathetic to Catholicism. He delighted in the electoral triumphs of the Democrats over "vagabond natives" and "Know-Nothings." "The Know-Nothings did not fail to make some recruits in Central Missouri, [especially] among the free-thinkers of the county," Helias conceded, but the Democrats outnumbered them, and anti-Catholic agitation did not "interrupt a single day of work." He proudly identified himself as "antirevolutionary."[121]

Bernhard Bruns, Helias's longtime opponent, moved in the opposite direction. Tellingly, he shifted in one 1848 letter from discussion of freedom and slavery in the United States to the topic of the European revolutions. He wished that Germans in Europe would put the "middle ages" behind them, remove obstacles placed in their way by "perfidious" princes, and embrace republican government and "political freedom."[122]

In 1850, Bruns endorsed efforts to make Missouri a "free state, without offending the slave owners." (That same year he accused Fr. Helias of "interfering in politics.") After the defeat of the antislavery Democratic candidate for senator, Thomas Hart Benton, Bruns explained to his German relatives that "the intelligent

German population voted as a man for emancipation candidates." He lambasted "the power of the Catholic vote, mainly the Jesuits," who supported the Democratic Party. These Catholics voted "unanimously for slavery—nice brothers in Christ."[123]

In 1854, Bruns ran an unsuccessful campaign for a seat in the Missouri legislature as a candidate of the Benton (antislavery) wing of the Missouri Democratic Party. He rejected the Kansas–Nebraska Act, and opposed any alliance with the "nullifiers and seceders of the Southern states."[124]

Bruns was elected alderman in 1857. One letter that year from Bruns's brother-in-law included complaints about Catholic priests "who condemn right away all who think differently." These priests attempted to revive "old customs, which were useful maybe a hundred years ago." Fortunately, even "these gentlemen cannot hinder the stream of progress and only hurt themselves, by losing their influence more and more."[125]

By 1860 Bruns and many German immigrants had become Republicans. Bruns attended the Republican Party national convention in Chicago that nominated Lincoln and served on the platform committee. In Osage County, an unusually high number of voters—24 percent—supported Lincoln in the general election in 1860, inspired, perhaps, by Bruns's leadership. One politically active German radical later extolled Bruns as "very enlightened and freethinking" with "great influence" in the region, despite the efforts of his Jesuit opponents.[126] After the election, Bruns referred to the revolt against papal rule then sweeping through much of Italy: "We Republicans take Garibaldi's side. The pro-slavery-Catholic clergy, especially the Jesuits and the Irish priests are of course for oppression, therefore for the Pope and [emperor] Franz II. of Naples." Two days later, discussing the desire of some southerners to secede from the Union, he added that "the Catholics" were "on the side of the disunionists."[127]

VII

The Father General of the Jesuits, Beckx, did not want to choose sides. In the weeks after the attack on Fort Sumter, as Börnstein and Hecker took positions as commanders in the Union army, and as Eliot blessed Union troops, Beckx insisted that Jesuits not "manifest or entertain any leaning or partiality towards either party in national difficulties." (He had already forbade Jesuits from voting in the 1860 election—at a time when the type of ballot requested publicly identified the voter as a member of a particular party—to avoid any hint of partisanship.) Or as De Smet summarized, "We do not positively know on which side rights and justice exist. The Prelates and Theologians of the Church are divided as to the question."[128]

Most Missouri Jesuits hewed to their leader's instructions—one Jesuit boasted that Jesuit service as chaplains for both the Union and Confederate armies proved their interest in "souls not parties"—but the intensity of the conflict made partisanship unavoidable.[129] Jesuits knew both Union and Confederate soldiers and families, and in June 1861, nervous Jesuits began searching for a safe house in Illinois in the event Missouri was "overrun in all directions."[130]

A handful of Jesuits such as De Smet and Weninger supported the Union, and they could point to the principle, often invoked by Jesuits opposed to nationalist revolts in Europe, that Jesuits (and southern secessionists) should obey "lawful government."[131] Both De Smet and Weninger admired Lincoln, with Weninger given to speculation that Lincoln had been baptized a Catholic.[132]

More Jesuits sympathized with the Confederacy. An influential Saint Louis Catholic close to the Jesuits expressed his dismay in 1861 that "there are so many secessionists amongst priests who have been sworn to support the general government. It looks to me like perjury."[133] One Jesuit leader, William Murphy, thought that by the "principles of international law and the example set by the [American founding] Fathers in formerly driving out the English, the Southern states have seceded with the best of right."[134] He expressed his dismay that "a rabble of non-Catholic Germans" had taken leadership roles in the Union army.[135]

Indeed, a frustrated De Smet complained to Beckx in 1861 that "several of Ours without regard to [your] instructions . . . as published by our Provincial continue to manifest secessionist sentiments, at least in the house."[136] An Italian Jesuit visiting Saint Louis in 1862 also noted that the "reputable element of the city with the Archbishop and his clergy does not give allegiance to this government, which is for the Union." He confirmed that "the open imprudence of some of [the Jesuits] has brought it about that Ours in that city are regarded in public opinion as Secessionists."[137]

Even if Jesuit Unionists and Jesuit Confederates disagreed on the specific question of whether secession was justified, they agreed on the continuing danger posed by Republican Party radicalism. When newspapers sympathetic to the Republican Party attacked Catholicism—one 1861 article in the *New York Times* defined popery and slavery as "incompatible with the spirit of the age" and "doomed" to "speedy destruction"—these comments circulated throughout the Catholic world as proof of the threat posed by a strong Republican state.[138]

Weninger, atypically, advocated the abolition of slavery early in the war and deflected charges from German–Catholic controversialists that he indiscriminately favored the Union cause.[139] But even Weninger informed readers in Germany in 1863 that "Democrats are the real conservatives" while "Puritans, the ubiquitous Methodists and the 48ers will band to crush us. Keine Sklaven, kein Pfaffen [no slavery, no priests]."[140]

De Smet made a similar assessment. American abolitionists and Republicans, he explained to a Belgian correspondent, "belong indeed to the [French revolutionary] class of '93." Sadly, "one must acknowledge that the liberalism of our young America exceeds that of its elder brothers in Europe."[141] Alexander Garesché, a local attorney whose brother, Ferdinand, served as a Jesuit priest in Saint Louis, agreed. He remained in Saint Louis during the war despite his sympathy for the Confederacy, and felt "hunted down and persecuted" by Missouri's wartime Unionist government. In 1865, the Jesuits at Saint Louis University awarded him an honorary degree. Ferdinand's vocal support for the Confederacy prompted his Jesuit superiors to ship him from Saint Louis to a more congenial Louisiana.[142]

The military draft authorized by President Lincoln seemed yet another example of an overreaching state. De Smet and other Jesuit leaders negotiated exemptions for individual priests through personal appeals to Secretary of War Edwin Stanton, but the necessity of doing so rankled. Fr. Joseph Keller, S.J., one of the men drafted, complained to Rome that "alone among the nations [the United States] has dared to drag with violence the ministers of peace from the altars of God."[143]

These suspicions of Republican Party radicalism reached Westphalia. There the new pastor, John Goeldlin, another 1848 exile, noted in 1862 that some of his parishioners had wondered whether a Catholic could vote for the "black Republican ticket." He conceded that they could, but in his diary added that such questions naturally grew out of Republican alliances with the "Spirit and deed of an infidel and religious-hating set of people." This "New Englander party" shows "of late a hatred for [the] cath. Religion." A year later he feared continued conflict between "Radicals and Democrats."[144]

The old central Missouri foe of the Jesuits, Bernhard Bruns, died in 1864 while serving as a surgeon in the Union army medical corps. Just before his death, Bruns had joined German radicals and some Missouri Republicans in urging the Lincoln administration to emancipate all slaves (including slaves not freed by the Emancipation Proclamation in border states such as Missouri) and support revolutionary movements in Europe. Bruns's relatives arranged for a requiem Mass in his honor in Germany. But the long-standing enmity between Bruns and the local Jesuits also meant that Fr. Goeldlin mistakenly assumed that Bruns and his allies had "died as infidels though born catholic."[145]

Jette, mourning her husband, son, and nephew, and burdened by debt and surviving children, turned her Jefferson City home into a boardinghouse for Republican legislators (or as she put it, "nothing but 'Radicals' ").[146] She remained a faithful Catholic, but accepted her daughter's decision to marry a German radical in a civil ceremony, even though she "would have preferred a Catholic wedding." She buried her husband and son in the public cemetery, not the Catholic cemetery. This decision prompted reflection. "I have gotten into conflict with the priests," she mused, "but in the meantime I am getting calmer." After her youngest child took his first communion, she explained, "The church education of the children will be finished. Our priests here are not like those back home."[147]

She was not alone. Orestes Brownson had allied himself with the Jesuits after his conversion to Catholicism in 1844, and decried their expulsion from Switzerland and other European countries.[148] Over time, though, Brownson had become worried that the Jesuits and immigrant Catholics more generally were not assimilating to American mores. Disillusionment turned to despair in the first years of the war, as Jesuits hesitantly supported the Union. Bapst, an old friend and Brownson's onetime confessor, distressed Brownson by refusing to admit him to a Jesuit house in Boston because of Brownson's controversial support for immediate slave emancipation.[149]

The deaths of two sons—one who died fighting for the Union, and another killed while traveling to enlist—were the final straw. In 1864, Brownson unleashed an attack on the Jesuits in the pages of his influential *Brownson's Quarterly Review*. He first ridiculed the Jesuits for allying themselves with that part of the Catholic world—notably Pope Piux IX in his 1864 Syllabus of Errors—willing to denounce "modern civilization." He continued:

> In the United States, [the Jesuits] sympathize to a man with the southern rebels not because they love negro slavery, but because they hate the republic, and wish to see it broken up and its influence destroyed. In France they to a man favored the re-establishment of the empire on the ruins of the republic because they flattered themselves that the new emperor [Napoleon III] would favor exclusively their church, suppress her enemies, and permit her pastors to bask once more in the sunshine of the court. In Italy they to a man reject the freedom offered to the church, because it is offered alike to the sects, and is coupled with constitutional liberty in the state.[150]

Jesuit neutrality during the American Civil War seemed to him inexcusable. "The Society boasts," Brownson observed, "that it has no country, no nationality, is at home nowhere and everywhere." But did not the Jesuits possess civic duties, along with "all the rights and immunities of American citizens"? He wondered whether "the education of the Catholic youth of the nation should be intrusted to a society so destitute of loyalty that it could look on with indifference and see the nation rent asunder." The Jesuits did not seem "adapted to our age, and especially to our country."[151]

VIII

At just this moment, Fr. Helias concluded his own study of the American Constitution. On reflection, Helias sketched two paths for American political development. In the first, Catholics, "the first to discover this continent," would flourish under a regime of "constitutional liberty and the true principles of independence." In the second, the Americans would rue the hubris that encouraged "protesters and revolutionaries" in the 1840s to emigrate to "these States, formerly so united and happy."[152]

Helias's anxieties had a specific source. With supporters of the Confederacy unable or unwilling to vote, a Radical Union party swept the Missouri state elections in November 1864, electing a governor and majority in both houses of the legislature. ("Too bad," wrote Jette a few months after her husband's death, "that [Bernhard] Bruns did not live to see this.")[153] These new representatives convened a state constitutional convention in January 1865, and enacted a more sweeping Reconstruction program than in any other southern or border state.[154]

The convention first freed the state's slaves, many of whom had already left their masters during the chaos of the last year of the war. It then required the General Assembly to maintain free public schools in order to enhance the "rights and liberties of the people."[155] Prominent Republicans such as minister Eliot urged Missourians to view public education as the "leading characteristic" separating disloyal from loyal states.[156]

This unprecedented Republican emphasis on public education in the years after the Civil War—not only in Missouri, but also among ex-slaves in the South, Mormons in Utah, and on Indian reservations—reflected a conviction that only universal public education could produce loyal citizens. The focus on public education, as opposed to any form of parochial education, further distanced many Catholics from Republican Party leaders not above using antagonism toward Catholicism as a tactic for rallying its voter base.[157]

The delegates at the Missouri constitutional convention required churches to limit the amount of nontaxable property that any church could own—a transparently anti-Catholic gesture since only Catholic churches owned large quantities of land beyond the church building itself—and insisted on an "ironclad" loyalty oath for lawyers, teachers, and clerics. If they hoped to appear in a Missouri court, teach in a Missouri classroom, witness a Missouri marriage, or preach in a Missouri church, lawyers, educators, and ministers had to swear that they had never "by act or deed, manifested any sympathy with those engaged in rebellion against the United States."[158]

The moving spirit of the constitutional convention was Charles Drake, the leader of the state's Republicans. Drake had attended Jesuit schools and even toyed with converting to Catholicism in the 1830s, but by the 1840s he was a member of the Second Presbyterian Church in Saint Louis. There Drake's pastor, William Potts, drew on Michelet and other European sources for a series of well-publicized sermons on the dangers posed by the Jesuits and Catholic schools "designed to pull down the institutions of freedom under which you live."[159]

In the 1850s, Drake had joined the Know-Nothing or American Party, and described the "public school [as] the most fatal foe of despotism."[160] In debates over the 1865 constitution, Drake did not disguise his views. Taxing Catholic property made sense since the wealth generated by such property supported a hierarchy with "unqualified allegiance to its absolute head in Rome and whose organization, instincts and purposes are not in alliance with democratic liberty or in sympathy with the spirit of Republican institutions."[161]

Loyalty oaths for ministers and priests made sense too. Drake could not sympathize with a Catholic church "whose members *in St. Louis* have, from the first, been universally understood to be disloyal. I say the great mass; for there are many Roman Catholics here who are undoubtedly loyal and patriotic; but that that body has been, and is, pervaded by a rebellious and treasonable spirit, is as notorious in St. Louis as any other fact about any other portion of our people."[162] He could not recall a leading Catholic uttering a "single word of love for the Union or of loyalty to the Government." When criticized by an anonymous author in a local newspaper, Drake concluded that the author must be an "unscrupulous Jesuit."[163]

Local Jesuits reacted to the so-called Drake laws with alarm. (The leader of the Missouri Jesuits sent a copy of the new state constitution to Father General Beckx in Rome with the loyalty oath marked in red.)[164] Predisposed by their experience in Europe to equate demands for national loyalty with persecution, and quick to see loyalty oaths as repeating attacks on Catholicism during the French Revolution, Jesuits insisted that religious liberty required freedom to preach and administer the sacraments without prior permission from the state. The freedom of the church—*libertas ecclesiae*—seemed at risk. Helias explained that a missionary should avoid "political decisions," but added that even a missionary could not remain neutral when politicians threatened "the liberty of conscience guaranteed by the Constitution." "It is wonderful," De Smet observed in a letter to his nephew in Belgium, "that a land so proud and jealous of its liberty can hatch so many tyrants of the lowest and most detestable kind."[165]

Saint Louis archbishop Peter Kenrick forbade his priests from taking the oath, and the Jesuits agreed with Kenrick's view of the oath as an "impediment to freedom of religion."[166] Some of the state's Baptist and Episcopalian ministers also refused to take the oath, with Baptists especially emphatic about resisting government involvement in religious affairs.[167] Edward Bates, Lincoln's former attorney general and a Saint Louis legal eminence, thought the oath "foolish and unjust," and described the radicals as obsessed with the "suppression of the power of the papacy."[168] De Smet agreed, informing Father General Beckx in Rome that "it is only the Catholic religion to which the 'parti radical' refers."[169]

Other clergy, including most African American ministers, did take the oath, and Missouri's governor, Thomas Fletcher, insisted that "religious liberty is a political right, and when these outraged gentlemen go to the Supreme Court of the United States with their complaint, they will be told that there is not a sentence or a word in the Constitution of the United States which gives them the right to preach at all."[170]

The law remained a dead letter in Saint Louis even after the deadline for taking the oath passed, and local Jesuits informed Beckx, "Our professors continue to teach, [and] our preachers to preach without being molested by the government."[171] The situation in other parts of Missouri was more volatile and De Smet worried about places "where the radicals are in a majority" and "religious persecution is beginning to seethe." The arrest of several Catholic priests for preaching without state permission began a fierce legal battle. The pastor of Westphalia, Goeldlin, along with two other Jesuits, was ordered in spring 1866 to appear before a judge, and all were charged with preaching without taking the loyalty oath. This "persecution," Goeldlin complained to Beckx in Rome, is "contrary to American liberty and hostile to the freedom of the Church."[172]

In the meantime, two other cases involving men who had refused to take loyalty oaths, another Catholic priest, Fr. John Cummings, and a Catholic lawyer, Saint Louis' Alexander Garesché, made their way into the Missouri court system.[173] The Missouri Supreme Court, its members all appointed by Republican governor Fletcher, ruled that requiring a loyalty oath from clergymen still permitted "conscience" to be "perfectly free in the enjoyment of its natural rights of independent, religious action."[174]

The case then moved to the US Supreme Court. First argued in March 1866, the case divided the justices sharply enough to persuade them to hold it under advisement even as rumors swirled in the press about the likely outcome. Finally, on January 14, 1867, a bare majority of the Court declared the test oath unconstitutional. The four dissenters, all Republicans, offered a withering rebuttal, arguing that "to suffer treasonable sentiments to spread here unchecked is to permit the stream on which the life of the Nation depends to be poisoned at its source."[175] They denied that state restrictions on the ability of ministers to conduct their duties damaged the "inviolability of religious freedom in this country."[176]

In accordance with the Supreme Court ruling, the cases against the Jesuits in central Missouri were dropped. Or as Fr. Goeldlin explained to Roman superiors, local opinion "considered the summons to be contrary to American liberty. Thus the whole matter was concluded to the honor, rather than to the shame, of our religion."[177] De Smet expressed relief that Catholics could "preach the Lord's gospel without being exposed to fines or imprisonment."[178]

IX

The tensions on display in Missouri at the end of the war—revolving around the extent to which a government could require loyalty of its Catholic citizens—convulsed nation-states on both sides of the Atlantic during the next decade. In the United States, Republicans convinced that Catholicism threatened national unity sparred with Jesuits ever more committed, in Rome and Missouri, to a church independent of government control. The most prominent legal scholar in the United States, Columbia professor Francis Lieber, in correspondence with leading scholars in France and Germany, praised attacks on the "anti-national" and "anti-liberty" Jesuits.[179]

The most provocative episode occurred in Rome, where bishops gathered for the first Vatican Council. The primary agenda item was whether to declare the pope infallible, only in specific (and ultimately rarely used) matters of doctrine, but infallible nonetheless. Underpinning the claim of infallibility was a yearning to reaffirm the doctrinal and organizational independence of Catholicism—a provocation to nationalist leaders already uneasy with such a powerful corporate body in their midst. Transnational religious orders, most prominently the Jesuits, were the most visible manifestation of this corporate independence, and endured vitriolic attacks from politicians across Europe and the Americas. In turn, Jesuits promoted the doctrine of infallibility, and indeed saw it as a necessary counterweight to the dangers posed by modern nationalism and a check on liberal Catholics eager for more autonomy from Rome.

Exiled Jesuits in the United States played a role in this global discussion.[180] In advance of the council, Weninger traveled to Europe and drafted a book in defense of papal infallibility, much of it drawn from an 1841 study he had composed while in Innsbruck. His endorsement of the doctrine—necessary in these "unstable times" as ammunition in the clash between "Truth and Error"—was translated into German, Italian, and French, and favorably reviewed in *Civiltà Cattolica*.[181] The book seemed to him an "ironclad" defense of papal infallibility and a dam against the "modern flood" of excessive nationalism.[182] Catholics must avoid, Weninger explained in a letter to Father General Beckx, a "national and schismatic" church along with the "spirit of unbridled liberty."[183] Beckx, in turn, kept Weninger informed of the activities of opponents of infallibility in Italy.[184]

Other Jesuits in the United States and Europe also followed the discussion carefully. John Miège, the one American Jesuit serving as a bishop, and himself an exile from Rome in 1848, vowed to battle "intrigues and underhanded dealings" in order to assure the "personal infallibility of the Pope" for the "happiness of the children of the Church."[185] Similarly, an American Jesuit based in Maryland wrote the Father General on the topic. "We think," he said, "that the article [infallibility] can be proclaimed by acclamation. Let it happen! For whoever knows well the idea of the Church as the body of Jesus Christ can not doubt for a moment the infallibility of its head."[186]

The passage of the doctrine persuaded Germany's Otto von Bismarck, England's William Gladstone, and Italian leader Camillus Cavour that Catholics led by an infallible pope could not be trusted. It led directly to Bismarck's Kulturkampf or war against Catholicism, and his expulsion of the Jesuits as enemies of Germany and opponents of religious toleration. Italian leaders also expelled the Jesuits (yet again) from Rome. The *London Times* editorialized in favor of Bismarck's expulsion of the Jesuits since they seemed "the most zealous and active instrument of a power that hates German unity." Or as a prominent French liberal put it, the Jesuits were "citizens of Rome, yes; subjects of the pope, yes; but Frenchmen, or Belgian, or Italians, certainly not!"[187]

Another nationalist leader, President Ulysses S. Grant, devoted the most publicized speech of his presidency to the subject. Briefly a member of the Know-Nothing Party when he lived in Saint Louis in the mid-1850s, Grant told an audience of fellow veterans in 1875, at the height of disputes over Catholic influence in education and politics, "If we are to have another contest in the near future of our national existence, I predict that the dividing line will not be Mason and Dixon's but between patriotism and intelligence on the one side and superstition, ambition and ignorance on the other."[188] A few months later, Grant urged Congress to pass a constitutional amendment banning aid to religious schools and a tax on "vast amounts of untaxed church property." Grant's Methodist minister and confidant, John P. Newman, compared him to Bismarck and Gladstone, and then explained that the United States, too, found itself at war with "the uncompromising claims of a politico-religious hierarchy, whose head is in Rome, whose body is in America."[189]

Events in Missouri mirrored these national and international patterns. Washington University president Eliot, like Grant, now saw Catholicism as newly poised to destroy national unity. The declaration of papal infallibility seemed to Eliot "the culmination of the supreme folly and arrogance of centuries." Catholic efforts to influence local politicians meant "war to the knife."[190]

Eliot's fellow Saint Louis minister, Truman Post, worried about "foreign superstition and spiritual despotism" as evidenced in the "reactionary evils of the papal crusade on our country."[191]

German anticlericals again joined in. Like many 1848 German exiles still in the United States, Hecker criticized Bismarck for not including a bill of rights in the new German Constitution. But he thought Bismarck's expulsion of the Jesuits and regulation of Catholic activities entirely justified. The new German nation could not tolerate a "Jesuitism against all progress and every civil freedom."

Remember, Hecker warned his audiences in Germany and the United States, "a mass of Roman faithful" continued to immigrate to the United States. Or as he explained to one friend in Switzerland, "You have no idea of the growth of Roman power in the U.S. . . . All the scum that you and Germany have run out nest here. . . . None of their adherents is allowed to read any paper, pamphlet or book that has not received the blessing of the Church, on penalty of confession . . . and *not even one* may vote anything but the Democratic ticket."[192] Hecker also published a pamphlet attacking papal infallibility and wrote fiercely anti-Catholic articles for the leading German-language newspaper in Saint Louis. He placed particular emphasis on the "blind faith" and mendacity of the Jesuits.[193]

X

Even as the national discussion about Catholic loyalty reached a new intensity, the turmoil that had marked Westphalia's religious affairs subsided. In 1864, Fr. Weninger claimed remarkable effects for yet another parish mission attracting "all with the exception of a few." (This despite Weninger rebuking Westphalia's Catholics for their meager contributions to the collection basket.) While Weninger preached by day, the town's Catholic farmers agreed to work "at night by the light of the moon." Storekeepers signed a pledge not to open on Sunday (or if they did, to pay into a fund for support of the parish school), women formed an altar society, and a men's group began a parish library.[194]

In heavily Catholic central Missouri, the distinction between public and private education had long been obscure. Initially, the only formal education in the region had occurred at schools funded by parishes, with the schoolmaster hired by Fr. Helias. Jesuits preached against support for an "infidel" or nonsectarian public school.[195] In 1864, the Jesuits persuaded local merchants and parishioners to fund an expanded Catholic school, despite the difficulty of any new venture "when expenditure is involved."[196]

In 1866, Jesuits recruited the School Sisters of Notre Dame to staff a German-language Catholic school in Westphalia. The overwhelmingly Catholic town soon agreed to pay the nuns to become certified by the state and teach in a nominally public school. The "schools of Westphalia," noted one early historian in 1889, "are virtually a union of public and parochial."[197] Only over time did a secular system of public education emerge, but the name of the town's public school, Fatima, after the site of a Marian apparition in Portugal, slyly reinforced the enduring importance of Catholicism for the town's identity.[198]

Parish reports became more routine. By 1867, Jesuit Goeldlin felt confident that his Westphalia parishioners had abandoned a formerly "protestant anti-church spirit, almost infidel."[199] The town celebrated the feast of Corpus Christi with a large procession "as in Europe," with houses decorated along the main street, and during May almost all of Westphalia's Catholics gathered for a daily rosary.[200] One chronicler described St. Joseph in New Westphalia as a "gem of a parish where the young men, one and all, belong to the Sodality, numbering at their monthly meeting about 120 communicants."[201]

One local freethinker, Gert Goebel, admitted defeat. "The many Catholic settlements," he complained, "are spread out over long routes and yet form a vast, closed community; those who are not believers are either completely absent or only in small and dwindling numbers." Sophisticated men in the region offered opinions in private that "they would never allow a Jesuit priest to overhear," but their wives and sisters were uniformly "fanatics." "After the Jesuits arrived," Goebel grumbled, "all spiritual independence vanished." He speculated that the Jesuits had begun to "brandish the rod" to diminish the circulation of the *Anzeiger des Westens* and other radical German-language newspapers, even as they forced townspeople to subscribe to "ultramontane" journals.[202]

Goebel's frustration demonstrated the success of Fr. Helias and his contemporaries: their ability to bring millions of Catholic immigrants and their children into the institutional milieu of nineteenth-century Catholicism through parishes, schools, and associations. Those Catholics such as Bernhard and Jette Bruns who mistrusted Helias, a significant minority, and those Catholics who publicly attacked Jesuits and episcopal leaders, a smaller group, had counterparts in Europe and among other Catholic immigrants. But the achievement of Helias and like-minded colleagues was to narrow the remembered Catholic experience of the nineteenth century to an undeniable, if incomplete, narrative of faith triumphing over adversity. That Jesuits in Europe denounced modern notions of religious liberty, even as exiled Jesuits in the United States demanded "liberty of conscience" as guaranteed by the US Constitution, was an irony left unremarked. Helias and other Jesuits now understood their battle against the excesses of the modern nation-state as one shared by Jesuit contemporaries across Europe, North America, and South America.[203]

Helias settled into a quiet rhythm. He persuaded his superiors to allow him to return to his parish in Taos after the end of the Civil War and the successful resolution of the lawsuits against Jesuits for refusing to take loyalty oaths. Living in the rectory of the church that he had built, he rang the church bells each morning, noon, and night. The bells "serve two roles," he explained, "calling those who dwell scattered far and wide to the [Mass] at set times," and "reminding the town dwellers" to pray to Mary.[204]

Ignoring Jesuit colleagues worried about his frail health, Helias continued to carry the eucharistic host as the leader of the annual Corpus Christi procession through the town and surrounding fields. When the church bells did not ring on the evening of August 11, 1874, neighbors found his dead body slumped over a table, next to a half-written sermon. Shortly before his death, he had gently warned his Belgian family that the "shadow lengthens" and his body had "worn out."[205]

Characteristically, Helias had already composed a detailed obituary before his death.[206] He translated it into German and Flemish, and ended it with the admonition, "Take heed, watch and pray, because you know not when the time will come."[207] On preprinted holy cards, he insisted on his devotion to his flock, despite "ingratitude and bad treatment." He also composed a Latin epitaph, signaling that he understood his "cosmopolitan" life as one episode in a global Catholic story.

Flandria nos genuit docuit nos Gallia; Romae
Teutoniae, Helvetiaeque sinus peragravimus omnes
Post varios casus, terraeque marisque labores
Sistimus; atque novae fundamina fiximus urbis
Westphaliae, septemque dicatas numinis aedes.
R.I.P.

Flanders bore me; France taught me. I wandered
through every corner of Rome, Germany and Switzerland.
After many misfortunes, many trials on land and sea
I came to a stop and laid the foundations of the city of
    New Westphalia
and dedicated seven churches to God.
R.I.P.[208]

GRAND COUTEAU, LOUISIANA:

MIRACLE

I

Mary Wilson described her childhood in London, Ontario, as one of "innocent tranquility." She loved her parents and family, and fondly recalled her mother reading Bible stories to her. At sixteen, she ventured outside Canada for the first time, joining her newly married cousin and her cousin's husband on a trip that concluded with a leisurely visit to Saint Louis.[1]

A few days after arriving in Saint Louis, Wilson agreed out of "curiosity" to accompany a "very pious" new acquaintance, Mary Dooley, to the funeral of a Jesuit priest, Fr. Peter König, in the Saint Louis University church. She did so with hesitation, remaining "very much opposed to the Catholic Church and especially so to priests and nuns."[2]

Entering the church, Wilson saw König's exposed body, "with a number of Priests around the coffin." When Dooley "and a great many persons put their hand on the face of the dead Father," Wilson did the same, quelling her fright. She began visiting the church without informing her cousin, drawn by the "majestic beauty of the ceremonies." With trepidation—"how frightened I was to speak to a Catholic priest. I had heard so many dreadful things about them"—she started meeting with a "zealous Jesuit father." After two weeks of instruction, she "begged to be baptized."

FIGURE 7. Mary Wilson, ca. 1862. Courtesy of Provincial Archives, United States—Canada Province, Society of the Sacred Heart.

On May 2, 1862, she was. She made her decision "without suspicion of the consequences that were to follow." Although she initially pledged to keep her baptism "secret from her family," her parents, staunch Presbyterians, eventually learned of her decision and demanded that she recant. She decided to abandon family ties and remain in Saint Louis, working as a maid and seamstress. The Jesuit who baptized Wilson identified her in the sacramental record as eighteen when she was only sixteen, perhaps indicating a desire to make Wilson less vulnerable to her parents' will.[3]

In 1866, she entered the Society of the Sacred Heart, a women's religious order. Already unwell when she joined the order, she fell desperately ill after beginning her training at a Sacred Heart convent north of New Orleans. Her superior then moved her to another Sacred Heart convent 145 miles west of New Orleans, in the tiny hamlet of Grand Couteau. There Sacred Heart nuns ran a school for Catholic girls, living less than a mile from a community of Jesuits, primarily exiles from France, who managed a small school for boys and walked along a picturesque path lined with oak trees to hear the confessions of the nuns and say Mass.

Wilson's illness delayed her formal admission into the order. After her condition worsened in October, doctors experimented with various medicines, using chloroform to stop her violent headaches, and placing hot glass on her arms and legs in hopes of drawing her disease away from the internal organs. These conventional remedies failed. Given her inability to keep down food or drink, her "feeble" pulse, and her cold hands and feet, the doctors despaired. During the last weeks of her illness she took little food or water, and could only swallow the communion host with agonizing difficulty. Her physician now visited the patient only out of respect for the wishes of the other nuns, not with any "prospect of [e]ffecting a cure."[4]

On December 5, 1866, the Sacred Heart nuns in her community began a nine-day novena or sequence of prayers on Wilson's behalf, pleading for the intercession of John Berchmans, a seventeenth-century Jesuit beatified by Pope Pius IX in 1865. Wilson now seemed near death. Her eyes were rimmed with blood from an infection. Blood oozed from her mouth, her body emitted a "disagreeable odor," and she shuddered in shock every two or three minutes.[5] Even as she orchestrated the novena, the Mother Superior asked the convent handyman to begin carving a coffin.[6]

On December 14, Berchmans himself appeared to Wilson, standing next to her bed just after she had placed a picture of Berchmans on her lips. He whispered, "Open your mouth." He then touched her aching, swollen tongue with his finger. "Immediately," she wrote, "I was relieved." Berchmans reassured her that she would receive the white veil of a novice and asked her to "be faithful, have confidence." "I come by the order of God," he said. "Your sufferings are over, fear not."[7]

When one of the nuns caring for Wilson entered the infirmary, she was stunned to see Wilson, skin unblemished, sitting upright and ready for a meal. When Wilson climbed out of bed and stood up, one observer reported, "The miracle was incontestable."[8] She drank a glass of water without difficulty as astonished nuns and the doctor dashed into the sickroom.

Word of Wilson's recovery spread quickly beyond convent walls, and two weeks later one Jesuit reported that accounts of the miracle had created a "sensation" among the "simple country people" in the region.[9] In collaboration with the Sacred Heart nuns and with the encouragement of New Orleans archbishop Jean-Marie Odin, the Jesuits began an investigation, asking those close to Wilson to write accounts of all they had witnessed.

These accounts survive, as does Wilson's own narrative, in forty-two neat, handwritten pages. Also surviving are Wilson's diary entries from summer 1867, memories of Wilson composed by her godmother in Saint Louis and other nuns living in the convent, letters from Jesuits and Sacred Heart nuns to contemporaries in France and Rome, several letters from Wilson, the proceedings of an initial investigation soon after the miraculous healing and a formal archdiocesan investigation twenty years later, and the Jesuit and Vatican files on the canonization of Saint John Berchmans.

Nothing about Wilson's saga was typical, as she and her contemporaries understood. But probing her experience illuminates the contours of nineteenth-century Catholic piety—a subject usually treated in isolation from debates over community formation and national identity, but in fact complementary to both. The devotions inspiring Wilson's conversion, a shared belief in the miraculous, a distinctive understanding of suffering and healing, and the era's renewed interest in saints and the canonization process helped constitute a global Catholic community, stretching from tiny Grand Couteau to Rome and beyond.

II

Nineteenth-century Catholic piety became simultaneously more populist and sectarian. Evidence for a more populist style lies in the tracts, prayer books, and periodicals that constitute the Catholic component of the nineteenth-century publishing revolution as well as the objects that accompanied them. Sales figures are elusive, but the number of religious titles increased dramatically in the 1850s and 1860s.[10] Missionary priests such as Francis Weninger distributed and sold thousands of devotional books and pamphlets each year, bringing Catholic texts to the most remote sections of the country. Most of these texts were first printed in Europe and then reprinted in the United States, with English and translated French titles the most widely distributed. These were supplemented by German-language texts published through an extensive German Catholic publishing network. Stained glass, crosses, statues, rosaries, and paintings came from Munich and Paris, mass-produced by the over one hundred firms that sprang up to meet the global Catholic demand. A German firm, Benziger Brothers, became the largest distributor of religious goods in the United States, with items ranging from inexpensive figurines and prints affordable to even working-class Catholics to life-size statues of saints. The house diary of the Grand Couteau convent repeatedly mentions the arrival of new religious goods, including Sacred Heart pendants, statues of the infant Jesus, holy medals, and scapulars.[11]

That Jesus suffered along with his followers was the most important message distilled from this avalanche of books, pamphlets, and devotional objects. Judgment was not absent from the sermons and instructions of the nineteenth-century Catholic clergy, of course, and priests frequently viewed individual failings as a reflection of divine unhappiness. "God's angry hand" seemed evident to Fr. Helias, for example, in the village skeptic crushed by a falling tree on Christmas Day or the lapsed Catholic forced to amputate a limb.[12]

Still, instead of the more distant God the Father characteristic of Catholic life in the eighteenth century, Wilson and other Catholics prayed, confessed their sins, and took communion with the expectation that Jesus, Mary, and the saints understood their plight. Disdaining Calvinist doctrines of the elect, the French Jesuit Henri Ramière insisted that "the sinner . . . as well as the just man" can expect God to answer their prayers. "Christian humility" should not translate into "despair."[13] "God wills," he concluded, "the salvation of all."[14]

This empathetic vision of Jesus permeated the Society of the Sacred Heart, the religious community that Wilson joined in 1866. Founded in 1800 by Madeleine Sophie Barat, the Society of the Sacred Heart, like so many nineteenth-century Catholic initiatives, emerged as a response to the French Revolution. Barat's brother had joined the seminary before the revolution and was imprisoned in Paris at the height of the terror.

That these women decided to found a new religious order did not distinguish them. Between 1800 and 1880, nuns (and a few priests and bishops) founded four hundred new women's religious orders in France alone, with over two hundred thousand women entering religious life. Ireland, Germany, and other parts of Catholic Europe registered similar increases.[15] Among the most successful of these new religious orders, the Society of the Sacred Heart numbered three thousand women by 1865, with houses in Europe, North Africa, and North and South America.

The name of the religious order—Society of the Sacred Heart—hints at the centrality of the devotion to the Sacred Heart in nineteenth-century Catholicism. In its modern form, the devotion began in the late seventeenth century with the visions of Sr. Margaret Mary Alacoque, a French nun. Alacoque claimed to have had multiple visions of Jesus in which he encouraged devotion to his heart, and recognition of the love pouring out from that heart toward humanity. Alacoque's confessor, Jesuit priest Fr. Claude de la Columbière, publicized these miraculous events, and interest in the devotion spread from France across Europe.

By the late eighteenth century, the image had become central to one of the most important struggles over the character of Catholic piety since the Reformation. Those sympathetic to the devotion argued that individuals must respond to God's sacrifice of Jesus, his son, with acts of devotion, contemplation, and pilgrimage. The fleshy, realistic character of the Sacred Heart revealed God's love for sinful humans, and the warmth of the

FIGURE 8. Sacred Heart of Jesus, lithograph, ca. 1870s. Courtesy of the Library of Congress.

image became juxtaposed against the corrupt state of the modern world after the Reformation, Enlightenment, and French Revolution.[16]

The devotion's Catholic opponents thought the image of the Sacred Heart and the piety favored by the Jesuits reeked of baroque excess. These opponents tended to be bishops, priests, and laypeople hostile to the Jesuits and eager to see Catholicism reconciled with Enlightenment ideals. One bishop termed the devotion "fantastical" and an offense to all "learned theologians."[17] Even Jesuits in the distant British North American colonies, such as John Carroll, equated enemies of the Jesuits with enemies of the Sacred Heart.[18] Father General Roothaan, too, later recalled that "the very men who continued to inveigh against the devotion to the Sacred Heart . . . proved to be the fiercest assailants of the Society."[19]

Over time the Jesuits and the supporters of the devotion triumphed. As early as 1767, the Jesuits arranged for a painting of the Sacred Heart to be installed in their home Church of the Gesù in Rome. In 1794, Pope Pius VI described criticism of the devotion as "false, rash and injurious to the merits of Christ."[20] One Jesuit historian of the devotion described the pope's words as a "clear and precise response to Jansenists, Gallicans, libertines, atheists . . . and bad Catholics."[21]

The central image of the devotion—Jesus gazing directly at the viewer, with his pulsing red heart exposed and pierced by a lance—became one of the most distributed of the nineteenth century, stamped, printed, carved, or engraved onto countless holy cards, stained glass windows, statues, tracts, and pamphlets. Here Jesus came neither as a conquering savior nor a wise teacher. Instead, he empathized and suffered with the devout. The occasional intellectual such as the convert Orestes Brownson thought the "wounded and bleeding heart" sentimental. "We have yet to see," Brownson acerbically remarked, "that love and fidelity to Jesus keep pace with the spread of the devotion." Far more representative was Jesuit Weninger, who retorted to Brownson that the Sacred Heart represented Christ's "love to mankind."[22] During his final days John Bapst reportedly carried a manual of devotion to the Sacred Heart "and could not be induced to give [it] up."[23]

The devotion's mass popularity rested on the work of nineteenth-century Jesuits, who preached the importance of the devotion across the world. "In all our wants," wrote one French Jesuit exiled to the United States in his private retreat notes, "we will find help in the Sacred Heart of Jesus . . . [especially in] the times of our life most charged with suffering."[24] Roothaan spoke and wrote about the devotion repeatedly, keeping a hand-painted copy of the Sacred Heart on his table.[25]

When nineteenth-century Jesuits reflected on the suffering and persecution they endured, they repeatedly turned to the Sacred Heart. While "we are anxiously looking around for solace and support in the present catastrophe," wrote Roothaan during the turmoil of the 1848 revolutions, "a prospect of relief is afforded us in the most Sacred Heart of Jesus, the ever-open refuge, the universal home of every misery."[26] In the United States, pondering the pain of exile in an unfamiliar land, they habitually linked their suffering to the Sacred Heart. In Philadelphia in 1860, for example, the city's Jesuits organized three days of prayers to "the Sacred Heart of Jesus that he might bless the Church and the Society in these adverse times."[27] In Chicago, during the great 1871 fire, Jesuits prayed to the Sacred Heart for protection.[28]

Roothaan also encouraged a Lyon Jesuit, Fr. Ramière, to take a small French devotional group named the Apostolate of Prayer and transform it into an international movement devoted to the Sacred Heart, an organization that numbered four million dues-paying adherents by 1900. In 1861, Ramière founded the *Messager du Coeur de Jésus*, the most influential Catholic devotional periodical of the nineteenth century. By 1926, Catholics in sixty-nine countries published versions of the *Messager* in forty-five languages.[29] An exiled Italian Jesuit began an English-language *Messenger of the Sacred Heart* in Washington, DC, in 1866, and Peter Arnoudt, a Belgian Jesuit living in Saint Louis, composed one of the most reprinted texts on the Sacred Heart, originally in Latin, and then translated into German, English, Spanish, Flemish, Hungarian, and Portuguese.[30]

Unsurprisingly, then, just nine days after her baptism, Wilson joined a Saint Louis group dedicated to the devotion.[31] She admired the Jesuit who received her into the church for his unstinting "devotion to the Sacred Heart."[32] One of her diary entries, written on the feast of the Sacred Heart, captures the mixture of obligation and empathy that structured not only the devotion but also nineteenth-century Catholic piety more generally:

> I am sensible to a certain extent, of the immense gratitude I owe to Our Lord for so many graces, and really, Dear Mother, when I feel my utter incapacity of doing any thing in return, and my want of generosity, I sometimes feel afraid, terrified almost at myself. I hope God will have pity on my weakness.[33]

This more populist nineteenth-century Catholic piety sharpened confessional lines. The Catholic world that Wilson joined, with its devotion to the Sacred Heart, fascination with the saints, veneration of Mary, and enthusiasm for once-neglected doctrines such as purgatory, became more isolated from other Christian communities over the course of the nineteenth century.

The focus on Mary was especially divisive. Nothing more alarmed American Protestants than what they saw as idolatrous worship of Christ's mother, and nothing so marked nineteenth-century Catholicism.[34] Interest in the rosary, the dedication of the month of May to Mary, and the endless stream of devotions, paintings, and churches named in Mary's honor made her presence inescapable in ways that would have surprised many eighteenth-century Catholics. In Grand Couteau, Sacred Heart nuns frequently made processions in Mary's honor in times of drought. Wilson identified the "Sacred Heart, and my Sweet Mother, the Blessed Virgin," as her primary spiritual guides.[35]

In 1854, Piux IX defined Mary as immaculate or conceived without original sin. While belief in Mary's Immaculate Conception did have a popular following, the definition's dubious scriptural pedigree and enormous attention given to the ceremonies marking the event in Rome placed yet another wedge between Catholic and Protestant. One group of American Protestant ministers thought the doctrine proof of the corruption of "Romanism in our times," and educator Horace Mann compared the doctrine to Ptolemaic astronomy and "Hindoo cosmogony."[36]

The reaction in Louisiana was more celebratory. In New Orleans, the Jesuits decided to name their grand new church and college Immaculate Conception, and offered a series of public lectures on the new doctrine. (One Jesuit from Lyon mischievously remarked that focusing on the doctrine will "scare" the "rich American Protestants.")[37] At Grand Couteau, the nuns and students rejoiced. "Rome is filled with joy," reported the house diarist in French, "and Grand Couteau, also."[38] When listing important dates in her life, Wilson noted her delight at receiving in 1862 a scapular, a small cloth devotional item hung around the neck, in honor of the Immaculate Conception.[39]

Wilson's own spiritual narrative reflected this divide between Catholic and Protestant. She begins with an affectionate description of her parents. But her parents' stinging assessment of her conversion to Catholicism—"a disgrace"—led to a permanent rift. After her conversion, Wilson moved out of the boarding-house occupied by her cousin and refused to provide her new address to relatives. By 1866, when she composed her miracle account, she referred to her parents' Presbyterianism as the religious community "in which it was their misfortune to have been born." During Wilson's illness, observers portrayed Wilson as "haunted" by fear that her parents would not reach heaven because of their mistaken religious convictions. On her deathbed Wilson reportedly prayed for "my parents' conversion."[40]

By this time the nuns in the Society of the Sacred Heart had replaced her biological family. Familial metaphors governed all religious congregations, with Jesuits referring to their leader as the Father General, and Sacred Heart nuns professing obedience to the Mother Superior, Révérende Mère, in the convent and the leader of the Society, Trés Révérende Mère, in Paris. But Wilson's abrupt break with her biological family and absorption into a Catholic milieu made the familial metaphor unusually powerful. When she visited a Saint Louis church before her conversion, she spent much time meditating in front of a painting of Mary. During one reverie, her friend Mary Dooley whispered to her, "Is not our Mother lovely?" Mary responded, "But she is not *my* mother, since I am not a Catholic." The evening of her conversion, distraught by a letter from her parents denouncing her decision that had arrived the same day, she claimed to have had a brief vision of Mary, dressed in white, whispering, "Do not cry, for I will be your Mother."[41] Even her last letter to her parents explained that joining the Sacred Heart community enabled her to find "not only friends, but Mothers and Sisters," and one of her final prayers, according to a nun sitting beside her deathbed, invoked Mary, who "has always shown herself my Mother, She will not abandon me."[42]

Also distinguishing Catholics from other Christians was an emphasis on suffering as redemptive. Certainly the novels of Protestants such as Harriet Beecher Stowe celebrated the willingness of Christians to dedicate their suffering to a divine will. But this

Protestant respect for the usefulness of suffering faded over the course of the nineteenth century, rejected by both liberal Protestants unwilling to accept suffering as a necessary sacrifice to a sovereign God and evangelicals convinced that suffering could be relieved by instantaneous faith cures.[43]

Within nineteenth-century Catholicism, by contrast, belief in suffering as necessary and productive penetrated every corner of devotional life. The custom of participating in the stations of the cross, meditating on Christ's suffering through fourteen carvings or paintings within Catholic churches, became more common during Lent and on Fridays. Recitation of the rosary, also increasingly common, included a long meditation on the sorrowful mysteries of Jesus.

If Puritans once saw worldly success and good fortune as a mark of God's favor, Catholics took the opposite tack. One Boston Jesuit informed his listeners in 1863 that "God can give us no greater proof of His love than by sending afflictions—I am aware that this proposition may seem false or exaggerated but I trust to be able to convince you of its truth."[44]

Undergirding this Catholic fascination with suffering was the belief that Jesus, too, in the words of a French Jesuit, endured "anguish, tribulations, poverty, diseases of the body, affliction of spirit." Another author insisted that God the Father, "in His divine nature, could have easily heard our prayers, pardoned our fault, heaped all manners of blessing on us." God also sent Jesus, who could be "moved to tears on account of our miseries." Jesus knew "hunger, thirst [and] want." Jesus knew "the want of food necessary for our children."[45]

Nineteenth-century Protestants recoiled from what they regarded as a morbid fixation. That Jesuits doing the *Spiritual Exercises* spent part of their time imagining the "writhing and burning souls of the lost" in hell seemed a step toward "perpetual slavery."[46] Grimly realistic crucifixes, with tiny drops of painted blood dripping from the nail holes in Jesus's hands and feet, appalled Protestant visitors to Catholic schools and churches.[47]

The burden of this Catholic suffering fell disproportionately on women. Mothers, one Jesuit noted, should "regard every affliction which may fall to your lot as an opportunity of proving your love of God."[48] When priests spoke to nuns they lingered on this theme.[49] During a retreat to the nuns at Grand Couteau, for example, one Lyon Jesuit preached the "practice of solid virtues: mortification, humility, abnegation and obedience." Three months later, another Jesuit preached on the "mortification of the passions" as the "essential preparation for prayer."[50] In Missouri, yet another Jesuit urged Sacred Heart nuns to cultivate "humility and the love of suffering."[51]

Wilson, too, absorbed the message that suffering served a noble purpose and the sense that God stood beside her on an unpredictable journey. She responded with particular enthusiasm to a meditation on the phrase, "My life is so short and its term uncertain."[52] Even her miraculous cure, after months of illness, did not relieve her from an obligation to honor God through continued suffering. If anything, it made her welcome or at least understand her ongoing health struggles. As she explained, God had the "good purpose [of] making me suffer for the last week, and He alone knows how much I did suffer." After Wilson's death, her Mother Superior wrote a long letter to her parents, encouraging them to "weep not for your darling child, she is no doubt in the enjoyment of her God, secure from all the trials, cares and vicissitudes of this miserable life."[53]

The sociological consequence of this devotional style—prayers to the Sacred Heart of Jesus, devotion to Mary, and a focus on suffering—depended on the place of Catholicism in a particular society. Everywhere, though, the Sacred Heart became associated with support for the papacy. One Italian Jesuit exiled to the United States saw the devotion as a counterweight to the "virulent attacks" on Pope Pius IX "from the mighty of the world." He especially disliked "those, who, nominally Catholics, are really in rebellion against the authority of the Church."[54]

In religiously divided countries such as Germany and the Netherlands, the style strengthened a confessional identity that included not only devotion to the Sacred Heart but also resistance to interfaith marriages and an insistence that Catholics form their own schools and associations. Where confessional divisions were of less importance—in Spain, Austria, France, Italy, and parts of Latin America—devotions such as the Sacred Heart became associated with the ultramontane, even royalist, side in the ongoing struggle between Catholics and anticlerical republicans.[55]

Louisiana's religious grid absorbed both patterns. On the one hand, Protestants and Catholics competed for souls and clashed over educational issues. In contrast to Bapst's solidly Protestant Maine, white Protestants outnumbered Catholics in Louisiana only after a wave of migration from New York, Pennsylvania, and the upper South in the 1820s.[56] These "American" newcomers brought with them anti-Catholic prejudices, and New Orleans was the site for an 1841 nativist convention attracting delegates from across the state.[57] Near Grand Couteau, one correspondent reported loose talk of "lynching the Fathers [Jesuits] or driving them out of the country."[58] New England natives, disciples of Horace Mann and suspicious of Catholicism, founded the first New Orleans public schools. In turn, as in New England but with greater success, Catholics in Louisiana fought to prohibit the use of the King James Bible in classrooms.[59]

At the same time, Louisiana Catholics developed their own version of the divide between those sympathetic to and those unenthusiastic about the nineteenth-century revival. By 1850, German and Irish Catholic migrants numbered just under half of the city's foreign-born population.[60] Bishops and Jesuits also migrated to the region, and even if French, allied themselves with the newly arrived Irish and German Catholics against the long-standing French-speaking Creole Catholic residents. One Grand Couteau Jesuit recalled struggles against not only "Freemasons" and "Protestant bigots" but also "renegades from the Church."[61]

These renegade Creoles, especially men, resented what they perceived as an authoritarian spirit among the new clergy. One Creole editor explained that "the Irish Catholics are, almost to a man, papists. The French Catholics are generally anti-Papal.

Hence, the French Creoles of this city are true Americans; the Papal Irish are not; and cannot be, until they abjure, as the French have abjured, the tyranny of the Jesuit and other orders of Papal Priests."[62] The same editor added that "republican Catholics" must battle "ultramontane and Jesuit priests" eager to prevent marriages between Protestants and Catholics, or form independent "social and political organizations."[63]

Many Louisiana Creoles even joined the southern wing of the Know-Nothing or American Party in the mid-1850s because they endorsed the party's attacks on foreign Catholics. Congressman and historian Charles Gayarré used anti-Catholic stereotypes to convince his fellow congressmen that Louisiana Catholics posed no threat to national unity since they did not tolerate the "gross superstitions" favored in Rome. In fact, "Louisianians are enlightened Catholics who would not permit the most distant ecclesiastical interference with politics."[64]

Most of Louisiana's Jesuits, by contrast, came from Lyon.[65] They favored an especially fervent piety, which they exported to Syria, Lebanon, Libya, Madagascar, and French-speaking Canada as well as Louisiana.[66] François Gautrelet and Ramière, the French Jesuits most responsible for the modern devotion to the Sacred Heart, came from Lyon, and Gautrelet's younger brother, Francis de Sales Gautrelet, also a Jesuit, spent most of his career in Alabama and Louisiana.

Indeed, the Lyon Jesuits felt the ideological tensions of the period with unusual vividness. Swiss Jesuits, including Bapst, poured into Lyon after their expulsion from Switzerland in 1847, and Italian Jesuits expelled from Rome and the Piedmont soon followed. Father General Roothaan lived with Lyon Jesuits for a time during his exile from Rome.[67]

Unsurprisingly, the Lyon Jesuits allied themselves with French ultramontanes in the battle against not only "libéralisme" but also "libéralisme catholique."[68] They distanced themselves from bishops known to have moderate views (they thought the archbishop of Paris especially suspect), and even Parisian Jesuits seemed insufficiently orthodox. Jesuit leaders in Rome eventually transferred the editorial offices of the Jesuit journal *Études* from Paris to the more ideologically reliable Lyon.[69]

So, too, in Louisiana; there, Jesuits assessed native-born Creoles as dangerously lax. They referred to them as "our infidels," and complained of their "stupendous indifference."[70] When a copy of Pius IX's Syllabus of Errors reached Grand Couteau in spring 1865, in the final days of the American Civil War, its contents were read aloud (in French and Latin) to the assembled Jesuits.[71]

Briefly expelled from their homes and schools during the revolution of 1848—American Protestant ministers applauded the expulsion since Lyon had become "the French metropolis of Popery" and Jesuit obedience to "foreign masters" violated the norms of republican citizenship—Lyon Jesuits became more interested in establishing beachheads abroad, and over the next two decades a steady stream of Lyon Jesuits crossed the Atlantic to an American "refuge."[72] On arrival, these Jesuits, as in France, worried about anticlericals, including a onetime French priest living in Louisiana and author of the tract *The Jesuit Unveiled*, a text reportedly influential with "even the Catholics."[73]

As in Maine and Missouri, Louisiana's Jesuits quietly identified themselves with the Democratic Party as the least hostile to Catholicism and disparaged the radicalism of the "partie abolitioniste." The "abolition of slavery," explained Fr. Felix Benausse, the Jesuit who coordinated the investigation into Wilson's healing, "is a complicated question and not as simple as it ordinarily appears in Europe."[74] Another French Jesuit dismissed Lincoln in 1860 as the "candidate of abolitionism."[75]

After Union army troops occupied New Orleans in 1863, a local judge fined the Jesuits at Immaculate Conception school for allegedly allowing their pupils to draw Confederate flags in their schoolbooks. (One account suggested that the Jesuits had refused to raise the American flag over the school building, choosing instead a French flag, since most of the Lyon Jesuits living in New Orleans remained French subjects.)[76] A Union army doctor who enrolled his thirteen-year-old son in Immaculate Conception school claimed that the boy was the only one of two hundred pupils who dared "to avow himself a Yankee." "Secessionist boasts and principles, songs, and flags," were said to be "commonly heard and seen, with contemptuous expressions about the Yankees, the Federal Union, the President." The Jesuits "are too cunning to say much, but it is easy to see that they do not discourage the treasonous sympathies of their pupils and principal patrons."[77] Privately, New Orleans Jesuits complained to colleagues in France of the "depredations of the Federal troops."[78]

After the war, Jesuits criticized the policies of congressional Republicans and regretted the "extreme Republicanism" evident in Congress after Lincoln's death.[79] In 1867, one Grand Couteau Jesuit contrasted the anticlerical "volcano" disrupting Jesuit life in Europe with the situation in Louisiana, where native-born white Protestants now admired the Jesuits. "The results of the war," he explained, "have been happy in this respect."[80] Near Grand Couteau, one Jesuit recalled that some Catholic slaves "apostasized" after the arrival of federal armies "because they were told that the Protestants had liberated them whilst the Catholics had kept them in bonds."[81]

IV

If the course taken by the nineteenth-century Catholic revival in Louisiana offers one context for the events at Grand Couteau, the Catholic understanding of illness provides another. To read the letters, diaries, and parish histories of nineteenth-century Catholics is to enter a precarious world, where death strikes without explanation, where mild illnesses turn severe, and where epidemics terrorize cities.

In this Catholics were little different from other Americans—just more impoverished and more vulnerable. This vulnerability did not lead nineteenth-century Catholics to disparage modern medicine, as suggested by the gravity with which Catholics promoting miracle accounts weighed physician testimony. Indeed, the first account of Wilson's healing stressed that the Sacred Heart nuns had lavished on Wilson not only "spiritual and supernatural aid" but also "all possible care, natural and professional."[82]

Instead, illness supplied yet another opportunity for Catholics to see themselves as a united body. Just as Catholic schools seemed necessary to combat the animus of Protestant public officials, and just as Catholics worried about excessive deference to the nation-state at the expense of religious bonds, so, too, did illness and healing depend on communal action. In moments of crisis, as epidemics swept cities, and friends and relatives lay dying, prayer became less the plea of an individual than a plea from one community (the devout) to another (God, Mary, and the saints). Here communal life intertwined with devotional life, with the same priests and nuns who built schools and founded parish associations rallying parishioners for marathon prayer sessions.

The priest was the pivotal person in the devotional economy because only the priest could provide the sacraments on which eternal salvation depended. The depth of this conviction among the Jesuits and, over time, the Catholics they catechized is remarkable. It explained the desire of Catholics to baptize their children soon after birth, since, as one Jesuit put it, an unbaptized child "would never be permitted to enter Heaven, the home of all the blessed."[83] It underlay the structure of the parish mission, where priests listened to a steady stream of penitents fearful about their final judgment should their serious sins not receive absolution in the confessional. It impelled priests such as Bapst and Helias to travel long distances under harsh conditions to place their hands and holy oil on the faces of dying Catholics. Bapst once pleaded with his superiors to send more Jesuits to Maine to prevent parishioners dying "without sacraments when they call after us in their last moments."[84] Similarly, when Wilson fell ill several months after her miraculous cure, she begged her Mother Superior to permit her to "make a general confession."[85] "I hope I will receive the last Sacraments, Mother," she worried, "but if I should die during the night, I cannot."[86]

When ordinary means of succor failed, God answered prayers through the miraculous, or direct intervention in human affairs. Before testifying at the archdiocesan investigation into Wilson's cure, each witness listened to a local Jesuit provide a careful definition of a miraculous healing. An ordinary healing, like ordinary grace, "uses nature." A miracle, by contrast, "acts without it."[87]

The era's most celebrated action without nature occurred in 1858 at Lourdes, a remote village in the Pyrenees, when a poor fourteen-year-old girl named Bernadette Soubirous claimed to see Mary, who, tellingly, uttered the phrase, "I am the Immaculate Conception"—a reference to the controversial doctrine approved in Rome in 1854. Word of the apparition reached the United States not long after it reached Paris, and in New Orleans the local Catholic press immediately reprinted accounts from the same journals read by French Catholics.[88]

Imitation Lourdes grottoes, often built by Jesuits, quickly appeared across the world. In Paris, for example, Jesuits installed the city's first Our Lady of Lourdes altar soon after the apparition, even as Jesuits also from Paris but working in Shanghai constructed altars and grottoes in China.[89] Jesuits helped organize the first American pilgrimage to Lourdes and began distributing Lourdes water as part of the Catholic healing arsenal. When one Jesuit collapsed of a stroke in Maryland, his colleagues tried to revive him with bleeding, mustard plasters, electric current from a battery, and croton oil. Then they tried Lourdes water, recently arrived from France. "Instantly," they reported, "the sick man recovered sense and speech."[90] By this time, priests at Bapst's parish in Boston reported daily requests for Lourdes water, with an especially fervent desire coming from women about to give birth.[91]

The attention lavished on Lourdes was unprecedented, but it was only the most visible manifestation of an interest in apparitions and miraculous healings saturating the Catholic world. Beneath the iceberg tip of the great nineteenth-century European and Latin American apparition pilgrimage sites lay a vast block of now-forgotten apparitions, miracles, and healings.

In Saint Louis alone, accounts of at least three miracles circulated through the city's Catholic networks in less than a decade. Wilson would undoubtedly have heard of the 1863 healing of a local baker, Ignatius Strecker, whose chest had been ripped open in a worksite accident and who had been cured after Jesuit Weninger touched him with a relic of the beatified Jesuit Peter Claver.[92] In 1867, the Sacred Heart nuns in Saint Louis informed colleagues around the world of the miraculous healing of a child from a prominent local Catholic family who had been touched with a piece of cloth worn by their founder, Sophie Barat.[93] In 1871, the city's residents debated whether Therese Schaeffer, a young German American woman, had seen Mary and whether her cure could be judged miraculous.[94]

Church authorities never required Catholics to believe in any of these apparitions and healings, including the miracle at Lourdes. But they insisted that basic religious truths, including miracles, remained accessible to all men and women.[95] This conviction about the accessibility and reasonableness of miracles made Catholics eager to enlist scientific allies in the investigations conducted to assess the authenticity of cures. In Lourdes, Catholics publicized the reluctance of the physicians employed by the Bureau des Constatations Médicales to identify miraculous healings, and in Grand Couteau, local Jesuits required detailed testimony from Wilson's physicians.[96] Miraculous healings, in fact, proved far less troubling than apparitions to church authorities, since medical experts could verify healings while apparitions rested on the credibility of a potentially troublesome beholder.

Jesuits such as Weninger voiced this simultaneous faith in scientific investigation and the miraculous. He conceded that "premature reports of miracles" before they had been "duly authenticated" invited charges of "encouraging credulity and superstition." But he also believed that once an event had withstood the "severe test of a Roman investigation, then the truth of a real miracle shines forth with dazzling brilliancy."[97] In Grand Couteau, similarly, Jesuit investigators asked that local magistrates, not Jesuits, witness the affidavits to Wilson's healing so as to forestall accusations of biased testimony.[98]

This Catholic assimilation of the miraculous, from theological treatises to popular piety, is distinctive. Certainly belief in the miraculous crossed denominational lines, and Seventh-day Adventists, African American Christians, and Mormons all claimed to effect miraculous healings.[99]

Still, most Protestant intellectuals believed miracles had ceased with the death of the apostles, and miracles occupied an uncertain space in mainstream Protestant churches. Miraculous healings, in particular, became discredited by association with Catholic superstition, and in the later nineteenth century became understood by educated elites as incompatible with a belief in modern science or even human reason.[100]

When Catholics publicized a cluster of alleged miraculous events in the 1840s and 1850s—including the exhibition of Christ's Holy Robe in Treves in Germany in 1844, which drew one million visitors and many claims of miraculous healing; the appearance of the Virgin to three children in LaSalette in France in 1846; and the winking Madonna in Rimini on the Adriatic coast in 1848—Protestant ministers and editors derided their credulity. Theodore Parker hoped that "science" as well as investigation into the "human origin of the Churches and the Bible" would end foolish tales about the appearance of the Virgin in LaSalette and charades such as the Holy Robe in Treves.[101] Traveling in Switzerland during the commotion caused by the Holy Robe in Treves, American minister George Cheever thought the episode proof of Protestantism's "clear intellect, and uniform logical passion" as opposed to Catholicism's "miracle-working enthusiasm."[102]

Even in tiny Ellsworth, Maine, residents accused Bapst of claiming to have "wrought a miracle" and healed a member of the town's leading Catholic family. Bapst denied the accusation. But as one Bapst opponent insisted, "Papists of the present do believe in miracles. Furthermore, they insist that Protestants have not the power to perform miracles because [they are] not of the true church."[103]

This accusation was accurate. That God, Mary, and the saints made themselves visible to coreligionists seemed to Catholics decisive for the era's confessional scorecards. The Abbé Gaume, author of the catechism studied by Wilson, put it bluntly: "The religion in favour of which miracles are performed is the true religion."[104] Just three days after Wilson's cure, one of the Louisiana Jesuits who witnessed the event explained to an acquaintance, "The time of miracles is not entirely passed away. [This] is nothing astonishing for us Catholics, since we know that the saints are powerful with God, and that nothing is impossible with God."[105]

Even in the eighteenth century, Jesuits had ignored mocking essays by Voltaire, and outstripped other religious orders in their production of hagiographic texts and their scholarly investigation of miracles and holy legends. The suppression temporarily displaced the Jesuits from this role, but by the mid-nineteenth century, working from influential perches in Rome, Jesuits again promoted miracle accounts as means for Catholics to know the saints, especially Jesuit saints, and through them to know God.[106]

Joseph Kleutgen, the most influential Jesuit philosopher of the nineteenth century, authored an important 1846 text insisting on the possibility of God's direct, miraculous intervention into human affairs. "The gift of miracles," Kleutgen wrote, "is one of the favors bestowed upon the Church by its Divine Benefactor." (Kleutgen later began a sexual relationship with a female visionary who claimed to receive divine messages—a relationship concealed by Jesuits and Roman authorities up to and including Pius IX.)[107] Jesuit Weninger and other prominent American Catholics as well as Catholic leaders from Poland, Austria, Italy, England, and even Australia visited the home of Maria von Mörl, the woman in the south Tyrol whose claim to possess the stigmata helped ignite the Catholic revival in Germany.[108]

The Jesuits were especially influential in the cultivation of a sensibility attuned to the miraculous in the United States.[109] The most celebrated miraculous claim in the United States in the early nineteenth century, the healing of Ann Mattingly in Washington, DC, involved local Jesuits, one of whom publicized the miracle to great effect in Europe, and discussed the event with fascinated Catholic nobles in Vienna, Munich, and Turin. (Two Jesuits dubious about Mattingly's veracity were denounced to Roman authorities and eventually left the Society.) The memory of the Mattingly cures endured, even in remote Grand Couteau, and after Wilson's initial cure, the local doctor recounted Mattingly's story to the Sacred Heart nuns.[110]

Other Catholics marveled at—and complained about—the ease with which Jesuit candidates made it through the canonization process. "Look at the number of saints they have already secured," complained one non-Jesuit priest in 1890, "and think of the others whose case is [slowly] advancing by stages."[111] This Jesuit fascination with miracles and their ease with the system for moving from investigation to beatification to canonization explains another puzzle of Wilson's healing: Why Berchmans? Wilson herself, when first told by the other nuns that they had begun a novena to Berchmans on her behalf, wondered "if there was any saint left."[112]

It was a fair question. Berchmans's short life—born in 1599, raised in what is now a Flemish-speaking area of Belgium, and dead at the age of twenty-two in Rome after six years as a Jesuit in training—is unprepossessing. After a flurry of interest in the seventeenth century, his canonization cause faded from even Roman memory. Pope Benedict XIV reopened an investigation into Berchmans's cause in 1745, but he was generally unsympathetic to the Jesuits, and refused to beatify or canonize any of the many proposed Jesuit saints. He reportedly worried that to canonize Berchmans would mean sainthood for all virtuous members of religious orders.[113]

The suppression of the Jesuits halted progress on Berchmans's canonization. Only in the early 1840s, spurred by Father General Roothaan, who believed Berchmans to be his special protector, do we again find Jesuits making "fervent prayers" for Pope Gregory XVI to reopen the canonization process.[114] Gregory XVI obliged in 1843, and in 1865 Pius IX declared Berchmans "blessed" or one step away from sainthood.

Berchmans's humility made him typical of the saints favored by Pius IX and Fr. Giuseppe Boero, the Italian Jesuit who alternated between engaging in polemics with Italian nationalists and shepherding Jesuit candidates through the beatification and canonization process.[115] (And Jesuits in the United States knew to contact Boero with notices of miraculous cures.) Berchmans, one commentator stressed, "made himself eminent in endeavoring to pass unnoticed among men. He has risen to heaven by avoiding everything that could exalt him in the estimation of others."[116]

Closely allied to humility was obedience, or what another commentator termed Berchmans's "full subjection, both interiorly and exteriorly, to the will of his superiors."[117] (One New York diocesan priest disenchanted with the Jesuits thought this focus on the "absolute obedience" of Berchmans yet another way the Jesuits worked against the "progress of the country and the times.")[118] Statues and portraits of Berchmans dating from the nineteenth century invariably show him clutching not only a rosary and a crucifix but also the book of rules for the Jesuit order. After Wilson's cure, the other nuns compared her scrupulous observance of her order's rules to that of Berchmans, and Wilson began the penitential practice of kissing the feet of the other nuns on the first Friday of the month in honor of "Blessed Brother John."[119]

The ceremonies surrounding Berchmans's beatification in 1865 received extensive coverage in the Catholic press. Pope Pius IX traveled across Rome to the Jesuit Collegio Romano to mark the occasion, and Jesuits encouraged pilgrims to visit Berchmans's home in Belgium and his tomb in Rome.[120] Once beatified, Berchmans's cause needed two miracles to advance him toward canonization. Jesuits had been collecting reports of miracles attributed to the intercession of Berchmans since the early 1840s, but publicity surrounding the beatification inspired Catholics around the world to report instances of prayers to Berchmans leading to unexplained healings. A cluster of reports from Belgium especially, but also from Italy and France, arrived in Rome within a year after the beatification. A child with eyes swollen shut in Mechelen opened them without pain on the ninth day of a novena to Berchmans; a doctor in Leuven reported the inexplicable healing of a local woman; a Belgian nun suffering from chronic inflammation and paralysis suddenly felt no pain. Most of the miracles involved Jesuits as either witnesses or local experts, and within a year of the beatification the Jesuits arranged

for the publication of a book describing six recent miracles attributed to the intercession of Berchmans.[121]

The Father General of the Jesuits made a point of highlighting the beatification of Berchmans in letters sent to the Jesuits in
the United States. One Missouri Jesuit responded by promising
financial support for the effort necessary to move the canonization forward, and a Philadelphia Jesuit arranged for the reprint-
ing of a recent Berchmans biography.[122]

This Jesuit ability to simultaneously appeal to the Catholic public and maneuver the levers of Roman authority shaped events at
Grand Couteau. Like contemporaries around the world, Grand
Couteau's Jesuits spent three days of prayer in support of Berchmans's canonization in April 1866. They welcomed the Sacred
Heart nuns and their students to the prayer services, along with local townspeople, so that all could profit from the "great festival."[123]

Prompted by this event, aware that Berchmans's life in a religious order made him an apt role model, and having just finished reading a biography of Berchmans that stressed his ability
to "make great account of small things," Mother Victorine Martinez ordered the thirty-eight nuns in the convent to conduct a
novena requesting Berchmans to cure Wilson after her illness
worsened. She placed a large picture of Berchmans in the chapel
of the convent surrounded by flowers and candles along with a
small picture next to Wilson's bed.[124] As Wilson writhed in pain,
the assembled nuns repeatedly made the following prayer:

> O God! Glorify Thy Servant Johns Berchmans by reliev-
>   ing our Sister, and if it
> Be to the glory of the Sacred Heart of Jesus that she re-
>   cover, let it be through
> The intercession of Blessed John Berchmans, that hereby
>   his canonization may be forwarded.[125]

Berchmans happened to be the Jesuit saint of the moment, but
the communal Catholic response to Wilson's illness, the sense
that an entire religious community must rally around an ill mem-

ber, was unexceptional. During the global cholera epidemic of the late 1840s, Jesuits in locales as diverse as Marseilles and Madura organized large devotional services to pray for good health and the victims, before tending to the sick and dying. (Cholera ravaged the Jesuit mission in Madura, killing five young Jesuits recently arrived from Lyon, and requiring the Lyon provincial to send Jesuits initially destined for Grand Couteau to India.)[126] When cholera passed through Saint Louis, killing six thousand residents, the Jesuits at Saint Louis University gathered the students into the university chapel, where they placed a silver crown over a statue of the Blessed Virgin Mary. After the epidemic passed, they installed the following plaque in the chapel: "This great confidence in the Mother of God pleased her Divine Son; for the devastating scourge, through the intercession of Mary, was not allowed to enter within the walls of the university; and to the admiration of the entire city, not even one, out of two hundred and more boarders, was infected with the plague."[127]

New Orleans, like Rio de Janeiro, Havana, and other tropical ports, endured outbreaks of not just cholera but also yellow fever, with newcomers to the region especially at risk. The 1853 yellow fever epidemic killed 10 percent of the city's population—almost all immigrants.[128] The toll taken on priests and nuns, often new to the region and vulnerable to the disease, was severe. One Jesuit superior from Lyon lasted less than a year; three Jesuits died from yellow fever in 1853, two in 1854, and four in 1855.[129] That same year, in one brutal seven-week span, yellow fever killed sixteen Sacred Heart nuns at a convent north of New Orleans.[130] The first years in Louisiana, admitted Fr. Benausse, "are always more or less critical."[131]

Yellow fever again swept through Louisiana in 1866 and 1867, killing over three thousand residents. In Grand Couteau, nuns and priests delayed the opening of the school year since few parents would allow students to leave homes, and civic officials imposed a quarantine for the Grand Couteau villagers, "priests and physicians excepted."[132] Two of the Jesuits in Grand Couteau, including one who testified in support of Wilson's miraculous cure, died from yellow fever contracted when they visited dying parishioners.[133]

Wilson did not suffer from yellow fever. Her illness was chronic, preceding her arrival in Louisiana. (In fact, her personal notebook suggests that she first received the last rites in 1865 while still living in Saint Louis).[134] Still, the quick resort to community prayers and novenas rested on hard experience of disease and death. Sr. Moran patiently told archdiocesan investigators that "sensing that all human help was in vain, the members of the Community who, one and all professed the most lively interest in the case of the invalid," offered "violence, as it were, to heaven to obtain from God a cure."[135]

This Catholic imploring of the divine, even "violent" pleas for assistance, saturated Catholic Louisiana.[136] In New Orleans, one French émigré priest vowed to build a church in honor of Saint Roch, a medieval saint noted for healing victims of the black plague, if his parishioners were spared. They were and he did, after touring Rome and the Rhineland for architectural inspiration. The chapel immediately became a healing site. And as in Lourdes, the healed immediately began to line the walls with their crutches and bandages.[137]

Also in New Orleans, a popular Redemptorist priest, Franz Xavier Seelos, died of yellow fever in fall 1867. Like the Jesuits, the nineteenth-century Redemptorists became leaders of popular missions and opponents of what they understood as an anti-Christian enlightenment. Raised in a small, Catholic town southwest of Munich, and taught at the University of Munich by Joseph Görres, one of the central figures in the German Catholic revival, Seelos emigrated to the United States in 1843 and joined the Redemptorist order.[138]

After his death, his colleagues immediately moved Seelos's body to St. Mary's Church, and large crowds came throughout the night to touch the corpse. Reports of miracles—a sixteen-year-old girl relieved of "nerve fever" after her family prayed before a crucifix used by Fr. Seelos; a six-month-old baby brought to see the body of Seelos during his funeral and cured of a mysterious illness—began circulating immediately after his death.

"The people loved and revered him as a holy priest," reported one Redemptorist priest to Seelos's sister in Germany, "and now after his death they want relics of him, decorate his grave with candles and flowers, and even are talking about miracles that have occurred."[139]

The crowds touching Fr. Seelos, the devout marching into Saint Roch's church with their crutches, and the Grand Couteau residents pestering the Jesuits and Sacred Heart nuns for paintings or holy cards of Berchmans all reflect interwoven ties among the Catholic community, sick bodies, and the divine—bonds evident even in the earliest Christian communities.[140] This fascination with the miraculous set Catholics apart, connecting them to other Catholics in ways inaccessible to their Protestant and Jewish neighbors. In this way the Catholic community extended from the natural to the supernatural, from parishioners in this world to the communion of saints in the next.

IV

Wilson's cure led to euphoria in the Sacred Heart and Jesuit communities. The nuns commenced yet another novena to Berchmans and moved the picture of Berchmans from the chapel to the main church. "Every day," according to one account, "a Mass was said in thanksgiving and prayers were said in public." The Grand Couteau Jesuits, isolated from the main Jesuit community in New Orleans, and aware that superiors in New Orleans and Rome were even then contemplating the closing of their school due to low enrollments, pleaded with the Father General in Rome to view the miracle as a sign of God's favor on "poor Grand Couteau."[141] When the Father General in Rome agreed to keep their college open, they attributed his decision to "a novena that the officers of this house made [to Berchmans] on the interests of our college."[142]

The day after her cure, Wilson officially took the white veil of a novice with "the Doctor and a number of the important families of Grand Couteau . . . present to witness the marvels of God's power."[143] Fr. Benausse preached. He urged Wilson to "consecrate this new life to the glory of the Sacred Heart." Her healing meant she must "die to the world and its vanities," allowing nothing to block "this perfect union which the Heart of Jesus wishes to contract with you."[144]

News of the miracle spread across Louisiana, where "the great sensation" attracted comment not just in Grand Couteau but also in Lafayette, Opelousas, and "other places where its fame has traveled." The local Acadians demanded their own pictures of "Le Bienheureux" or "the Blessed."[145]

When Odin, another French missionary priest from Lyon and now the archbishop of New Orleans, received the first report of the miracle from the Jesuits and the Sacred Heart nuns, he responded with "great joy." He thought the "finger of God" evident in Wilson's cure. The miracle also demonstrated God's obvious desire to "hasten the moment of [Berchmans's] canonization."[146]

In the first months after the miracle, both the Sacred Heart nuns and the Jesuits decided not to publicize Wilson's claim to have seen Berchmans. Wilson told only Mother Martinez and Sr. Moran, who did not inform the other nuns. Fr. Benausse, the Jesuit who began the official investigation of the case, requested that Wilson provide an "attestation" or testimony of her experience, and Mother Martinez later prodded Wilson for even more details, including a precise description of Berchmans's appearance.[147]

When Benausse conveyed Wilson's testimony along with fourteen other depositions to the archbishop of New Orleans, however, he explained that he thought it imprudent to publicize the apparition. Indeed, he termed this aspect of her testimony "less miraculous."[148]

Why? Benausse worried, first, about the "malicious criticism of heretics and bad Catholics."[149] "While contenting the pious curiosity of some," he explained, directing attention to the apparition "will make it more difficult for others to adhere entirely to the principal, important fact [of her cure]." Complaints by locals that the healing was "humbug" circulated after the event, and the very fact that some Jesuits saw the miracle as a refutation of local "petit philosophers" suggests an anticlerical presence in the villages of Catholic Louisiana.[150]

For less skeptical Catholics, details about the apparition might have the oppositive effect, fostering a "certain dangerous exaltation of spirit." As Benausse noted, "In this same convent at Grand Couteau, a little while after the extraordinary healing, a novice experienced mystical exaltation very similar to insanity; she had to leave the convent."[151] A Grand Couteau Jesuit, too, claimed a miraculous cure through the intercession of Berchmans only weeks after Wilson's cure.[152]

Benausse's short history, published soon after Wilson's cure in both English and French, did not mention the apparition. As Benausse explained to his readers, he aimed only to demonstrate the gravity of Wilson's illness, her "instantaneous and perfect" cure, and the "connection between the cure and the intercession of Blessed John Berchmans." (Here he noted the novena in Berchmans's honor and Wilson's touching her own tongue with the small painting of Berchmans.)[153] After requesting from the archdiocese copies of any available canonical investigations of miracles or "similar occurrences," Benausse copied the fourteen attestations, in French or English depending on the first language of the witness, and then translated all the documents into Latin—"a prodigious work"—at the request of the New Orleans archbishop.[154]

The New Orleans Catholic newspaper publicized Benausse's discreet version of events, despite having "heard various statements" in the weeks after the miracle.[155] When the Louisiana Jesuits publicized the miracle to colleagues in Europe, they stressed only the "incontestable" and "truly miraculous" account of Wilson's initial conversion and healing.[156] Mother Martinez and Wilson also apparently agreed to say nothing of the "special favor" of Berchmans's appearance, and Martinez's first account, circulated to Sacred Heart nuns around the world, did not mention it.[157]

During the months after her cure, Wilson did not deviate from the standard routine of work and prayer. She frequently expressed joy at the "graces Our Lord has bestowed on me," even as she again battled illness a few months after her cure.[158] When asked to describe Berchmans—"a smiling countenance, he looked so pure and heavenly!"—she proudly declared to Mother Martinez that "I wish you could see him as I did; it would increase your desire of Heaven!"[159]

But life as a visionary also took a toll. Wilson's status as what one nun admiringly termed an "eminent and privileged soul" made her an object of intense scrutiny, with many local Jesuits, Sacred Heart nuns, and laypeople asking for one-on-one meetings.[160] She found herself burdened by repeated requests to answer questions in writing. Wilson apologized for her inability to "explain myself well," perhaps anticipating that Sacred Heart nuns would later correct her occasionally awkward grammar.[161] When she destroyed some "little papers" she had written during retreats and meditation, she again apologized, knowing that Mother Martinez insisted on reading everything she wrote about her spiritual experience. "I am sorry now that I did not keep some of them to show you, but it is too late now, they are gone; but I was afraid anyone would see them."[162]

Wilson claimed to see Berchmans a second time on January 27, 1867, six weeks after the first apparition, while praying in the convent infirmary at the exact spot of Berchmans's first appearance. This time she asked Berchmans about two topics giving her "great uneasiness of mind": first, whether he was pleased with her testimony at the initial investigation of the healing, and second, whether she would die a novice. Berchmans placed his hand on her head, making her feel "as if I was in Heaven." He assured her that her testimony pleased him and urged her to abandon her fears. But he also said Wilson would die a novice. Wilson immediately asked: Within the first year? He answered: "Yes, be faithful; I will see you again and make known the time."[163]

Wilson informed Mother Martinez of this vision five days later, but Martinez again declined to report this apparition to the other nuns, informing only Fr. Benausse. Rumors of an apparition apparently did circulate, but when queried Wilson deflected discussion of the topic.[164] Even twenty years later, many of the nuns marveled at Wilson's reticence, and she herself, six months after her cure, calmly noted "how little idea" the other sisters had of her experience.[165]

Wilson apparently moved through the next few months with a joyous aura, and in fact Mother Martinez thought Wilson's "joy increased as the hour of deliverance approached."[166] In June 1867, Wilson became convinced that she would die by August 15, the Feast of the Assumption of Mary into heaven. Her diary entries, directed to Mother Martinez, and Mother Martinez's own notes on Wilson's conduct provide some indication of her state of mind. She began to approach each communion and confession with greater fervor. She continually reassured Mother Martinez that she did not "dread [death] at all: it is with joy and an ardent desire of being more closely united to my Blessed Mother and the Adorable Heart of Jesus, that I hail the coming day."[167]

At the same time, Wilson registered an undercurrent of fear. The entire diary entry for July 25 is the following: "Time is short. I must do something to repair my badness." Five days later, as her health continued to deteriorate: "I feel that time is short. I have felt it more to-day and I have been thinking that Our Lord has sent me this sickness to make me begin to be good."[168] A week later: "Every hour I desire more and more to be in Heaven, not that I am tired of living, but I am so much afraid of offending Almighty God."[169]

On July 31, she felt too weak to get out of bed. "I believe it is the beginning," she told Mother Martinez.[170] Her condition briefly improved, but by August 9, Mother Martinez agreed to her request to stop attending classes. Even as her condition worsened, visitors to the convent begged to meet her. On August 10, she met with a former student at the Sacred Heart school who had "heard of the miraculous cure of the Sister." Two days later, "notwithstanding her great fatigue," Wilson visited with the father of one of the other novices, "a gentleman of exemplary piety" eager to discuss the miracle.[171]

Wilson's last diary entry—marked "Adieu to the Journal!!!"—was August 12, 1867. She spent the next day, the feast day of Berchmans, in prayer at the foot of the altar where Berchmans's picture had been placed. That evening, she listened to Fr. Benausse "excite our devotion and gratitude towards Blessed John Berchmans."[172] On August 14, Mother Martinez prevailed on Dr. Campbell, the physician of the convent and one of the two doctors who treated Wilson during her first illness, to visit Wilson in the infirmary. Campbell thought her condition inexplicable though not life threatening. Puzzled when Wilson declined to take any medicine—she claimed "she would be cured but in Heaven"—Campbell asked for an explanation. She pointed to a picture of Berchmans with the comment that "there was her physician." As Campbell later testified, "We first thought Wilson's remark a joke, but she remarked that he was the only one who could do her any good."[173]

Later that day, Wilson slipped out of consciousness. She endured three more days of fever and convulsions. Dr. Campbell prescribed mustard, turpentine, blistering, and the usual "remedial agents." Witnessing the agonies of this "privileged soul" were Fr. Benausse, usually kneeling at her side and reciting various prayers, including "the litanies of the Sacred Heart."[174] All of the convent members crowded into the infirmary to pray for another cure. Mother Martinez stood at the head of her bed clutching a crucifix in front of Wilson's eyes.

Finally, Martinez reported, on August 17, 1866, two days after the Feast of the Assumption, Wilson "left this land of exile for heaven."[175] Then a "profound and religious silence" entered the room. One by one, the other nuns went to the chapel and made the stations of the cross in Wilson's honor. They begged Wilson, now with the saints, "to intercede for us near the Heart of Jesus." Martinez spoke with an exhausted Fr. Benausse near the infirmary. "Allez, vous avez à faire" (Go, you have enough to do), he told Martinez. The nuns placed white roses around Wilson's body, and clad her in her beloved habit. They then placed a crown on her head, and a tableau of Berchmans on the wall above the bed so that Berchmans could watch "the mortal remains of one who had been so devoted to him." They buried her in the convent cemetery, where five days previously Wilson had indicated she wished to be buried in the neat rows of identical gravestones. At that time, the other novices had laughed in response, teasing her with the observation that "that row will be filled up long before you die, Sister Wilson!"[176]

V

Instead of prompting doubts about Wilson's veracity, the saga of what one Jesuit, reporting back to colleagues in France, explained as a "truly extraordinary conversion, healing and death" only fueled greater interest.[177] Sr. Martinez finally told the nuns of the appearances of Berchmans to Wilson, and Wilson's own conduct during the past six months, "silently faithful" as well as "so simple and unassuming," became an inspirational model.[178] The other nuns frequently compared Wilson's own humility and cheerfulness to that of Berchmans, and one nun later declared that she could "never separate one from the other." "When I pray aloud," she explained, "'Blessed John Berchmans, pray for us,' I immediately add (to myself) 'Dear Sr. Wilson pray for us.'"[179]

Wilson's vision of Berchmans now became widely known outside the convent. The Grand Couteau Jesuits relayed the full story, including the multiple apparitions of Berchmans, to Jesuits around the world, with the caveat that they left assessment of the authenticity of the miracle "entirely to the judgment of Rome."[180]

Each year the nuns celebrated Wilson's cure on December 14, and the anniversary of the second apparition of Berchmans on January 27. Pilgrims continued to visit, including in 1868 New Orleans archbishop Odin, who asked "with interest for more minute details of the miracle."[181]

The miracle itself became part of the region's religious fabric, as proof of God's concern for Catholic Louisiana. A Jesuit from New Orleans spoke to the Sacred Heart nuns in 1868 "on the subject of the miracle of which we had been witnesses, and proved to us that this miracle was as much for us as for the one upon whom it had been worked."[182] That same year, Fr. Benausse requested another relic of Berchmans for display in the church in Grand Couteau as well as pictures of Berchmans and the Sacred Heart.[183] In 1872, the Sacred Heart nuns converted the

FIGURE 9. Shrine at the spot where John Berchmans appeared to Mary Wilson, Grand Couteau, Lousiana. Courtesy of Provincial Archives, United States—Canada Province, Society of the Sacred Heart.

infirmary where Wilson saw Berchmans into a small shrine and chapel, and received permission from the archbishop to admit those they deemed "suitable" to the site. A small wicker basket on the exact spot of Berchmans's appearance became the receptacle of handwritten requests for favors. Another New Orleans archbishop, Napoleon Perché, chose to take a summer vacation at the site.[184]

Once filed, the bulky dossier on Wilson's cure disappeared into a lengthy sainthood queue. Already papal officials investigating the canonization cause had decided that one of the two miracles for Berchmans's cure would be the miraculous healing of another nun, Sr. Mary Denis Lyon, in Brussels. The nuns in Brussels, too, prayed a novena to Berchmans as Lyon lay on her apparent deathbed and credited Berchmans with Lyons's unexpected recovery.[185]

In the mid-1880s, the case reached the docket of the Sacred Congregation for Rites, the Roman congregation charged with making recommendations to the pope. The congregation used as initial documentation the testimonies gathered in 1867 by Fr. Benausse, but requested an additional formal investigation conducted by the archdiocese.

Conducted in the episcopal residence in New Orleans with great solemnity, this investigation included each witness testifying to tell the truth on pain of excommunication. New Orleans Jesuits ran the proceedings and collected new statements from witnesses, including surviving Jesuits and Sacred Heart nuns, two of whom traveled from Mexico City to New Orleans for the hearing.

The Jesuit managing the process cajoled the Mother Superior of the Grand Couteau convent to assist him, despite "all the trouble and inconvenience and expense." After all, "the Saints in Heaven, like God Himself, never allow themselves to be outstripped in generosity, the more we do for them, the more will they do for us—indeed a most singular privilege has been conferred upon your Mission in Louisiana in having performed in one of your houses the Miracle which is to bring about the Canonization of Blessed Berchmans."[186]

The Grand Couteau Jesuits also sent pleas to Rome. "We hope," one Jesuit explained to a Roman Jesuit handling the case, "that the Sacred Congregation will not reject the miracle of our Blessed Brother, which seems to have been performed, with a view almost exclusively to his Canonization."[187]

Not everyone accepted Wilson's version of events. The fourteen testimonies taken in the initial 1867 investigation, including that of the two doctors, several nuns and Jesuits, and Wilson herself, included no significant dissonant notes. But even Sr. Moran, Wilson's most determined advocate, admitted that "dissensions or doubts" existed about Wilson's account of the apparition.[188]

One particular dissenter, Sr. Mary Jane Miller, stepped forward in 1886. Miller testified that while she, too, thought Wilson's healing miraculous, she had never believed Wilson's account of Berchmans's apparition or, in her words, "the reality of this phantom." Miller had moved to Grand Couteau three months after the miraculous cure, in March 1867. She thought Wilson's visions of Berchmans the product of a "stimulated imagination." She described Mother Martinez, whom she had known since 1840, as credulous, having a "fairly pronounced penchant . . . for miraculous and supernatural things." She acerbically noted that Wilson's prediction, via Berchmans, of her own death had been three days premature. Even Dr. Campbell seemed to Miller "overly excited."

Miller also informed investigators that Wilson had attempted to enter the Sacred Heart convent in Chicago before she had entered the convent in Saint Louis, but had been "asked to leave the house" because of her work "in service," or as a maid. (Miller was almost certainly distinguishing Wilson's humble background from the more socially elevated origins typical of Sacred Heart nuns.) A tone of disdain is evident in Miller's astonishment that Wilson described herself as "belonging to a family that was well-placed in the world." Miller thought Wilson willed her own death by eating only "a morsel of bread" each day.[189]

Papal officials seem to have judged the other testimonies convincing on the specific subject of Wilson's inexplicable cure. They described Wilson as a woman of "great zeal" and emphasized the suddenness of her cure, without mentioning her death eight months later. In contrast to initial Jesuit and episcopal hesitation, the official account of the miracle briefly mentioned the first appearance of Berchmans. (In Louisiana, sensitivities on this point were such that a local Jesuit cautioned a Catholic editor not to use the phrase "mental apparition," which might imply that the appearance of Berchmans was a figment of Wilson's imagination.) Even Pope Leo XIII may have had some hesitations, since, as the official account explained, he at first delayed "giving his opinion" on the question of Berchmans's canonization, and requested further prayer and deliberation.[190]

In any event, Leo XIII authorized the canonization. In spring 1886, local Jesuits and Sacred Heart nuns learned of the pope's decision. "You will convey to the witnesses the agreeable news that their tongues are loosed," wrote one Jesuit to the Mother Superior of the Grand Couteau convent, "and that the oath of secrecy no longer binds them: they can make known everything they said as witnesses and everything that was said, if they please."[191] When American Jesuits visited Rome, they reported back on the relics and notebooks of Berchmans now displayed in the Jesuit church of St. Ignatius.[192]

On January 15, 1888, Pope Leo XIII canonized Berchmans along with two other Jesuits, Alonso Rodriguez, a seventeenth-century Spanish theologian, and Peter Claver, a seventeenth-century Spanish missionary to the slaves in the South American port city of Cartagena. The official statement conceded that Berchmans's life contained no "truly extraordinary" episodes, but stressed his holiness and ability to achieve the "highest perfection" of the ordinary virtues.[193]

Celebrations across the world at Jesuit parishes and schools marked the canonizations, but the ceremonies in Rome were a Jesuit triumph, demonstrating the renewed strength of the Society near the end of a turbulent century. Thirty-six cardinals and 265 bishops processed into St. Peter's, followed by members of the papal court and thousands of pilgrims, all waiting for the moment during the canonization ceremony when Pope Leo XIII signaled for the dropping of a curtain to reveal paintings of the three Jesuit saints held high above the main altar.

"Time and again," Father General Anderledy explained to his fellow Jesuits, "[Pope Leo XIII] urged me to gather the evidence of documents" in support of the canonizations. When Leo XIII, educated by Jesuits and with a Jesuit brother, met privately with Anderledy and other Jesuit leaders to celebrate the canonizations, he spoke "most feelingly of his warm attachment to the society, of the glorious work it was doing for the Church, of the persecutions it was suffering, and of the consolation God had sent it in the recent canonization."[194]

PHILADELPHIA, PENNSYLVANIA:

AMERICANS

I

Burchard Villiger, S.J., first surveyed the section of North Philadelphia just east of the Schuylkill River in the late 1860s. At
that time the area included a number of small farms, and Villiger found himself scaling fences and chasing "flocks of geese
from his path." His decision to purchase a plot of land (eventually a full city block) to locate a new church building and
Saint Joseph's College there was controversial. "Many a head was
shaken doubtfully at the project," wrote one parish historian,
and "prophets of ill were not wanting to scout it as visionary."[1]

A decade of fund-raising then began—a blur of "fairs, lectures,
concerts, festivals, excursions, collections in the church and also . . .
contributions of our church-building association."[2] Even the Father General sympathized with Villiger's difficulties in "moving
forward with a new church and a new school" in this era of "turmoil" for Jesuits worldwide.[3] But the population of Philadelphia
was growing rapidly, and blocks of rowhouses soon surrounded a
temporary church building and school.

The initial parishioners were predominantly first- and second-
generation Irish, a string of McKennas, Donovans, Murphys,
and Carrolls. Matching parishioner names to those in the Philadelphia city directory indicates that most were skilled and un-

FIGURE 10. Burchard Villiger, SJ. Courtesy of Archives and Special Collections, Saint Joseph's University.

skilled workers, with a sprinkling of business owners, doctors, and lawyers.[4]

In 1879, Villiger laid the cornerstone for a new church, to be named the Gesu, after one of the world's most famous churches, the sixteenth-century baroque masterpiece and headquarters of the Society of Jesus, the Gesù in Rome. A new round of fund-raising commenced, especially as the scale of the church that Villiger envisioned became clear. Parish announcement books included a steady diet of lectures to support the "building fund," and admonitions from Villiger "not to leave such a heavy burden upon their Pastor [so] it will be impossible for him to build either the Church or anything else." A recurring cycle of debt incurred to build the next section of the church, and then pleas for assistance in reducing the debt ensued. Villiger insisted to his parishioners that he refused to "run after money," but he also asked, "How many years will it take, if for want of money we shall be obliged to stop the work?"[5] Only in the late 1880s did Villiger finally obtain funds to "put the roof" on the Gesu.[6] The total cost of the church was $426,548, roughly $25 million in today's dollars, and the parish groaned under the burden of building loans for a generation, with debt reduction campaigns launched at regular intervals.[7]

The expenses began with decorations. One of the first Jesuits to visit the United States after the order's restoration in 1814 had regretted that the nation's Catholic churches were "unpretending structures, without ornament."[8] Even in the 1830s Constance de Maistre, the daughter of the famous Catholic polemicist Joseph de Maistre, had sent funds from Turin to Philadelphia for Jesuits unable to afford clerical vestments and a monstrance.[9]

By the 1870s, Catholics could raise their aesthetic sights. Like so many of his Jesuit contemporaries, Villiger used European contacts to outfit the church with statues and devotional items, ordering crucifixes from Munich and candelabras from Switzerland. He even negotiated the purchase of a collection of life-size paintings of famous Jesuits done by the distinguished Mexican artist Miguel Cabrera and moved them to the adjoining Jesuit residence.

An enthusiast for virtually every dimension of the devotional culture that the Jesuits helped transfer to the United States, Villiger founded a Sacred Heart sodality in the parish.[10] He was unusually interested in relics, and here, too, connections with European Jesuit networks were obvious. Most of the over four hundred relics brought to the Gesu—and displayed every Friday during Lent in a wooden box with Roman attestations to their authenticity—came from Italy via European Jesuit friends, such as Fr. Joseph Keller, from Saint Louis but based in Rome, or Fr. Charles Picirillo and Fr. Benedict Sestini, exiled Italian Jesuits. One batch of relics allegedly came from a "noble" Roman family "fallen into poverty" because of their generous financial support of an embattled Pius IX. Villiger proudly noted that the parish owned relics from all periods of Christian history (including tiny fragments from the bodies of John Berchmans, Saint

FIGURE 11. Interior of the Church of the Gesu, Philadelphia. Courtesy of Tom Crane Photography.

FIGURE 12. Interior of the Church of the Gesù, Rome. Courtesy of Scala/ Art Resource, New York.

Patrick, John the Evangelist, and Andrew the Apostle), a nail that had touched a nail used on the cross (and located in Jerusalem), and three slivers of the true cross itself.[11]

The most striking characteristic of the Philadelphia Gesu was its size. One of Villiger's notes on the project lists the heights of large buildings and monuments—including the Washington Monument, St. Peter's in Rome, St. Paul's in London, and Cologne Cathedral—evidently with the idea that Gesu would rank among their number. Villiger chose a Philadelphia Catholic architect with expertise in a variety of architectural styles, but ultimately modeled the church after the Roman Gesù, itself an inspiration for dozens of Jesuit churches from Munich to Buenos Aires.[12]

Like the Roman Gesù, the Philadelphia church had a vast interior, with 84-foot-high walls supporting the arched ceiling. The length of the Philadelphia Gesu was 252 feet; the length of the Roman Gesù was 255 feet. (When Villiger visited Rome a few years after the completion of the Philadelphia Gesu, he made "exact comparisons between both edifices in various dimensions of length and breadth.")[13] The 70-foot-high baroque main altar in the Philadelphia church mimicked the style of the altar in the Roman Gesù, itself reconstructed only after the Jesuits regained control of the church after their restoration in 1814 (and before their expulsion from Rome). One Philadelphian described the main altar as "completed in the traditional and recognizable style of many Jesuit churches."[14]

The front of the Philadelphia Gesu, with its two towers instead of a more balanced facade, only loosely reflected its Roman namesake. The interior was more faithful. Running up both lengths of the church, as in the Roman Gesù, was a series of eight side altars, four on each side. (One altar was dedicated to the just-canonized Berchmans.) Two large sanctuary altars, dedicated to Saint Ignatius and Saint Francis Xavier, adjoined the main altar. A pulpit jutted from the side of the church and towered directly over the pews, conforming exactly with the Roman model.[15]

This baroque aesthetic was controversial, and another topic for religious polemic. Gothic architecture—the style of most Catholic churches built in the late nineteenth century—drew the support of both Catholic and Protestant patrons, even if its medieval origins disquieted austere Protestants.[16] The baroque crossed fewer denominational lines. Its lavish statuary, stained glass, and painted ceilings, frequently associated with the Jesuits because of the Gesù, had a defiantly Catholic provenance. The Swiss historian Jacob Burkhardt coined a derogatory term "Jesuit Style" in 1845 to connote the "degenerate" Jesuit effort to bedazzle the Catholic masses through "great pomp" aimed at "raw effect."[17]

American and British visitors to Rome in the nineteenth century shared these prejudices. When recounting their Roman sojourns, they downplayed the baroque city—including the sculptures in the Piazza Navona and even St. Peter's—preferring classical ruins such as the Forum and Colosseum. The American novelist William Dean Howells poked his head inside the Gesù—"the most baroque church in Rome"—and retreated with the verdict that the "soul shrinks, dismayed."[18]

Villiger and his parishioners had a different view. At the Philadelphia Gesu dedication ceremonies on the morning of December 2, 1888, twelve hundred "pew holders and friends" jammed into the church, and a much larger crowd estimated at twenty thousand milled about in the street. The event commenced with a procession of fifty clergy and forty altar boys leading the crowd around the entire city block taken up by the new church, two grade schools (one for boys, and one for girls), a high school, and Saint Joseph's College (both for boys) as well as a rectory housing fifty Jesuit priests and brothers.

For Villiger and his contemporaries, the completion of the Gesu and other churches across the country, all with their side altars, relics, and statues, all towering over urban neighborhoods now dominated by the same Catholics whose sacrifices had built them, signaled the consolidation of a genuinely Roman and Catholic community. In Chicago, Jesuits celebrated the completion of Holy Family Church, for a time the highest structure in the city. In Boston, Jesuits delighted in the tableau of "New England boys and girls" entering the new Immaculate Conception Church, "almost under the shadow of Bunker Hill."[19]

In Philadelphia, as one Jesuit chronicler happily reported, when viewed from the city's tallest building, City Hall, the Church of the Gesu was now the "most striking figure in the whole city." It rises "like a veritable giant, head and shoulders above the vast area of buildings round about it."[20]

II

Villiger was born in 1819 in a Catholic district within a Swiss Protestant canton. At age ten he walked twenty-seven miles with his mother, praying the rosary aloud, to Einsiedeln, one of Europe's most visited Marian shrines. (When the American evangelical Cheever witnessed an Einsiedeln pilgrimage, his heart "ache[d] to see the mournful superstition of the people.")[21] The solemn demeanor of Catholics making the journey made a vivid impression, and Villiger decided to become a priest during that trip. He entered the Jesuits in 1838 and was sent to Fribourg, where he studied and was later ordained.

Like Bapst, he fled Fribourg after the armies of the Protestant cantons defeated the Catholic cantons in the 1847 Swiss civil war, and troops ransacked the Jesuit school and church. Villiger explained the war as originating from a "radical anti-Catholic government" that exploited popular misconceptions—"how rich those Jesuits are!"—to further its own ends.

Villiger fled to a Jesuit house near Turin, but there, too, crowds encircled the house, chanting "down with the Jesuits." He was again expelled, just three months after his expulsion from Switzerland. (Even fifty years later, he still judged these expulsions fundamental to his Jesuit identity.)[22]

He made it across the French border to Toulouse, but the June revolutions in France alarmed him, and he retreated to Switzerland to beg for funds to support himself. Finally, along with forty-four other expelled Jesuits, he traveled to Antwerp to begin a several week voyage to the United States.

He then took on a string of parish and college assignments, his success in each tempting superiors to give him yet another challenging task. In Fredericksburg, Maryland, he challenged local Know-Nothings while pastor of the town's sole Catholic parish. In Philadelphia, he worked at Saint Joseph's parish. In Washington, DC, he organized the building of St. Aloysius Church and delighted in the attendance of the president, Democrat James Buchanan, at its dedication. Two years later he moved to Santa Clara College as its president. Distressed by the squat adobe buildings constituting the campus, he began a building campaign that as in Philadelphia resulted in a cluster of new buildings, including a baroque facade for the college church.[23]

He moved back to Philadelphia in 1868. There he held the dual titles of president of Saint Joseph's College and pastor of the Gesu. He focused on the two educational issues preoccupying nineteenth-century Jesuits: secondary and collegiate education for a male Catholic elite, and primary education for the Catholic masses. In both realms the goal was identical: to establish Catholic institutions that would at once shelter and form Catholic young people.

That collegiate education would become central to Jesuit work in the United States was not inevitable. Certainly the Jesuit history in education, with the Society running 800 schools or colleges in Europe and Latin America at the time of the suppression, pointed in that direction. But in the United States the Jesuits began otherwise. The first waves of European Jesuit missionaries desired above all else to work with Indians, and many did, including Bapst with the Penobscots in Maine as well as other Jesuits with the Pottawatomie in Kansas, and the Blackfeet and the Flathead in the Pacific Northwest. Those Jesuits deflected by their superiors from the Indian missions worried among themselves that working with European Catholic immigrants did not have equivalent "prestige."[24]

Only over time did the needs of the millions of immigrant Catholics in the urban centers pull the majority of Jesuits away from Indian Territory and rural parishes into educational work. In this the Jesuits were not alone, and the second half of the nineteenth century saw the founding of a staggering 357 colleges in the United States, religious and secular, public and private. The mortality rate for these colleges was high, and many survived only a few years. Still, by 1900, the state of Ohio counted 37 degree-granting institutions; England had 4.[25]

Even in this entrepreneurial context the Jesuits were ambitious. (The contrast with Europe and Latin America, where state control eventually left less room for a Jesuit presence in developing systems of higher education, is notable.) By 1900, Jesuits managed 25 colleges (which at the time usually included a corresponding high school) in the United States—more than any other single group—with institutions located in almost every major city.[26] That Jesuits emigrated to the United States in large numbers at exactly the moment of the development of the American system of higher education allowed them to carve out an enduring niche. Jesuits founded Santa Clara University in California (1851), for example, well before the University of California at Berkeley (1869), and Saint Louis University (1818) in advance of Washington University of Saint Louis (1853).

This Jesuit focus on higher education generated controversy. Starting in the 1830s and 1840s, prominent Protestant ministers such as Lyman Beecher had warned Americans against complacency as Jesuits—"the most powerful [order of men] that ever conspired against liberty"—began opening American colleges. Another Beecher, novelist Harriet Beecher Stowe, worried about the "political power" the Jesuits might wield.[27] The *Chicago Tribune* similarly editorialized against a possible Jesuit college (ultimately Loyola University) since "the Society of Jesus is the most virulent and relentless enemy of the Protestant faith and Democratic government."[28]

Even within the Society a handful of Jesuits argued that collegiate education for those few Catholics able to benefit from it distracted from parish work. One Boston Jesuit complained of the decision to found Boston College with only a small number of faculty and students. He urged the Jesuit provincial not to bless the stones of Boston College's first building "as long as they are heaped up out of the sweat of the poor and by the bread of the poor." Better to work with Catholics requesting assistance

TABLE 1. JESUIT COLLEGES IN THE UNITED STATES IN 1893

College (current name if still in existence)	Location	Year founded
Georgetown University	Washington, DC	1789
Saint Louis University	Saint Louis, MO	1818
Gonzaga College	Washington, DC	1821
Spring Hill College	Mobile, AL	1830
Xavier University	Cincinnati, OH	1831
Fordham University	Bronx, NY	1841
College of the Holy Cross	Worcester, MA	1843
St. Francis Xavier College	New York, NY	1847
Saint Joseph's University	Philadelphia, PA	1851
Santa Clara University	Santa Clara, CA	1851
Loyola University (Maryland)	Baltimore, MD	1852
University of San Francisco	San Francisco, CA	1855
Boston College	Boston, MA	1863
Canisius College	Buffalo, NY	1870
Loyola University (Chicago)	Chicago, IL	1870
Saint Peter's University	Jersey City, NJ	1872
Regis University	Denver, CO	1877
University of Detroit-Mercy	Detroit, MI	1877
Creighton University	Omaha, NE	1878
Marquette University	Milwaukee, WI	1881
St. Mary's University	Galveston, TX	1884
John Carroll University	University Heights, OH	1886
Gonzaga University	Spokane, WA	1887
University of Scranton	Scranton, PA	1888
Seattle University	Seattle, WA	1891

in the Protestant-dominated almshouses. Or to help Catholic "servant girls."[29]

Still, by the early twentieth century Irish and German Catholics attended college at close to the same rate as their non-Catholic peers, and a recurring theme among Jesuits was concern about the number of Catholic students attending non-Catholic institutions.[30] Over three hundred Catholic men attended Harvard College in the 1890s, for example—more than enrolled at any single Catholic institution in the United States.[31] As one Saint Joseph's president noted, "One of the complaints made by some Catholics [in Philadelphia is] that there are not enough schools for the better conditioned Catholics and for those who form the elite of our society."[32]

Musings about a Jesuit college in Philadelphia dated back to the eighteenth century, but only in 1851 did local Jesuits overcome their hesitations and found Saint Joseph's College as an annex to Saint Joseph's parish, located in an alley a few blocks from Independence Hall. The founding generated little public discussion, although a local minister had recently given a widely reprinted lecture on the alleged Jesuit conspiracy to change the stars and stripes on the American flag "into the yellow folds of Rome."[33] Father General Roothaan learned of the decision to found Saint Joseph's belatedly; he presciently told the Maryland provincial that he feared the "too hasty acceptance of colleges."[34]

Saint Joseph's lurched in its first decades from crisis to crisis. Its first president, Felix Barbelin, S.J., knew little about higher education, and a visiting Jesuit provincial was concerned that "discipline and finances have gone down under him. . . . [H]e is a good, indeed a holy man; he knows and sincerely believes that he is not fit to govern a College, and desires only to be a parish priest."[35]

Forty boys enrolled in the school in its first year, most already members of Saint Joseph's parish. Enrollment grew for a brief moment in the 1850s—despite "the persecutions of our Know-Nothings"—but the college effectively closed in 1859, opened again briefly in the early 1860s, closed again, reopened briefly in the late 1860s, and then closed yet again until Villiger had completed the building of the Gesu church.[36] At that time the college received a gift of $72,000 from the estate of Catholic banker Francis Drexel, allowing it to reopen on a bare-bones budget. Even forty years later, some Philadelphia Jesuits grumbled about Villiger's "manifold and bewildering ambitions" along with his neglect of the college for the magnificent Gesu church. The college had in this view "suffered grievously" until the appointment of leadership focused less on the parish and more on higher education.[37]

The atmosphere at Saint Joseph's and other nineteenth-century Jesuit colleges was distinctive. European Jesuits staffed most faculty positions, and of the twenty-five founding presidents of Jesuit colleges in the nineteenth century all but two were born outside the United States.[38] Many faculty members struggled to communicate in English. At Spring Hill, a Jesuit college in Alabama, students endured a faculty member said to be "unintelligible in four languages." At Canisius in Buffalo, the president alerted the Father General in Rome to the fact that while students "speak only English . . . I have only a few fathers who can teach this tongue or teach in it."[39]

Every Jesuit did command one language, Latin, and much of the curriculum at Jesuit colleges was still based on the 1599 Ratio Studiorum, or plan of studies, reestablished as authoritative by Roothaan in 1832. The seven-year curriculum of the Ratio focused on the ability to read and speak Latin with fluency, emphasizing Latin prose in one year, and Latin poetry in another. (Advanced students studied Greek as well as Latin.) The reading list included Cicero, Homer, Virgil, and Horace.[40] Daily Latin drills took up much of the school day, with "constant repetition," as one Gesu parish bulletin noted, "familiar to every Jesuit professor."[41] Suggestions that "American boys" could not learn to speak fluent Latin were dismissed. Courses in mathematics and science, and more controversially, Romance languages, history, and English, supported this classical core.[42]

The goal was the educated Catholic gentleman—an ideal with deep roots in Renaissance humanism, and one that nineteenth-century Jesuits thought transferable to even the most remote

HOURS	SENIOR	JUNIOR	SOPHOMORE	FRESHMAN	1st ACADEMIC	2nd ACADEMIC	3rd ACADEMIC	4th ACADEMIC	SPECIAL CLASSICS
A. M. 9 to 10	M., W., Metaphysics. T., F.—Physiological Psychology, Geology. S.—Evidences of Religion.	M., T., W., F., Latin. S.—Logic and Metaphysics.	M., T., W., F., Latin. S.—Evidences of Religion.	M., T., W., F., Latin. S.—Evidences of Religion.	M., T., W., F. S.—Latin.	M., T., W., F., S.—Latin.	M., T., W., F., S.—Latin.	M., T., W., F., S.—Latin.	M., T., W., F., S.—Latin.
10 to 10.40	M., W.—Political Economy. T., F., S., Principles of Law.	M., W.—Latin. T., F.—Greek. S.—Analytic Chemistry.	M., T., W., F., English. S.—Later Modern History.	M., T., W., F., English. S—Mediæval History.	M., W., S., English. T., F.—U. S. History and Civics.	M., W., S., English. T., F.—English History.	M., W., S., English. T., F.—Roman History.	M., T., W., F., S.—English.	M., T., W., F., S.—English.
11 to 12	M., W.—Early Modern History. T., F., Metaphysics. S.—Circle in Metaphysics.	M., W.—Early Modern History, U. S. Constitut. T., F.—Advanced English. S.—Advanced Physics.	M., T., W., F., Astronomy, Mechanics. S.—Latin.	M., T., W., F., Trigonometry and Analytic Geometry. S.—Latin.	M., T., W., F., Solid Geometry and Higher Algebra. S—Latin Sodality.	M., T., W.. F., Plane Geometry. S.—Latin Sodality.	M., T., W., F., 1st Algebra. S.—Latin Sodality.	M., T., W.. F., 2nd Algebra. S.—Latin Sodality.	M., T., W., F., Algebra or Plane Geometry. S.—Latin Sodality.
P. M. 12.30 to 1 30	M., T., W., F., Ethics. S.—Circle in Ethics.	M., T., W., S., Adv. Physics. F.—Analytic Chemistry.	M., T., W., F., S.—Greek.	M., T., W., F., S.—Greek.	M., T., W., F., S.—Greek.	M., T., W., F., S.—Greek.	M., T., W., F., S.—Greek.	M., W., S., Grecian History T., F., Latin.	M., T., W., F., S.—Greek.
1.30 to 2 30	W.—Sodality. S.—Elocution.	M.—Ad. English. T.—Evidences of Religion. W.—Sodality. F.—Physics. S.—Circle in Logic or Metaphysics.	M.—Later Modern History. W.—Sodality. T., F.—General Chemistry. S.—Latin, Elocution.	M.—Med. Hist. W.—Sodality. T., F., 1st French, 1st German. S.—Latin, Elocution.	M.—Latin. W.—Elocution. T., F., S., 2d French, 2d German.	M.—Latin. W.—Elocution. T., F., S., 3d French, 3d German.	M.—Elocution. T., F., S., 4th French, 4th German.	M.—Grec. Hist. W.—Bible Hist. T.—English. F.—Phys. Geog. Elocution. S.—Latin, Physical Geography.	M —Elocution. W.—Latin. T., F., S., French, German.

ST. JOSEPH'S COLLEGE.
Daily Schedule of Lectures and Recitations, 1905-1906.

On Mondays and Wednesdays, Military Drill.

FIGURE 13. Typical course schedule for a student at Saint Joseph's College in 1903. Note the emphasis on Latin grammar and texts. Courtesy of Archives and Special Collections, Saint Joseph's University.

locales. (Roothaan told a Louisiana bishop that he hoped to see the "classical" course implemented in a proposed college in frontier Baton Rouge, then boasting a population of two thousand residents.)[43] "The aim," announced one Saint Joseph's catalog, "is not to give a technical or business training, or to produce specialists in any line—but to give a liberal education which is the best foundation for the specialist."[44]

As Villiger explained, producing Catholic gentlemen meant that the college must first cultivate virtue and only then "human learning." Edification trumped "curiosity."[45] Religion entered the curriculum only obliquely, but was omnipresent in student life through daily Mass and various Catholic devotions. One of the college's first students remembered the "splendid ceremonies" held to celebrate the declaration of the dogma of the Immaculate Conception in 1854, and this student later had the opportunity to visit two of his former professors who had returned to work in Rome.[46]

Villiger urged students to imagine themselves as part of an extended tradition. After an opening of the school year Mass at the Gesu, he informed the assembled student body that they could count themselves among the "more than 60,000 Jesuit students [around the world] who, like you, are studying under the direction of men who for the last 300 or 400 years have been distinguished as educators. . . . You are being trained along the principles of the Ratio Studiorum of the Society of Jesus."[47]

The confidence of Villiger and other Jesuits in a classical curriculum isolated them from their educational peers. Most college students in the late nineteenth century studied classical texts, but most colleges also allowed students to choose electives, and had drifted away from a singular focus on Latin and Greek authors. In Europe as early as the 1840s, the classical curriculum of the Jesuits came under criticism from nationalists convinced, as one Jesuit living in Rome reported, that the Jesuits were "impeding progress, [and] suffocating the young people committed to us under a heap of Latin and Greek rubbish."[48]

In the United States, the most prominent dissenter from the ideal of the classical curriculum was Harvard president Charles W. Eliot. Eliot loudly proclaimed the virtues of student curricular choice, and in 1893 the governing body of Harvard Law School, under Eliot's aegis, quietly decided not to admit the graduates of Jesuit colleges, given the classical focus of their curricula and what Eliot deemed an insufficiently varied "programme of studies." He thought the education available at Jesuit colleges "the education of priests."[49]

When queried, Harvard administrators first evaded the topic and then added two Jesuit institutions to the approved list, although not Saint Joseph's. Eliot then took to the pages of the *Atlantic Monthly* to defend high school and college programs enhancing student choice through elective courses. Only "Moslem countries" and "Jesuit colleges" now favored "uniform prescribed education." "That these examples are both ecclesiastical," Eliot concluded, "is not without significance." Such colleges could only provide "trifling concessions" to inductive disciplines such as "natural science." Indeed, "direct revelation from on high would be the only satisfactory basis for a uniform prescribed school curriculum."[50]

A pamphlet war ensued, with Jesuits and graduates of Jesuit colleges defending their alma maters. Jesuit Timothy Brosnahan offered an elegant riposte, marshaling Eliot's many critics within the universe of "non-Catholic colleges" to oppose the "dogmatic intensity" of Eliot's belief in curricular choice.[51] The keynote speaker at an alumni banquet for graduates of Jesuit colleges was more blunt. Eliot, not his opponents, was a "dogmatizing bigot." In fact, "the liberal, broad-minded president of Harvard University, in his venomous sneers at the Jesuit colleges, now displays a spirit of intolerance which up to this time he has wisely restrained."[52] The Jesuit president of Boston College worried that Eliot planned to "crush" Catholic education.[53]

Eliot's suggestion that the Jesuits opposed science, a common jibe often bolstered by references to seventeenth-century Jesuit criticism of Galileo, reflected the polemical climate of the late nineteenth century, where advocates of science juxtaposed Catholic dogmas, notably papal infallibility, with their own putatively inductive claims. This was unfair. One characteristic of the exiled nineteenth-century European Jesuits was their relative sophistication in scientific training, and almost every Jesuit college, however impoverished, had its own rudimentary laboratory and often an observatory.[54] Like many nineteenth-century intellectuals, Jesuits approached evolutionary theory with caution—Charles Darwin's writings did not even appear in the catalog of one Jesuit college library—but cultivated interest in botany and astronomy. At Saint Joseph's, Jesuits opened a small museum of natural history as early as 1854. Science clubs were the first student academic organizations, and the college later took pride in opening the first radio station in Philadelphia, with the call letters "S.J."[55]

Eliot's claim that Jesuit colleges offered students few curricular options was more accurate. When Roothaan reinstated the Ratio Studiorum in 1832, he had specifically rejected curricular innovation as "self-contradictory and mutually repugnant."[56] Not a single elective was available to students in the first years of Saint Joseph's. Jesuits understood this uniformity as advantageous (and

economical)—a proper distinction between a prescribed collegiate education and vocational postcollegiate training. By contrast, they saw Eliot's musings about electives as part of a "systematic and deliberate intention on the part of these gentlemen
to discredit Catholic education, and to drive us from the field."[57]
Even the Father General in Rome denounced the "shallow" inno-
vations now "prevailing in modern colleges and universities."[58]

A tension between Jesuits insistent on the Ratio Studiorum in
its pure form and parental requests for practical subjects such as
bookkeeping marked the history of every Jesuit college. When a
Roman Jesuit visitor ordered the dismantling of the "commercial"
course at the Jesuit University of San Francisco, some parents
reacted with outrage, withdrawing their sons. "Oh what a waste
of time are Latin and Greek," one father wrote, "for so many students that I now see working for a living—as grocer, butcher, and
who knows what else!"[59]

Jesuits in the Midwest, such as those at Saint Ignatius (now
Loyola) in Chicago, seemed more likely than their counterparts
on either coast to accept a commercial course, although even in
the Midwest the pattern was not consistent. (Jesuits in Detroit, for
instance, first accepted a commercial course but then dropped
it to focus solely on the classical curriculum.) European trained
Jesuits especially wished their colleagues "would confine [them-
selves] to the classics. The English, or Commercial course is
humbugging."[60] Roothaan, too, did not think Jesuit institutions
"called" to vocational tracks.[61]

Villiger was defiant on the topic. He required the classical curriculum for all Saint Joseph's students and thought the "universal manner of studies" (or fixed curriculum) embodied in the Ratio Studiorum a useful barrier to each student following his own
methods according to an "arbitrary will."[62]

III

Villiger's role as pastor pushed him into another dimension of
Jesuit work: primary and secondary education. As important as
establishing Saint Joseph's College, in Villiger's view, was the task

of ensuring Catholic education for the boys and girls of North Philadelphia, and he authorized the construction of a school building and recruited women religious to teach in the lower grades (with Jesuits running a high school for boys, and nuns running a high school for girls) immediately after accepting his new role. He repeatedly urged parents to avail themselves of the benefits of Catholic education for the sake of their children. "We cannot say our work in the parish is done satisfactorily," Villiger announced, "until every Catholic father and mother fully realize their responsibility to God and giving their children the best Catholic training that can be had."[63]

In this Villiger and the Jesuits were on one side of a multi-pronged debate that began in the 1840s and continued until the turn of the century. In the first phase, in the 1840s and 1850s, Jesuits such as Bapst, joined by like-minded bishops, priests, and laypeople, fought to eliminate the reading of the King James Bible in the public schools. At the same time, Jesuits were at the forefront of the effort to found Catholic schools because of their conviction about the inseparability of religious faith and morality. In Philadelphia, Villiger's predecessor urged on the Father General the importance of Catholic schools, "in this nation especially," to combat "free schools which are paid for and favored by the government." Attending government schools caused Catholic young people to become "indifferent to the practice of religion and even ashamed of it."[64]

In the second phase, in the 1870s, Catholics, often led by Jesuits, floated the idea of public funding for Catholic schools, and again worried that public education in the United States would isolate Catholicism from its youth. Villiger regretted the "infidel and demoralizing tendency of the Public Schools," and another Jesuit based in Philadelphia, a German exile, termed public schools the "curse of our free land."[65] Or as Bapst complained: "At the Capitol in Washington as well as in the legislatures of certain states . . . they are bent on monopolizing for the State the management of public instruction, as well as that which pertains to the higher studies."[66]

By this time elite American opinion had hardened, with lead-ing statesmen and editors willing to eliminate all religious teach-ing in the public schools to thwart the possible public funding of Catholic schools. Even in frontier New Mexico, where Neapolitan Jesuits had written the first textbooks (in Spanish) and founded the region's first schools, Republican Party territorial officials led a ferocious attack on public funding for religious schools. One New Mexico public official wondered how the state's residents could allow Jesuits—"expelled from every civilized nation"—to become the region's leading educators, especially Italian Jesuits ejected from a "free Italy" due to "conspiracy and treason."[67]

Tensions eased only when the political impossibility of pub-lic funding for Catholic schools became clear, and when public schools became less explicitly Protestant. The occasional old-line Republican liberal such as New Hampshire senator Henry Blair, a leading supporter of Reconstruction and other reforms, could unleash an attack on the Jesuits on the floor of the US Senate in 1888 as he tried to rally support for the federal funding of public schools. "The Jesuits had been expelled from the countries of the old world," Blair thundered, "and the time would come when they would be looked upon as enemies of this country, and when the question of their expulsion would have to be considered."[68]

But these tirades drew little response, with Catholics and many of Blair's fellow Republicans agreed that education should re-main a local matter. This agreement permitted the emergence of the third phase of the school debate, between two groups of Catholics. A new generation of Catholic leaders came to the fore in Europe and North America in the 1880s and 1890s. They were more open to compromise with once-anticlerical governments, more assertive in their patriotism, and more willing to accept state-funded schools.[69]

In the United States, the key figure was Archbishop John Ireland of Saint Paul, Minnesota. A former Union army chap-lain and friend to a number of leading figures in the Republi-can Party, Ireland spent his career arguing for a basic harmony between Catholic and American ideals, and experimented with schemes to teach the basics of Catholicism in the public schools, either with nuns paid by the state or through voluntary religion classes taught at the end of the school day. "The burden," he explained to Cardinal James Gibbons of Baltimore, "upon our Catholics to maintain parish schools up to the required standard for all the children of the Church is almost unbearable."[70] At his most provocative, he proclaimed the public school as the nation's "pride and glory. . . . The Free school of America! Withered be the hand raised in sign of its destruction."[71]

To Jesuits these were fighting words. Already 2,400 Catholic schools enrolled 500,000 students, and the American bishops, encouraged by leading Jesuits in Rome, had vowed in 1884 to provide places in Catholic schools for each Catholic child—a momentous decision leading to the world's largest private school system. That system absorbed tremendous Catholic energy over the next century, most prominently the energy of hundreds of thousands of nuns working for token wages and now dedicating their lives to the education of children. Catholic schools never enrolled more than half, and at various points in the nineteenth and twentieth centuries far fewer than half, of Catholic schoolchildren. But they became the church's most potent symbol of Catholic identity and, for Jesuits, a vital marker of independent Catholic institutions juxtaposed against a potentially hostile state.

This suspicion of state power derived from the Jesuit experience in an often-anticlerical Europe. As one French Jesuit told an American counterpart, "The Republican party [in France] wishes centralized government which tends to absorb all in the God-State: power, wealth, science, religion. Such is the tendency of the party which triumphed over the Sonderbund in Switzerland, of Bismark [*sic*] in Germany. This is the purpose seen in Italy: Despotism presents itself under the mask of liberty."[72]

The growth in the American state seemed to fit the European pattern. An Italian Jesuit who began his career in Turin but ended it in California sarcastically explained that "you know the State is every thing & every thing should be for the benefit of the State, cost what it may. Thanks to heaven, we have succeeded in this glorious 19th in getting rid of that old-fogish maxim that the State is made for men."[73] When a group of exiled German Jesuits working in South Dakota learned of attempts to eliminate federal funding for religious schools on Indian reservations, they immediately termed it a Kulturkampf, a reference to Bismarck's attacks on German Catholics and particularly German Jesuits in the 1870s.[74]

Ireland's nationalism—he once referred to the "sacred stigmata of patriotism"—seemed to Jesuits wholly excessive. Saint Louis Jesuits were offended when at a banquet attended by both Archbishop Ireland and many local Jesuits, a group of Catholic laymen pleaded with Ireland to give an impromptu speech following a toast to "Our Country."[75] A number of Buffalo Jesuits—almost all exiled from Germany—expressed vehement dislike of a "liberal" or "democratic ethos" in the United States, or what they termed the "spiritus Americanus." They wrote the Father General complaining of "excessive nationalism" exhibited by bishops such as Ireland. They disliked clergy lauding "American progress, American institutions, American liberty etc. in innumerable speeches, articles and public appeals to the government."[76]

Two remarkable essays on the United States by Italian Jesuit Matteo Liberatore and published in *Civiltà Cattolica* also registered concern about the related problems of an overweening state and secular education. Liberatore was the most important Catholic social theorist of the late nineteenth century, and his works became staples in the curricula of Jesuit Scholasticates around the world, with Bapst, in fact, arranging for their dispersal among American Jesuits.[77]

Liberatore first favorably contrasted American founding principles with those of "modern liberalism" in Europe. He thought the separation of powers provided for in the Constitution a salutary contrast to the unchecked popular sovereignty on display in European parliaments. Liberatore admired the ability of federal courts to revoke "unjust pronouncements of a legislature." He contrasted the freedom of religion from governmental interference in the United States with the situation in Switzerland, Germany, and "even here in Italy," where liberals "brag loudly about their freedoms of conscience and religion," but imprison priests, seize church property, and disband religious orders. "Wouldn't it be nice," Liberatore concluded, if we could "send Bismarck or even our honorable judges from Montecitorio [the seat of the Italian Parliament] to the American school of jurisprudence?"

Liberatore was less admiring as he analyzed recent American politics. He lamented that the southern refusal to eliminate slavery "little by little" opened the door to a radical Republican Party. This party, led in part by German immigrants "imbued with socialist theories," had "raised the banner of abolition" as a mechanism to "break down local autonomy and the sovereignty of the states." Republican policies during Reconstruction seemed a "military tyranny." The unraveling fabric of American society, with increasing rates of divorce, women demanding the vote, and corruption in the Grant administration, marked a decline of the virtues that distinguished the American founders. Making "education a state monopoly" only made the "poison of modern liberalism" more debilitating. He worried about American liberals imitating Europeans and making "war on Catholicism." What would be the long-term effect of "compulsory education without God[?]"[78]

Archibishop Ireland's most determined opponent was Salvatore Brandi, a Neapolitan Jesuit. After his expulsion from Naples, Brandi came to the United States in 1875, taught at the Woodstock Jesuit theologate, and then returned to Rome as editor of *Civiltà Cattolica* in 1891, eventually becoming a Roman cardinal and member of Pope Leo XIII's inner circle.

Brandi used the pages of *Civiltà Cattolica* to criticize Ireland's schemes. To Brandi it seemed obvious that a non-Catholic ("atheistic, or Protestant, or altogether indifferent") state would make religious instruction a meaningless "appendix" to long days spent in classrooms run by "teachers who are Protestants, or Jews, or unbelievers, appointed by the State."[79]

The debate was not for the faint of heart. Ireland and his supporters as well as Brandi and his supporters rallied bishops to their side, and lobbied influential cardinals in an effort to influence the pope. Privately, Brandi assured a French Jesuit based in New York that "Archbishop Ireland is now well known in Rome as a liberal and revolutionary bishop. I have had occasion to speak of him to Cardinals Rampolla, Monaco and Maz[z]ella." (Camillo Mazzella, too, was exiled from Italy to the United States, taught at Woodstock, and then returned to Rome, first working as a professor at a Jesuit university and then after 1886 serving as a curial cardinal.)[80]

Brandi and his Jesuit allies in the United States and Rome helped quash Ireland's dream of sustained cooperation between religious groups and public school leaders. That American politicians and leaders resolutely opposed aiding Catholic schools from the tax fund still seemed to Jesuits regrettable, and confirmed for them the view that the American version of separation of church and state should not become a Catholic ideal. (And indeed, Liberatore had denounced efforts by "liberal Catholics" in Europe to open up discussion of the separation of church and state.) Jesuits might admit the practical benefits of the American church–state arrangement. But in the same breath they warned against the "lost souls" of the unrestricted religious marketplace. Liberatore held to the view that the First Amendment to the US Constitution permitted "freedom of worship" less as a natural right then as a "political expedient." That Catholics in colonial Maryland had once favored religious freedom, Liberatore claimed, had been a tactical decision in a majority Protestant society, and had backfired when Protestants flooded into the colony and passed anti-Catholic laws. Better not to open the "doors to heresy."[81]

Another Italian Jesuit exiled to the United States, Mazzella, was even more blunt. He authored a Latin textbook, *De Religione et Ecclesia*, written in the United States yet circulated throughout the Catholic world, urging a unity of church and state since "not only individuals, but society itself, must profess the true religion." In his correspondence, Mazzella casually contrasted the many "religious sects" in the United States with the "one, true Church."[82]

An unusual affirmation of Catholic orthodoxy on church–state questions occurred in 1890. The occasion was a Grand Act or formal disputation in which a Jesuit seminarian would defend church teaching as outlined in various theses before a panel of bishops and ecclesiastical dignitaries serving as examiners. The theses included a discussion of whether Pope Pius IX's 1864 Syllabus of Errors was an infallible teaching of the church (the view of the seminarian) or merely authoritative (as alleged by a questioner).

The day's final discussion revolved around teaching on church and state—a provocative choice in the presence of some bishops, notably Baltimore's Cardinal Gibbons, uneasy about broadcasting the traditional Catholic view in an American setting. A report says that the young Jesuit "easily maintained" the orthodox position favoring a unity of church and state. After the formal disputation, Gibbons asked the the student if he "would maintain his proposition on liberty of conscience as applied to this country where all religions are equal before the law." The student "modestly acknowledged that he would."[83]

In 1895, Brandi drafted an encyclical for Pope Leo XIII, *Longinqua Oceani* (Across a wide ocean). "Of course," he told an ally, Archbishop Michael Corrigan of New York, the liberals "had to be disappointed."[84] It not only reaffirmed the importance of independent parochial schools but also rejected the assertion that "it would be universally lawful or expedient for State and Church to be, as in America, dissevered or divorced." In fact, it would be preferable if "in addition to liberty, [the church] enjoyed the favor of the laws and the patronage of the public authority."[85]

These debates over schools and church–state doctrine evolved into a dispute between Ireland and the Jesuits over a set of ideas (for Ireland and his allies), or heresies (for Ireland's opponents), termed "Americanism." At its core, Americanism included an embrace of patriotic rituals and sympathy for ecclesiatical innovation. As Ireland insisted, in a jab at the Jesuits' stress on the writings of Aquinas, Catholics should know more about the discoveries of the nineteenth century than those of the thirteenth century. "We should live our age, know it, be in touch with it," he added. "Let no one dare to paint [the church's] brow with a foreign taint or pin to her mantle foreign linings."[86]

The willingness of Ireland and his allies to suggest that church–state separation as practiced in the United States might be a global model drew grateful applause from leading American citizens. Republican Theodore Roosevelt, a friend of Ireland's, saw him defending the "wing [of the Catholic Church] which is liberalized and Americanized, and is always the object of the inveterate hostility of the ultramontane section."[87]

In the late 1890s, Ireland's ideas circulated on both sides of the Atlantic, where American ideas about a more modern church and church–state separation meshed with those of liberal European Catholic intellectuals, already immersed in discussions about the literal truth of scripture, the significance of individual religious experience (as opposed to an emphasis on dogma), and the need to reconcile modern science, including evolutionary theory, and Catholicism. A French priest, Felix Klein, and a German priest, Franz Xavier Kraus, translated Ireland's writings, and German and Italian theologians eager to see a more modern church mobilized their scholarly and publishing contacts in Ireland's support.

From the beginning, Ireland and his allies identified the Jesuits as their chief opponents. "The Jesuits and their ilk," Ireland told a sympathetic German professor, "are killing the church."[88] Ireland's allies explained that "both in America & Europe," the Jesuits were "saying to enter American ways was to abandon the church or to go towards indifferentism," and hoped that "the 'Fathers of the S.J.' . . . will be left for the rear."[89] A French sympathizer worried that any condemnation of Americanism "will be interpreted in France as a joining together of *Catholicism* with the *Society of Jesus*," demonstrating Catholicism's incompatibility with "democracy, the republic and liberty."[90]

Ireland's suspicions were well founded. Jesuits in both Europe and the United States viewed "what is called 'Americanism'" as "a real and not unimportant danger."[91] German Jesuits, especially, supported by Fr. Luis Martín, the Jesuit Father General, explicitly rejected the "doctrines of American liberalism."[92]

To Martín and like-minded colleagues, Americanists seemed to have absorbed the "liberal and progressive" view, denying obedience as the "first duty of a true Catholic." Indeed, one anxious Italian Jesuit in New York, a witness to anticlericalism in both Italy and Nicaragua, warned Roman authorities that the Americanists planned a "full ecclesiastical revolution."[93] Ireland and his allies from the "Catholic liberal party" seemed to Martín naive in their support for the "separation of Church and State" as an ideal, enthusiasm for "freedom of the press," and sympathy for public (or secular) education as opposed to Catholic schools. These "errors" contradicted the Syllabus of Errors, and promoted a false "modernization of the Church to adapt to the needs and exigencies of the modern state."[94]

Just as Ireland and his allies cultivated European allies, Martín vowed to deflect charges that the Jesuits opposed "modernity and progress."[95] Brandi worked furiously behind the scenes to ensure a papal condemnation. In October 1898, Brandi told a confidant, the archbishop of New York, that "Americanism will soon receive a blow . . . in the shape of a pontifical document addressed to the Bishops of the U.S." Two months later, he exulted in the fact that the "encyclical against Americanism is, at last ready." There had been "great difficulties to overcome" from the Americanist "clique."[96]

On February 2, 1899, George Washington's birthday, Pope Leo XIII issued the apostolic letter *Testem Benevolentiae*. The letter included a tribute to the "characteristic qualities that reflect honor on the people of America," but the caution against "excessive liberty" was clear. The Jesuit-sponsored Spanish-language newspaper published in New Mexico, *Revista Católica*, expressed "immense satisfaction."[97] Fr. Brandi was satisfied, too, and took to the pages of *Civiltà Cattolica* to articulate his delight at the condemnation of a heresy originating in the United States but now evident in much of Europe. Surely no one could now believe that Americanists "were the only true Americans and the only genuine representatives of the Church."[98] Father General Martín reported, again with satisfaction, that the pope himself had approved Brandi's article. A year later, Martín chastised English Jesuits for permitting Ireland to speak in a hall owned by the Society.[99]

IV

Busy with parish and college life in Philadelphia, Villiger did not leave any reflection on the Americanist controversy, but he surely supported his Jesuit colleagues. To Villiger, as for Brandi and

Martín, the challenge for the Jesuits was to remain true to their heritage, disdaining calls for adaptation in a frequently anti-Catholic milieu.

In his old age, in several hundred closely written pages, Villiger made notes on the history of the Society and its manner of proceeding. There he warned against "innovation and change" within the Jesuits, and against a nineteenth-century spirit that "always disdains what is old, always seeks novelty and never is at rest in anything." He rejected the notion that "since the world has changed, the Society, of course, must change. The world has changed, I grant it and experience shows that the world has changed not for the better but for the worse."[100]

Even the suppression of the Jesuits in 1773, in Villiger's view, purified the Society so as to retain its "essential portions." As one friend recalled, "He [Villiger] had a childlike devotion to the Church and to the orthodox teaching of the Church, had the greatest dread of liberalism, and was always distrustful of books by Protestants; his great passion was to explain the catechism."[101]

When Villiger returned to Europe in the 1890s for the first time since his expulsion in 1847, he turned the journey into a Jesuit grand tour. In Spain, he concluded that the country's ordinary Catholics were "far better educated than the accounts of Protestant or Infidels would have us believe, it being the exception to find one who does not know how to read."[102] In Rome he had the honor, along with his friend and onetime fellow exile Cardinal Mazzella, of serving as a deacon at St. Peter's Basilica at a Mass celebrating the fiftieth anniversary of Pope Leo XIII's priestly ordination. He dined with Fr. Brandi at the *Civiltà Cattolica* editorial offices. When he visited Paris, he prayed at an altar commemorating the deaths of five Jesuits in 1870 at the hands of radicals leading the Paris Commune. When he visited an altar in Belgium honoring Berchmans, he marveled at a man who "became a saint without doing anything wonderful, only by doing ordinary things perfectly." When he returned to Philadelphia after an almost two-year journey, a large delegation from the Gesu greeted him at the train station and escorted him back to the parish, where he lectured on the impressions made by his trip.[103]

In 1898, Villiger marked sixty years as a Jesuit with a grand celebration. By this time his stature in the parish was such that some parishioners thought his prayers could heal their illnesses. Up to a dozen people would crowd the parlor of the Jesuit residence, and "his practice on these occasions was to make the callers kneel down, then to say some prayers of the Church over them and require them to make a novena or say some prayers, sometimes also to enjoin on them the use of Holy Water of Ignatius."[104]

Villiger's final illness drew the respectful attention on the front page of the *New York Times* as crowds milled about the streets outside his beloved Gesu church. At his funeral, on November 5, 1902, one hundred priests filled the altar for his funeral Mass, and fifty-five policemen managed the crowds. Saint Joseph's College and Gesu school closed for the ceremonies. In the hour preceding the funeral services, as Villiger lay in an open casket in the church, a number of mourners "pressed forward and succeeded in touching [Villiger's body] reverently" in the hope that a touch could cure the sick. "One woman," according to a newspaper account, "begged the undertaker to lay her [rosary] beads on father Villiger's hands. He did so, and when he handed the rosary back to her, her face lit up with an expression of religious joy."[105]

V

The crowds pouring into the Gesu church on the morning of Villiger's funeral marked Jesuit consolidation and triumph. The construction of a vast Catholic subculture of parishes and schools, the cultivation of a global Catholic sensibility centered in Rome, the widespread adoption of devotional practices such as the Sacred Heart and architectural styles such as the baroque, and a renewed fascination with the miraculous did not depend solely on exiled Jesuits. But they are unimaginable without them, as recognized in obituaries praising these "remarkable men" when they passed from the Catholic scene in the early twentieth century.[106]

This Catholic milieu endured, and even strengthened, into the 1960s. But the combative ethos underlying it became more muted. If the first instinct of the exiled nineteenth-century Jesuits was to isolate themselves, their congregations and students—as late as 1887, the Jesuit Father General warned against "contracting even the slightest taint of liberal opinions"—their successors, born in the United States, took a more measured approach.[107] To them it seemed self-evident, for example, that American Jesuits needed a reporting line directly to the Father General in Rome, not through Italian, French, or German superiors. After all, wrote one New York Jesuit, "We are not Italians, nor Frenchmen, nor Germans. . . . We are Americans with our peculiar traits." "Surely," one California Jesuit exclaimed, "you wouldn't for a moment imagine that I could direct any superior in Milan or in Genoa. I've been in both cities, but cannot measure the spirit of that part of the world." Italian superiors "do not and cannot appreciate the true nature of affairs in the United States, and particularly in California."[108]

As the migration of Jesuits from Europe to the United States ceased, the desire for greater autonomy took organizational form. In 1892, the Maryland–New York and Missouri Jesuit missions were elevated to the status of provinces, fully equal to those in Europe. In 1893, New Orleans separated from Lyon; Buffalo separated from Germany in 1907. Turinese Jesuits working in an anticlerical Italy relied on subsides from American Jesuit colleges to support themselves and so hesitated to break ties with their colleagues in California. But Americans complained that "the missions in Turin in America have more [Jesuits] than the European Province of Turn," and so Jesuit superiors in Rome severed the link. A decade later, Jesuit leaders consolidated the last of the European missions in the United States, the Naples mission to the desert Southwest, into the work of existing American provinces.[109]

The political climate in both Europe and North America also became more welcoming. In 1895, after a thirty-year absence, the Italian government permitted the Jesuits to reestablish themselves at the Gesù in Rome. Anticlerical governments in Portugal (1901) and France (1905) expelled the Jesuits yet again, but the relative stability of the first decades of the twentieth century contrasted favorably with repeated nineteenth-century dispersions. Only in Mexico (in the 1920s) and Spain (in the 1930s), where bitter civil wars divided the populace into Catholic and republican factions, would large groups of early twentieth-century Jesuits endure the chronic instability so defining for their nineteenth-century predecessors.

Working at *Civiltà Cattolica*, Jesuits such as Brandi continued to insist on adherence to Roman norms, even on controversial issues such as the union of church and state. In the United States, the tone became less defiant. One American Jesuit dutifully endorsed the orthodox doctrine on a union of church and state, but only "in the abstract."[110] At Saint Joseph's, students occasionally completed a miniature version of a Grand Act. As part of the exercise the students formally rejected "separation between church and state." Yet this rhetorical task must have seemed peculiar since Saint Joseph's College Jesuits even then boasted of their most celebrated alumnus, Joseph McKenna, who in 1898 took a seat as the second Catholic justice in the history of the US Supreme Court.[111]

If American Jesuits and their students (quietly) clung to an orthodox view of religious freedom and church–state relations, they and their liberal opponents found unexpected common ground on economic questions. A Catholic peasantry pulled from Europe by the magnets of the great manufacturing centers—Irish to New York, Glasgow, and Liverpool, Italians to Milan, New York, and Buenos Aires, Poles to Warsaw and Chicago, and Germans to the Ruhr, Milwaukee, and Saint Louis—constituted much of the late nineteenth-century working class, and Catholic families bore much of the dislocation endemic to a period of both rapid economic growth and increasing inequality.

Precisely the same European Jesuits who expressed skepticism about religious individualism also criticized an individualist market capitalism, with Germany's Theodor Meyer authoring a series of articles on the "social question" as early as the 1870s.[112] A decade later, the even more influential work of Italian Jesuit Liberatore criticized Adam Smith and laissez-faire economics. "Free competition," he concluded, "is a terrible weapon, most effectual to crush the weak and reduce whole populations to economic slavery under a rod of iron wielded by the potent rulers of social wealth."[113] Liberatore was the primary drafter of *Rerum Novarum*, Leo XIII's 1891 papal encyclical decrying the "misery and wretchedness pressing so unjustly on the majority of the working class."[114]

Liberatore had long held that unrestrained competition had especially regrettable consequences in the United States, where "notwithstanding the republican spirit, the rich, the wealthy and the carefree look with indifference upon the misery and pathetic situation of the poor." In Protestant and secular circles in the United States, challenges to laissez-faire economics entered reform circles through cadres of graduate students studying at German universities, often under the tutelage of Adolph Wagner and Gustav Schmoller, the leading economists at the University of Berlin.[115]

Catholic scholars made similar journeys. The most important Catholic social theorist of the early twentieth century, German Jesuit Heinrich Pesch, studied with Wagner and Schmoller in Berlin, and became a fierce opponent of so-called natural laws, including the "unrestrained nature of the free economic system based on economic individualism."[116] American Jesuits studied in Germany with Pesch and returned to the United States enthusiastic about his approach. By that time references to a just wage—contrasted with the lowest wage that a market would bear—and *Rerum Novarum* regularly appeared in the Saint Joseph's College newspaper.[117]

By that time, too, Roman Jesuits had become almost effusive in their descriptions of the United States. The occasional letter from Rome might caution against a "spirit of Americanism," but the more consistent message was delight at Jesuit achievements in parishes such as the Gesu or colleges such as Saint Joseph's.[118] "There is not enough modernism in the United States," Brandi declared in 1909, "for us to write three words about it."[119]

Jesuit colleges and schools, too, beneath rhetoric of adherence to timeless ideals, adapted to American mores. When they first arrived in the United States, some European Jesuits made the disconcerting discovery that collegiate life in America included ice skating parties, dancing, and athletics. One English Jesuit reacted with dismay after witnessing a Jesuit rector at Georgetown boast about the triumphs of the baseball team to a room of cheering students.[120]

The same competitive pressures of the American educational marketplace shaped finances and curricula. When Villiger had reopened Saint Joseph's, he had insisted on following the Ratio Studiorum to the letter, which meant charging no tuition since Ignatius of Loyola had recommended against tuition or fees. The ironic effect of no tuition charges, however, was to make parents suspicious of the quality of the "charity" education provided. Saint Joseph's administrators, desperate for income, began collecting fees soon after Villiger stepped down as president.[121]

Other pressures came from American educational officials. Jesuit anxiety that "our colleges will be forced to affiliate with state institutions or come under state control" proved overwrought. But recognition that "what we are doing is being more and more closely scrutinized and compared with that done by [public] high schools and colleges" was realism. Prodded by accrediting agencies and state education boards, the structures of Jesuit high schools and colleges—including new organizing principles such as the credit hour and majors—began to mimic secular counterparts.[122]

These educational reforms were only one piece of a new identification with modern nation-states. In 1909, the Jesuits in the United States founded a weekly journal of opinion. In a decision that would have astonished their predecessors, so many of whom were European exiles uneasy about nationalist sentiment, they unhesitatingly named it *America*.

More disturbingly, a nascent Catholic nationalism and modern exaltation of "race" fostered Jesuit anti-Semitism. Jesuit writers for *Civiltà Cattolica*, for example, had long relied on commonplace anti-Semitic tropes. Yet in the early twentieth century, in central Europe most emphatically but in the United States occasionally as well, Jesuits newly comfortable in nation-states made derogatory references to Jews as racially inferior and a worrisome "nation within a nation."[123]

VI

In 1914, the Jesuits inaugurated a centenary celebration.[124] The Society now numbered over sixteen thousand—a remarkable increase from the several hundred survivors of the suppression who celebrated the restoration in 1814. Beginning with a handful of beleaguered institutions, Jesuits now ran 234 colleges in forty-three countries, sponsored dozens of scholarly, devotional, and missionary journals, ran multiple scientific observatories, served as advisers to the pope and in various high ecclesiastical positions, and as a collective constituted the most significant Catholic intellectual resource.[125] Such accomplishments decisively refuted, in the Jesuits' view, critics who had accused them of opposition to "civilization and progress."[126]

The celebration was ill timed, since it coincided exactly with the assassination of Archduke Franz Ferdinand and his wife, Sophie, in Sarajevo (with an Austrian Jesuit delivering last rites) and the beginning of World War I. In this sense, too, the celebration marked a transition, as the war demonstrated more powerfully than any other event an identification with the modern nationalism that Jesuits had once rejected. During the 1859 war between France and Austria, some Jesuits had evaded military service by enlisting doctors with ties to the Society to declare them unfit. During both the American Civil War (1861–65) and Franco-Prussian War (1870–71), Jesuits did volunteer as chaplains, but only after making a point of their neutrality and resisting claims that a state could draft Jesuits into military service. In Germany especially, Jesuits occasionally encountered accusations of disloyalty simply became of their membership in an international—and to many Germans notorious—religious order. They were men "without Fatherland."[127] And in fact, German Jesuits repeatedly stressed the incompatibility of nationalist fervor with "a global Order. As such we should be prepared to go out into the world, being everywhere at home."[128]

The First World War was different. Those Protestants inclined to see their religious heritage as tightly bound to particular nation-states quickly rallied to support their political leaders, most famously in Germany, where many leading churchmen and theologians fiercely defended Kaiser Wilhelm's Reich. More surprisingly, just as international socialism crumbled on the willingness of one country's workers to slaughter another's, so, too, did an international Catholicism struggle to contain ethnic nationalism.[129] Even the Jesuits were not immune. Despite the Father General's efforts to sustain Jesuit solidarity across battle lines, in part by moving his offices to neutral Switzerland during the war, Jesuit patriotism became more evident than at any point in the Society's history. In Italy, 300 Jesuits labored in the army of a government still in a standoff with the pope over the independence of the Vatican. Twenty-six German Jesuits died in service, and 535 German Jesuits served as chaplains and stretcher bearers despite extant anti-Jesuit laws. (The laws were repealed in 1917 because of Jesuit willingness to sacrifice for the German war effort, and as Prussian officials sought to placate Catholics.)[130]

In France, less than fifteen years after their expulsion, Jesuits evinced little hesitation about serving in the trenches of the western front as well as with French armies in North Africa and the Middle East. One hundred sixty-three French Jesuits died in battle or from illnesses contracted during the war. Their surviving Jesuit colleagues repeatedly invoked the notion of France as the eldest daughter of the church, and the need to serve one's country and sacrifice one's life. They expected that a chastened French populace would return after the war "to the altar."[131]

French and Belgian Jesuits openly condemned German aggression; a few even expressed uneasiness about the 1915 election of a Father General, Wlodimir Ledóchowski, of Polish origin but a member of the German province.[132] That a French Jesuit denounced German militarism and imperialism as French soldiers died in ghastly numbers is predictable. That the same French Jesuit identified so completely with the nation-state is startling. God desired, he claimed, "national homelands" for all people. Indeed, "a soldier who dies for his country accomplishes an eminently religious act." It is as natural to love one's "country as one loves a holy thing."[133]

STUDENTS' ARMY TRAINING CORPS, ST. JOSEPH'S COLLEGE.

FIGURE 14. Students undergoing military officer training at Saint Joseph's College, Philadelphia, in 1918. Courtesy of Archives and Special Collections, Saint Joseph's University.

The war also bound Jesuits to the American nation-state. Even before American entry into the war in 1917, Jesuit educational leaders had written President Woodrow Wilson offering their assistance.[134] At Saint Joseph's and other Jesuit colleges, large numbers of students volunteered for military duty (or later, were drafted), and Jesuit administrators were delighted when the US Department of War designated Saint Joseph's and a number of other Jesuit colleges as a site for the Students' Army Training Corps. The Department of War took over almost every classroom on the Saint Joseph's campus—paying welcome rent—and the first class of recruits began their program with a High Mass in the Gesu followed by a swearing-in ceremony. By the time of the armistice in 1918, 240 current students and another roughly 500 alumni had served in the military. Fourteen died in service.[135]

American entry into the war had curricular consequences. Like their counterparts at secular colleges, Jesuits responded to government requests and developed materials for a required short course on American war aims. Designed for use in Jesuit colleges, the syllabus is a primer on the ways in which long-standing Jesuit antagonism to liberalism now nestled inside a more assertive patriotism. According to the course outline, a disposition toward force explained German militarism—a problem beginning with the philosophical errors of Immanuel Kant and deepening with Friedrich Nietszche. A mistaken German veneration of the state had permitted the Kulturkampf and attacks on Catholic institutions in the 1870s as well as the authoritarianism on display during the war. Even in this course outline, Jesuits still registered concerns about the dangers posed by mass democratic politics— concerns animated by nineteenth-century anticlericalism and Jesuit expulsions—but these cautions now paled beside the threat from German aggression.[136]

Amicable relationships developed with American government officials during the war further propelled Jesuit educational ambitions. Until the war, one New York Jesuit leader, Joseph Rockwell, explained, "We have been ostracized in the educational world and as educational factors we have been either entirely overlooked or purposely set aside as antiquated and of narrow vision by men who are the recognized leaders and spokesmen in educational movements."

American educational leaders impressed by the "quick adaptability" of Jesuit college leaders now had a more positive view. Would it endure? Jesuits, Rockwell conceded, had once devoted all their "energies to the imparting of a knowledge of the Classics." Yet few students desired the classical course. Indeed, "the Classics were not in popular demand and in many instances the number of students attending our Colleges hardly justified the keeping of a staff of professors." Rockwell wondered if Jesuits "should offer a greater range of courses in our Colleges."[137] Colleges such as Saint Joseph's modified the Ratio Studiorum to coexist with American standard practices such as the four-year high school and four-year college cycle instead of the seven-year curriculum mandated by the Ratio. Required Greek courses began to disappear after

World War I. Required Latin fell away in most schools—although not without controversy—in the 1960s.[138]

Patriotic gestures extended beyond the schools to other facets of Jesuit life. Just after the declaration of war, the editors at *America* urged fellow citizens to "dedicate ourselves" to "our beloved country." Only "basely recreant" Catholics would refuse.[139] Jesuit leaders requested summaries of the patriotic accomplishments of alumni of Jesuit parishes and schools, since they understood themselves to be "living in abnormal times when one must give external manifestation of his patriotism, in order that he may avoid suspicion."[140] At a Jesuit church a few blocks from the US Capitol, a priest organized a rally to combat "apathy." Five thousand people gathered in front of the church for speeches and the singing of the Star Spangled Banner.[141]

The leaders of both Gesu parish and Saint Joseph's College left no doubt of their support for the war effort. The Gesu parish bulletin described itself as "second in loyalty to none," pointing to 119 men from the parish "who have answered their country's call."[142] One Jesuit instructor at Saint Joseph's asked his former students serving abroad in the military for accounts of their experience. The letters of these students turned soldiers, plucked from Philadelphia parishes and classrooms, testify to their patriotism—the United States is the "only real nation"—and their delight in bumping into friends from North Philadelphia in French villages. The horrors of combat are present in the letters, along with a simultaneous confidence in the "victory of America's ideals." The hope that the war would wrench an often-irreligious Europe back toward Catholicism appeared in the conviction of one soldier that "the fires of war shall have purged [France] of all dross and recreated her [as] 'the eldest daughter' of the Church."

The most vivid theme was pride in both their nation and their Catholicism. Or as one recruit explained, the "very intimate relation between my presence in the Army today and the training I received at St. Joseph's." That Catholic soldiers attended church services more frequently than other Christians, that the Gesu hosted several packed Masses each Sunday, and that the parochial grade school, Jesuit high school, and Jesuit college thrived all suggested that American Catholics might export successful institutions to a war-torn globe. As another Saint Joseph's alumnus put it, perhaps he and his friends might join President Wilson as "makers of a democratic world."[143]

6

MANILA, PHILIPPINES: EMPIRE

I

Just how American Jesuits might further democratic ideals became more evident in the first decades of the twentieth century. By that time, American Jesuits constituted roughly 15 percent of the sixteen thousand Jesuits worldwide. And instead of receiving European Jesuits, a process that had begun in the sixteenth century, Jesuits from the United States now started to venture in small groups into their own mission territories, including Jamaica, India, British Honduras, Chile, and China.

The largest American Jesuit missionary enterprise was in the Philippines. In spring 1898, after the mysterious sinking of the *USS Maine* in the Havana harbor, Pope Leo XIII asked Archbishop Ireland to use his ties with leading Republicans to negotiate a settlement, and prevent war between the United States and Spain. Ireland appealed to President William McKinley, but to no avail. Congress declared war in April, the US Navy sank the bulk of the Spanish fleet in Cuba and the Philippines, and American diplomats pressured Spain into selling its remaining colonial territories. American Catholics, eager to demonstrate their patriotism, generally supported the war effort, although Irish Americans antagonistic toward the British Empire evinced some reluctance to support any American colonial presence. Still, as Ireland explained, "No true American Catholic will think of espousing the cause of Spain against that of this country because the former is a Catholic nation."[1]

Convinced that the United States would play a providential role in world history, Ireland and his allies understood the conflict as one between the future and the past. They did not join prominent scholars such as Philadelphia's Henry Lea, who attributed Spanish weakness to an "all pervading" Catholicism.[2] But a more muted chauvinism informed their conviction that Italian and Spanish churchmen must acknowledge an American ascent. "If the Pope is in the future to have any world-wide prestige," Ireland boasted to one longtime clerical ally, Denis O'Connell, "he must deal as never before with America." The church in the Philippines and Cuba "will be organized along the lines of Americanism."[3]

O'Connell's reply merits quotation:

It is the question of two civilizations. It is the question of all that is old & vile & mean & rotten & cruel & false in Europe against all this [*sic*] is free & noble & open & true & humane in America. When Spain is swept of [*sic*] the seas much of the meanness & narrowness of old Europe goes with it to be replaced by the freedom and openness of America. This is God's way of developing the world.[4]

O'Connell specifically linked Spanish decadence to the Jesuits, whose founder, Ignatius of Loyola, was a Spanish nobleman. The war, he told an Italian correspondent, was "sure to transfer the center of influence and thus [move] the new ideas to the forefront. . . . The home of Ignatius and the Inquisition is about to be stripped of its influence. The future belongs to men such as Ireland."[5]

The response of Jesuits in the United States to the war was more nuanced. They stressed obedience to "civil constituted authority"—and as a result support for the war effort—but also had close ties to Spanish Jesuit colleagues in Cuba.[6] When compared to statements praising America's divine civilizing mission coming from Protestant pulpits—one survey suggested that Protestant clergy were more supportive of the American war effort and subsequent occupation than any other group—Jesuits were less bellicose. "Let us realize our duty," argued one New York Jesuit, "to prevent a strong nation from trampling and preying upon the weak."[7] In New Mexico, exiled Italian Jesuits writing for a Spanish-language newspaper distinguished between "patriotism" and "fanaticism."[8]

A Jesuit in the United States writing for *Civiltà Cattolica* was more blunt. He lamented the "aggressive" turn in American foreign policy and attacked the "humanitarian hypocrisy" of the American press for circulating legends about the Spanish Inquisition at the exact moment that an "imperial" American force took over the Philippines. (The same correspondent noted the irony of Americans dredging up sixteenth-century tales of Spaniards torturing heretics even as press reports from Texas circulated of an African American burned to death by a white mob.)[9] When, uncharacteristically, a native-born American Jesuit—Thomas Sherman, the son of Civil War general William Sherman—publicly urged American military intervention, the Father General in Rome, Spaniard Luis Martín, thought Sherman spoke "like a madman."[10]

European Jesuits made little pretense of neutrality. In the run-up to the war, the Spanish correspondent for *Civiltà Cattolica* condemned "creeping American imperialism." In Spain, as one Spanish Jesuit informed Father General Martín, the war "inflamed the spirit of the youth" studying in Jesuit colleges and led to public demonstrations of "love for country."[11]

An entire chapter of Martín's memoirs is devoted to what he termed the war "against Cuba and the Philippines" (not the Spanish-American War), and although obligated to make no public comments as the head of an international religious order, Martín privately donated funds to support the Spanish war effort. He regretted that American and British Jesuits in Rome seemed sympathetic to the American cause, and fumed at the arrival of routine letters from American Jesuits "mentioning nothing about the injustice of the war." Martín only reluctantly allowed American Jesuits to serve as chaplains for the American military, and struggled to overcome "the great love I felt for Spain and the great hatred for America." He later termed 1898 a "year of martyrdom."[12]

II

The victory of the United States along with the subsequent decision to purchase and occupy the Philippines placed Americans in two of the era's most powerful transformations: the expansion of Christianity, and the strengthening of global empires. The practical questions were immediate: How should a country with a sense of nationhood powerfully shaped by Protestantism rule several million Catholic subjects? How would those Catholic subjects respond to American rule?

The Jesuits faced equally complex dilemmas. Many Jesuits—including Italian Jesuits in Ceylon and Guatemala, German Jesuits in Japan and Brazil, and Irish Jesuits in Australia and Hong Kong—scattered to the corners of the globe independent of their relationship with local governments. And precisely because many European nation-states had expelled Jesuits and leaders of the Society disparaged contemporary nationalism, missionary Jesuits often tried to disentangle Christianity from national cultures. As Father General Beckx instructed French Jesuits heading for Syria, "Our missionaries are sent to make Christians and not Europeans or Frenchmen etc. The point is of the highest importance."[13]

Separating religion from nation, however, proved more difficult for Jesuits in areas where compatriots exercised imperial power. Over time, Jesuits once accused of impeding the "progress of liberty and civilization" began to see themselves as bringing civilization to indigenous peoples.[14] As Spanish Jesuits ventured to Cuba and the Philippines, Portuguese Jesuits to Mozambique, Italian Jesuits to Libya, British Jesuits to India, Guyana, and Rhodesia (modern Zimbabwe), and Belgian Jesuits to the Congo, they developed close, if fraught, relationships with colonial leaders. Often Jesuits ran the schools that educated the sons of colonial officials and traders, and mingled at public events with other expatriates.

French Jesuit missionaries provide the most striking example of the overlap between colonial and religious missions. More than in almost any European country, Jesuits in France continued to endure hostility from government officials eager to close Jesuit schools and limit Jesuit influence, with anticlerical governments expelling the Jesuits in 1880 and 1901.

Relationships overseas were vastly more cordial, especially after Pope Leo XIII urged French Catholics to reconcile themselves to republican government in France. Imperial competition between France and Britain made Jesuit sympathy for the French language and loyalty to France as the oldest "daughter of the church" attractive to even anticlerical colonial officials. (French Protestants, formally granted equality with Catholic missionaries, frequently complained of favoritism toward Jesuits, and even indifference to principles of religious freedom, in locales such as Polynesia and Madagascar.) In Beirut and across the Ottoman Empire, French governmental officials in the foreign ministry funded Jesuit schools even as legislators in Paris fumed about Jesuit influence. In turn, Jesuits, along with other Catholic missionaries, took patriotic pride in a French "civilizing" mission.[15]

In the United States, the imperial vision of Jesuits bringing civilization to indigenous peoples also became more widespread. The first nineteenth-century European Jesuits to work with the Indians, including De Smet and Bapst, lauded them as noble counterpoints to an increasingly corrupt European civilization. After first meeting the Penobscots in Maine, Bapst described them as possessing a "savage eloquence" freed from "all trammels to which overwrought civilization often subjects our greatest orators."[16]

By the end of the century, exiled Jesuits struck a different note. They still protested the efforts of American Protestant missionaries to send Indian children hundreds of miles away to boarding schools instead of to nearby Catholic schools accessible to parents and family members. But the need to civilize Indians now seemed pressing. One Italian Jesuit working among the Blackfeet described Indian life as a form of "uncivilization."[17]

Another lauded the movement of the Coeur d'Alene tribe away from "foolish superstitions" and "degraded habits."[18]

Along with American policy makers, Jesuits glided from promoting civilization among North American Indians to promoting it among the peoples of the Philippines.[19] Jesuits had first reached the Philippines in 1581, and had become the island's leading educators and most prominent missionaries. Following Spain's suppression of the Society in 1767, Spanish Jesuits had returned to the islands, still under the control of the Spanish government, in 1859. Their numbers and influence increased over time, especially when, as in 1868, Jesuits were expelled from Spain. (A few Spanish Jesuits moved at this time to work in the United States as well.)[20] By 1898, Spanish Jesuits again ran some of the country's most prominent schools, had founded a famous observatory, and had sent a new generation of missionaries to Mindanao and more remote parts of the archipelago.

The letters of these Spanish Jesuit missionaries echo those of Bapst in Maine or Helias in Missouri, as they self-consciously placed themselves in the footsteps of seventeenth- and eighteenth-century predecessors, and cataloged native languages and customs. Like their counterparts in Europe and North America, they encountered anticlericalism—one Filipino antagonist of the Jesuits had carefully read Sue's *Le Juif Errant*—and bemoaned "liberals" disfiguring Spain and the contemporary world. Like their counterparts, they paid homage to Pius IX—honored as "Pontiff and King" with a nod to endorsing his temporal power in Italy—and organized parish missions, Lourdes shrines, and devotions to the Sacred Heart.[21] Like other Jesuits allied with imperial authorities, they saw their work as in part "patriotic" (for Spain) and in part "civilizing" (for Filipinos).[22]

The Filipino revolution against Spanish colonial rule beginning in 1896 and the 1898 war disrupted the Jesuit mission.[23] Some Jesuit-educated Filipinos, such as the novelist and writer José Rizal, became leading symbols of resistance to colonial rule. Despite affection for his Jesuit instructors, Rizal absorbed free thought ideals during his studies in Spain and Germany. His correspondence with Jesuit mentors after returning to the Philippines is, on the Jesuit side, an extended effort to bring their onetime pupil back to recognition of "true religion" and the scientific validity of miracles, such as in Lourdes.[24] Rizal, by contrast, chided the Jesuits for not accepting the "liberal principles of progress, etc., for example, freedom of the press, freedom of thought, freedom of religion."[25] He was polite, but incredulous, when one Jesuit mentor sent him a text influential among Spanish Catholic conservatives, titled "Liberalism Is a Sin."[26]

Spanish Jesuits in the Philippines endured criticism from more nationalist Catholics in Spain for an overly "cosmopolitan" and insufficiently Spanish curriculum. They initially responded with the argument that Jesuit education was less a "national" education than an immersion in classical texts suitable for all Catholic students anywhere. Under pressure, and increasingly embarrassed by the prominence of Rizal and some of his Jesuit-educated contemporaries in the struggle against Spain, they attempted to demonstrate that the "cause of Spain here is the cause of the Catholic religion."[27] They urged Filipinos to "love Spain and to respect and bless her paternal sovereignty."[28]

That the Spanish defeat at the hands of the American military prompted a new reckoning for Jesuits in four locales—Rome, the Philippines, Spain, and the United States—suggests the challenge of managing a global religious order in an imperial age. In Rome, Father General Martín, appalled by American militarism, urged the Spanish Jesuits to remain "close to the Indians [i.e., native Filipinos] and not appear to the Spanish as less in love with and faithful to their own country." He worried that Spanish Jesuits might trust "too much in the Americans" and depend on "their protection." Much better, he thought, for Jesuits "to appear Spanish" as opposed to "appearing to be American." After all, in the missions outside Manila the Jesuits might prove "useful" to the Americans, but only as a means of "preparing for [Americans] the lands that they will exploit and the Indians who they will exterminate." Martín insisted that Spanish Jesuits, not Americans, would control the Philippine mission, and viewed American Jesuits as necessary for their English-language skills, yet untested in missionary work. He cautioned against rapid "Americanization."[29] He feared that an American colonial regime meant an aggressive "Protestant spirit" capable of destroying a Catholic culture.[30]

In Spain, demonstrations against the militarily inept government inspired anticlericals to vandalize Jesuit residences and led to renewed calls among Spanish republicans for yet another Jesuit expulsion.[31] News of these demonstrations also reached the United States. "What makes me anxious," worried one American Jesuit leader, "is the outcome in Spain. If a republican revolution breaks out we shall hear of 3000 S.J.s turned adrift, and we shall not be able to offer hospitality."[32]

In the Philippines, Spanish Jesuits regretted the "disgrace" of their country, and feared a "Yankee" occupation in part because the United States was thought not to respect church property and President McKinley was (accurately) believed ready to separate church from state. One Spanish Jesuit thought "the future of the archipelago" destined to be "dark, bad all throughout."[33] Soon after the conclusion of the war, roughly one-third of the 158 Spanish Jesuits in the Philippines, generally older or unwell, left for assignments in Spain or Spanish-speaking South America.[34] The remaining Spanish Jesuits requested English grammar books (from Spain) to better prepare themselves for the new regime, and fretted about an occupying power—the United States—ignorant of Spanish religious traditions and customs as well as willing to distribute "propaganda" against the "Spanish and the Catholics."[35]

In the United States, American Jesuits belatedly realized that the expansion of the American overseas empire meant the expansion of their responsibilities. The percentage of American Jesuits serving in foreign missions had always been tiny, certainly when compared with Spanish, French, or German Jesuits, in large part because of the vast opportunities for Jesuit work within the growing United States.[36] Now the situation was different. "For the first time in the history of our Province," explained one New York Jesuit, "God seems to open up to us a real foreign Mission."[37]

From the earliest days of the war, reports circulated in the American Catholic press of desecrations of Catholic churches by

FIGURE 15. Spanish Jesuits Learning English in Manila, ca. 1898, after
the victory of the United States over Spain in the Spanish-American War.
Courtesy of the Archives of the Philippine Province, Society of Jesus.

American soldiers and commanders. In part to alter the tone of
the occupation, American Jesuit leaders resolved to send a few
men to Manila to minister to Catholic American officials, sailors,
and soldiers, and assist Spanish Jesuits in adjusting to the new
regime. It seemed imperative to make "our relations with the
United States Government more cordial and successful."[38]

This blended Jesuit community—mostly Spanish with a handful of Americans—played a significant role in the first years of the
occupation. Crucially, they helped manage the transition from
Spanish to American rule by emphasizing respect for Spanish
Catholic culture in the Philippines, understood not as decadent
or corrupt but rather as vital to a civilizing mission. In this view
Catholicism, instead of thwarting progress toward liberal ideals
of autonomy or the emergence of the nation-state, had elevated
Filipino culture to a high, if precarious, plateau. The achievements of the modern Philippines depended on the "Catholic civilization of Spain," and the Filipinos had been essentially
a "happy and contented people" until "a few natives educated

in Europe returned without faith or morals." This Jesuit vision of a beneficent Spanish Catholic heritage entailed minimizing religious diversity. Muslims in particular, one Spanish Jesuit argued in a report written for American policy makers, constituted a barrier to the "colonization and civilization of Mindanao."[39]

That most Filipinos were Catholic should not, American Jesuits assured their fellow citizens, create anxiety. Instead, Americans should take pride in the fact that Catholicism was not only the "religion of practically the whole Filipino people" but also the religion "of the largest body of professing Christians in the United States."[40]

This portrait of a civilized Catholic Philippines was in part prompted by religious competition. American Protestant missionaries saw victory in the Spanish-American War as an evangelical opportunity, with even President McKinley openly discussing his desire to "Christianize" the already-Christian but Catholic population of the islands.[41] Dozens of American Protestant missionaries sailed to the Philippines after the war, provoking nervous exchanges between Spanish and American Jesuits. One New York Jesuit urged his colleagues to challenge "American Bible Associations and American proselytizing Societies" certain to use "money, guile and false teachings to rob this simple people of their faith and to implant error in their souls." American Jesuits in the Philippines chided Protestant fellow citizens for "spreading rumors that students in Jesuit schools such as the Ateneo de Manila were not loyal to the United States.[42]

To Jesuit dismay, some American Protestant missionaries in the Philippines also encouraged the emergence of a schismatic movement led by a onetime Filipino Catholic priest and nationalist Gregorio Aglipay that resulted in the establishment of an independent Filipino church, the Iglesia Filipina Independiente. The Aglipay movement at its height counted roughly two million adherents—and as late as 1939, almost 10 percent of the Filipino population—and along with the Polish National Catholic Church founded in the United States was one of two major Catholic schisms at the turn of the twentieth century. Adherents of both churches—the Polish National Catholic Church and Iglesia Filipina Independiente—attacked the Jesuits as the epitome of an international, unpatriotic religious body. In turn, an American Jesuit ascribed hurricanes in Aglipayan regions of the Philippines to God's anger with "infidelity."[43]

The practical challenge, from the American Jesuit point of view, was to publicly defend the Spanish Catholic heritage of the islands—a "stupendous accomplishment of rescuing from barbarism and bringing to a remarkably high state of civilization a people originally not far removed from savagery"—while transferring the successful institution-building strategies developed in the United States.[44]

One obstacle, again, was orthodox Catholic teaching on church and state. Spanish Jesuits had worked in two societies, Spain and the Philippines, where the Catholic Church claimed a privileged, official role. Now the overlap between the goals of American politicians and military officials and the evangelical aspirations of American Protestant ministers threatened to make Protestantism the official island religion in practice, if not in law.

When queried by American military authorities, the Spanish Jesuits tried to sustain a distinctive place for Catholicism. Certainly, the Spanish Jesuits conceded, no state should mandate conversion to Catholicism.

> But if by liberty of religions is understood the granting to all religions—for example, the worship of Confucius, or of Mohammed—and to all the Protestant sects equal rights to open schools, erect churches, create parishes, have processions and public ceremonies, with the Catholic Church, we believe that it would not only not be advisable, but it would be a lamentable measure for any government which may rule the destinies of the Filipinos.[45]

The Spanish Jesuits recognized that Filipino rebels inspired in part by the US Constitution had "proclaimed liberty of religions and separation of church and state" during the brief interval between Spanish and American rule. (And even then, Spanish Jesuits had opposed the separation and pondered denying absolution in the confessional to Filipino revolutionaries who supported it.) But the same rebels had also demanded Filipino independence. "Will the Americans," the Spanish Jesuits pointedly asked, "therefore give it to them?"[46]

Despite Spanish Jesuit objections, American colonial officials authored a constitution for the Philippines ensuring freedom of religion and the disentanglement of church from state along the American model. As in the United States, the most volatile issue was education, and the colonial government ultimately refused to provide aid for Catholic schools in the Philippines, in contrast to the Spanish practice, and to the frustration of American Jesuits who kept receiving hints that such aid might be forthcoming from prominent figures such as the Philippine governor general—and future president—William Howard Taft.[47]

The colonial government did formally adopt Archbishop Ireland's scheme, never implemented in the United States, to allow religious instruction by nuns and priests in public schools after regular school hours. While many American Protestants condemned even this concession, Jesuits insisted, again as in the United States, that after-hours instruction was insufficient. Instead, they turned their once publicly funded institutions, including the Ateneo de Manila, into private, Catholic schools. "American Jesuits," one early Filipino Jesuit historian wrote, "*knew* [that after-hours instruction] was not sufficient . . . because they had seen the effects upon the Catholic communities in their own country of the American public school system upon which the public school system of the Philippines had been so slavishly modeled."[48]

The respectful attitude expressed by American officials toward Catholicism was, however, more striking than ongoing tensions over religious freedom or education policy. American colonial officials tried to hire Catholic teachers for public schools (after Catholics complained about the high percentage of Protestants, often recruited from the United States, serving as instructors), and ensured that college scholarships for Filipino students funded by the US government could be used at Jesuit and other Catholic colleges.[49] Theodore Roosevelt's reasoning was straightforward:

> I am very strongly of the opinion that the uplifting of the people in these tropic islands must come chiefly through making them better catholics and better citizens, and that on the one hand we shall have to guard against the reactionary catholics who would oppose the correction of abuses in the ecclesiastical arrangements of the islands, and on the other hand, guard against the Protestant fanaticism which will give trouble anyhow more or less.[50]

These remarks deserve emphasis: twelve years after the country's leading political scientist declared the Jesuits "unnational" an American vice president (and soon president), insisted on the need to make American subjects better Catholics.[51]

The Jesuits changed as well. Into the late nineteenth century, the faculty at the Jesuit theologate in Maryland—mostly exiled Italians, but also exiled Spaniards, Frenchmen, and Germans—had declined to permit their American students to vote or celebrate holidays such as the Fourth of July or George Washington's birthday. (On the day of the 1884 presidential election, the diarist at Woodstock noted that "only the Negroes [i.e., the housekeeping and grounds crew] voted.") In Buffalo, exiled German Jesuits held classes on Memorial Day and did not register to vote until the early twentieth century, and even then only at the instruction of their rector.[52]

By contrast, American Jesuits traveled to the Philippines as informal representatives of a conquering authority and enjoyed access to high diplomatic circles. One New York Jesuit reported back to his American colleagues his hope that "our great country, as [it has] sent soldiers and sailors to protect her material interests, will send also spiritual laborers to advance the eternal interests of her citizens and subjects."[53] Another American Jesuit in Manila, having absorbed the rhetoric of American colonial leaders, explained to a friend back in the United States that American troops were necessary in the Philippines to prevent a descent into "perfect savagery."[54] Taft met with American Jesuits once they arrived in Manila and contemplated sending his son to the Ateneo de Manila, declining to do so only to avoid accusations of favoritism toward Catholics. Other officials reported that leading American public officials had abandoned "old feelings of rancor" because of the good work already accomplished by American Jesuits in Manila.[55]

One Spanish Jesuit even became an influential figure in the colonial regime. After Admiral George Dewey, the conqueror of the Spanish fleet, sailed into Manila harbor, watched by curious students gathered on the roof of the Ateneo de Manila, one of his first visitors was Fr. José Algué, a scientist and the director of the Manila Observatory. (In yet another marker of global Jesuit networks, Algué had completed his scientific training at Georgetown's observatory, and was well known and admired by American Jesuits.)[56]

Algué delighted in the fact that the American government, like its Spanish predecessor, agreed to fund the Manila Observatory.[57] He reported that Admiral Dewey praised "the care with which the Spanish Government has fostered and enlarged an institution [the observatory] which did so much honor to their colony and said that it was the duty of the United States to show a like interest in its welfare." Dewey then queried Algué about the military situation in the Philippines, and Algué responded with a briefing on the "work our missionaries were doing for the conversion and civilization of the various tribes that people the Islands."[58]

Algué eventually threw himself into the effort to preserve Catholic influence. He cooperated directly with the various American commissions sent to the islands by coordinating the writing and publication of ethnographic descriptions of the various peoples of the islands and detailed atlases.[59] He visited Washington, DC— staying at Georgetown—and met with top military officials, Senator Albert Beveridge (the leading congressional advocate of the

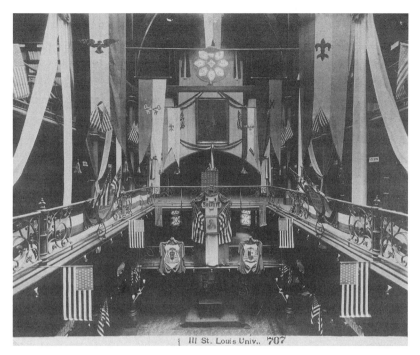

FIGURE 16. An auditorium at Saint Louis University decorated with American and Vatican flags in honor of the 1903 Grand Act and the presence of President Theodore Roosevelt. Courtesy of Jesuit Archives of the Central United States.

American colonial presence), and President McKinley himself. McKinley reportedly greeted Algué with the observation that his presence would be "very useful" for the Americans, even as Algué highlighted the Jesuit desire to assist American leaders in the Philippines.[60] A few years later, one American Jesuit admiringly said of Algué that he can "get whatever he wants from the government."[61]

As president, Roosevelt similarly cultivated the Jesuits. When visiting Saint Louis to open the World's Fair of 1904, Roosevelt chose to attend a Grand Act or formal disputation with a seminarian answering questions posed by church dignitaries and theologians—the third held in the United States. There, Jesuits reveled in Roosevelt's "boyish" demeanor and applauded his entrance into the lecture hall. "This meeting of Church and State," enthused one Saint Louis Jesuit, "might be described as energetically amicable."[62]

The Jesuit student defending church teaching in front of Roosevelt, Joaquin Vilallonga, a Spanish native, was one of three Spanish Jesuits sent to the United States to learn English, and would move to the Philippines months after the Grand Act, eventually becoming the leader of the Jesuit community in Manila. Vilallonga answered questions in Latin on topics such as the Church, the papacy, and the sacraments. His bravura performance was reported in detail to both American and Spanish Jesuits.

The rector of the Saint Louis theologate assured President Roosevelt that Vilallonga had absorbed "an ardent love and admiration for the United States and her institutions, which he is now preparing to carry back with him to Manila." He then thanked Roosevelt "for the eminent fairness with which you have striven to handle that most difficult of questions, our island possessions, and [expressed] our admiration for the broadminded generosity with which both in Rome and Manila you have striven to do justice to the large Catholic interests involved." Roosevelt himself requested to meet Vilallonga and queried him about conditions in the Philippines.[63]

At the World's Fair, the largest and one of the most popular exhibits—funded entirely by the American government—was dedicated to the recently acquired Philippines. Fr. Algué spent almost a year in Saint Louis—staying at Saint Louis University—preparing the part of the exhibition highlighting the work of the Jesuit-run Manila Observatory. Algué and other Jesuits also frequently said Mass at an altar set aside on the exhibition grounds. Ultimately, the US government awarded the Jesuits gold medals for their maps and the quality of the exhibit.[64]

Algué was also invited to deliver one of the main addresses at the exhibition opening. He stressed the importance of Catholicism for the history and future of the islands as well as the necessity of Americans recognizing that their new possessions in the Pacific included "7,000,000 Christian Catholics." Algué escorted Taft (now secretary of war) around the exhibit, and a grateful Taft spoke at the World's Fair and the University of Notre Dame on the significance of the Jesuits and other Catholic religious in bringing "Christianity and European civilization" to the Philippines.[65]

III

Over the next fifteen years, a small group of American Jesuits in the Philippines worked with their Spanish colleagues at the Ateneo de Manila and staffed missionary parishes across the archipelago. Initially the two groups collaborated with ease, and one American Jesuit, after noting that the Latin textbooks used in Manila classrooms were the same as those used in classrooms in the United States, boasted to American colleagues, "The Society is still the same all the world over, and national and local differences are after all mere trifles which should not disturb a man's peace of soul."[66]

Over time, however, disputes reflecting a heightened sense of national identity undermined communal harmony. The sharpest arguments occurred over language. Early in the occupation, American colonial authorities decided to make English the language of instruction at all public schools, even as teachers at the Ateneo and other Jesuit schools continued to use Spanish.[67]

The Spanish Jesuits were divided, with a few "americanistas"— usually those who had studied in the United States—favoring English, and a larger number convinced that abandoning Spanish meant abandoning a Catholic culture. Advocates of Spanish agreed that English should be taught, and might be tolerable in science and history classes. (It seems to have been the language of instruction for one hour each day.) But they insisted that Spanish should be the medium for the classical course mandated by the Ratio Studiorum.[68] One Spanish Jesuit complained that in the public schools, the language "with which Filipinos learned religion, has been almost completely put aside, or has become just an adornment. Public instruction knows no God and this is so as though the students had no soul in need of salvation or religious obligations to fulfill."[69]

American Jesuits held the opposite view. One American, James Monaghan, sent a lengthy report to Rome in 1908 assessing the situation. He began by regretting the influx of American Protestant missionaries—well organized, with "ample financial resources"—determined to wreak "great havoc in the Catholics' ranks."[70] Jesuit schools could be an important counterweight, but not if students had such weak English that they were unprepared for university studies, could not obtain positions as a "clerk in any of the government offices," and could not even "obtain a position in any business house where a knowledge of English is required." That the native language of some students entering the Ateneo's lower grades was Tagalog, and that these students would presumably find English no more difficult than Spanish, clinched the case.

Spanish Jesuits resisted the linguistic transition because, they claimed, too few Spanish Jesuits spoke English, or because the Ateneo de Manila remained popular with Filipino parents. Monaghan thought such objections specious. Many zealous Catholic parents, he warned, now declined to send their boys to the Ateneo because of inadequate preparation for a commercial and civic world conducted in English. Regrettably, Spanish Jesuits displayed a "spirit of nationalism" at the expense of Filipino students desiring not only Catholic training but also "career advancement." They declined to display the American flag at events attended by American public officials, and subtly favored the red and yellow colors of the Spanish flag in decorations displayed at the school. Even some of the Spanish Jesuits who had spent time in the United States, Monaghan complained, "instead of exerting their influence against this spirit of nationalism seem to fear the accusation of having adopted American ideas."[71]

Other leading Catholics and American government officials agreed. The Vatican's representative in the islands pleaded with Father General Franz Wernz to recognize the vanity of thinking "that Spanish is going to dominate here in the near future [since] the Americans are giving every proof that they are here to stay." He thought only English-speaking Jesuits could combat the influence of the "government schools where no religion is taught."[72] The American governor general William Cameron Forbes bluntly assessed the failure of Catholic high schools as stemming from the inability of graduates to "compete successfully" for jobs requiring English.[73] A decade later, American Jesuits still complained that at the Ateneo de Manila, "they might as well be in Spain, as far as any American Spirit is concerned."[74]

Language questions intertwined with cultural differences. One Spanish Jesuit was dismayed by the enthusiasm of American Jesuits for the Knights of Columbus, a popular, American Catholic fraternal organization then founding its first chapters in the Philippines.[75] *America* magazine's decision to hire a Spanish correspondent eager to report on divides within Spanish Catholicism and not aligned with the traditionalist views favored by Spanish Jesuits seemed an act of "harsh" criticism better kept behind closed doors. That the same correspondent casually reported to American readers that Spaniards "in general" care more about "the most popular bullfighter" than "grave political questions" was slander. Or as a Spanish Jesuit working in Manila explained in a ten-page letter to superiors in Barcelona and Rome, "As if in the United States there were not people who live only for the result of an encounter between two boxers!"[76]

Political questions were equally fraught. From the beginning of the colonial occupation, most American Jesuits dismissed the idea that the United States might soon permit Filipino independence. Monaghan, for example, bolstered the case for English-language instruction by predicting that there was "no possibility" of Filipino independence "within the space of one generation" and "little probability" of independence during the twentieth century.[77]

Another American Jesuit, Philip Finegan, offered a similar analysis. Like all Jesuits and most American governmental officials, he publicly stressed the success of the Spanish missionary effort, bringing a people "from the lowest grade of savagery to the highest grade of civilization." But Finegan, too, worried about the impact of American Protestant missionaries and claimed that fifty had been on his steamer across the Pacific. The American government's insistence on the separation of church and state seemed to him troubling because of the "religious disadvantages of the public school."[78]

Still, Finegan noted progress. He thought it hopeful that young Filipino men "quick to grasp the need of educational advantages" recognized the necessity of English. He expressed pleasure that a "growing class" of such men had even adopted American patterns of dress instead of slouching "along with their shirt outside their trousers."[79] He underscored the need of "priests, American priests, to do the great work of the Society" in the Philippines.[80]

None of this made Finegan sanguine about political independence. Soon after his arrival, he expressed his disappointment at the electoral strength of Filipino nationalists and welcomed American-led rallies in opposition to independence. "The Americans have told them," he explained, "that there will be [no] independence, at least for a few centuries after the present generation is in the grave."[81] In Manila newspapers, he later expressed his belief that Filipinos were not ready for independence—a view in contrast to that of Democratic presidential candidate Woodrow Wilson, who campaigned on a platform opposed to "a policy of imperialism and colonial exploitation in the Philippines as elsewhere."[82]

Spanish Jesuits, scarred perhaps by their opposition to the Filipino revolt against Spain in the 1890s, took a more measured view of both Filipino independence and Finegan. One Spanish Jesuit wrote to Barcelona to advise removing Finegan from the Philippines. "Fr. Finegan has been here in our mission for about five years working hard and well," he explained. "But because he has put himself before the public eye through the papers as being opposed to Philippine Independence, there is here, at the present time, among the Filipinos, a very strong current of antipathy against him, and for this very reason we are inclined to believe that perhaps it would be better for him to delay for a while his return to these Islands." After extending Finegan's "necessary and convenient" fund-raising trip to the United States, the Maryland–New York provincial again queried the Spanish leader of the Jesuits in the Philippines as to whether he should allow Fr. Finegan to return to Manila. The one word Latin reply, "Retinendus" (retain), ended Finegan's missionary career.[83] Ripples from the episode extended back to Manila, as American Jesuits complained that Finegan's banishment meant that they were "not wanted here." Even eight years later the Father General, Ledóchowski, referred to "those people from the congregation of Quezon [outside Manila] who once claimed that [Fr. Finegan] was opposed to Philippine independence."[84]

IV

If World War I solidified the loyalty of the graduates of Saint Joseph's College as well as other Catholic parishes and schools to the United States, it pushed Filipino activists in the opposite direction. In 1916, President Wilson maneuvered a bill through Congress promising Filipino independence, insisting that the United States must not imitate European imperial powers. Less than a year later the United States was at war, and Filipino activists, like their Vietnamese, Egyptian, and Korean counterparts, saw Wilson's advocacy of self-determination for small nations, most notably in his famous fourteen points address, as an opportunity to gain independence. Filipinos eagerly volunteered for the US military, and Filipino soldiers took over military duties from regular US Army troops pulled out of Manila and sent to Europe.[85]

The gap between Wilson's anticolonial rhetoric and the outcome of the postwar negotiations at Versailles, with French, British, and Japanese empires left largely intact, disillusioned the nationalists he had once inspired. Wilson's successor, Warren Harding, had fewer ideals to betray, and on becoming president in 1921 Harding chartered a commission to examine Filipino policy. Staffed by old hands from the first days of the American occupation, the commission predictably deduced that independence should wait "until the people have had time to absorb and thoroughly master the power already in their hands."[86]

Even as Harding's commissioners toured the islands, Father General Ledóchowski notified all Jesuits of his desire to switch formal responsibility for the Philippines from the Aragón (Spain) Province to the Maryland–New York Province. The origins of the decision were complex. In the first years of the war, the Father General had sent a handful of American Jesuits to Bombay to replace German Jesuits forced by the British colonial authorities to return to Germany. He had then requested more American volunteers, but British authorities alert to revolutionary tensions in another British colony, Ireland, mistrusted Irish American Jesuits. Or as one English Jesuit and future archbishop of Bombay explained, Irish American Jesuits seemed overly eager to spread "republican principles and practices" among Indian students.[87] The Father General then decided to send most of the remaining Spanish Jesuits in the Philippines to Bombay, since "the English government will have no difficulty with Spaniards."[88]

To replace the Spaniards in the Philippines, the Father General then decided to send Americans. Caught off guard by the decision, and confronted with the abandonment of a mission they had cultivated since the sixteenth century, often at great personal sacrifice, Spanish Jesuits were, according to a sympathetic American observer, "quite distressed." The Father General himself conceded that the decision was "difficult and heart-breaking."[89]

American Jesuits urged caution in public statements about the shift from Spanish to American leadership since by this time most educated Filipinos favored independence. Indeed, "if the Filipinos heard of this change they would immediately jump to the conclusion that they were not going to get independence and [the Americans] were coming to strengthen the American cause. And we would surely be set down as enemies of Filipino Independence."[90] The leader of the Spanish Jesuits in the Philippines agreed. "Of course," he explained to a Jesuit colleague in New York, "the general sentiment of the people is that sooner or later independence will come, at most 25 years."[91]

Surprising, too, was Father General Ledóchowski's insistence that a group of American Jesuits leave immediately for Manila. American Jesuit leaders called for volunteers, first acknowledging the Spanish Jesuits for their willingness to leave the mission "they have cultivated for centuries with their labors, prayers, sufferings, sweat and blood—even death." "But they cannot go to India," the New York provincial stressed, "until we arrive in the Philippines."[92]

Twenty-one American Jesuits volunteered, much as European Jesuits had once volunteered for service in the United States. After a candlelit steak dinner and high Mass, the Jesuits left New York City for the Philippines with photographers documenting their departure. Groups of Jesuits greeted the missionaries at train stops in the United States—Jesuits from Loyola University in Chicago, Creighton University in Omaha, and the University of Seattle. The men then sailed across the Pacific—noting American Protestant ministers in the main cabin and "sixty Asiatics" traveling in steerage—and visited sites associated with the most famous Jesuit missionary, Saint Francis Xavier, at their initial stop in Japan. They then traveled to Manila, where Jesuits and students from the Ateneo de Manila greeted them as they walked off the ship.[93]

The arrival of a large group of American Jesuits accentuated the ongoing tensions between Spaniards and Americans. Even those Americans appreciative of the accomplishments of the Spanish Jesuits, and willing to recommend that their peers learn Spanish since "it is necessary for any bit of work outside the school," worried about the Spanish focus on raw memorization in the classroom and a general reluctance to adapt to American mores.[94] They suspected that the Spaniards—despite the orders of the Father General—had "no intention" of leaving their beloved Manila and were concocting visa difficulties. The Spanish fathers, explained one American, think of the Americans as "half trained worldly minded Jesuits."[95]

Other American Jesuits were more blunt. They repeatedly wrote the Father General in Rome and their immediate superiors in New York City, registering their concerns about their Spanish brethren. Two of these men, Arthur Hohman and Charles Connor, had served as army chaplains during World War I, and Connor had worked as a priest at Gesu parish in Philadelphia, just before transferring to the Ateneo de Manila. As much as

FIGURE 17. Ateneo de Manila faculty in 1921, evenly divided between Spanish and American Jesuits. Courtesy of the Archives of the Philippine Province, Society of Jesus.

any other set of documents, their letters testify to the distance Jesuits had traveled from the anti-nationalist ethos of the mid-nineteenth century.

Connor wrote to Father General Ledóchowski in English since "I have had little or no time to exercise myself in Latin in the busy life of an American Jesuit." He conceded that his interpretation of the situation might not be "the correct one," but felt an obligation to convey his views.

It seemed absurd to Connor to maintain Spanish Jesuit customs in the Philippines because they differed so dramatically from successful methods "of saving souls in the United States." Spanish Jesuits had failed to produce a vibrant Catholicism in "Cuba, in South America, in Puerta Rica [sic], in Mexico and these islands." Calling the Philippines a "Catholic country" seemed to Connor "a joke" given infrequent Mass attendance (especially among men). "Why," he asked, "were we [Americans] brought here?" "If you want the old useless methods then call the Spanish Fathers back." He described himself as from the "Irish Race" where priests are "part and parcel with the people, they live with them, they mingle with them." Spanish Jesuits seemed willing to "bar the doors with great bolts and rarely if ever visit their people."[96] Hohman made much the same complaint: Filipino men did not "partake of the sacraments," and Spanish priests had limited "contact with the people."[97]

Few Filipinos had become Protestants, Connor admitted, despite the best efforts of American Protestant missionaries. But they "had left the Church in large numbers," and Hohman estimated that half the graduates of the Ateneo were "apostates." The association of Catholicism with Spain meant an association between "the downfall of Spain" and "downfall of Catholicism." American Protestants, not Spanish Catholics, stood for "sanitation, for educational progress and liberty." Only the energetic work of Jesuits such as Fr. Finegan, raising money for dormitories for Catholic students at the secular national university, ameliorated this dismal situation. The Spanish Jesuits, by contrast, seemed willing to "eat, drink and sleep and preach to a handful of reactionary Spaniards."

Connor had more specific grievances that again reveal the merging of national identity and religious practice even among members of Catholicism's most international religious order. American Jesuits should not be expected, as Spanish Jesuits insisted, to wear robes in public, as opposed to more conventional suit-like clerical attire. "Let us appear before [the Filipinos] dressed as men," Connor implored, "and not as poor imitations of our own sisters." This "relic of medievalism" ensured that Jesuits would not be "held in respect." Another Jesuit maintained that priests should dress "as we do in America," and yet another refused to wear the robes unless directly ordered to do so since Manila effectively "is America."[98] (Seventy years earlier, Villiger in Philadelphia and Italian Jesuits in New Mexico had urged their Jesuit colleagues to wear their robes in public, despite anti-Catholic attacks in the press and anti-Catholic violence in the streets, so as to avoid losing the "spirit of the Society.")[99]

Sports were similarly important. The Protestant men running the Manila YMCA understood the value of athletics for boys,

Connor explained, but Spanish Jesuits did not. Hohman contrasted a Spanish tolerance for boys "moping" about during school recess with the character-building function of organized athletics. Spanish Jesuits, in turn, thought it bizarre that "athletic exercise" allegedly constituted such a significant part of Catholic identity.[100]

Boxing especially, forbidden by the Father General after lobbying from the Spanish Jesuits, seemed to Connor crucial to developing "manly and vigorous Catholics." He had run a successful youth boxing program at the Gesu in Philadelphia and yearned to develop such a program in Manila. Like many Americans of the era, including most prominently Theodore Roosevelt, Connor thought boxing effective in teaching "fairness, self control, self reliance." How could Spanish Jesuits applaud bullfighters and yet denounce boxing? One American Jesuit reported that a Spanish Jesuit confessor told one boy that to box was a "mortal sin."[101] He circulated a copy of a Manila Catholic newspaper with reports of boxing matches to demonstrate episcopal approval of the sport's "moral training."[102]

In Connor's view, too, only student organizations where the boys did charitable works—instead of saying "prayers all day long and making meditations"—would create a vibrant faith. "Our idea of piety," he explained, "is something active, vigorous, full of energy and zeal." By contrast, the Spanish Jesuits favored "boys who are not boys at all but sweet pious Girls who go around the house with their eyes down and look of abject submission . . . and who of course never take part in the rough games always in favor with real boys." Again, the contrast with the Gesu in Philadelphia seemed stark. There, Catholics were willing to "pay a double tax to preserve the faith of their children by erecting parochial schools." There lines for the confessional were long, as opposed to the handful receiving the sacrament in this "so-called Catholic country."[103]

Father General Ledóchowski's response to the Americans was measured. In a letter to the entire Society, he had already reminded Jesuits to balance a desire to be "sincere patriots"—demonstrated by the sacrifice of Jesuit "life blood" during World

War I—with a need to model "love [for] those of other nations."[104]
He had privately chided American Jesuits for their zeal in advocating for Irish independence from Britain, with the American
Jesuits grudgingly agreeing in response to criticize only the "English government" and not the "English as a nation."[105]

Now Ledóchowski challenged American Jesuits in Manila,
asking them to "respect the Spanish discipline and traditions"
in the Philippines mission.[106] He hoped that when it came to
"changing things" the Americans might "make haste slowly," and
recommended no change on the "serious matter" of whether Jesuits should wear robes in public.[107]

Ledóchowski counseled patience to Connor since "as the
Spanish Fathers would be in error were they to hold as irregular
all that was peculiarly American, so, dear Father, are you wrong
after a brief experience of the Spanish Fathers in severely condemning them and the Latin nations in general as hopelessly
inefficient."[108] Perhaps Divine Providence would allow Americans to help Europeans "adapt themselves to modern needs."
But at the same time, Americans could benefit from a focus on
"internal things." In particular, he worried that Connor would
insist on making Filipinos "themselves American" and in that
sense not be a "true Jesuit." "Americans," he concluded, "need
to be told that they should not expect to change overnight or
even radically . . . a characteristic deceptiveness in peoples of
the East."[109] He pleaded with the Jesuits to "set aside inconve-
niences" stemming from the "diversity of the provinces."[110]

Connor lasted only two years in the Philippines, and both
Spanish and American Jesuits came to regret his "radical" approach to policy at the Ateneo and "bitter tongue." Hohman's superior diagnosed him as "depressive" and used heat exhaustion
as a pretext for sending him back to the United States.[111]

Still, the anxieties expressed by the two men were not idiosyn-
cratic. Only over time did a blended community of Spanish and
American Jesuits forge a new accord, and then largely on Ameri-
can terms. Francis X. Byrne, S.J., the first American rector of the
Ateneo de Manila, managed to install a more self-consciously
American atmosphere without entirely alienating his Spanish

colleagues. He knew that the Father General had finally resolved the language question at the Ateneo in favor of English as part of the transition to American Jesuits, and "present urgencies and necessities."[112] He knew that the Spanish resented the "so-called spirit of American independence." So Byrne began his assignment by promising his superiors to examine disputed issues "very carefully [and] proceed very, very slowly and gently."[113] For a time he aggravated his American compatriots by enforcing the Father General's edict prohibiting boxing.[114]

Notwithstanding his diplomatic style, though, Byrne privately betrayed a nationalist impatience. Even on the boat crossing the Pacific, he wrote a plaintive letter regretting that the superior of the Jesuit community in Manila would still be a Spaniard. "How can a Spanish Provincial and a Spanish superior," he asked, "understand our American ways and ideas?"[115] He refused to "forget that I am an American," and bemoaned "strange customs that often are repulsive and seem so childish to Americans." Byrne disparaged the Spanish Jesuit habit of wearing robes. He made a point of noting that the American Governor General Leonard Wood, "regretted we had to wear them because he said they would make it hard to move in certain circles where our influence would be good." He thought it regrettable that the Spanish Jesuits—"in an American colony"—treated the Spanish Consul with marked deference, as "in Europe."[116]

Byrne replaced soccer with basketball as the official school sport and instituted a popular cadet corps, with Ateneo students trained by officers on loan from the American military, leading to an informal designation of the Ateneo as the "West Point of the Philippines."[117] He developed a close friendship with Wood, an unpopular figure among Filipino nationalists because of Wood's resistance to independence. Byrne boasted to a colleague, "The Governor General very often calls upon me for advice on all things Catholic." On Byrne's departure from Manila, Wood declared that the islands had lost their "best known and most efficient leader."[118]

Byrne's successors continued to mediate between the two Jesuit groups. A few Jesuits of the "older Spanish generation" apparently complained about both Ateneo boys participating in local dances and an abandonment of "strict discipline" by the Americans.[119] When the Spanish Jesuits ceded control of a local seminary to the American Jesuits in 1930, the American leader at the Ateneo rejoiced. It had been "NINE YEARS" since the first large group of Americans had sailed into Manila Bay. Now, the Society of Jesus in Manila finally could become "an American institution."[120]

These tensions eventually eased. The Ateneo had begun to attract more students and build new facilities under American leadership—a fund-raising campaign after a devastating fire generated remarkable enthusiasm—and American Jesuits took pride in government reports describing the Ateneo as a model school despite the hardship caused by the absence of public funding.[121]

The more farsighted, or realistic, Spanish Jesuits had conceded from the American arrival in 1921 that the Philippines would eventually become an American mission even as they complained about Americans disrespecting Spanish customs. The Spanish superior in Manila, Vilallonga, lauded as a young man by Roosevelt for his performance at the 1903 Grand Act in Saint Louis, recommended sending young Spanish and Filipino Jesuits to the United States for theological training. Spanish Jesuits must "get in the midst of our American brethren, study the language and build their character to be able to live with Americans with the right spirit of the Society."[122]

A more self-consciously American devotional style also emerged. Sympathy toward popular Catholic devotions was characteristic of nineteenth-century Jesuits, and Italian Jesuits in New Mexico, for example, took to the pages of their journal, *Revista Católica*, to defend the pious customs of their Mexican American parishioners. (At the same time, they expressed disappointment with the irregular Mass attendance of their Italian compatriots.) Italian Jesuits in New York City encouraged *feste* and processions, and regretted the tendency of the city's Irish American pastors to shunt Italians toward chapels in church basements.[123]

A generation later in Manila the tone was more ambivalent. An undercurrent of embarrassment often marked American Jesuit descriptions of native Filipino Catholic shrines and religious practices, indicating absorption of modern notions of what constituted authentic religion.[124] One popular procession, organized by Filipino laypeople, seemed to have "deteriorated into superstition or near-superstition." The costumes, the music, and the rush to touch a statue of Jesus in the middle of the procession provided "a source of scandal to non-Catholic Americans who think that these things are true Catholicism and do not realize that they are abuses which the Church authorities are trying prudently to eradicate." The popular practice of kissing a statue at a Filipino Marian shrine, Our Lady of Antipolo, led to nervous jokes about the transfer of germs.[125]

A few years after their arrival the American Jesuits wrested control of San Ignacio parish, next to the Ateneo, from the Spaniards. By 1932 the Sunday Mass schedule included just one service in Spanish, one in Tagalog and two in English. Until then, according to one American, the Spaniards had thought of it as "a church for the Spanish speaking people and they resent now that the Americans have taken charge and are introducing some services for the English-speaking young men and women." Under American Jesuit leadership the parish became known as a "modern" church where "no one walked on their knees or prayed aloud with arms outstretched." One Filipino communicant recalled this as a "thrilling novelty" in the period "when Filipinos were just beginning to pray the Our Father instead of the Padre Nuestro, to confess in English, and to prefer the American Jesuit style in sermons."[126]

By the 1930s, twice as many American as Spanish Jesuits worked in the Philippines.[127] Reports from Manila now dwelled on the ordinary events of parish and school life, including the development of new academic programs and internal debates on whether students transferring from other schools would have to make up required Latin courses. (As in Jesuit schools around the world, parental uneasiness placed Jesuits teaching the "peculiarly difficult" classical texts of the Ratio Studiorum on the defensive.)[128] Some American Jesuits still doubted the wisdom of political independence for the Phillipines, but they did so privately, hastening to recognize that "the great majority of the Filipinos want to consider themselves a free people and to do things their own way." In this less volatile atmosphere, the Jesuits agreed to reintroduce Spanish-language courses as electives, since "many of the [Filipino] parents resented strongly the elimination of Spanish from the curriculum." This decision apparently caused no discord since the language was now one of "sentimental associations" and "not necessary in the Philippines at the present time." A "holy union of wills" now marked the Jesuit community. Indeed, according to another American Jesuit in 1935, "The spirit of union and fraternity is remarkable."[129]

CONCLUSION

One of the most important Catholic intellectuals of the twentieth century, John Courtney Murray, S.J., taught English literature and Latin at the Ateneo de Manila from 1927 to 1930. We know little about Murray's experience in Manila, his first assignment after attending Jesuit schools in New York City and Boston. We do know that his first published article was on the topic of governmental supervision of schools in the Philippines. There, Murray expressed concern about Protestant public officials, in both the United States and the Philippines, predisposed to dislike Catholic schools. The situation in the Philippines was worrisome because of the "absolute power" invested in colonial officials, and he applauded the American Jesuit superior in Manila for using his "high estimation and influence" to fight onerous regulations. Murray insisted that government supervision should extend only to ensuring "minimum academic standards" and not to advance the mistaken goal of separating religion from the "education of the nation."[1]

Murray's writings over the next two decades addressed the puzzle of articulating Catholic doctrine in American society. Religious diversity in the United States made it tempting, Murray thought, to discard truth claims for an easy pluralism. The consequent tendency of even sophisticated Americans to forgo conversation about first principles seemed a step toward barbarism. Indeed, Murray later claimed, the contemporary barbarian "may wear a Brooks Brothers suit and carry a ball point pen to write his advertising copy."[2]

Murray agreed to give after-dinner remarks at a 1949 New York benefit for Jesuit schools and missions in the Philippines. He began by noting that Jesuit missionary work reflected the ideal of Catholic unity, the conviction that Catholicism "has not retired to one corner of the world nor shut her self off from any segment of humanity." Neither had Catholicism "consented to a permanent apportionment of the world between the followers of Christ and the followers of the great Buddha or of the Prophet of Islam or of any other prophets. Nor has she admitted that there may yet be fashioned some 'religion of mankind' whose faith would be more catholic than hers."

Then Murray moved in a different direction. Instead of insisting on the need for separate Catholic institutions in a hostile society, Murray challenged his audience, enjoying coffee and dessert in a New York hotel ballroom, to imagine themselves as missionaries. He wondered if "we American Catholics have been hitherto working too exclusively . . . erecting our churches and our own schools and our own hospitals, creating our own societies and organizations of all kinds, pursuing our own interests." The creation of this Catholic subculture "was, and still is, a necessary task." But the next "missionary journey" for American Catholics must be "a voyage into the heart of all the problems of American democracy." The goal in this missionary journey would be civic, not religious, unity. And civic unity, in Murray's view, was nothing less than the "Christian ancestry to the grand old American concept, We the People."[3]

Murray's evolution from defending Catholic institutions against a potentially hostile state to encouraging Catholics to take on leadership roles in a democratic society mirrors a wider pattern. If the upheavals of the late eighteenth and early nineteenth century convinced Catholics, often led by Jesuits, to build their own institutions and associations as a refuge, the fading of old antagonisms between Catholics and Protestants and Catholics and their secular neighbors allowed mid-twentieth-century Catholics to take a wider view. And too, the sour aftermath of modern fascism's emergence in the 1920s and 1930s, followed by the cataclysm of the Second World War, seemed to have demonstrated the limits of a subcultural strategy. Many Catholics ensconced in their own institutions, after all, willing to condemn modern liberalism as overly individualist or lacking a moral compass, had welcomed or condoned authoritarian or fascist governments in Austria, Argentina, Spain, Portugal, and Italy. In the mid-1930s, leading American Jesuits acknowledged that even the Father General in Rome "will not approve a direct stand against Fascism." Some French Jesuits endorsed the authoritarian (and strongly oriented toward Catholicism) Vichy government after the Nazis defeated the French in 1940.[4]

In retrospect, Catholic sympathy for authoritarian regimes suggested the dangers of insufficient attention to political philosophy. Leading Jesuits in the nineteenth century felt compelled to publicly announce that they did not view monarchies as preferable, and that they *could* work with constitutional or democratic governments. But this formal neutrality naturally diminished appreciation for democratic politics, still disparaged among many European Catholics by association with the French Revolution.[5]

The tone after the Second World War was different. Many Jesuits followed the lead of Pope Pius XII, who in his influential Christmas messages of 1942 and 1944 traced a Christian lineage for human rights and democracy. By the late 1940s, the vast majority of Jesuits in the North Atlantic had also come to terms with nonsectarian public education (as long as Catholic schools were permitted), religious liberty (in practice), and modern science (while sustaining a belief in the miraculous).[6]

Jesuits in the Philippines fit this pattern. Up until the last days before the Second World War, they had speculated as to whether authoritarian (and Catholic-influenced) governments in Portugal or Austria might prove useful models in Manila. When the leader of the commonwealth government in the Philippines, Manuel L. Quezon, floated the idea of eliminating political parties, American and Filipino Jesuits did not recoil, and even published tributes to the authoritarian Portuguese Catholic leader António de Oliveira Salazar. In response, the editor of the leading English-language newspaper in the Philippines charged the Jesuits with undermining democratic governments.[7]

The war obscured these debates. After 1945, all Jesuits assumed the necessity of democratic politics, and indeed supported the formation of largely Catholic Christian Democratic parties in much of Europe and Latin America. The war also deepened the identification of American Jesuits with the democratic United States. Imprisoned American Jesuits in the Philippines annoyed their Japanese captors during the war by breaking into impromptu choruses of "God Bless America." At the Mass celebrating their release, the homilist, an American Jesuit who himself had been held in a Japanese camp, invoked a "divine approval for patriotism" and "thanked God" that he was an American.[8]

In this patriotic context, long-standing Catholic customs prohibiting cooperation with Protestants and Jews in religious and even civic organizations seemed ridiculous. Many Jesuits had served in the military with ministers and rabbis as chaplains, and in the Philippines in particular the shared ordeal of internment had brought Jesuits into friendly contact with Protestant ministers. Murray published an important essay during the war encouraging interreligious cooperation and agreed with correspondents frustrated by the reluctance of bishops to recognize the "fact of pluralism among us." More broadly, Murray and other Jesuits joined the Christian consensus stretching from Reinhold Niebuhr and John Foster Dulles in the United States to Konrad Adenauer in West Germany and Pius XII in Rome, all defending the West against Soviet Communism. A startling number of American liberals disparaged Catholicism as an authoritarian threat to basic freedoms in the late 1940s, but this tension, too, eventually dissolved in the solvent of a common anti-Communism and official Catholic sympathy for the emerging African American civil rights movement in the US South.[9]

Murray even hoped that the Philippines might offer a moral example. One American Jesuit friend in the Philippines asked Murray after the war to assess the free speech rights of American Jehovah's Witnesses, some of whom had traveled to the Philippines, where they denounced Catholicism in a plaza in front of a Filipino Jesuit church. Murray declined to venture into the thicket of US Supreme Court jurisprudence on freedom of speech, populated, as Murray knew, by cases of Jehovah's Witnesses proselytizing in a similarly provocative manner in the United States. The subject was not "suitably simple." Yet he wondered if the newly independent Philippines, freed from American control in 1946, might provide a workable model for the "crucial, complicated question" of how to allow individual freedoms while sustaining a deeper sense of communal purpose. In contrast to intellectuals in the United States and "other Western societies," Filipinos had not substituted the "sense of the political community as a spiritual and moral community" with mere "forms of freedom, in matters of process, procedure, method." Indeed, "if the Filipino people wed their ancestral Christian wisdom to their hard won political wisdom, there is hope they will show triumphant leadership in today's crisis."[10]

Regret over Catholic sympathy for fascism, then, and a weakening of denominational divides inspired a generation of European and North American Jesuits, including Karl Rahner (Germany), Henri de Lubac (France), Bernard Lonergan (Canada), and Augustin Bea (Germany) to work on bridging the gap between individual piety and responsibility for public life. De Lubac regretted the "servility" of the French episcopate during the war and urged Catholics to view their faith as social, not private. Rahner thought Catholicism needed to avoid a "defensive mentality, [a] turning of the Church in on itself against the world."[11]

Murray's fame derives from his work on the thorny problem of religious freedom, or how to reimagine the claim, developed in the nineteenth century by successive popes (and their Jesuit advisers), that in an ideal situation, the state would support Catholicism because the state would recognize that Catholicism was true. In the interwar period, this position continued to inform the work of Vatican diplomats, who favored treaties or concordats between the Vatican and particular governments outlining the responsibilities of "Catholic States" in areas such as education, family law, and censorship. In Italy, following the 1929 Lateran Pact with Benito Mussolini, with Catholicism defined as the "only state religion," religious freedom for Protestants and Jews existed as a form of toleration, not constitutional right.[12] As late as 1937, Irish Jesuits urged that country's prime minister, Éamon de Valera, to use the revision of the country's Constitution to recognize the "special position" of Catholicism, as in other "Catholic constitutions."[13]

The centrality of religious freedom to Allied rhetoric during the Second World War and need for Christian unity against Communist foes made the orthodox Catholic position less tenable. During the Versailles negotiations, Woodrow Wilson had struggled unsuccessfully to write protections for religious freedom into the constitutions governing new European states after World War I. After World War II, similar American efforts in Japan and elsewhere met little resistance.[14] Similarly, over the objections of some Jesuits in Italy and Spain, countries where Catholicism continued to play a privileged civic role, Murray now saw an opportunity to position religious freedom as a good arising out of a universal human dignity, not a tactical concession to religious pluralism. Denunciations of religious freedom by nineteenth-century popes and Jesuits, Murray argued, should be read against anticlerical attacks then sweeping Europe and resulting in Jesuit expulsions, not the more temperate religious climate of the mid-twentieth century.

If the experience of Catholicism in the democratic United States demonstrated the advantages of a principled government refusal to endorse any faith, so, too, did the manipulation of churches by fascist or Communist regimes. In the Philippines, Jesuit experience with Japanese state-sponsored religion during World War II had been illuminating. Japanese leaders had begun limiting the freedoms of small religious groups—both Buddhist and Christian—in the late 1930s as part of an effort to create a more cohesive, unified society in contrast to what they perceived as the decadent, individualist West. These Japanese ideas came to the Philippines in 1942 along with the conquering Japanese army. As Murray probably knew, when pressed to demonstrate their loyalty to the Greater East Asia Co-Prosperity Sphere and a "new Philippines" during the Japanese occupation of Manila, Jesuits responded by defending the American model of church–state separation—a model their predecessors had denounced as heterodox when introduced in the Philippines forty years before.[15]

In the 1950s, Murray came under suspicion from Vatican officials, who demanded that several Catholic theologians, including two prominent Jesuits, Murray, and de Lubac, refrain from publishing on sensitive topics.[16] Only a decade later, however, at the Second Vatican Council, Murray exerted a decisive influence on one of the most important conciliar documents, *Dignitatis Humanae* (1965). Here the assembled bishops shifted Catholic teaching from favoring a unity of church and state to a defense of religious freedom as inseparable from human dignity. Here, too, in another conciliar document, *Gaudium et Spes* (1965) the bishops urged Catholics to move out from their own institutions to share in the "joys and hopes" and "griefs and anxieties" of the wider world.[17]

The triumph of this outward vision is well known. With it came obscurity for the subjects of this book. After all, Jesuits focused on building Catholic institutions, promoting devotion to the Sacred Heart, defending papal infallibility, and writing miracle accounts seemed out of step with the conciliar ethos—a detour from the theological road leading to the 1960s.

Now they seem in some ways less alien. The Catholic challenge as understood by nineteenth-century Jesuits—how to sustain religious faith in a diasporic community—is acute in the twenty-first century not just for Catholics but also for Muslims and other members of global religions. (And contemporary accusations that Muslims are inherently authoritarian or antidemocratic echo claims made about nineteenth-century Catholics.)[18]

Similarly, the Jesuit desire to use institutions as a vehicle for the training of Catholic leaders endures. St. Joseph's Preparatory high school, for example, founded in 1851, continues to thrive, still located next to the Gesu church in one of Philadelphia's most impoverished neighborhoods. Students read some of the required Latin texts read by the first St. Joseph's students in the 1850s, or for that matter, students at Jesuit institutions in the sixteenth century. When students attend Mass, they do so in the massive baroque church building constructed so lovingly, and at such expense, by Fr. Burchard Villiger. Two of Philadelphia's past five mayors are graduates. After his election in 2007, Mayor Michael Nutter visited his alma mater. "I think it should be clear to you what your mission is," he told a cheering group of students. "You're being trained right here to be leaders of your community."[19]

Parallel anecdotes dot the history of the Ateneo de Manila, founded in 1859, eight years after St. Joseph's Preparatory. The Ateneo's grade school, high school, and college, destroyed during the battle for Manila in 1945, were rebuilt in part through donations from American Catholics along with reconstruction aid from the US government (lobbied for by American Jesuits). Like their counterparts in Philadelphia, graduates of the Ateneo constitute a significant portion of Manila's elite, and alumni include the country's president, Benigno Aquino, and the current cardinal archbishop of Manila, Luis Tagle.[20]

If training Catholic leaders connects nineteenth- and twenty-first-century Jesuits, so, too, does a global orientation. That Manila now matters more to the future of Catholicism than Milan, and Kampala more than Cologne, is in part an achievement of nineteenth-century Jesuits and their missionary peers. Their hesitations about democracy and religious liberty did not equip them for the challenges of the twentieth century. But their success as institution builders, along with their linguistic facility and a willingness to travel to all corners of the globe, seem oddly contemporary. The career of a Jesuit expelled from Sicily in 1848 who moved to Ireland, then to Spain, then to the Philippines, and then to France before ending his career in New Mexico resembles that of a contemporary management consultant or international aid worker. A newly self-aware and global Catholic community bounded his life and work far more than any particular nation-state.[21]

This Jesuit global ethos, like globalization generally, has its own history. Peaking in the nineteenth century as exiled European Jesuits carried an international Catholic style across the world, it waned during the era of the First World War. Notably, the percentage of Jesuits serving as missionaries halved in

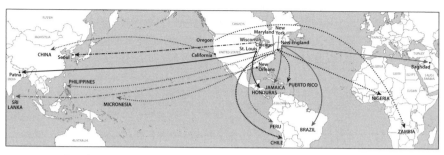

MAP 2. Jesuit Migration from the United States, 1890s–1960s

the immediate aftermath of the war, although the number of American Jesuits on mission assignments grew, as they began taking on new responsibilities around the world.[22]

Only the horrors of another global war reinvigorated a global Jesuit vision. The exaltation of "race" in Adolf Hitler's Germany and Benito Mussolini's Italy, in particular, provoked a handful of European and American Jesuits to insist that scientifically inaccurate ideas of inferior or superior races could not order the human community. One American Jesuit, John LaFarge, authored a fundamental text, admired by Pope Pius XI, on Catholic "interracialism." (He also helped silence fellow Jesuits at the Gesu in Philadelphia who into the early 1940s discouraged African Americans from registering in the parish or enrolling at the parish school in a futile effort to prevent white flight.)[23]

The first Jesuits trained in the new discipline of anthropology amplified this vision. One American Jesuit anthropologist sent in 1941 to work in the Philippines began his career with a sense of the natives as exotic and explicitly hoped to place his work in *National Geographic* magazine as "local color." A decade later, he organized Catholic missionaries from across the United States to challenge "ethnocentrism."[24]

More practically, Jesuits confronted the profound challenge of missionary work in an era of decolonization. As early as 1948, the Jesuit Father General, Belgian Jean-Baptiste Janssens, had noted the importance for the Society of the "push toward independence" made by "people of color." French Jesuits in particular paid increasing attention to Francophone Africa in the 1940s and 1950s, spurred by efforts to integrate Algerians into French society as well as more general questions of economic development. German Jesuits in India pondered how to avoid an "excessive legalism" in their missionary approach.[25]

By that time, many Jesuits had become more sympathetic than their predecessors to indigenous religious practices. As European colonial empires collapsed, many Jesuits urged their colleagues to distinguish conversion to Christianity from conversion to Western mores. A Jesuit General Congregation in 1946 could still refer in rote fashion to "missions among the infidels." One decade later, another Jesuit General Congregation insisted on striving to "understand [the] culture, history and religious teachings" of indigenous peoples.[26] A Belgian Jesuit coined a verb—"inculturate"—that became talismanic for missionaries, signaling a turn away from soul-by-soul conversion to "inculturating" Catholicism into local societies.[27]

Markers of successful inculturation—even collaboration—were evident in the Philippines. From the beginning, the Father General had stressed lifetime commitment, unlike "civil officials or merchants," and dozens of American Jesuits, men raised in Brooklyn or Buffalo, spent their careers on the islands. They brought with them an interest in Catholic social thought, as suggested by social action clubs on *Rerum Novarum* and concern about "landholders of enormous tracts" exerting too much political influence.[28]

Some of these American Jesuits united with the growing number of Filipino Jesuits to chide American colleagues who focused only on the "curious and grotesque" when describing life in the Philippines. They also responded to the Father General's prodding to "look for and foster vocations among the Filipinos themselves."[29] One American Jesuit insisted that "native Filipino Jesuits" must eventually take over positions "now manned largely by American and Spanish Fathers."[30]

The shared experience of the Second World War was again decisive. In the uncertain days of the Japanese occupation American Jesuit leaders planned for Filipinos to take their place if the Japanese deported (or killed) the Americans.[31] The Americans survived the war, but the transition from American to Filipino leadership eventually took place with noticeably less rancor than the transition from Spaniards to Americans. By the late 1950s the province's 440 Jesuit members were evenly divided between Americans and Filipinos, with a few remaining Spaniards. The crucial transitional figure, and the first Filipino leader of the Jesuits in the Philippines, was Horacio de la Costa. De la Costa had graduated from the Ateneo de Manila, had participated in a Grand Act, the first in the Philippines, had been interned by the Japanese during World War II, and had obtained a PhD in history from Harvard before returning to Manila. As early as 1952, de la Costa insisted that Catholicism should not be viewed as a Western import but instead belonged "fully as much to Asia as to Europe."[32]

An official turning point in the emergence of a more global church occurred at the Second Vatican Council, where nationalism and the nation-state received virtually no attention, even or especially at the height of the Cold War. The bishops endorsed a "generous and loyal" patriotism, but only with an immediate caution against "narrow-mindedness" and a plea to focus on the "welfare of the whole human family."[33]

Geographic diversity made the council more global, too. For the first time bishops born in Africa, Asia, and Latin America participated with their European colleagues. (At the first Vatican Council in 1869–70 only a handful of missionary bishops, all born in Europe, represented the Roman church east of Russia, south of Naples, and west of Galway.)

Inspired by the council, Jesuits from the global South, notably Latin America, South Asia, and the Philippines, where de la Costa was a key interlocutor, reflected on theological insights they might bring to the wider church. Pedro Arrupe, the Jesuit Father General immediately after the council, spent much of his career as a missionary in Japan and survived the dropping of the atomic bomb on Hiroshima. Visiting the Philippines in the early 1970s, he explained that he could no longer distinguish between "mission" and "non-mission" territories. Filipino Jesuits must "answer the needs of the Philippines in the theological language and thought of the Philippines."[34]

The German Jesuit Karl Rahner consolidated and furthered the idea of a global church in an important essay that began as a lecture, delivered partially in German and simultaneously translated, to faculty and students at a Jesuit theologate in Cambridge, Massachusetts. The Second Vatican Council for Rahner signified the emergence of a "world Church in a fully official way." In the nineteenth century, the church "exported a European religion as a commodity it did not really want to change . . . together with the rest of the culture and civilization it considered superior."

The Council was different. Its primary practical achievement, after all, had been requiring the translation of the liturgy into the vernacular. "The victory of the vernacular in the church liturgy," Rahner argued, "signals unmistakably the coming-to-be of a world Church whose individual churches exist with a certain independence in their respective cultural spheres, inculturated, and no longer a European export."

Rahner recognized that a contemporary global Catholic sensibility would emerge with frequent starts and stops. Wary of Vatican offices with the "mentality of a centralized bureaucracy which thinks it knows best," Rahner would now presumably regret the absence of a more dialogic process for articulating Catholic doctrine.[35]

Nonetheless, Rome has become a global hub, where orthodoxy as defined in curial offices jostles against pleas for expanded leadership roles for women in the North Atlantic, competition with Pentecostalism in Mexico, South America, and the Philippines, and tension (and cooperation) with Islam in the Middle East, Africa, and Southeast Asia. Catholic leaders now veer between assessing the church's diminished prospects in a secular Europe—along with an increasingly secular North and South America—and hoping to propel Catholic growth in Africa, India, and China. In the middle of the twentieth century, the single-largest group of Jesuits came from the United States. Since the 1980s, the single-largest group has come from South Asia.

FIGURE 18. Pope Francis at the Gesù in Rome, celebrating the bicentennial of the restoration of the Jesuits in December 2014. Courtesy of Catholic News Service.

The Jesuit Father General, Adolfo Nicolás, understands this global church firsthand. Born in Spain, he studied in Tokyo and Rome, and then returned to Asia, including a six-year stint at the Ateneo de Manila, for the bulk of his ministerial career. Following his election in 2008, he urged the world's Jesuits to develop a more self-consciously global orientation. "Can we not go beyond the loose family relationships we now have as institutions," he asked, "and re-imagine and re-organize ourselves so that, in this globalized world, we can more effectively realize the universality which has always been part of Ignatius's vision of the Society?"[36]

Another globally minded Jesuit, Jorge Mario Bergoglio or Pope Francis, is not only the first Jesuit pope but also the first modern pope from outside Europe. Or as he explained with a smile to the throng in St. Peter's Square on the evening of his election, "from the end of the earth." In the early 1970s, he urged analysis of the "habits, values, [and] cultural references" of the poor, and the "many and unique" manifestations of human culture. He has installed an advisory cabinet of nine cardinals representing seven continents. He contrasts a "globalization of indifference" marking the current divide between rich and poor with a "globalization of fraternity."[37]

Global connections forged in the twenty-first century will not simply replicate those sketched in this volume, but Jesuit networks created in the era of text messages and Skype do follow already-laid paths. Just as the restoration of the Jesuits in 1814 led to a surge of missionary activity, Pope Francis used the occasion of the restoration's bicentennial, speaking to several hundred Jesuits from around the world at the Gesù in Rome, to encourage an "outbound" ethos within the Society.

Nine months later, visiting Philadelphia, the pope made a surprise visit to Jesuit St. Joseph's University, where he blessed a statue commemorating the Second Vatican Council. He then said Mass before a crowd of one million people, standing just over a mile from the Philadelphia Gesu church, modeled on the Roman Gesù, and constructed in the nineteenth century by his exiled predecessors. He urged his listeners to respond to contemporary global challenges as "part of the great human family." And as Catholics, and all people of good will, absorb Francis's plea for a "globalization of hope," these forgotten Jesuit tales may possess an unexpected resonance.[38]

ABBREVIATIONS USED
IN THE NOTES

Manuscript collections, archives, and periodicals cited in the notes are identified by the following abbreviations.

Individual pieces of correspondence identified with a Roman numeral, Arabic numeral, and lowercase letter (e.g., III-2-p) are located in the correspondence collection, Archives of the University of Notre Dame.

Documents located in the Archivum Romanum Societatis Iesu, the Jesuit archives in Rome, are identified by the abbreviation ARSI. That abbreviation is preceded by the Latin name for the relevant Jesuit province—Neo-Aurelensis for New Orleans—and then the box number, folder number, and if relevant, document number.

AAB	Archives of the Archdiocese of Boston, Massachusetts
AANO	Archives of the Archdiocese of New Orleans, Louisiana
AAS	American Antiquarian Society, Worcester, Massachusetts
ABPSJ	Archives of the Belgian Province, Society of Jesus, KADOC, Leuven, Belgium
ADP	Archives of the Diocese of Portland, Maine

ADPSJ	Archives of the Postulator General, Jesuit Curia, Rome, Italy
ADR	Archives of the Diocese of Richmond, Virginia
AFPSJ	Archives of the French Province, Society of Jesus, Vanves, France
AHSI	*Archivum Historicum Societatis Iesu*
ANPSJ	Archives of the New Orleans Province, Society of Jesus, Loyola University, New Orleans
APPSJ	Archives of the Philippine Province, Society of Jesus, Quezon City, Philippines
ARSI	Archivum Romanum Societatis Iesu, Jesuit Curia, Rome, Italy
ASV	Archivio Segreto Vaticano, Rome, Italy
AUND	Archives of the University of Notre Dame, Notre Dame, Indiana
BCANNO	Processus Apostolicus Pro Canonizatione B. Joannis Berchmans, S.J., 1886, Archives of the Archdiocese of New Orleans, Louisiana
BW	Bernardin Wiget Papers, Special Collections Research Center, Georgetown University, Washington, DC
CFP	Cheever Family Papers, American Antiquarian Society, Worcester, Massachusetts
DD	David Dunigan Papers, Bapst Library, Boston College, Boston, Massachusetts
FW	Francis Weninger Papers, Jesuit Archives, Central United States, Saint Louis, Missouri
GBC	George Burrell Cheever Papers, American Antiquarian Society, Worcester, Massachusetts

GCJA	Grand Couteau Jesuit Archives, Grand Couteau, Louisiana
GUA	Georgetown University Archives, Washington, DC
HFP	Hunt Family Papers, Missouri Historical Society, Columbia, Missouri
HUA	Harvard University Archives, Cambridge, Massachusetts
JACUS	Jesuit Archives, Central United States, Saint Louis, Missouri
JB	John Bapst Papers, Burns Library, Boston College, Boston, Massachusetts
JCM	John Courtney Murray Papers, Special Collections Research Center, Georgetown University, Washington, DC
JF	John Fitzpatrick Papers, Archives of the Archdiocese of Boston, Massachusetts
MP	Maryland Province Archives of the Society of Jesus, Special Collections Research Center, Georgetown University, Washington, DC
MPC	Maryland Province Collection, Special Collections Research Center, Georgetown University, Washington, DC
NOPSJ	Archives of the New Orleans Province, Society of Jesus, New Orleans, Louisiana
NYPSJ	Archives of the New York Province, Society of Jesus, New York
PPSJ	Documents Relating to the Jesuit Mission in the Philippines, 1914–30, microfilm copy, original at Rizal Library, Ateneo de Manila, Quezon City, Philippines

RSCJ	Society of the Sacred Heart Archives, United States–Canada, Saint Louis, Missouri (the material used in chapter 4 concerning Mary Wilson is located in Saint Louis Province, series IV-E, box 6)
RSCJ–Rome	Society of the Sacred Heart Archives, Rome, Italy
SHEA	John Gilmary Shea Papers, Special Collections Research Center, Georgetown University, Washington, DC
SJU	Saint Joseph University Archives, Philadelphia, Pennsylvania
TM	Thomas Mulledy Papers, Manuscripts and Archives, Special Collections Research Center, Georgetown University, Washington, DC
VSJP	Villiger Archives, St. Joseph's Preparatory School, Philadelphia, Pennsylvania
WCA	Woodstock College Archives, Woodstock Library, Georgetown University
WGE	William Greenleaf Eliot Papers, Washington University, Saint Louis, Missouri
WL	*Woodstock Letters*

NOTES

INTRODUCTION

1. [John Adams], "The Jesuits," *North American Review* 6 (November 1817): 129–34, quote on 130; [John Adams], "The Jesuits," *North American Review* 6 (March 1818); 405–8. On the suppression, see Jonathan Wright, "The Suppression and Restoration," in *The Cambridge Companion to the Jesuits*, ed. Thomas Worcester (Cambridge, UK, 2008), 263–77; Pierre Antoine Fabre and Patrick Goujoun, *Suppression et rétablissement de la Compagnie de Jésus (1773–1814)* (Paris, 2014); Robert A. Maryks and Jonathan Wright, eds., *Jesuit Survival and Restoration: A Global History, 1773–1900* (Leiden, 2015).

2. Hilario Azzolini, S.J., "Prospectus numericus Societatis Iesu: Ab anno 1814 AD 1932," *AHSI* 2 (1933): 88–92.

3. Margaret Lavinia Anderson, "The Limits of Secularization: On the Problem of the Catholic Revival in Nineteenth-Century Germany," *Historical Journal* 38 (1995): 647–70; Austin Iverveigh, ed., *The Politics of Religion in an Age of Revival* (London, 2000).

4. Roger Aubert, *Le Pontificat de Pie IX (1846–1878)* (Paris, 1952), 457.

5. Sodality of Immaculate Conception to Fr. Beckx, January 25, 1858, in Marylandiae, box 1009, X-9, ARSI.

6. John Breuilly, "On the Principle of Nationality," in *The Cambridge History of Nineteenth-Century Political Thought*, ed. Gareth Stedman Jones and Gregory Claeys (Cambridge, UK, 2011), 77–109.

7. Quoted in James F. Sanders, *The Vanguard of the Atlantic World: Creating Modernity, Nation, and Democracy in Nineteenth-Century Latin America* (Durham, NC, 2014), 142. On the general question, see Pierre Rosanvallon, *The Demands of Liberty: Civil Society in France since the Revolution*, trans. Arthur Goldhammer (Cambridge, UK, 2007), 195–99; Matthew P. Fitzpatrick, *Purging the Empire: Mass Expulsions in Germany, 1871–1914* (New York, 2015), 39–66.

8. Paolo Chenillo Alazraki, "Liberalismo a prueba: La expulsión de 'extranjeros perniciosos' en México durante la República Restaurada (1867–1876)," *Revista de Indias* 72 (2012): 377–408. Anti-Jesuitism has attracted much

attention from historians, although the absence of a synthetic work has submerged the topic's importance. On France, see Geoffrey Cubitt, *The Jesuit Myth: Conspiracy Theory and Politics in Nineteenth-Century France* (Oxford, 1993); Michel Leroy, *Le mythe jésuite: De Béranger à Michelet* (Paris, 1992). On Italy, see Giacoma Martina, S.J., "Motivi e radici dell'opposizione piemontese alla Compagnia di Gesù: 1818–1848," in *La Compagnia di Gesù nella provinica di Torino: Dagli anni di Emanuele Filiberto a quelli di Carlo Alberto*, ed. Bruno Signorelli and Piero Uscello (Turin, 1998), 411–27. On the Czech lands, see Marie-Élizabeth Ducreux, "L'antijésuitisme tchèque au XIXe siècle," in *Les Antijésuites: Discours, figures et lieux de l'antijésuitisme à l'époque moderne*, ed. Pierre-Antoine Fabre and Catherine Maire (Rennes, Fr., 2010), 518–36. On Germany, see Michael B. Gross, *The War against Catholicism: Liberalism and the Anti-Catholic Imagination in Nineteenth-Century Germany* (Ann Arbor, MI, 2004), 259–91; Róisín Healy, *The Jesuit Specter in Imperial Germany* (Leiden, Neth., 2003). On Latin America, see Susana Monreal, Sabina Pavone, and Guillermo Zermeno, eds., *Antijesuitismo y filojesuitismo: Dos identidades ante la restauración* (Mexico City, 2014).

9. Quoted in Henry Winter Davis, *The Origin, Principles, and Purposes of the American Party* (Baltimore, 1856), 35.

10. Charles Taylor, *Modern Social Imaginaries* (Durham, NC, 2004), 31–68.

11. On the Catholic milieu, see Christopher Clark and Wolfram Kaiser, eds., *Culture Wars: Secular-Catholic Conflict in Nineteenth-Century Europe* (Cambridge, UK, 2003). See also Christopher Clark, "From 1848 to Christian Democracy," in *Religion and the Political Imagination*, ed. Ira Katznelson and Gareth-Stedman Jones (New York, 2010), esp. 190–96; Olaf Blaschke, "Das 19. Jahrhundert: Ein Zweites Konfessionelles Zeitalter?" *Geschichte und Gesellschaft* 26 (2000): 38–75. On China, see Henrietta Harrison, *The Missionary's Curse and Other Tales from a Chinese Catholic Village* (Berkeley, CA, 2013), 65–91.

12. Simon Ditchfield, "Decentering the Catholic Reformation: Papacy and Peoples in the Early Modern World," *Archiv für Reformationgeschichte* 101 (2010): 186–208; Luke Clossey, *Salvation and Globalization in the Early Jesuit Missions* (Cambridge, UK, 2008).

13. Alexandre Brou, *Cent ans de missions, 1815–1934: Les Jésuites missionnaires au XIXe et au XXe siècle* (Paris, 1935), 297–98.

14. Jean-Marie Kreins and Josy Brisens, S.J., "Les jesuites luxembourgeois et l'experience missionnaire dans le monde aux XIXe et XXe siècles," in *Le Face-à-Face des Dieux: Missionnaires luxembourgeois en Outre-Mer*, ed. Andre Neuberg (Bastogne, Bel., 2007), 127–31.

15. Roothaan to Luigi Fortis, August 25, 1823, in Ioannis Phil. Roothaan, *Epistolae* (Rome, 1935), 1:225.

16. For data analysis, see Antonio F. B. De Castro, S.J., "Jesuits in the Philippines: From the Revolution to the Transition from the Spanish Jesuits to the American Jesuits, 1898–1927 (PhD diss., Pontifical Gregorian University, 2000), 684.

17. Ferdinand Coosemans to Peter Beckx, July 29, 1870, Missouriana, box 1007, VII-1, ARSI. More generally and brilliantly, see C. A. Bayly, *The Birth of the Modern World, 1780–1914* (Malden, MA, 2004), 325–65.

18. David Hempton, *Methodism: Empire of the Spirit* (New Haven, CT, 2005), 151–77; Seema Alavai, *Muslim Cosmopolitanism in the Age of Empire* (Cambridge, MA, 2015). See also Abigail Green and Vincent Viaene, eds., *Religious Internationals in the Modern World: Globalization and Faith Communities since 1750* (London, 2012).

19. E. Laveille, *The Life of Father De Smet, S.J.: Apostle of the Rocky Mountains, 1801–1873* (New York, 1928), 368. On the papacy, see, for example, Claude Prudhomme, *Stratégie missionnaire du Saint-Siège sous Léon XIII (1878–1903): Centralisation romaine et défis culturels* (Rome, 1994). I borrow the term "register" from Lisabeth Cohen, "Re-viewing the Twentieth Century through an American Catholic Lens," in *Catholics in the American Century: Recasting Narratives of U.S. History*, ed. R. Scott Appleby and Kathleen Sprows Cummings (Ithaca, NY, 2012), 53–54.

20. For a sterling exception to this generalization and a book on which I have relied heavily, see Gerald McKevitt, S.J., *Brokers of Culture: Italian Jesuits in the American West, 1848–1919* (Stanford, CA, 2007). On Maryland Province Jesuits, see Robert Emmett Curran, *Shaping American Catholicism: Maryland and New York, 1805–1915* (Washington, DC, 2012). The standard, monumental source on midwestern Jesuits remains Gilbert Garraghan, S.J., *The Jesuits of the Middle United States*, 3 vols. (New York, 1938).

21. Louis Hartz, *The Liberal Tradition in America* (New York, 1955). On the United States in global history, the standard account is now Thomas Bender, *A Nation among Nations: America's Place in World History* (New York, 2006). The specific topic of Catholicism in the United States has attracted an international group of collaborators. In English, among others, see Luca Condignola, "Roman Catholic Conservatism in a New North Atlantic World, 1760–1829," *William and Mary Quarterly*, 3rd ser., 64 (October 2007), 717–56; Kathleen Cummings, "Citizen Saints: Catholics and Canonization in American Culture" (forthcoming); Steven W. Hackel, *Junipero Serra: California's Founding Father* (New York, 2013); Thomas W. Tweed, *Our Lady of the Exile: Diasporic Religion at a Cuban Catholic Shrine in Miami* (Oxford, 1997); Peter R. D'Agostino, *Rome in America: Transnational Catholic Ideology from the Risorgimento to Fascism* (Chapel Hill, NC, 2004); John T. McGreevy, *Catholicism and American Freedom: A History* (New York, 2003);

Gerald McKevitt, *Brokers of Culture: Italian Jesuits in the American West, 1848–1919* (Stanford, CA, 2007); Timothy Matovina, *Guadalupe and Her Faithful: Latino Catholics in San Antonio from Colonial Origins to the Present* (Baltimore, 2005). In French, see Florian Michel, *La pensée catholique en Amérique du Nord: Réseaux intellectuels et échanges cuturels entre l'Europe, le Canada et les États Unis (années 1920–1960)* (Paris, 2010); Tangi Villerbu, "Faire l'histoire catholique e l'ouest américain au 19 siècle: Une terre de missions à réévaluer," *Revue d'Histoire Ecclesiastique* 101 (2006), 117–42. In German, see Michael Hochgeschwender, *Wahrheit, Einheit, Ordnung: Die Sklavenfrage und der amerikanische Katholizismus 1835–1870* (Paderborn, Ger., 2006). In Italian, see Matteo Sanfilippo, *L'Affermazione del Cattolicesimo nel Nord America: Elite Emigranti e Chiesa Cattolica negli Stati Uniti e in Canada, 1750–1920* (Viterbo, It., 2003).

CHAPTER 1: NINETEENTH-CENTURY JESUITS AND THEIR CRITICS

1. "Massachusetts Bay Passes an Anti-Priest Law, May 26, 1647," in John Tracy Ellis, ed., *Documents of American Catholic History, Volume 1* (Chicago, [1961] 1967), 110–12; Thomas Hughes, *History of the Society of Jesus in North America: Colonial and Federal, Volume II, 1645–1773* (London, 1907–17), 109; James D. Rice, "Bacon's Rebellion in Indian Country," *Journal of American History* 101 (December 2014): 746; Francis X. Curran, *Catholics in Colonial Law* (Chicago, 1963), 76–77. On colonial anti-Catholicism more generally, see Owen Stanwood, *The Empire Reformed: English America in the Age of the Glorious Revolution* (Philadelphia, 2011), 1–21.

2. Caroline Winterer, "Where Is America in the Republic of Letters?" *Modern Intellectual History* 9 (November 2012): 615–17; Luca Condignola, "Benjamin Franklin and the Holy See, 1783–4: The Myth of Non-Interference in Religious Affairs" (copy in author's possession).

3. John Carroll to Daniel Carroll, September, 11, 1773, in R. Emmett Curran, S.J., ed., *American Jesuit Spirituality: The Maryland Tradition, 1634–1900* (New York, 1988), 129; John Carroll to Charles Plowden, January 5, 1815, in Thomas O'Brien Hanley, ed., *The John Carroll Papers: Volume 1, 1755–1791* (Notre Dame, IN, 1976), 316.

4. For sixty million—a gross figure that does not count return—between 1820 and 1920, see Kevin O'Rourke and Jeffrey Williamson, *Globalization and History: The Evolution of a Nineteenth-Century Atlantic Economy* (Cambridge, MA, 1999), 119. For comparisons, see Adam McKeown, "Global Migration, 1846–1940," *Journal of World History* 15 (2004): 155–89. Irish immigrants to the United States were roughly 90 percent Catholic; Germans were roughly 50 percent. Kerby A. Miller, *Emigrants and Exiles: Ireland and*

the Irish Exodus to North America (New York, 1985), 297, 569; Kevin Robert Ostoyich, "The Transatlantic Soul: German Catholic Emigration during the Nineteenth Century" (PhD diss., Harvard University, 2006), 159–60.

5. Fr. Cornelius Smarius, [June 1863], quoted in Rev. Joseph P. Conroy, S.J., *Arnold Damen, S.J.: A Chapter in the Making of Chicago* (New York, 1930), 231.

6. Roothaan to Fr. Peter Beckx, February 25, 1842, Corr. #347, and Roothaan to Fr. Peter Beckx, March 25, 1843, Corr #348, in Roothaan papers, ARSI.

7. On the links between eighteenth- and nineteenth-century anti-Jesuitism, see Dale Van Kley, "From the Catholic Enlightenment to the Risorgimento: The Exchange between Nichola Spedalieri and Pietro Tamburini, 1791–1797," *Past and Present* 224 (August 2014): 154. See also Sabine Pavone, *The Wily Jesuits and the Monita Secreta: The Forged Secret Instructions of the Jesuits* (Saint Louis, 2005); note the list of editions, including many in the nineteenth century, on 234–41.

8. On Sue, see Michel Leroy, *Le Mythe jésuite: De Béranger à Michelet* (Paris, 1992), 261–338. See also Jorge Enrique Salcedo Martinez, S.J., "The History of the Society of Jesus in Colombia, 1844–1861" (PhD diss., Oxford University, 2011), 134; Vincent Viaene, *Belgium and the Holy See from Gregory XVI to Pius IX (1831–1859): Catholic Revival, Society, and Politics in 19th-Century Europe* (Brussels, 2001), 339–400; Roothaan to Joseph Antonio de Pilat, October 4, 1845, in Ioannis Phil. Roothaan, *Epistolae* (Rome, 1940), 5:910; Roberto DiSteano, "El antijesuitismo porteño del siglo XIX," in *Antijesuitismo y filojesuitismo: Dos identidades ante la restauración*, ed. Susana Monreal, Sabina Pavone, and Guillermo Zermeno (Mexico City, 2014), 141–43; Susanna Monreal, "'Catolicismo y antijesuitismo son un misma cosa': campañas antijesuiticas en Montevideo, 1893–1913," in *Antijesuitismo y filojesuitismo: Dos identidades ante la restauración*, ed. Susana Monreal, Sabina Pavone, and Guillermo Zermeno (Mexico City, 2014), 166.

9. John Wolffe, "The Jesuit as Villain in Nineteenth-Century British Fiction," in *The Church and Literature*, ed. Peter Clarke and Charlotte Methuen (Woodbridge, UK, 2012), 309.

10. Jules Michelet and Edgar Quinet, *Des Jésuites* (Paris, 1843), 196; Geoffrey Cubbitt, *The Jesuit Myth: Conspiracy Theory and Politics in Nineteenth-Century France* (Oxford, 1993), 137.

11. Michelet and Quinet, *Des Jésuites*, 33, 71.

12. Jorge Enrique Salcedo, "La recepción de la leyenda anti-jesuita y pro-jesuita en la Nueva Granada, 1842–1850," in *Antijesuitismo y filojesuitismo: Dos identidades ante la restauración*, ed. Susana Monreal, Sabina Pavone, and Guillermo Zermeno (Mexico City, 2014), 159–60, 167–75; quote on 159.

13. Cristián Gazmuri, "Las revoluciones europeas de 1848 y su influencia en la historia politica de Chile," in *The European Revolutions of 1848 and the Americas*, ed. Guy Thomson (London, 2002), 166–67.

14. Ari Joskowicz, *The Modernity of Others: Jewish Anti-Catholicism in Germany and France* (Stanford, CA, 2014), 53, 55; Eugenio F. Biagini, "Mazzini and Anticlericalism: The English Exile," in *Guiseppe Mazzini and the Globalization of Democratic Nationalism, 1830–1920* (Oxford, 2008), 145–66; Michaela Tomaschewsky, "Dress Rehearsal for 1848: Johannes Ronge and the German Catholic Movement," *Consortium on Revolutionary Europe, 1750–1850: Selected Papers* (Tallahassee, FL, 1994), 116–22; Róisín Healy, *The Jesuit Specter in Imperial Germany* (Leiden, Neth., 2003), 40.

15. Klaus Schatz, *Geschichte der deutschen Jesuiten, Vol. 1, 1814–1872* (Münster, Ger., 2014), 131.

16. Vicenzo Gioberti, *La Suisse, Pie IX et les jésuites: Extraits traduits du Gesuita moderno de Vicenzo Gioberti* (Lausanne, Switz., 1847), 2; Salcedo, "La recepción de la leyenda anti-jesuita y pro-jesuita en la Nueva Granada," 113.

17. Quoted in Antonio De Meo, *I Gesuiti Nell'Italia Meridionale Dal 1848 Al 1859* (Palermo, It., 1991), 59.

18. Fr. Roothaan, "On Present Calamities and on Zeal for Perfection" (1847), in *Select Letters of Our Very Reverend Fathers General to the Fathers and Brothers of the Society of Jesus* (Woodstock, MD, 1900), 270.

19. John Baptist Miège, S.J., to Urban Miège, [1847], in Herman J. Muller, S.J., *Bishop East of the Rockies: The Life and Letters of John Baptist Miege, S.J.* (Chicago, 1994), 10.

20. See, for example, C. Larère, S.J., "La suppression de la mission de la Guyane Française (1763–1766)," *AHSI* 9 (1940): 208–26; François Philibert Watrin, "Bannissement des Jésuites de la Louisiane," in *The Jesuit Relations and Allied Documents, 1610–1791*, ed. Reuben Gold Thwaites (Cleveland, 1890), 70:211–300. On Jesuit understandings of the suppression, see Gustave-Xavier de Ravignan, S.J., *Clément XIII et Clément XIV* (Paris, 1854); Roothaan to Fr. Gustave-Xavier de Ravignan, December 31, 1852, in Ioannis Phil. Roothaan, *Epistolae* (Rome, 1940) 2:82.

21. Giovanni [John] Grassi to John McElroy, June 8, 1848, folder 2, box 70, MP.

22. Roothaan to Fr. Leonardo Fava, February 1, 1848, in Ioannis Phil. Roothaan, *Epistolae* (Rome, 1940), 3:173.

23. François Guizot, *The History of Civilization in Europe* (New York, [1828] 1997), 209.

24. Roothaan to Joseph Anthony De Pilat, September 4, 1847, in Ioannis Phil. Roothaan, *Epistolae* (Rome, 1940), 5:940.

25. The term "askew" is drawn from Robert A. Orsi, "U.S. Catholics between Memory and Modernity: How Catholics Are American," in *Catholics in the American Century: Recasting Narratives of U.S. History*, ed. R. Scott Appleby and Kathleen Sprows Cummings (Ithaca, NY, 2012), 15. See also Boris Vilallonga, "The Theoretical Origins of Catholic Nationalism in Nineteenth-Century Europe," *Modern Intellectual History* 11 (August 2014): 307–31;

Richard Schaeffer, "Program for a new Catholic *Wissenschaft*: Devotional Activism and Catholic Modernity in the Nineteenth Century," *Modern Intellectual History* 4 (2007): 433–62. More broadly, see Charles Taylor, *A Catholic Modernity? Charles Taylor's Marianist Award Lecture*, ed. James Heft (New York, 1999), 3–37; S. E. Eisenstadt, "Multiple Modernities," *Daedalus* 129 (Winter 2000): 1–29.

26. On nineteenth-century Jesuits, see John W. Padberg, "A Body Brought to Life Again: Organization, Spiritual Vitality, and Missionary Dynamism in the Restored Society of Jesus in the Nineteenth Century," *Center for Ignatian Spirituality* 24 (1993): 30–45.

27. Marcel Chappin, "John Philip Roothaan: 'The General of the Spiritual Exercises?'" *Center for Ignatian Spirituality* 24 (1993): 46–56.

28. Fourth Exhortation to the Community in New York, November 10, 1889, in folder 9, box 1, Philip Cardella, S.J., papers, Georgetown University. On individualism, see Klaus Schatz, *Geschichte der deutschen Jesuiten, Vol. 2, 1872–1917* (Münster, Ger., 2014), 82–88.

29. "Father James Perron: A Sketch of His Life, Part II," *WL* 20 (1891): 257, 263, 267; Cubbitt, *The Jesuit Myth*, 280–82; Joannes Philippus Roothaan, ed., *The Spiritual Exercises of St. Ignatius of Loyola*, trans. Charles Seager (Baltimore, 1850), 143–44.

30. Schatz, *Geschicte der deutschen Jesuiten, Vol. 1*, 146; circular letter and decree, Maryland Province, October 1, 1870, in file Ia 3.3a, box 1, WCA.

31. Roothaan, "On Desire for the Missions" [1833], in *Renovation Reading*, revised and enlarged edition (Woodstock, MD, 1931), 58.

32. Roothaan to Joseph Anthony de Pilat, April 12, 1844, in Ioannis Phil. Roothaan, *Epistolae* (Rome, 1940), 4:298.

33. C. F. Smarius, S.J., "Des État-Unis D'Amérique," in *Mélanges Litteraires et Scientifique* (Brussels, 1865), 65.

34. Philip Gleason, *Contending with Modernity: Catholic Higher Education in the Twentieth Century* (New York, 1995), 36.

35. Ulrich L. Lehner, "The Many Faces of the Catholic Enlightenment," in *A Companion to the Catholic Enlightenment in Europe*, ed. Ulrich L. Lehner and Michael Printy (Leiden, Neth., 2010), esp. 30–32; Dale K. Van Kley, "Jansenism and the International Suppression of the Jesuits," *The Cambridge History of Christianity, Volume VII: Enlightenment, Reawakening, and Revolution, 1660–1815*, ed. Stewart J. Brown and Timothy Tackett (Cambridge, UK, 2006), 302–28.

36. John W. O'Malley, "The Historiography of the Society of Jesus: Where Does It Stand Today?" in *The Jesuits II: Cultures, Sciences, and the Arts, 1540–1773*, ed. John W. O'Malley, S.J., Gauvin Alexander Bailey, Steven J. Harris, and T. Frank Kennedy, S.J. (Toronto, 2005), 3–37; Simon Ditchfield, "Of Missions and Models: The Jesuit Enterprise (1540–1773)

Reassessed in Recent Literature,"*Catholic Historical Review* 93 (2007): 325–43.

37. Agustin Udias, "Observatories of the Society of Jesus, 1814–1898," *AHSI* 69 (January 1, 2000): 151–78.

38. "Father Kenny on Scholasticism," in Kenny file, IIC 127a, box 82, WCA.

39. General Congregation 21, decree 14 [1829], in John W. Padberg, S.J., Martín D. O'Keefe, S.J., and John L. McCarthy, S.J., eds., *For Matters of Greater Moment: The First Thirty Jesuit General Congregations. A Brief History and a Translation of the Decrees* (Saint Louis, 1994), 440.

40. Wlodimir Ledóchowski, S.J., "On Following the Doctrine of St. Thomas" [1917], in *Selected Writings of Father Ledóchowski* (Chicago, 1945), 498–99. More generally, see Oliver P. Rafferty, "The Thomistic Revival and the Relationship between the Jesuits and the Papacy, 1878–1974," *Theological Studies* 75 (December 2014): 746–73.

41. Pierre Blet, "Jésuites gallicans au XVIIe siècle?" *AHSI* 29 (1960): 250–61.

42. Memoria Del P. Carlo Maria Curci, December 25, 1849, copy in Francesco Dante, *Storia Della 'Civiltà Cattolica' (1850–1891): Il laboratorio del Papa* (Rome, 1990), 141; Angelo Paresce to C. C. Lancaster, March 19, 1856, in folder 10, box 20, MP; Gerald McKevitt, *Brokers of Culture: Italian Jesuits in the American West, 1848–1919* (Stanford, CA, 2007), 236.

43. Burkhart Schneider, "Der Syllabus Pius IX und die deutschen Jesuiten," *Archivium historiae pontificiae* 6 (1968): 317–69.

44. An Account of the Audience Granted to the Holy Father Leo XIII to Our Rev. Procurators on October 5, 1896, compiled from the notes of Rev. Frs. Chandlery and Others of the Fathers Present, in folder 1, box 5, MP.

45. Newman to Mrs. John Mozley, July 25, 1847, and Newman to Mrs. John Mozley, September 15, 1847, in Charles Stephen Dessain, I. T. Ker, and Thomas Gornall, eds., *The Letters and Diaries of John Henry Newman* (London, 1961), 2:103–4, 117.

46. Schatz, *Geschichte der deutschen Jesuiten, Vol. 1*, 228.

47. "Ripugnanza del Concetto di Cattolico liberale," *Civiltà Cattolica*, 7th ser., 8 (1869): 5; Keller to Peter Beckx, January 6, 1870, in Marylandiae, box 1010, X-2, ARSI.

48. General Congregation 23, decree 12 [1883], in John W. Padberg, S.J., Martín D. O'Keefe, S.J., and John L. McCarthy, S.J., eds., *For Matters of Greater Moment: The First Thirty Jesuit General Congregations: A Brief History and a Translation of the Decrees* (Saint Louis, 1994), 465.

49. Broadly, see Darrin M. McMahon, *Enemies of the Enlightenment: The French Counter-Enlightenment and the Making of Modernity* (New York, 2001).

50. Roothaan, "Filosophia (psuedo)," #122a, box 1007, Roothaan papers, ARSI; Roothaan to P. Gustave-Xavier de Ravignan, December 31, 1852, in Ioannis Phil. Roothaan, *Epistolae* (Rome, 1940), 2:82.

51. R. P. Rozaven, S.J., Votum, [1831], in M. J. Le Guillou and Louis Le Guillou, eds., *La Condamnation de Lamennais: Dossier Présenté* (Paris, 1832), 121, 125.

52. Jaime Balmes, *Protestantism and Catholicity Compared in Their Effects on the Civilization of Europe* (Baltimore, 1851), 269; Nicholas Point, S.J., to Fr. Fremiot, S.J., March 18, 1850, in Lorenz Cadieux, ed., *Lettres des nouvelles missions du Canada, 1843–1852* (Montreal, 1973), 614–15. Into the twentieth century, *Protestantism and Catholicity Compared* was read out loud in Jesuit residences at mealtimes. See Prefect of Reading List, October 4, 1904, in file Ia 3.3a, box 1, WCA.

53. Michael Printy, "Protestantism and Progress in the Year XII: Charles Villers' *Essay on the Spirit and Influence of Luther's Reformation* (1804)," *Modern Intellectual History* 9 (August 2012): 303–29; Giovanni Perrone, *Il Protestantesimo e la regola di Fede* (Turin, 1854), 401–71; Fr. Friedrich, "Quelque Notices sur l'Amerique" July 15, 1849, copy in Gilbert Garraghan papers, JACUS.

54. Fr. John Larkin to unknown, March 20, 1848, John Larkin papers, NYPSJ.

55. Fr. Roh to Fr. Rubillon, January 1848, in Ferdinand Strobel, S.J., *Jesuiten und die Schweiz im XIX Jahrhundert* (Olten, Switz., 1954), 1062.

56. Ignace Brocard to Roothaan, [1848], in Marylandiae, box 1009, VIII-2, ARSI.

57. "Father Roothaan's Visit to Maynooth College, 1848," *Letters and Notices* 20 (1890): 353.

58. Schatz, *Geschichte der deutschen Jesuiten, Vol. 1*, 46; Roothaan to Ignace Brocard, April 6, 1848, in file 13, box 93, MP.

59. Holy card with prayer composed by Pierre De Smet, S.J., undated, copy in JACUS; André Boland, S.J., "Roothaan," *Dictionnaire de Spiritualité* (Paris, 1988), 13:920–31.

60. "Fr. Beckx, on BB. Canisius and Berchmans" [1865], in *Renovation Reading* (Woodstock, MD, 1886), 351.

61. Anthony Anderledy to Society of Jesus, May 16, 1884, in Roman file, SJU.

62. Luis Martín, "On Some Dangers of Our Times" [1896], in *Select Letters of Our Very Reverend Fathers General to the Fathers and Brothers of the Society of Jesus* (Woodstock, MD, 1900), 503.

63. John Thornton Kirkland, "On the Errors of the Romish Church" [1813], in HUC 5340.113, HUA; John Tierce, *The Right of Private Judgment in Religion, Vindicated against the Claims of the Romish Church and All Kindred Usurpations in a Dudleian Lecture Delivered before the University in Cambridge, 24 October, 1821* (Cambridge, UK, 1821), 4.

64. Susan M. Griffin, *Anti-Catholicism and Nineteenth-Century Fiction* (Cambridge, UK, 2004); Jenny Franchot, *Roads to Rome: The Antebellum Protestant Encounter with Catholicism* (Berkeley, CA, 1994).

65. "Freedom of Inquiry and Romanism," *Christian Observatory* 3 (April 1849): 158; Donald F. Crosby, S.J., "Jesuits Go Home: The Anti-Jesuit Movement

in the United States, 1830–1860," *WL* 97 (1968): 225–40; Francis X. Curran, "Tentative Bibliography of American Anti-Jesuitiana," *WL* 81 (1952): 293–304.

66. Noah Webster, *Webster's Dictionary of the American English Language* (New York, 1829), 473. On other European languages, see Harro Höppfl, *Jesuit Political Thought: The Society of Jesus and the State, c. 1540–1630* (Cambridge, UK, 2004), 1.

67. Lyman Beecher, *A Plea for the West* (New York, [1835] 1977), 135; Samuel F. B. Morse, *Imminent Dangers to the Free Institutions of the United States through Foreign Immigration* (New York, [1835] 1969), 12.

68. *Dangers of Jesuit Instruction Comprising: I. Sermon on Jesuit Instruction by W.S. Potts. II. Review of Dr. Potts' Sermon, by O. A. Brownson. III. Reply to Dr. Brownson's Review, by W.S. Potts* (Saint Louis, 1846), 17; *Independent,* January 5, 1854.

69. Michel Leroy, *Le mythe jésuite De Béranger à Michelet* (Paris, 1992), 53–56; Cubbitt, *The Jesuit Myth,* 132–33; Sir Charles Lyell, *A Second Visit to the United States of North America, Vol. 2* (London, 1849), 340.

70. *Dangers of Jesuit Instruction,* 17; Michel Leroy, *Le mythe jésuite De Béranger à Michelet* (Paris, 1992), 85–87.

71. Edwards Lester to Jules Michelet, November 1, 1846, in Jules Michelet, *Correspondance Génerale, Vol. 5, 1846–1848,* ed. Louis Le Guillou (Paris, 1996), 204. More broadly, see Timothy Verhoeven, *Transatlantic Anti-Catholicism: France and the United States in the Nineteenth Century* (New York, 2010), 29–32.

72. Stowe quoted in Verhoeven, *Transatlantic Anti-Catholicism,* 109; Noah Porter, *The Educational Systems of the Puritans and Jesuits Compared* (New York, 1851), 15–17.

73. December 31, 1847 dispatch to the *New York Tribune,* in Margaret Fuller, *"These Sad But Glorious Days": Dispatches from Europe, 1846–1850,* ed. Larry J. Reynolds and Susan Belasco Smith (New Haven, CT, 1991), 184.

74. Charles Waterton to Fr. Tomei, December 27, 1848, in folder 1, box 69, MP.

75. Leonard G. Kroeber, "Anti-Catholic Agitation in Milwaukee, 1843–1860" (Marquette, MA, 1960), 56–57.

76. Eugene Lawrence, "The Jesuits," *Harper's Weekly* 10 (October 26, 1872): 829.

77. *Petition to the Legislature of Pennsylvania to Prohibit Charters to Churches Not Having Lay Trustees, Debarring Bishops from Appointing Other Than Lay Trustees and the Clergy from Receiving Legacies,* in *American Catholic Historical Researches* 11 (July 1894): 131.

78. Gerald McKevitt, *The University of Santa Clara: A History 1851–1977* (Stanford, CA, 1979), 19.

79. Entry of July 11, 1865, in Richard Lalor Burtsell and Nelson J. Callahan, ed., *The Diary of Richard L. Burtsell, Priest of New York: The Early Years, 1865–1868* (New York, 1978), 100.

80. Tyler Anbinder, *Nativism and Slavery: The Northern Know-Nothings and the Politics of the 1850s* (New York, 1994), 3–51.

81. C. S. Tarpley to head of Jesuit order, July 6, 1855, in folder 22, box 75, MP; Speech of Hon. Bayard Clarke of New York, July 24, 1856, appendix to *Congressional Globe*, [1856]: 955–57.

82. Fr. Anthony Minoux, Historia Province a 1847–1849, [1850?], in Gilbert J. Garraghan, S.J., *The Jesuits of the Middle United States: Volume I* (New York, 1938), 526; Michael Accolti to Roothaan, March 28, 1850, quoted in Gilbert J. Garraghan, S.J., *The Jesuits of the Middle United States: Volume II* (New York, 1938), 408.

83. Roothaan to Fr. Leonard Fava, February 1, 1848, in Ioannis Phil. Roothaan, *Epistolae* (Rome, 1940), 3:173; Fr. Hus, quoted in Joseph Burnichon, S.J., *La Compagnie de Jésus en France: Histoire d'un Siècle 1814–1914 Tome Troisième: 1845–1860* (Paris, 1919), 183–84; Fr. Larkin to unknown, August 14, 1849, in Larkin file, NYPSJ.

84. Georges Goyau, ed., "Un inédit du P. de Ravignan" [1844], reprinted in *Le Correspondant* 330 (January 25, 1933): 199.

85. Roothaan to Fr. Jacob Curley, February 15, 1844, in Ioannis Phil. Roothaan, *Epistolae* (Rome, 1940), 2:484.

86. Roothaan to Rev. Father Peter Spicher, April 14, 1851, in Ioannis Phil. Roothaan, *Epistolae* (Rome, 1940), 2:504–5; Augustus Langcake, Letter of December 1, 1863, in *Letters and Notices* 2 (1864): 65.

87. Anthony Minoux to Roothaan, August 3, 1848, quoted in Schatz, *Geschichte der deutschen Jesuiten, Vol. 1*, 113; Stephen Dubuisson to Luigi Fortis, January 26, 1825, quoted in Cornelius Michael Buckley, S.J., *Stephen Larigaudelle Dubuisson, S.J. (1786–1864) and the Reform of the American Jesuits* (Lanham, MD, 2013), 112.

88. Thomas Mulledy, S.J., "On Liberty," July 4, 1852, in folder 1, box 4, TM.

89. De Smet to Fr. Michael Accolti, April 26, 1850, in file 16707, ABPSJ.

90. Anonymous preface to [Giovanni Perrone's] *The Jew of Verona: An Historical Tale of the Italian Revolutions of 1846–9* (Baltimore, 1854), 1:xix.

91. Letter from R. P. Perron to R. P. Fouillot, n.d., *Lettres d'Aix* (January 1876): 17.

92. John Louis Ciani, "Across a Wide Ocean: Salvatore Maria Brandi, S.J., and the 'Civilta Cattolica' from Americanism to Modernism, 1891–1914" (PhD diss., University of Virginia, 1992), 80.

93. Charles Gresselin, S.J., to Angelo Paresce, S.J., October 1861, in folder 27, box 76, MP.

94. Benedict Sestini, introduction [1866] to *American Jesuit Spirituality: The Maryland Tradition, 1634–1900*, ed. Robert Emmett Curran, S.J. (New York, 1988), 272, 277.

95. P. Keller, "Exhortation at the Opening of the Scholasticate at Woodstock, Sept. 23, 1869," in Marylandiae, box 1010, X-2, ARSI.

CHAPTER 2: ELLSWORTH, MAINE:
EDUCATION AND RELIGIOUS LIBERTY

1. W. Murphy, "Ellsworth, June 3, 1854: Doings of the Mob," copy in ADP; "Housekeeper's Account," *WL* 18 (1889): 136-40; *Ellsworth Freeman*, June 16, 1854.

2. Meeting of July 8, 1854, Ellsworth town records, 1850 to 1863, copy in Bapst file, DD.

3. Interview with Mr. Maguire conducted by Fr. Casson, June 20, 1904, in Bapst file, DD.

4. "Protestant Friend of Mr. Bapst," *WL* 18 (1889): 307.

5. Accounts of the Bapst incident include, especially, Allan R. Whitmore, "Portrait of a Maine 'Know-Nothing': William H. Chaney (1821–1903); His Early Years and His Role in the Ellsworth Nativist Controversy, 1853–1854," *Maine Historical Society Quarterly* 14 (Summer 1974): 1–57; Nancy Skoglund, "Assault on John Bapst," in *A Handful of Spice: Essays in Maine History and Literature*, ed. Richard S. Sprague (Orono, ME, 1968), 107–25; William Leo Lucey, S.J., *The Catholic Church in Maine* (Francestown, NH, 1957), 99–136; James H. Mundy, *Hard Times and Hard Men: Maine and the Irish, 1830–1860* (Scarborough, ON, 1990), 156–62.

6. Quoted in Kathleen Ashe, *The Jesuit Academy (Pensionat) of St. Michel in Fribourg, 1827–1847* (Fribourg, Switz., 1971), 184; Bruno Dumons, "Exils jésuites, réseaux romains et mémoires 'blanches': La naissance d'une fraternité politique au collège Saint-Michel de Fribourg (1827–1847)," *Schweizerische Zeitschrift für Religions und Kulturgeschichte* 106 (2012): 51–64.

7. Quoted in Ashe, *The Jesuit Academy*, 65.

8. Joachim Remak, *A Very Civil War: The Swiss Sonderbund War of 1847* (Boulder, CO, 1993), 28; Gordon A. Craig, *The Triumph of Liberalism: Zurich in the Golden Age, 1830–1869* (New York, 1988), 69–70, 244.

9. Baptist W. Noel, *Notes of a Tour in Switzerland in the Summer of 1847* (London, 1847), 157.

10. Ashe, *The Jesuit Academy*, 128–29, 67–69.

11. *Univers*, November 11, 1847; *Univers*, November 21, 1847.

12. John Padberg, *Colleges in Controversy: The Jesuit Schools in France from Revival to Suppression, 1815–1880* (Cambridge, MA, 1969), 137; Henri-Domenique

Lacordaire to Charles de Montalembert, January 19, 1848, in Louis Le Guillou, ed., *Lacordaire-Montalembert Correspondance inédite (1830–1861)* (Paris, 1989), 613.

13. Bernardin Wiget, "La derniere belle nuit a Fribourg" [1849], in box 1, BW.

14. Bapst to Joseph Duverney, June 10, 1850, in *WL* 17 (1888): 223.

15. Roothaan, "On Desire for the Missions" [1831], in *Renovation Reading*, revised and enlarged edition (Woodstock, MD, 1931), 58.

16. On the desire to work with Indians, see Michael Pasquier, *Fathers on the Frontier: French Missionaries and the Roman Catholic Priesthood in the United States, 1789–1870* (New York, 2010), 114–23. On Jesuits, see Eleanor C. Donnelly, *A Memoir of Father Felix Joseph Barbelin, S.J.* (Philadelphia, 1886), 14. On 1848 Jesuit exiles working with Indians in Canada and the United States, see John Mack, "Osage Mission: The Story of Catholic Missionary Work in Southeast Kansas," *Catholic Historical Review* 96 (April 2010): 262–81; Olivier Servias, *Des Jésuites chez les Amérindiens ojibwas: Histoire et ethnologie d'une rencontre XVII–XX siècles* (Paris, 2005).

17. On Xavier, see Hippolyte De Neckerere to Ignace Brocard, November 20, 1851, in folder 14, box 72, MP. On Râle, see Emma Willard, *History of the United States* (New York, 1831), 103; Thomas S. Kidd, " 'The Devil and Father Rallee': The Narration of Father Râle's War in Provincial Massachusetts," *Historical Journal of Massachusetts* 30 (Summer 2002): 159–80.

18. Robert H. Lord, John E. Sexton, and Edward T. Harrington, *History of the Archdiocese of Boston in the Various Stages of Its Development, 1604 to 1943, in Three Volumes* (New York, 1944), 1:132; James Axtell, *The Invasion Within: The Contest of Cultures in Colonial North America* (New York, 1985), 251–54.

19. Bapst to Joseph Duverney, June 10, 1850, in *WL* 17 (1888): 223; "Corrispondenza di America," *Civiltà Cattolica*, 1st ser., 8 (February 3, 1852), 113–17.

20. Emma Anderson, *The Death and Afterlife of the North American Martyrs* (Cambridge, MA, 2013), 102–3; William Leo Lucey, S.J., *The Catholic Church in Maine* (Francetown, NH, 1957), 74–75; Laura M. Chmielewski, *The Spice of Popery: Converging Christianities on an Early American Frontier* (Notre Dame, IN, 2012), 269–78.

21. Benedict Fenwick to George Fenwick, April 13, 1842, in folder 4, box 67, MP.

22. Bapst to Ignace Brocard, August 16, 1848, in folder 23, box 69, MP.

23. Bapst to unknown, April 2, 1849, in file II C 44a 1885, box 84, WCA.

24. Bapst to Swiss fathers, October 24, 1849, in *Lettres de Laval* (1850).

25. English Jesuits in the 1630s created the only surviving document in an Algonquian language. Maura Jane Farrelly, *Papist Patriots: The Making of an*

American Catholic Identity (New York, 2012), 107. On the nineteenth century, see Gerald McKevitt, "Jesuit Missionary Linguistics in the Pacific Northwest: A Comparative Study," *Western Historical Quarterly* 21 (August 1990), 281–304; Ines A. Murzaku, *Catholicism, Culture, Conversion: The History of the Jesuits in Albania (1841–1946)* (Rome, 2006), 76–77.

26. Bapst to Swiss fathers, October 24, 1849, in *Lettres de Laval* (1850).

27. Bapst to Duverney, June 10, 1850, in *WL* 17 (1888): 365. Index of sacramental records prepared by Richard D. Kelly Jr., copy in ADP.

28. Bapst to the directors, [1855], in Archives of the Propagation of the Faith, microfilm reel 21, AUND.

29. Bapst to unknown, November 10, 1851, in *WL* 17 (1888): 370. The tabulation of marriages and baptisms is drawn from Bapst's pocket record book, preserved at St. John's Catholic Church in Bangor, Maine.

30. Bapst to Charles Stonestreet, May 6, 1852, in file 14, box 73, MP; Gustave Eck to Charles Stonestreet, July 5, 1852, in folder 22, box 73, MP.

31. See, for example, Robert Haly, S.J., to Frank Haly, January 29, 1857, in *Collectanea Hibernica* 43 (2001): 231.

32. Bapst to Angelo Paresce, January 29, 1863, in file 18, box 77, MP.

33. Mary Heimann, "Catholic Revivalism in Worship and Devotion," in *The Cambridge History of Christianity: World Christianities c. 1815–c. 1914*, ed. Sheridan Gilley and Brian Stanley (Cambridge, UK, 2006), 77. On Shanghai, see Paul Mariani, S.J., "The Phoenix Rises from Its Ashes: The Restoration of the Jesuit Shanghai Mission," in *Jesuit Survival and Restoration: A Global History, 1773–1900*, ed. Robert A. Maryks and Jonathan Wright (Leiden, Neth., 2015), 299–314.

34. Bapst to Swiss fathers, October 24, 1849, in *Lettres de Laval* (1850); Bapst to unknown, April 2, 1849, in file II C 44a 1885, box 84, WCA.

35. Bapst to Ignace Brocard, copied in Brocard to Peter Beckx, April 21, 1851, in Marylandiae, box 1009, VIII-2, ARSI.

36. Louis Châtellier, *The Religion of the Poor: Rural Missions in Europe and the Formation of Modern Catholicism, c. 1500–c. 1800*, trans. Brian Pearce (Cambridge, UK, 1997). On Italy, see Armando Guidetti, S.J., *Le Mission Popolari: I Grandi Gesuiti Italiani* (Milan, 1988), 218–302. On France, see Ernest Sévrin, *Les Missions Eeligieuses en France sous la Restauration*, 2 vols. (Saint-Mandé, Fr., 1948–59). On the United States, see Jay P. Dolan, *Catholic Revivalism: The American Experience, 1830–1900* (Notre Dame, IN, 1977).

37. Bapst to Ignace Brocard, n.d. copied in Ignace Brocard to Peter Beckx, April 21, 1851, in Marylandiae, box 1009, VIII-2, ARSI.

38. Bapst to Fr. Charles Billet, April 27, 1850, in *WL* 17 (1888): 362.

39. Owen Chadwick, *The Popes and European Revolution* (Oxford, 1980), 426.

40. Bapst to Charles Billet, April 27, 1850, in *WL* 17 (1888): 362.

41. Bapst to Charles Stonestreet, August 17, 1853, in folder 10, box 74, MP; "A Mission Band's Spring Campaign, 1851," in Robert Emmett Curran, S.J., ed., *American Jesuit Spirituality: The Maryland Tradition, 1634–1900* (New York, 1988), 212.

42. Bapst to Joseph Ashwanden, July 18, 1852, in folder 13, box 73, MP. While traveling in Maine, Bapst made a point of not eating meat on Fridays if Protestants were dining with him. When a group of "six Trustees" in Waterville, Maine, encouraged by an "enraged Congregationalist," proposed putting the title to the land for the Catholic chapel in their own name instead of Bishop Fitzpatrick's, a common practice in the early nineteenth century, Bapst refused to do so. "Fr. John Bapst: A Sketch," *WL* 18 (1889): 85–86; Bapst to Ignace Brocard, August 5, 1851, in Marylandiae, box 1009, IX-22, ARSI.

43. Roothaan to Fr. Stephen Dubuisson, May 15, 1841, in Ioannis Phil. Roothaan, *Epistolae* (Rome, 1940), 3:482. See also John F. Quinn, "Father Mathew's Disciples: American Catholic Support for Temperance, 1840–1920," *Church History* 65 (December 1996): 624–40.

44. Bapst to Swiss Jesuit Fathers, October 24, 1849, in *Lettres de Laval* (1850).

45. Rev. Edwin Carey Whittemore, ed., *The Centennial History of Waterville* (Waterville, ME, 1902), 248.

46. Clement M. Giveen, ed., *A Chronology of Municipal History and Election Statistics, Waterville, Maine, 1771–1908* (Augusta, ME, 1908), 94.

47. Bapst to Charles Billet, April 27, 1850, in *WL* 17 (1888): 365.

48. Bapst to Ignace Brocard, n.d., copied in Ignace Brocard to Roothaan, April 21, 1851, in Marylandiae, box 1009, VIII-2, ARSI.

49. Bapst to Bishop John Fitzpatrick, May 14, 1851, copy in ADP; Mundy, 21.

50. "Fr. Bapst's Narrative," *WL* 18 (1889): 133. Hints of the tension caused by these conversions even marked the 1904 reminiscences of a Bangor resident acquainted with Bapst. See "Account of Mr. Maguire," in Bapst file, DD.

51. Mary Agnes Tincker, *House of Yorke* (New York, 1873), 98.

52. Ignace Brocard to Roothaan, April 21, 1851, in Marylandiae, box 1009, IX-22, ARSI.

53. Bapst to Ignace Brocard, August 29, 1851, in Marylandiae, box 1009, IX-22, ARSI.

54. Quoted in *Ellsworth Herald*, July 1, 1852; *Ellsworth Herald*, July 9, 1852.

55. See, for example, Roothaan to Fr. Nicholas Deschamps, December 24, 1850, in Ioannis Phil. Roothaan, *Epistolae* (Rome, 1940), 2:130–31.

56. Bapst to Swiss Fathers, October 24, 1849, in *Lettres de Laval* (1850).

57. Pauleena MacDougall, "Indian Island, Maine: 1780–1930" (PhD diss., University of Maine, 1995), 183–96. See also Pauleena MacDougall, *The Penobscot*

Dance of Resistance: Tradition in the History of a People (Lebanon, NH, 2004), 157–62.

58. Bapst to Bishop John Fitzpatrick, July 4, 1850, in John Fitzpatrick Papers, file 1.5, box 1, AAB.

59. Bapst to Bishop John Fitzpatrick, July 24, 1850, ADP; Bapst to Ignace Brocard, October 11, 1850, in *WL* 17 (1888): 369.

60. *Christian Mirror*, September 19, 1854. The school fell under Catholic control again in 1878. See MacDougall, *The Penobscot Dance of Resistance*, 133–38.

61. Bapst to unknown, November 10, 1851, in *WL* 17 (1888): 370.

62. Quoted in *Independent*, August 7, 1851.

63. Henry David Thoreau, *The Maine Woods*, ed. Joseph J. Moldenhauer (Princeton, NJ, 1972), 293–94; Fannie Hardy Eckstorm, *Old John Neptune and Other Maine Indian Shamans* (Portland, ME, 1945), 187.

64. Charles Lowell, quoted in *Eastern Freeman*, June 9, 1854; Bapst to Charles Stonestreet, October 24, 1853, in folder 10, box 72, MP.

65. Letter from New York, December 25, 1854, in *Lettres de Laval* (1854).

66. Quoted in *Bangor Daily Whig and Courier*, January 5, 1854.

67. Bapst to unknown, April 2, 1849, in file II C 44a 1885, box 84, WCA.

68. Quoted in *Ellsworth Herald*, December 12, 1853.

69. *Ellsworth Herald*, December 9, 1853.

70. Bapst to Charles Stonestreet, November 7, 1853, in folder 10, box 74, MP; Bapst to Charles Stonestreet, November 16, 1853, in folder 10, box 72, MP.

71. Bapst to Charles Billet, April 27, 1850, in *WL* 17 (1888): 362; Bapst to Stonestreet, August 3, 1854, in file 30, box 74, MP; *Ellsworth Herald*, January 6, 1854.

72. Quoted in *Ellsworth Herald*, December 12, 1853.

73. John McElroy to Bapst, November 8, 1854, in folder 34, box 74, MP.

74. Bapst to Ignace Brocard, October 11, 1850, in *WL* 17 (1888): 369.

75. Letter of October 1, 1847, to October 1, 1848, in Thomas C. Hennessy, S.J., *How the Jesuits Settled in New York: A Documentary Account* (New York, 2003), 79; *New York Freeman's Journal*, October 2, 1852.

76. Bapst to Charles Stonestreet, November 7, 1853, in folder 10, box 74, MP.

77. Bapst to Charles Stonestreet, February 10, 1855, in folder 19, box 75, MP.

78. Quoted in *Christian Mirror*, March 28, 1854.

79. Whitmore, "Portrait of a Maine 'Know-Nothing.'"

80. Bapst to Charles Stonestreet, February 10, 1854, in file 30, box 74, MP.

81. *Eastern Freeman*, June 9, 1854.

82. Herbert T. Silsby II, *A Church Has Been Gathered: A History of the First Congregational Church in Ellsworth, Maine* (Ellsworth, ME, [1962] 2004), 33, 41.

83. Quoted in *Ellsworth American*, April 27, 1855.

84. Quoted in *Eastern Freeman*, June 9, 1854.

85. On Orr in Scotland, see James E. Handley, *The Navvy in Scotland* (Cork, Ir., 1970), 5.

86. *New York Times*, May 9, 1854.

87. Harold A. Davis, *An International Community on the St. Croix (1604–1930)* (Orono, ME, 1950), 196–97; Allan R. Whitmore, "'A Guard of Faithful Sentinels': The Know-Nothing Appeal in Maine, 1854–1855," *Maine Historical Society Quarterly* 20 (Winter 1981): 156–58; Rev. John W. Cavanaugh, C.S.C., *Daniel E. Hudson: A Memoir* (Notre Dame, IN, 1934), 9–10; "The Riot at Bath, Me.," *New York Freeman's Journal*, July 15, 1854, 1.

88. "Street Preaching and Mobs," *New York Observer*, June 22, 1854, 194.

89. John S. Orr, *Freedom versus Despotism or Protestantism versus Romanism; Or Are the People of England, the United States, and Turkey, to Bow to the Despots of Russia, Austria, France, and Italy?* (Philadelphia, 1852), copy in AAS.

90. Quoted in *Ellsworth Herald*, February 3, 1854.

91. Bernard Aspinwall, "Rev. Alessandro Gavazzi (1808–1889) and Scottish Identity: A Chapter in Nineteenth-Century Anti-Catholicism," *Recusant History* 28 (May 2006): 129–52.

92. *Life of Henry Wadsworth Longfellow—with Extracts from His Journals and Correspondence*, ed. Samuel Longfellow (Boston, 1886), 2:237; James N. Sykes, *Common v. Catholic Schools: A Discourse before the Congregational, Methodist, and Baptist Congregations, Delivered Thanksgiving Day, Nov. 24, 1853 at the Meridian Street Church* (Boston, 1853), 12. On Gavazzi in the United States, see Matteo Sanfilippo, "Tra antipapismo e cattolicesimo: Gli echi della Repubblica romana e i viaggi in Nord America di Gaetano Bedini e Alessandro Gavazzi (1853–1854)," in *Gli americani e la Repubblica Romana del 1849*, ed. Sarah Antonelli, Daniele Fiorentino, and Giuseppe Monsagrati (Rome, 2000), 159–87.

93. Quoted in *Ellsworth Herald*, February 3, 1854.

94. Luigi Santini, "Alessandro Gavazzi e l'emigrazione politco-religiosa in Inghilterra e negli Stati Uniti nel decennio 1849–1859," *Rassegna Storica del Risorgimento* 41 (1954): 589.

95. G. F. Secchi to George Cheever, March 23, 1854, in folder 1, box 11, GBC.

96. *Father Gavazzi's Lectures in New York, Reported in Full by T.C. Leland, Phonographer*, trans. and rev. Madame Julie de Marguerittes (New York, 1853), 109–10, 268.

97. Parker to Dr. Convers Francis, March 18, 1844, in John Weiss, *Life and Correspondence of Theodore Parker* (New York, 1864), 231–32; Dean Grodzins, "A Transcendentalist's Know-Nothingism: The Anti-Catholic Thought of Theodore Parker" (paper in author's possession).

98. Parker to Dr. John Ronge, Boston, May 19, 1854, in John Weiss, *Life and Correspondence of Theodore Parker* (New York, 1864), 376.

99. Theodore Parker, "A Sermon of the Dangers Which Threaten the Rights of Man in America," July 2, 1854, in *Additional Speeches, Addresses, and Occasional Sermons, Volume II* (Boston, 1855), 242.

100. *Independent*, January 8, 1852; Robert M. York, *George B. Cheever, Religious and Social Reformer, 1807–1890* (Orono, ME, 1955), 43.

101. York, *George B. Cheever*, 58.

102. "Cheever's Letters from Spain, IV," January 31, 1837, in folio 1, GBC; "Cheever's Letters from Europe," *New York Observer*, [1838?], in folio 1, GBC.

103. George B. Cheever, *Wanderings of a Pilgrim in the Shadow of Mont Blanc* (New York, 1846), 20.

104. George B. Cheever, *The Pilgrim in the Shadow of the Jungfrau Alp* (New York, 1846), 23.

105. Cheever, *Wanderings of a Pilgrim*, 20. On d'Aubigne, see A. G. Dickens and John Tonkin with Kenneth Powell, *The Reformation in Historical Thought* (Cambridge, MA, 1984), 119. See also Elizabeth Fox-Genovese and Eugene D. Genovese, *The Mind of the Master Class: History and Faith in the Southern Slaveholders' Worldview* (Cambridge, UK, 2005), 651–52, 733–34.

106. Ray Allen Billington, *The Protestant Crusade, 1800–1860* (New York, 1938), 265.

107. George Cheever to his mother, November 17, 1853, in folder 5, box 10, CFP; George Burrell Cheever to Elizabeth Cheever, July 9, 1886, in folder 1, box 18, CFP.

108. Anne Lohrli, "The Madiai: A Forgotten Chapter of Church History," *Victorian Studies* 33 (1989–90): 29–50; Giorgio Spini, *Risorgimento e protestanti* (Milan, 1989), 285–95.

109. "A Letter to the Rev. John Hughes," *Christian Union* 4 (April 1853): 169.

110. Spini, *Risorgimento e protestanti*, 291.

111. Lewis Cass on May 15, 1854, in *Congressional Globe*, 33rd Cong., 1st Sess., appendix 681.

112. Martha Finnemore, *The Purpose of Intervention: Changing Beliefs about the Use of Force* (Ithaca, NY, 1993), 58–62. On Jews as a test case, see Abigail Green, "Intervening in the Jewish Question, 1840–1878," in *Humanitarian Intervention: A History*, ed. Brendan Simms and D.J.B. Trim (Cambridge, UK, 2011), 139–58.

113. *Religious Liberty and Protection of American Citizens Abroad: Proceedings of a Great Public Meeting at the Tabernacle* (New York, 1854), 7; Lewis Cass on May 15, 1854, in *Congressional Globe*, 33rd Cong., 1st Sess., appendix 685.

114. "Dr. Bacon's Speech at the Annual Meeting of the Society," *Christian Union* 4 (July 1853): 311–13.

115. *Gospel Banner*, November 15, 1854.

116. On Mortara, see Bertram Wallace Korn, *The American Reaction to the Mortara Case* (Cincinnati, 1957), 24; David I. Kertzer, *The Kidnapping of Edgardo Mortara* (New York, 1997).

117. Senator John Hale in appendix to the *Congressional Globe*, 35th Cong., 2d Sess., February 15, 1859, 165.

118. Quoted in *Independent*, March 2, 1854.

119. Enoch Pond, "Anniversary at Bangor," *Christian Mirror*, August 22, 1854; *Ellsworth Herald*, January 27, 1854.

120. *Ellsworth Herald*, February 11, 1854; *Congressional Globe*, January 9, 1856, 191; "Mr. Leo's Course of Lectures," *Christian Union* 5 (February 1854): 56.

121. *The Bible in Schools Argument of Richard H. Dana, Jr., Esq., and Opinion of the Supreme Court of Maine, in the Cases of Laurence Donahoe vs. Richards and al., and Bridget Donahoe . . .* (Boston, 1855), 32, 59. See also the description in Steven K. Green, *The Bible, the School, and the Constitution* (Oxford, 2012), 36–39.

122. *Ellsworth Herald*, January 13, 1854.

123. George B. Cheever, *Right of the Bible in Our Public Schools* (New York, 1854), 49–50.

124. Annual Letter to Rome, covering October 1, 1847, to October 1, 1848, in Thomas C. Hennessy, S.J., ed., *How the Jesuits Settled in New York: A Documentary Account* (New York, 2003), 78. German Lutheran and Dutch Reformed immigrants to the United States often agreed. See Jon Gjerde, *The Minds of the West: Ethnocultural Evolution in the Rural Middle West, 1830–1917* (Chapel Hill, NC, 1997), 59–63.

125. Bapst to Charles Billet, April 27, 1850, in *WL* 17 (November 1888): 366.

126. Lectures of Fr. Joseph Duverney, "De Rome Pontificae," folder 3, box 1, BW.

127. [Cardinal Karl August von Reisach], "Mormonism in Connection with Modern Protestantism," [1860], trans. Elizabeth Cramer, *BYU Studies* 45 (2006): 58.

128. "Fr. Bapst's Narrative," *WL* 18 (1889): 134–35; Bapst to Duverney, June 10, 1850, in *WL* 17 (1888): 222.

129. Bapst to Fitzpatrick, October 20, 1854, in folder 1.5, box 1, JF. On the watch, see James J. Walsh, *American Jesuits* (New York, 1934), 222.

130. Bapst to Beckx, January 10, 1855, in Marylandiae, box 1009, XXII-3, ARSI.

131. Stonestreet to Beckx, January 30, 1854, in Marylandiae, box 1009, VIII-3, ARSI.

132. Copy of letter sent to Cardinal Paul Cullen, November 23, 1854, box 1, JB; Italian translation of article in *Bangor Mercury*, in Marylandiae, box 1009, VIII-3, ARSI; *Tablet*, November 25, 1854, 742.

133. Fr. Pierre-Jean De Smet, S.J., to unknown, November 28, 1854, in *Freeman's Journal*, January 20, 1855.

134. M. J. Spalding, *Miscellanea: Compromising Reviews, Lectures, and Essays on Historical, Theological, and Miscellaneous Subjects* (Louisville, KY, [1855] 1858), xxi–xxii; *Propagateur Catholique*, November 11, 1854.

135. [Beckx] to Bapst, November 17, 1854, in Marylandiae, September 24, 1853, to June 26, 1886, ARSI.

136. Gustave Eck to Joseph Ashwanden, July 5, 1852, in folder 22, box 73, MP; Charles Stonestreet to Peter Beckx, October 26, 1854, in Marylandiae, box 1009, IX-22, ARSI.

137. Letter from United States, in *Lettres de Laval* (1859).

138. Bapst to unknown, [1861], in file 17307, ABPSJ.

139. *Boston Pilot*, November 11, 1854, quoting *Bangor Daily Journal*.

140. Louis Clinton Hatch, *Maine: A History* (New York, 1919), 1:306.

141. Bapst to Charles Stonestreet, April 28, 1856, in folder 35, box 75, MP; Bapst to Thomas White, February 8, 1858, in folder 7, box 1, Archdiocese of Boston collection, AUND.

142. Bapst naturalization record, microfilm copy in ADP; Bapst to Charles Billet, April 27, 1850, in *WL* 17 (1888): 366–67; Bapst to the directors, [1855], in Archives of the Propagation de la Foi, reel 21, AUND.

143. James F. Sanders, *The Vanguard of the Atlantic World: Creating Modernity, Nation, and Democracy in Nineteenth-Century Latin America* (Durham, NC, 2014), 139; John T. McGreevy, *Catholicism and American Freedom: A History* (New York, 2003), 59.

144. *Bangor Whig and Courier*, March 14, 1854; Theodore Parker, "An Address on the Condition of America, before the New York City Anti-Slavery Society, at Its First Anniversary," May 12, 1854, in *Additional Speeches, Addresses, and Occasional Sermons, Volume I* (Boston, 1855), 399–400.

145. Parker, "A Sermon of the Dangers Which Threaten the Rights of Man in America," 244.

146. *Oration of Hon. Anson Burlingame, Delivered at Salem, July 4, 1854* (Salem, MA, 1854), 13, 16–17.

147. Eden B. Foster, *The Rights of the Pulpit and the Perils of Freedom: Two Discourses Preached in Lowell, Sunday, June 25th, 1854* (Lowell, MA, 1854), 44.

148. *New York Freeman's Journal*, August 12, 1854; James Rodway, *Guiana: British, Dutch, and French* (London, 1892), 127–28.

149. Speech of Hon. Bayard Clarke, of New York, July 24, 1856, appendix to *Congressional Globe*, [1856], 957.

150. Quoted in *Ellsworth American*, August 31, 1855.

151. *The Maine Register and Business Directory for the Year 1857* (South Berwick, ME, 1857), 85.

152. *Ellsworth American*, August 17, 1855; *Ellsworth American*, August 24, 1855; *Ellsworth American*, August 31, 1855; John Claudius Pitrat, *Americans Warned of Jesuitism, or, the Jesuits Unveiled* (Boston, 1855).

153. Quoted in *Bangor Courier and Daily Whig*, July 16, 1855.

154. Quoted in *Ellsworth American*, January 25, 1856. On Maine politics, see William E. Gienapp, *The Origins of the Republican Party, 1852–1856* (New York, 1987), 389–94; Michael Holt, *The Rise and Fall of the American Whig Party: Jacksonian Politics and the Onset of the Civil War* (New York, 1999), 872–75.

155. McGreevy, *Catholicism and American Freedom*, 43–76; John T. McGreevy, "Catholicism and Abolitionism: An Historical (and Theological) Problem," in *Figures in the Carpet: Finding the Human Person in the American Past*, ed. Wilfred M. McClay (Grand Rapids, MI, 2007), 415–37.

156. Mark A. Noll, *The Civil War as a Theological Crisis* (Chapel Hill, NC, 2006), 147.

157. Thomas J. Murphy, *Jesuit Slaveholding in Maryland: 1717–1838* (New York, 2001); Maura Jane Farrelly, "American Slavery, American Freedom, American Catholicism," *Early American Studies* 10 (Winter 2012), 69–100.

158. Bapst to Charles Stonestreet, March 20, 1855, in file 19, box 75, MP.

159. Robert Emmet Curran, S.J., *The Bicentennial History of Georgetown University: From Academy to University, 1789–1989* (Washington, DC, 1993), 1:363; entry of June 6, 1862, in George M. Anderson, S.J., ed., "The Civil War Diary of John Abell Morgan, S.J.: A Jesuit Scholastic of the Maryland Province," *Records of the American Catholic Historical Society* 101 (Fall 1990): 38.

160. Bapst to Charles Stonestreet, November 16, 1853, in file 10, box 72, MP. Bapst does not name Jarvis in this letter, but other accounts including that of novelist Mary Tincker stress Jarvis's support for Bapst.

161. *Ellsworth American*, April 3, 1857; *Ellsworth American*, April 10, 1857; Charles Lowell, *Introductory Remarks More Particularly to Republicans* (Ellsworth, ME, 1856), 14.

162. Lowell, *Introductory Remarks*, 3.

163. Quoted in *Boston Pilot*, October 30, 1854; "The Ellsworth Outrage," *Metropolitan* 2 (December 1854): 676.

164. Quoted in *New York Freeman's Journal*, November 24, 1855.

165. Bapst to Charles Stonestreet, April 8, 1855, in file 19, box 75, MP.

166. Anatole O. Baillargeon, OMI, "Father John Bapst and the Know-Nothing Movement in Maine" (MA thesis, Ottawa University, 1950), 80.

167. Catholic women of Bangor to Burchard Villiger, S.J., [1858], in folder 5, box 76, MP.

168. "Nathaniel Bradsteet Shurtleff, Jr.," in *Harvard Memorial Biographies*, ed. Thomas Wentworth Higginson (Cambridge, MA, 1866), 46. Knowledge of Shurtleff's conversion reached Europe. See Letter from Maryland Province, n.d., in *Lettres de Vals* (February 1859).

169. "Fr. John Bapst," *WL* 20 (1891): 63–65; Fr. John McElroy to Fr. Angelo Paresce, September 30, 1862, in folder 22, box 76, MP.

170. Bapst to unknown, [1861], in folder 17307, ABPSJ; Bapst to Charles Billet, March 5, 1873, in *WL* 20 (1891): 243.

171. A. J. Coolidge and J. B. Mansfield, *A History and Description of New England General and Local* (Boston, 1859), 119–20.

172. John Bapst to John Gilmary Shea, October 24, 1854, in folder 27, box 1, SHEA; John G. Shea, *Catholic Missions among the Indian Tribes of the United States* (New York, 1855), 497–98.

173. A. M. to unknown, December 21, 1887, in *WL* 20 (1891): 413.

174. Bapst to Mrs. Samuel Gray Ward, April 7, 1869, in Bapst file, DD.

175. John Gilmary Shea, *A History of the Catholic Church within the Limits of the United States: Vol. 4* (New York, 1886–92), 536–37; Joseph Moreau, "Rise of the (Catholic) American Nation: United States History and Parochial Schools, 1878–1925," *American Studies* 38 (Fall 1997): 78; Prefect of Reading List, October 4, 1904, in file Ia 3.3a, box 1, WCA.

176. Bapst to Peter Beckx, October 16, 1870, in Richard J. Cronin, S.J., *The Jesuits and the Beginning of St. Peter's College* (n.p., 1983), 54–56.

177. Fr. John J. Ryan, S.J., "Our Scholasticate—An Account of Its Growth and History to the Opening of Woodstock, 1805–1869," *WL* 33 (1904): 134.

178. Death of Fr. Bapst at Mt. Hope Insane Asylum, Baltimore, November 4, 1885, in folder IIc 44.3, box 84, WCA.

179. Bapst to unknown, February 12, 1883, in box 1, JB.

180. "Father John Bapst," *WL* 20 (1891): 405–7; James Perron, S.J., to Daniel Lamson, March 11, 1884, in folder 15, box 1, Daniel S. Lamson Papers, GUA.

CHAPTER 3: WESTPHALIA, MISSOURI: NATION

1. Ferdinand Helias, S.J., *Mémoires du Rd. P. Ferdinand Helias D'Huddegem prêtre missionaire de la Compagnie de Jesus en Amerique* [ca. 1867], Helias biographical file, copy in JACUS.

2. Ibid.; Jean-Pierre De Smet to John Goeldlin, September 23, 1861, in IX d-I, 194, De Smet Letterbooks, JACUS.

3. Helias, *Mémoires*; Helias to Peter Beckx, December 13, 1863, in Missouriana, box 1006, VI-18, ARSI.

4. On the military history, see Mark A. Lause, *Price's Lost Campaign: The 1864 Invasion of Missouri* (Columbia, MO, 2011), 159.

5. Helias, *Mémoires*; preceeding two paragraphs.

6. Helias, *Mémoires*; Helias to family, January 29, 1864, in folder 16298, ABPSJ.

7. Editorial note on first page of Pierre-Jean De Smet, "Une Serment Tyrannique et La Liberté Americaine" [September 1, 1865], in *Melanges Litteraires et Scientifiques* (Brussels, 1865), 55.

8. Owen Chadwick, *The Popes and European Revolution* (Oxford, 1981), 476–80.

9. Auguste Lebrocquy, S.J., "Une Famille Flamande an XIX siècle," *Précis Historiques* 27 (1878): 85. See also Auguste Lebrocquy, *Vie Du R. P. Helias d'Huddughem: Le Fondateur des Missions Du Missouri Central* (Ghent, 1878); Auguste Lebrocquy, S.J., *Litterae Annuae Provinciae Belgicae Societatits Jesu Ab Anno 1873–1874 Ad Annum 1881–1882* (Brussels, 1908), 2–14.

10. Helias to Emmanuel Helias, April 14, 1865, in folder 16298, ABPSJ.

11. Emmanuel-Marie-Adrien-Ghislain Helias d'Huddeghem, in *Biographie Nationale Academie Royal* (Brussels, 1880–83), 8:894.

12. Gilbert J. Garraghan, S.J., *The Jesuits of the Middle United States: Volume I* (New York, 1938), 16.

13. E. de Moreau, S.J., "La vie secrete des Jesuites belges de 1773 a 1830," *Nouvelle Revue Theologique* 67 (1940): 32–69; Alfred Poncelet, S.J., *La Compagnie De Jesus en Belgique* (Brussels, 1907), 41–43; Louis Brouwers, S.J., *Le Retablissement de la Compagnie De Jesus en Belgique 1773–1832* (Brussels, 1980), 20–36.

14. Helias, Considerations sur la Belgique: Diverses formes de son government, [n.d.], in file 13657, ABPSJ.

15. Helias to parents, July 16, 1838, in letterbook, file 16373, ABPSJ.

16. Lebrocquy, *Vie Du R. P. Helias d'Huddeghem*, 27.

17. Helias, Souvenirs d'un voyage de Suisse en Italie, [1826], in file 13677, ABPSJ.

18. Helias, *Mémoires*; "Father Ferdinand Maria De Helias," *Letters and Notices* 10 (1875): 134–36.

19. Roothaan to Fr. McSherry, April 3, 1835, in Ioannis Phil. Roothaan, *Epistolae* (Rome, 1940), 2:478.

20. Joseph H. Schmidt, "Recollections of the First Catholic Mission Work in Central Missouri," *Missouri Historical Review* 5 (1910–11): 84, 86.

21. Fr. James Busschots to Roothaan, March 19, 1844, in Missouriana, box 1004, IV-1, ARSI; Busschots to Archbishop Vincent Eduard Milde, April 30, 1844, in Leopoldine Society microfilm, reel 10, #41, AUND.

22. Entry of October 11, 1838, diary of Bishop Joseph Rosati, in microfilm of the Archdiocese of Saint Louis, reel 1, AUND.

23. Helias, *Mémoires*.

24. James Farris, trans., *The Latin Memoirs of Fr. Ferdinand Helias*, 49 (copy in author's possession).

25. Fr. Ferdinand Helias, S.J., to Archbishop Vincent Eduard Milde, January 28, 1842, in Leopoldine Society Collection on Microfilm, reel 3, #250, AUND; Roothaan to Beckx, May 6, 1843, in letter #350, box 1023, Roothaan Papers, ARSI.

26. Helias to Pierre-Jean De Smet, September 14, 1854, in Helias biographical file, JACUS; Helias to Pierre-Jean De Smet, September 17, 1854, in file 16625, ABPSJ.

27. James S. Farris, trans., *The Latin Memoirs of Father Ferdinand Helias* (n.p., n.d.), 9–10; Helias to his mother, July 16, 1838, in letterbox, file 16298, ABPSJ; Lebrocquy, *Vie Du R. P. Helias d'Huddughem*, 66.

28. Farris, *The Latin Memoirs of Father Ferdinand Helias*, 47; Helias to his mother, July 16, 1838, in letterbox, file 16298, ABPSJ.

29. [Ferdinand Helias, S.J.], "Origo et progressus Missionis Centralis S.J. Missouri, 1838–1867," copy in JACUS.

30. Farris, *The Latin Memoirs of Father Ferdinand Helias*, 3.

31. Helias, in *Berichte der Leopoldinen Stiftung* 19 (1846): 66–76; Helias to Roothaan, January 6, 1845, in Missouriana, box 1004, V-11, ARSI.

32. Peter Verhaegen to Roothaan, September 1, 1842, quoted in Garraghan, *The Jesuits of the Middle United States: Volume I*, 464.

33. William Murphy to Beckx, January 1855, in Missouriana, box 1005, V-2, ARSI.

34. Felix Barbelin, letter of February 9, 1859, in *Lettres de Laval* (1859); Gerald McKevitt, *Brokers of Culture: Italian Jesuits in the American West, 1848–1919* (Stanford, CA, 2007), 244–45.

35. Farris, *The Latin Memoirs of Father Ferdinand Helias*, 6; Garraghan, *The Jesuits of the Middle United States: Volume I*, 459.

36. "Sur les missions Allemandes de la aux Etats Unis," [1843?], in Missouriana, box 1004, IV-2, ARSI. The verdict was similar twenty years later. Ferdinand Coosemans to Peter Beckx, May 18, 1864, in Missouriana, box 1007, VII-1, ARSI.

37. Thomas Mergel, "Ultramontanism, Liberalism, Moderation: Political Mentalities and Political Behavior of the German Catholic *Bürgertum*, 1848–1914," *Central European History* 29 (1996): 159–67; Eric John Yonke, "The Emergence of a Roman Catholic Middle Class in Nineteenth-Century Germany: Catholic Associations in the Prussian Rhine Province, 1837–1876" (PhD diss., University of North Carolina, 1990), 55–58.

38. "German Catholic Activity in the United States Seventy Years Ago," *Records of the American Catholic Historical Society* 20 (June 1909): 105; William

Murphy to Peter Beckx, December 8, 1853, in Missouriana, box 1005, V-2, ARSI.

39. Philip Hamburger, "Illiberal Liberalism: Liberal Theology, Anti-Catholicism, and Church Property," *Journal of Contemporary Legal Issues* 12 (2002): 722. More generally, see David A. Gerber, *The Making of an American Pluralism: Buffalo, New York, 1825–1860* (Urbana, IL, 1989), 280–96; Andrew P. Yox, "The Parochial Context of Trusteeism: Buffalo's St. Louis Church, 1828–1855," *Catholic Historical Review* 76 (October 1990): 712–33.

40. Farris, *The Latin Memoirs of Father Ferdinand Helias*, 3; Helias to his parents, January 10, 1839, in letterbook, file 16298, ABPSJ.

41. Garraghan, *The Jesuits of the Middle United States: Volume I*, 464–65.

42. *History of Cole, Moniteau, Morgan, Benton, Miller, Maries, and Osage Counties* (Chicago, 1989), 679.

43. Bernard Bruns to Caspar Geisberg, April 14, 1837 (copy in possession of author through the courtesy of Professor Walter Kampfhoefner); Adolf E. Schroeder and Carla Schulz-Geisberg, eds., *Hold Dear, as Always: Jette, a German Immigrant Life in Letters*, trans. Adolf E. Schroeder (Columbia, MO, 1988), 166

44. Bernhard Bruns to Caspar Geisberg, August 13, 1838, in Schroeder and Schulz-Geisberg, *Hold Dear, as Always*, 87.

45. Farris, *The Latin Memoirs of Father Ferdinand Helias*, 1.

46. Jette Bruns to Heinrich Geisberg, May 7, 1841, in Schroeder and Schulz-Geisberg, *Hold Dear, as Always*, 109.

47. Jette Bruns to Heinrich Geisberg, October 15, 1842, in Schroeder and Schulz-Geisberg, *Hold Dear, as Always*, 119.

48. Farris, *The Latin Memoirs of Father Ferdinand Helias*, 18, 32.

49. Ibid., 53.

50. Helias to John Elet, January 18, 1849, in folder 22, box 70, MP.

51. Franz X. Weiser, S.J., *Ein Apostel der Neuen Welt: Franz X. Weninger, S.J., 1805–1888* (Vienna, 1938), 55; Francis X. Weninger, S.J., *Memoirs: Events of My Life in Europe and America for 80 Years, 1805–1885*, trans. Susan X. Blakely (Columbus, OH, 1886), 60, copy in box 2B, FW.

52. Jette Bruns memoir [1848], in Schroeder and Schulz-Geisberg, *Hold Dear, as Always*, 128; Jette Bruns to Heinrich Geisberg, December 1850, in Schroeder and Schulz-Geisberg, *Hold Dear, as Always*, 155.

53. Fr. Friedrich, "Quelque Notices sur l'Amerique," July 15, 1849, copy in Gilbert Garraghan Papers, JACUS.

54. D. A. Brading, *The First America: The Spanish Monarchy, Creole Patriots, and the Liberal State, 1492–1867* (Cambridge, UK, 1991), 535–40.

55. Felix Dzierozynski, S.J., "Oppressed Poland" [1840], in folder 11, box 11, MPC.

56. Emiel Lamberts, "Religion and National Identities in Belgium," *Religion und Nation: Katholizismen im Europa des 19. und 20. Jahrhunderts* (Stuttgart, 2007), 37–49.

57. Helias, Considerations sur la Belgique: Diverses formes de son government, n.d., file 13657, ABPSJ; Vincent Viaene, *Belgium and the Holy See from Gregory XVI to Pius IX (1831–1859): Catholic Revival, Society, and Politics in 19th-Century Europe* (Brussels, 2001), 338.

58. Helias, *Mémoires*; William B. Faherty, S.J., *Better the Dream Saint Louis: University and Community, 1818–1968* (Saint Louis, 1968), 62–63.

59. Francesco de Maria to Roothaan, August 12, 1842, in Mont. Sax., Box 1001-III-4, ARSI.

60. Luigi d'Azeglio Taparelli, *Saggio teoretico di dritto naturale appoggiato sul fatto* (Rome, [1849] 1949), 478; Roothaan, in Giacoma Martina, S.J., "Motivi e radici dell'opposizione piemontese alla Compagnia di Gesù," in *La Compagnia di Gesù nella Provinica di Torino: Dagli anni di Emanuele Filiberto a quelli di Carlo Alberto*, ed. Bruno Signorelli and Piero Uscello (Turin, 1998), 421–22.

61. Tadeusz Brzozowski to Peter Kenney, April 23, 1819, quoted in Thomas Morrissey, *As One Sent: Peter Kenney, S.J., 1779–1841* (Dublin, 1996), 135.

62. Francesco Traniello, *Cultura Cattolica e vita religiosa tra Ottocento e Novecento* (Brescia, It., 1991), 62–64, 77–82. See also Taparelli, *Saggio teoretico di dritto naturale appoggiato sul fatto*, 455–85, quotes on 456, 458. For a model study, see James E. Bjork, *Neither German nor Pole: Catholicism and National Indifference in a Central European Borderland* (Ann Arbor, MI, 2008). On regional identity, see Christopher Clark, "From 1848 to Christian Democracy," in *Religion and the Political Imagination*, ed. Ira Katznelson and Gareth Stedman Jones (Cambridge, UK, 2010), 211–12.

63. Borja Vilallonga, "The Theoretical Origins of Catholic Nationalism in Nineteenth-Century Europe," *Modern Intellectual History* 11 (August 2014): 307–31.

64. Charles Lucas Hunt to Ann Hunt, March 12, 1848, in 1848 file, box 2, HFP; Ferdinand Helias to Emmanuel Helias, December 26, 1851, in file 16298, ABPSJ; Fr. John Larkin to unknown, March 20, 1848, in John Larkin Papers, NYPSJ.

65. Roothaan to Count Louis de Robiano, September 27, 1852, in Ioannis Phil. Roothaan, *Epistolae* (Rome, 1940), 5:586; Viaene, *Belgium and the Holy See*, 503.

66. "Elijah P. Lovejoy as an Anti-Catholic," *Records of the American Catholic Historical Society* 62 (September 1951): 172–80.

67. Bruce Levine, *The Spirit of 1848: German Immigrants, Labor Conflict, and the Coming of the Civil War* (Urbana, IL, 1992).

68. Hans L. Trefousse, *Carl Schurz: A Biography* (Knoxville, TN, 1982), 7–19, 172; Carl Schurz, "True Americanism" [1859], in *Speeches of Carl Schurz* (Philadelphia, 1865), 65–66.

69. Steven Rowan, "Franz Schmidt and the *Freie Blätter of St. Louis*," in *The German-American Radical Press*, ed. Elliott Shore, Ken Fones-Wolf, and James Danke (Urbana, IL, 1992).

70. Sabine Freitag, *Friedrich Hecker: Two Lives for Liberty*, trans. Steven Rowan (Saint Louis, 2006), 65, 384.

71. Lloyd S. Kramer, *Threshold of a New World: Intellectuals and the Exile Experience in Paris, 1830–1848* (Ithaca, NY, 1988), 123–27.

72. Adam-Max Tuchinsky, *Horace Greeley's New York Tribune: Civil War–Era Socialism and the Crisis of Free Labor* (Ithaca, NY, 2009), 88–95.

73. Quoted in *Anzieger des Westens*, February 15, 1851.

74. Quoted in ibid., March 29, 1851.

75. Engels to Joseph Weydemeyer, February 27, 1852, quoted in Henry Boernstein, *Memoirs of a Nobody: The Missouri Years of an Austrian Radical, 1849–1866*, trans. and ed. Steven Rowan (Saint Louis, 1997), 134.

76. *Anzeiger des Westens*, April 5, 1851.

77. On the *Revue de l'Ouest*, see Charles Van Ravenswaay, "Years of Turmoil, Years of Growth: St. Louis in the 1850s," *Bulletin of the Missouri Historical Society* 23 (July 1967): 308.

78. Quoted in *Anzeiger des Westens*, February 15, 1851.

79. Annuae Litterae, Domus Saint Louis, 1851, in JACUS.

80. Heinrich Boernstein, *The Mysteries of St. Louis*, trans. and ed. Steven Rowan and Elizabeth Sims (Chicago, 1990).

81. Gerhild Scholz Williams, "New Country, Old Secrets: Heinrich Börnstein's *Die Geheimnisse von St. Louis* (1851)," in *German Culture in Nineteenth-Century America: Reception, Adaptation, Transformation*, ed. Lynne Tatlock and Matt Erlin (Rochester, NY, 2005), 253.

82. Emil Klauprecht, *Cincinnati, or the Mysteries of the West*, trans. Steven Rowan (New York, 1996); Baron Ludwig von Reizenstein, *The Mysteries of New Orleans*, trans. Steven Rowan (Baltimore, 2002). On the United States and Britain, see Susan M. Griffin, *Anti-Catholicism and Nineteenth-Century Fiction* (New York, 2004), 91–114; John Wolffe, "The Jesuit as Villain in Nineteenth-Century British Fiction," in *The Church and Literature*, ed. Peer Clarke and Charlotte Methuen (Woodbridge, UK, 2012), 308–20; Maureen Moran, *Catholic Sensationalism and Victorian Literature* (Liverpool, 2007), 29–76. On France, see Michel Leroy, *Le Mythe jésuite De Béranger à Michelet* (Paris, 1992), 279–332. On central Europe, see Marie-Élizabeth Ducreux, "L'antijésuitisme tchèque au XIXe siècle," in *Les Antijésuites: Discours, figures et lieux de l'anti-jésuitisme à l'époque moderne*, ed. Pierre Antoine Fabre and Catherine Maire

(Rennes, 2010), 523–28. On Spain, for a slightly later period, see Manuel Revuelta Gonzàlez, S.J., *La Compañia de Jesús en la España contemporánea Tomo II expansion en tiempos recios (1884–1906)* (Madrid, 1991), 710–20.

83. *Hannah Corcoran: An Authentic Narrative of Her Conversion from Romanism, Her Abduction from Charlestown, and the Treatment She Received during Her Absence* (Boston, 1853), esp. 118–19. See also Joseph G. Mannard, "The 1839 Baltimore Nunnery Riot: An Episode in Jacksonian Nativism and Social Violence," *Maryland Historian* 11 (Spring 1980): 13–27. On Europe, see Caroline Ford, *Divided Houses: Religion and Gender in Modern France* (Ithaca, NY, 2005), 79–93.

84. Boernstein, *The Mysteries of St. Louis*, 160.

85. Gustav Freytag, *Debit and Credit* (New York, [1855], 1990), 173, 248. See Manfred Hinz, "Catholicism and 'Decadence' in Nineteenth-Century German Literature," in *Catholicism as Decadence*, ed. Marcello Fantoni and Chiara Continisio (Florence, 2008), 182–83; Ritchie Robertson, "Jesuits, Jews, and Thugs: Myths of Conspiracy and Infiltration from Dickens to Thomas Mann," in *In the Embrace of the Swan: Anglo-German Mythologies in Literature, the Visual Arts and Cultural Theory*, ed. Rüdiger Gorner and Angus Nicholis (Berlin, 2010), 130–31.

86. Thomas Bender, *A Nation among Nations: America's Place in World History* (New York, 2006), 127–30; Timothy Mason Roberts, *Distant Revolutions: 1848 and the Challenge to American Exceptionalism* (Charlottesville, NC, 2009), 129–30. On Catholics, see Donald S. Spencer, *Louis Kossuth and Young America: A Study of Sectionalism and Foreign Policy, 1848–1852* (Columbia, MO, 1977), 126–29.

87. N. M. Gaylord, *Kossuth and the American Jesuits: A Lecture Delivered in Lowell, January 4, 1852* (Lowell, MA, 1852), 14; Roy P. Basler, ed., *Collected Works of Abraham Lincoln* (New Brunswick, NJ, 1953), 2:116.

88. *Anzeiger des Westens*, January 3, 1852; *Anzeiger des Westens*, January 10, 1852.

89. Quoted in "Kossuth at St. Louis," *New York Tribune*, March 24, 1852, 6; *Missouri Republican*, March 15, 1852.

90. Louisville Platform, reprinted in Don Heinrich Tolzmann, ed., *The German-American Forty-Eighters, 1848–1998* (Indianapolis, IN, 1998), 97–105.

91. Quoted in *Atlantis* (May 1855): 325; *Anzeiger des Westens*, July 15, 1854.

92. Clipping of May 18, 1849, in notebook #2, box 1, WGE; Adam Arenson, *The Great Heart of the Republic: St. Louis and the Cultural Civil War* (Cambridge, MA, 2011), 53.

93. Selwyn K. Troen, *The Public and the Schools: Shaping the St. Louis System, 1838–1920* (Columbia, MO, 1975), 33.

94. William Greenleaf Eliot, "Lectures on Europe" [1852], in folder 18, box 1, WGE.

95. Truman M. Post, *Voices of History* (Saint Louis, 1851), 53.

96. Truman M. Post, *The Skeptical Era in Modern History; or, the Infidelity of the Eighteenth Century, the Product of Spiritual Despotism* (New York, 1856), 84, 218, 261.

97. Carl Wittke, *Refugees of Revolution: The German Forty-Eighters in America* (Philadelphia, 1952), 139–43.

98. W. Dean Burnham, *Presidential Ballots, 1832–1892* (Baltimore, 1955), 570, 592; Louis S. Gerteis, *Civil War St. Louis* (Lawrence, KS, 2001), 78.

99. Ronald Formisano, *The Birth of Mass Political Parties in Michigan, 1827–1861* (Princeton, NJ, 1971), 305; Walter D. Kamphoefner, "German-Americans and Civil War Politics: A Reconsideration of the Ethnocultural Thesis," *Civil War History* 3 (1991): 232–40.

100. Gustav Körner to Abraham Lincoln, July 17, 1858, in Abraham Lincoln Papers, Library of Congress, http://memory.loc.gov/ammem/alhtml/alhome .html (accessed August 18, 2015).

101. Annuae Litterae, Saint Louis University, 1851–52, in JACUS.

102. Pierre-Jean De Smet to Helias, April 4, 1851, in XI D-2, 229, De Smet Letterbooks, JACUS.

103. William Murphy to Beckx, August 2, 1855, quoted in Garraghan, *The Jesuits of the Middle United States: Volume I*, 563.

104. Pierre-Jean De Smet to Mr. Conway, October 10, 1855, in file 16702, ABPSJ. The letter is partially reprinted in Hiram Chittenden and Alfred Talbot Richardson, eds., *Life, Letters, and Travels of Father Pierre-Jean De Smet, S.J., 1801–1873, Volume 4* (New York, [1905] 1969), 1457.

105. Pierre-Jean De Smet, S.J., to a father at the Collège Saint-Michel, June 17, 1854, in *L'Ami de la religion* 165 (1854): 613.

106. Pierre-Jean De Smet to Peter Beckx, August 9, 1854, in Missouriana, box 1005, V-2, ARSI.

107. Pierre-Jean De Smet to Mr. Conway, October 10, 1855, in folder 16702, ABPSJ.

108. Annuae Litterae, Saint Louis University, 1854–55, translation in George Joseph McHugh, "Political Nativism in St. Louis, 1840–1857" (MA thesis, Saint Louis University, 1939), 161–63; John C. Schneider, "Riot and Reaction in St. Louis, 1854–1856," *Missouri Historical Review* 68 (January 1974), 172–75.

109. P. Weninger, S.J., *Amerika*, July 1, 1888, in Weninger letters and biographical data, English translation, FW.

110. Summary of House Notes, 1849–50, in St. Joseph parish files, JACUS; [Fr. Martín Seisl], Brevis historia ecclesiae et congregationis ad St. Josephi, St. Louis, Mo., ab anno 1846–1853, in St. Joseph parish files, JACUS.

111. *Anzeiger des Westens*, March 6, 1852.

112. McCormack, *Memoirs of Gustave Koerner*, 1:551.

113. Quoted in *Wahrheitsfreund*, February 27, 1851.

114. Weiser, *Ein Apostel der Neuen Welt*, 60; *Shepherd of the Valley*, December 27, 1851; *Shepherd of the Valley*, January 3, 1852; Weninger, *Memoirs*, 78, copy in box 2B, FW; J. Michael Phayer, "Politics and Popular Religion: The Cult of the Cross in France, 1815–1840," *Journal of Social History* 11 (1978): 346–65.

115. Francis Weninger, Relatio [1854], in Missouriana, box 1006, XXVII-25.

116. Brownson to Weninger, September 5, 1854, in I-3-1.

117. Weninger to Brownson, September 1, 1854, in I-3-1.

118. Pierre-Jean De Smet to Helias, April 4, 1851, in XI D-2, 229, De Smet Correspondence Collection, JACUS.

119. Helias, Considerations sur la Belgique: Diverses formes de son government [n.d.], in file 13657, ABPSJ.

120. Helias, *Mémoires*.

121. Ferdinand Helias to Henry and John Hocker, April 20, 1856, copy in St. Francis Xavier parish archives, Taos, MO; Helias *Mémoires*; Helias to his family, January 30, 1856, in file 16298, ABPSJ.

122. Bernhard Bruns to Heinrich Geisberg, October 28, 1848, in Carla Schulz-Geisberg, ed., *Ein Auswanderinnenschicksal in Briefen und Dokumenten* (Warendorf, Ger., 1989), 160–62.

123. Bruns to Caspar Geisberg, September 21, 1850 (copy in author's possession, courtesy of Professor Walter Kamphoefner); John Elet to Bernhard Bruns, July 18, 1850, copy in General and Father Provincial file, CM box, JACUS.

124. Schroeder and Schulz-Geisberg, *Hold Dear, as Always*, 164.

125. Franz Geisberg to Caspar Geisberg, May 13, 1857, in Carla Schulz-Geisberg, ed., *Ein Auswanderinnenschicksal in Briefen und Dokumenten* (Warendorf, Ger., 1989), 210–11.

126. Walter Dean Burnham, *Presidential Ballots, 1836–1892* (Baltimore, 1955), 588; Gert Goebel, *Länger als ein Menschenleben in Missouri* (Saint Louis, 1877), 50.

127. Bernhard Bruns to Caspar Geisberg, June 24, 1860, and November 21, 1860, in Carla Schulz-Geisberg, ed., *Ein Auswanderinnenschicksal in Briefen und Dokumenten* (Warendorf, Ger., 1989), 216–17; Bernhard Bruns to Heinrich Geisberg, November 23, 1860, in Carla Schulz-Geisberg, ed., *Ein Auswanderinnenschicksal in Briefen und Dokumenten* (Warendorf, Ger., 1989), 218.

128. Robert Emmett Curran, S.J., *The Bicentennial History of Georgetown University: From Academy to University, 1789–1889* (Washington, DC, 1993), 1: 227; Angelo Paresce to Joseph O'Callaghan, February 23, 1862, quoted in Nicholas Varga, *Baltimore's Loyola, Loyola's Baltimore, 1851–1986* (Baltimore, 1990), 553; Gilbert J. Garraghan, S.J., *The Jesuits of the Middle United States: Volume II* (New York, 1938), 156.

129. William Murphy to Peter Beckx, August 14, 1861, in Missouriana, box 1005, V-2, ARSI.

130. Pierre-Jean De Smet to William Murphy, June 13, 1861, in XI, 61, De Smet Letterbooks, JACUS.

131. Garraghan, *The Jesuits of the Middle United States: Volume II*, 157.

132. Francis Weninger, Annalen letter [1864], in Annalen file, box 2, FW.

133. M. L. Linton to Orestes Brownson, October 16, 1861, in I-4-a.

134. William Murphy to Peter Beckx, March 24, 1861, in Missouriana, box 1005, V-2, ARSI.

135. Ibid., May 17, 1861, in Missouriana, box 1005, V-10, ARSI.

136. Pierre-Jean De Smet to Peter Beckx, October 20, 1861, in Missouriana, box 1005, V-16, ARSI.

137. Felix Sopranis to Peter Beckx, February 1862, in Garraghan, *The Jesuits of the Middle United States: Volume II*, 158.

138. *New York Times*, May 5, 1861.

139. Michael Hochgeschwender, *Warhheit, Einheit, Ordnung: Die Sklavenfrage und der amerikanische Katholizismus, 1835–1870* (Paderborn, Ger., 2006), 367–68.

140. Weninger, Annalen letter [1863], in Annalen file, box 2. FW.

141. Pierre-Jean De Smet to Edmond De Bare, March 15, 1864, in IX D8, 212–14, De Smet Letterbooks, JACUS. De Smet had friendships with leading Missouri Confederates. See D. M. Frost to Pierre-Jean De Smet, August 8, 1865, reprinted in Joseph G. Knapp, S.J., *The Presence of the Past* (Saint Louis, 1979), 10–11.

142. Garraghan, *The Jesuits of the Middle United States: Volume II*, 158.

143. Joseph Keller to Peter Beckx, October 12, 1864, cited in Garraghan, *The Jesuits of the Middle United States: Volume II*, 161–64; Draft Notice for John Abell Morgan, June 25, 1864, in folder 9, box 10, MP.

144. Entry of November 11, 1862, and entry of October 13, 1863, in John Goeldlin, S.J., diary, 1859–71, in central Missouri files, JACUS.

145. Undated entry [1865?], in John Goeldlin, S.J., diary, 1859–71, in central Missouri files, JACUS.

146. Jette to Heinrich, May 31, 1868, in Schroeder and Schulz-Geisberg, *Hold Dear, as Always*, 216.

147. Ibid., May 28, 1866, in Schroeder and Schulz-Geisberg, *Hold Dear, as Always*, 208–9.

148. [Brownson] "The Expulsion of the Jesuits," *Brownson's Quarterly Review* 10 (July 1848): 415–16.

149. Charles Gresselin, S.J., to Orestes Brownson, February 19, 1862, in I-4-b.

150. [Brownson] "Civil and Religious Freedom," *Brownson's Quarterly Review* 1 (July 1864): 272.

151. [Brownson] "Some Explanations Offered to Our Catholic Readers," *Brownson's Quarterly Review* 1 (October 1864): 472–74.

152. Helias, *Mémoires*.

153. Jette Bruns to Heinrich Geisberg, January 4, 1865, in Schroeder and Schulz-Geisberg, *Hold Dear, as Always*, 199.

154. Arenson, *The Great Heart of the Republic*, 178–98.

155. William E. Parrish, *Missouri under Radical Rule, 1865–1870* (Columbia, MO, 1965), 142.

156. William Greenleaf Eliot, *Education as Connected with the Right of Suffrage* (Saint Louis, 1865), 2.

157. Ward M. McAfee, *Religion, Race, and Reconstruction: The Public School in the Politics of the 1870s* (Albany, NY, 1998); Michael F. Holt, *By One Vote: The Disputed Presidential Election of 1876* (Lawrence, KS, 2009), 51–53, 61–66.

158. Lucas P. Volkman, "Houses Divided: Evangelical Schisms, Society, and Law, and the Crisis of the Union in Missouri, 1837–1876" (PhD diss., University of Missouri, 2012), 544–89. See also Parrish, *Missouri under Radical Rule*, 329.

159. *Dangers of Jesuit Instruction Comprising: I. Sermon on Jesuit Instruction by W.S. Potts. II. Review of Dr. Potts' Sermon, by O. A. Brownson. III. Reply to Dr. Browson's Review, by W.S. Potts* (Saint Louis, 1846), 17.

160. Charles D. Drake, *Address Delivered March 24, 1856, at the Dedication of the First Public High School Building Erected in the City of St. Louis* (Saint Louis, 1856), 15.

161. "Autobiography of Charles D. Drake" [1888?], microfilm copy in Missouri State Archives, Columbia.

162. Quoted in *Daily Missouri Democrat*, April 28, 1865.

163. "Autobiography of Charles D. Drake."

164. Ferdinand Coosemans to Peter Beckx, January 19, 1865, in Missouriana, box 1007, VII-1, ARSI.

165. Helias, *Mémoires*; Pierre-Jean De Smet to Gustave, September 23, 1865, in Chittenden and Richardson, *Life, Letters, and Travels of Father Pierre-Jean De Smet*, 1444–45.

166. P. R. Kenrick to J. B. Goeldlin, S.J., [1865], quoted in Harold C. Bradley, "In Defense of John Cummings," *Missouri Historical Review* 58 (October 1962): 4; John McMullen, "Catholics and the Missouri Constitution," in *The Life and Writings of the Right Reverend John McMullen, D.D.*, ed. James Joseph McGovern (Chicago, 1888), appendix, cxx–cxxxiv.

167. Galusha Anderson, *The Story of a Border City during the Civil War* (Boston, 1908), 385.

168. Entry of July 19, and entry of July 21, 1865, in Howard K. Beale, ed., *The Diary of Edward Bates, 1859–1866* (New York, 1971), 492, 494.

169. Pierre-Jean De Smet to Peter Beckx, August 27, 1865, in Missouriania, box 1007, VI-28, ARSI.

170. Quoted in Parrish, *Missouri under Radical Rule*, 64.

171. De Smet to Gustave[?], September 23, 1865, in Chittenden and Richardson, *Life, Letters, and Travels of Father Pierre-Jean De Smet,* 1444–45; Ferdinand Coosemans to Peter Beckx, September 13, 1865, in Missouriania box 1007, VII-1, ARSI.

172. Annual letter of the Missouri central mission, July 1, 1866, to July 1, 1867, central Missouri mission, JACUS.

173. Douglas J. Slawson, "The Vincentian Experience of the Civil War in Missouri," *American Catholic Studies* 121 (2010): 58–60. For a personal narrative of another priest charged under the Test Oath Act, see Rt. Rev. John Joseph Hogan, *On the Mission in Missouri, 1857–1868* (Glorieta, NM, [1892] 1976), 123–48.

174. *State of Missouri v. J. A. Cummings, 36 Missouri 263* (1865), 7.

175. *Ex Parte Garland* 71 U.S. 277 (1866), 386. The dissent in *Cummings v. Missouri* (1867) was attached to the body of the case in *Ex Parte Garland.*

176. Ibid., 397.

177. John Goeldlin, S.J., Annuae Litterae, 1866–67, in central Missouri mission, JACUS.

178. Pierre-Jean De Smet to Ch. De Coster, January 26, 1867, in Chittenden and Richardson, *Life, Letters, and Travels of Father Pierre-Jean De Smet,* 1462.

179. Francis Lieber to Johann Bluntschili, February 8, 1868, in Thomas Sergeant Perry, ed., *The Life and Letters of Francis Lieber* (Boston, 1882), 379. Similarly, see Francis Lieber, *Fragments of Political Science on Nationalism and Inter-Nationalism* (New York, 1868), 7, 9, 12.

180. William V. Bangert, *A History of the Society of Jesus* (Saint Louis, 1972), 444–46.

181. F. X. Weninger, *On the Apostolic and Infallible Authority of the Pope When Teaching the Faithful, and on His Relation to a General Council* (New York, 1869), reviewed in *Civiltà Cattolica,* 7th ser., 5 (1869): 464–65.

182. Weninger to Archbishop John Purcell, [October] 2, 1868, copy in FW.

183. Weninger, 1868 Relationes, copy in FW.

184. Peter Beckx to Weninger, September 26, 1868, in Missouriana, April 27, 1853, to June 25, 1886, in ARSI.

185. Bernard McQuaid to James M. Early, December 1, 1869, in Harry J. Browne, ed., "The Letters of Bishop McQuaid from the Vatican Council," *Catholic Historical Review* 41 (January 1956): 412; John Baptist Miège to Canon Alliaudi, January 30, 1870, in Herman J. Muller, S.J., *Bishop East of the Rockies: The Life and Letters of John Baptist Miege, S.J.* (Chicago, 1994), 108–9.

186. Joseph Keller to Peter Beckx, January 6, 1870, in Marylandiae, box 1010, X-2, ARSI.

187. Francis A. Arlinghaus, "British Public Opinion and the Kulturkampf in Germany, 1871–1875," *Catholic Historical Review* 34 (January 1949): 388;

Charles Sauvestre, *Congrégations Religieuses Dévoilées Enquete*, 2nd. ed. (Paris, 1870), 83.

188. Tyler Anbinder, "Ulysses S. Grant, Nativist," *Civil War History* 43 (1997): 119–41.

189. John P. Newman, *Religious Liberty: A Free Church in a Free Country* (Washington, DC, 1875), 24.

190. William G. Eliot, October 27, 1875, in notebook #9, box 1, WGE.

191. T. A. Post, *Truman Marcellus Post, D.D., a Biography, Personal and Literary* (Chicago, 1891), 364.

192. Freitag, *Friedrich Hecker*, 379–82.

193. Friedrich Hecker, *Betrachtungen über den Kirchenstreit in Deutschland und die Infallibilitat* (Saint Louis, 1874), quoted in Freitag, *Friedrich Hecker*, 380–81.

194. Annual letter from the Jesuit Residence at Westphalia, Missouri, July 1, 1863 to July 1, 1864, in central Missouri files, JACUS; Annual letter of the central Missouri mission, July 1, 1864, to July 1, 1865, in central Missouri files, JACUS.

195. Entry of July 28, 1863, John Goeldlin diary, in JACUS.

196. Annuae Litterae, Missionis Centralis Missouriana, see copy and translation in FW.

197. *History of Cole, Moniteau, Morgan, Benton, Miller, Maries, and Osage Counties*, 686; Therese Rabstock, SSND, *Called and Sent: A Charism of Service* (Saint Louis, 2004), C253–54.

198. Rabstock, *Called and Sent*, C274. On debates in the 1950s, see Sarah Barringer Gordon, "'Free' Religion and 'Captive' Schools: Protestants, Catholics, and Education, 1945–1965," *DePaul Law Review* 56 (2006–7): 1177–220.

199. Entry of July 2, 1859, in John Goeldlin, S.J., diary, 1859–71, in central Missouri files, MP.

200. John Goeldin, S.J., Annuae Litterae, Missouri central mission, July 1, 1866, to July 1, 1867, in central Missouri files, JACUS.

201. Fr. N. L. Schlechter, S.J., "Missouri: A History of Osage County," *WL* 14 (1885): 360.

202. Goebel, *Länger als ein Menschenleben in Missouri*, 50.

203. Alison Clark Efford, *German Immigrants, Race, and Citizenship in the Civil War Era* (Cambridge, UK, 2013), 214.

204. Ferdinand Helias, "Origus et Progressus."

205. Ferdinand Coosemans to Peter Beckx, June 5, 1869, in Missouriana, box 1007, VII-1, ARSI; Lebrocquy, *Vie Du R. P. Helias d'Huddeghem*, 110–14.

206. Fr. De Smet to unknown, October 11, 1867, in file 16625, ABPSJ.

207. Mark 13:33.

208. Lebrocquy, *Vie Du R. P. Helias d'Huddeghem*, 114; Helias, *Mémoires*. My translation is more literal than the version in Lebrocquy.

CHAPTER 4: GRAND COUTEAU,
LOUISIANA: MIRACLE

1. Mary Dooley to Mother Victorine Martinez, September 20, 1868, 100, in Wilson compilation, RSCJ.

2. Ibid., 97.

3. The baptismal record is noted in M. A. Boland, RSCJ, "The Story of Mary Wilson," [ca. 1915], in RSCJ; Mary Dooley to Mother Victorine Martinez, September 20, 1868, 100, in Wilson compilation, RSCJ.

4. Testimony of Mother Mary E. Moran [1867], in BCANNO.

5. Testimony of Mother Mary E. Moran [1886], in BCANNO; testimony of Mme. Kate Moran [1886], in BCANNO.

6. Testimony of Mother Mary E. Moran [1886], in BCANNO; testimony of Stanislas Billard [1886], in BCANNO.

7. Mary Wilson account, February 15, 1867, 14, in Wilson compilation, RSCJ.

8. Letter from Spring Hill, Alabama, in *Lettres de Fourvière* (1867).

9. Felix Benausse, S.J., to Archbishop Jean-Marie Odin, December 28, 1866, in VI-2-I.

10. Ann Taves, *The Household of Faith: Roman Catholic Devotions in Mid-Nineteenth Century America* (Notre Dame, IN, 1986), 6. On Catholic print culture, see Charles L. Cohen, preface to *Religion and the Culture of Print in Modern America*, ed. Charles S. Cohen and Paul S. Boyer (Madison, WI, 2008), iv–v. For a comparison, see Claude Savart, *Les Catholiques en France au XIXe siècle: Le témoignage du livre religieux* (Paris, 1985).

11. *Grand Couteau House Journal*, November 10, 1850, January 1, 1853, July 18, 1860, copies in RSCJ. On Catholic religious artifacts, see Colleen Mc-Dannell, *Material Christianity: Religion and Popular Culture in America* (New Haven, CT, 1995), 167–73; Saul Zalesch, "The Religious Art of Benziger Brothers," *American Art* 13 (Summer 1999): 58–79.

12. James S. Farris, trans., *The Latin Memoirs of Father Ferdinand Helias* (n.p., n.d.), 3, 6–7.

13. Henri Ramière, *The Apostleship of Prayer* (Baltimore, 1874), 80; Henri Ramière, "Jesus Is Our Life," *Messenger of the Sacred Heart* 1 (August 1866): 148.

14. Henri Ramière, *The Apostleship of Prayer* (London, 1866), 31.

15. Claude Langlois, *Le catholicisme au féminin: Les congrégations francaises a supérieure generale au XIX siècle* (Paris, 1984).

16. Marina Caffiero, *La politica della santità Nascita di un culto nell'età dei Lumi* (Rome, 1996), esp. 183–243.

17. Daniele Menozzi, *Sacro Cuore: Un culto tra devozione interiore e restaurazione cristiana della società* (Rome, 2001); Charles A. Bolton, *Church Reform in*

18th-Century Italy (the Synod of Pistoia, 1786) (The Hague, 1969), 10–11. I
am indebted for this reference and wider context to David Morgan, *The Sacred Heart of Jesus: The Visual Evolution of a Devotion* (Amsterdam, 2008), 17.
See also the detailed account in Michael Printy, *Enlightenment and the Creation of German Catholicism* (New York, 2009), 128–38. Complaints about
the devotion to the Sacred Heart crescendoed again in the mid-twentieth
century. See McDannell, *Material Christianity*, 180–81.

18. John Carroll to Thomas Ellerker, January 23, [1773], in Thomas O'Brien
Hanley, ed., *The John Carroll Papers: Volume 1, 1755–1791* (Notre Dame, IN,
1976), 27; Eamon Duffy, "Ecclesiastical Democracy Detected, II (1787–
1796)," *Recusant History* (1969–70): 324.

19. Roothaan, "On Devotion to the Sacred Heart" [1847], in *Renovation Reading* (Woodstock, MD, 1886), 295.

20. Jon L. Seydl, "Contesting the Sacred Heart of Jesus in Late Eighteenth-
Century Rome," in *Roman Bodies: Antiquity to the Eighteenth Century*, ed.
Andrew Hopkins and Maria Wyke (London, 2005), 215–27. On Jesuit en-
thusiasm for the Sacred Heart, see Joseph de Guibert, S.J., *The Jesuits: Their
Spiritual Doctrine and Practice. A Historical Study*, trans. William J. Young,
S.J. (Chicago, [1953] 1964), 392–402.

21. A. Hamon, S.J., *Histoire de la dévotion au Sacré-Coeur IV: Luttes indécises*
(Paris, 1931), 277.

22. Quoted in *Brownson's Quarterly Review* 23 (July 1874): 421–24; [Francis
Weninger], letter to the editor, *Brownson's Quarterly Review* 23 (October
1874): 534.

23. "Father John Bapst," *WL* (20) 1891, 405–407.

24. Father James Perron, retreat notes, [ca. 1850s], in *WL* 20 (1891): 268.

25. A. Hamon, S.J., *Histoire de la dévotion au Sacré-Coeur IV: Luttes indécises*
(Paris, 1931), 253–60.

26. Roothaan, "On Devotion to the Sacred Heart" [1847], in *Renovation Reading* (Woodstock, MD, 1886), 293.

27. Diary of St. Joseph's College, 1853–60, trans. Frederick A. Homan, S.J., in
SJU.

28. "Special Protection of Our College and Parish during the 'Chicago Fire,'"
WL 1 (1872): 33.

29. Guibert, *The Jesuits*, 500.

30. C. J. Ligthart, S.J., *The Return of the Jesuits*, trans. Jan J. Slijkerman, S.J.
(London, 1978), 18. On Arnoudt, see Gilbert J. Garraghan, S.J., *The Jesuits
of the Middle United States* (Chicago, 1938), 2:106–7.

31. The date was May 11, 1862. Prayer book used by Mary Wilson, 17, copy in
RSCJ.

32. Mary Wilson to Fr. Coghlan, S.J., July 24, 1867, 48, in Wilson compilation, RSCJ.

33. Diary entry of July 28, 1867, 33, in Wilson compilation, RSCJ.

34. *American and Foreign Christian Union* 5 (June 1854).

35. Wogan and Bernard, *The Story of the Church of the Immaculate Conception (Jesuits), Baronne Street, 1847–1928* (New Orleans, 1928), 9.

36. "Characteristics of Romanism of Our Times," *American and Foreign Christian Union* 4 (May 1853): 193; Horace Mann, "Baccalaureate Address of 1857," in *Life and Works of Horace Mann, Volume V* (Boston, 1891), 492.

37. Parisian Jesuits also named their new church after the Immaculate Conception. Pierre-Marie Hoog, S.J., *L'Église Saint-Ignace* (Paris, n.d.), 12; *Propagateur Catholique*, February 3, 1855; Benausse, November 29, 1856, in Mission Nouvelle Orleans letters, FAM, box 56, AFPSJ.

38. Quoted in *Grand Couteau House Journal*, February 2, 1855, copy in RSCJ.

39. Small book used by Mary Wilson (hereafter MWd), n.p., in RSCJ.

40. Testimony of Mary Elizabeth Moran [1886], in *Processus Apostolicus Pro Canonizatione B. Joannis Berchmans, S.J., 1886*, in AANO; MWd, 33, in RSCJ.

41. "A Notice on the Life of Mary Wilson, Novice of the Sacred Heart," copy in RSCJ.

42. Mary Wilson to her parents, July 18, 1867, 37–40, in Wilson compilation, RSCJ; Mother Victorine Martinez, August 21, 1867, 95, in Wilson compilation, RSCJ.

43. Heather D. Curtis, *Faith in the Great Physician: Suffering and Divine Healing in American Culture, 1860–1900* (Baltimore, 2007).

44. "Edward Holker Welch: The Puritan as Jesuit," in *American Jesuit Spirituality: The Maryland Tradition, 1634–1900*, ed. Robert Emmett Curran (New York, 1988), 300–301.

45. "Devotion to the Sacred Heart of Jesus," *Messenger of the Sacred Heart* 2 (December 1867): 434–36.

46. "Freedom of Inquiry and Romanism," *Christian Observatory* 3 (April 1849): 158–59.

47. Ryan K. Smith, "The Cross: Church Symbol and Context in Nineteenth-Century America," *Church History* 70 (December 2001): 74; Charles Eliot Norton, *Notes of Travel and Study in Italy* (Boston, 1859), 210–11.

48. F. X. Weninger, *Original, Short, and Practical Conferences for Married Women and Young Maidens* (New York, 1883), 22.

49. Abbe Gaume, *The Catechism of Perseverance, an Historical Moral and Liturgical Exposition of the Catholic Religion*, trans. Rev. F. B. Jameson (Baltimore, 1864).

50. Quoted in *Grand Couteau House Journal*, July 22, 1848, October 5, 1848, January 30, 1874, copies in RSCJ.

51. "St. Charles," in *Lettres Annuelles* (1867–68), copy in RSCJ.

52. Mother Victorine Martinez notes, August 2, 1867, 46, in Wilson compilation, RSCJ.

53. M. E. Moran to parents of Mary Wilson [1866], 124, in Wilson compilation, RSCJ.

54. [Benedict Sestini], *Messenger of the Sacred Heart* 4 (October 1869): 455–57.

55. Laurence Cole, "The Counter-Reformation's Last Stand: Austria," in *Culture Wars: Secular-Catholic Conflict in Nineteenth-Century Europe*, ed. Christopher Clark and Wolfram Kaiser (Cambridge, UK, 2003), 294–95.

56. Joseph G. Tregle Jr., "Creoles and Americans," in *Creole New Orleans: Race and Americanization*, ed. Arnold R. Hirsch and Joseph Logsdon (Baton Rouge, LA, 1992), 154.

57. Marius M. Carriere Jr., "Anti-Catholicism, Nativism, and Louisiana Politics in the 1850s," *Louisiana History* 35 (Fall 1994): 459–60.

58. Pierce J. Connelly to Bishop Antoine Blanc, September 16, 1840, in V-4-k.

59. Robert C. Reinders, "New England Influences on the Formation of Public Schools in New Orleans," *Journal of Southern History* 30 (May 1964): 181–95.

60. Tregle, "Creoles and Americans," 164.

61. "Father John Francis Abbadie," *WL* 24 (1895): 21.

62. "The Jesuits as Educators," *Semi-Weekly Creole*, October 18, 1854; J. Edgar Bruns, "Antoine Blanc: Louisiana's Joshua in the Land of Promise He Opened," in *Cross, Crozier, and Crucible: A Volume Celebrating the Bicentennial of a Catholic Diocese in Louisiana*, ed. Glenn R. Conrad (New Orleans, 1993), 120–21; Cornelius M. Buckley, trans., *A Frenchman, a Chaplain, a Rebel: The War Letters of Pere Louis-Hippolyte Gache, S.J.* (Chicago, 1981), 19.

63. *Semi-Weekly Creole*, November 8, 1854.

64. *New Orleans Daily True Delta*, September 18, 1855, quoted in Leon Cyprian Soulé, *The Know-Nothing Party in New Orleans: A Reappraisal* (Baton Rouge, LA, 1961), 66.

65. Thomas H. Clancy, "The Antebellum Jesuits of the New Orleans Province, 1837–1861," *Louisiana History* 24 (1993): 327–423.

66. Yannick Essetel, *L'aventure missionnaire lyonnaise, 1815-1962* (Paris, 2001); Paul Duclos, ed., *Dictionnaire Du Monde Religieux Dans La France Contemporaine: Les Jésuites* (Paris, 1985), 17.

67. Joseph Burnichon, S.J., *La Compagnie de Jésus en France: Histoire d'un Siècle 1814–1914 Tome Troisième: 1845–1860* (Paris, 1919), 118–20.

68. Henri Ramière, S.J., *Les doctrines romaines sur le libéralisme* (Paris, 1870).

69. Bruno Dumons, "Jésuites lyonnais et catholicisme intransigeant, (1880–1950)," in *Les jésuites à Lyon xvi–xx siécle*, ed. Étienne Fouilloux and Bernard

Hours (Lyon, 2005), 133–36; Pierre Vallin, "La Nouvelle Compagnie En France," in *Les Jésuites: Spiritualité et activités* (Paris, 1974), 183–88.

70. Fr. Felix Benausse to Provincial, November 29, 1856, in Mission Nouvelle Orleans letters, FAM, box 56, AFPSJ; *Southern Standard*, July 15, 1855; *Southern Standard*, February 10, 1856; Weninger, Latin Relationes, 1852, in FW.

71. March 25, 1865, Ministerium Diarium (1837–80), in GCJA.

72. *Christian Union* 1 (June 1848): 367–68; Jean Baptiste Maisonnabe to Roothaan, May 13, 1848, in Neo-Aurelianensia, box 1002, I-8, ARSI.

73. Fr. A. Doyle to Archbishop Antoine Blanc, February 3, 1851, in VI-1-a.

74. Fr. Felix Benausse to unknown, November 29, 1856, in Mission of Nouvelle Orleans letters, FAM, box 56, AFPSJ.

75. Letter from Fr. Larnaudie, n.d., in *Lettres de Fourviere* (1861).

76. *New Orleans Picayune*, May 22, 1863; *New Orleans Bee*, May 23, 1863.

77. Samuel Kneeland to Brigadier General James Bowen, May 17, 1864, quoted in Thomas Clancy, S.J., and Donald Hawkins, S.J., "Father Theobald Butler (1826–1916): Americanizing the Jesuits," in *Religious Pioneers: Building the Faith in the Archdiocese of New Orleans*, ed. Dorothy Dawes and Charles Nolan (New Orleans, 2004), 118–19.

78. Letter from scholastic, May 14, 1862, in *Lettres de Fourvière* (1862).

79. Conrad Widman, "History of New Orleans Mission, 1566–1896," copy in NOPSJ; David T. Gleeson, "'No Disruption of Union': The Catholic Church in the South and Reconstruction," in *Vale of Tears: New Essays on Religion and Reconstruction*, ed. Edward J. Blum and W. Scott Poole (Macon, GA, 2005), 182–86.

80. Francis Nachon to Beckx, January 25, 1867, in Neo-Aurelianensia, box 1002, II-19, ARSI.

81. C. M. Widman, S.J., "Grand Couteau College in War Times, 1860–1866," *WL* 30 (1901): 44.

82. Francis Benausse, S.J., *Account of the Cure of Miss Mary Wilson, Novice in the Community of the Sacred Heart, Grand Coteau, Louisiana* (New Orleans, 1867), 9. More generally, see Jacalyn Duffin, *Medical Miracles: Doctors, Saints, and Healing in the Modern World* (New York, 2009).

83. Weninger, *Original, Short, and Practical Conferences for Married Women and Young Maidens*, 6.

84. Bapst to Charles Stonestreet, May 6, 1852, in file 14, box 73, MP.

85. Diary entry of August 6, 1867, 29, in Wilson compilation, RSCJ.

86. Diary entry of August 10, 167, 30, in Wilson compilation, RSCJ.

87. Summary of Tribunal, in *Processus Apostolicus Pro Canonizatione B. Joannis Berchmans, S.J., 1886*, in AANO.

88. *New York Freeman's Journal*, October 23, 1858; *Propagateur Catholique*, October 16, 1858.

89. Pierre-Marie Hoog, S.J., *L'Église Saint Ignace* (Paris, n.d.), 22; Jeremy Clark, S.J., "Our Lady of China: Marian Devotion and the Jesuits," *Studies in the Spirituality of the Jesuits* 41 (Fall 2009): 14–15.

90. Robert Emmett Curran, S.J., *The Bicentennial History of Georgetown University: From Academy to University, 1789–1989,* (Washington, DC, 1993), 1: 265; "A Favor of Our Blessed Lady," *WL* 1 (1872): 191.

91. "Residence of St. Mary's, Boston, Mass, 1868–1876," *WL* 6 (1877): 39; "An Account of a Miraculous Cure Effect at Boston, Mass. by the Use of the 'Water of Lourdes,'" *WL* 1 (1872): 69.

92. Fr. Ralph Reinner, S.J., and Fr. Dan O'Connell, S.J., trans., "History of St. Joseph's Parish, 1881–1896," in *Herold des Glaubens*, in St. Joseph's files, MPA. On this miracle, see Patrick Hayes, "Jesuit Saint Making: The Case of St. Peter Claver's Cause in Nineteenth-Century America," *American Catholic Studies* 117 (2006): 13–20.

93. "St. Louis," in *Lettres Annuelles* (1867–68), copy in RSCJ.

94. Alexander Gareshé to James McMaster, September 25, 1871, in I-1-c.

95. Dogmatic Constitution on the Catholic Faith, Dei Filius, Canons, sec. 3, English translation available at http://www.ccel.org/ccel/schaff/creeds2.v.ii.i .html (accessed October 30, 2015).

96. Ruth Harris, *Lourdes: Body and Spirit in the Secular Age* (New York, 1999), 320–56.

97. F. X. Weninger, letter to the editor, *Ave Maria*, March 13, 1886, 251.

98. Felix Benausse to Jean-Marie Odin, January 23, 1867, in VI-2-m.

99. See, for example, Sharla M. Fett, *Working Cures: Healing, Health, and Power on Southern Slave Plantations* (Chapel Hill, NC, 2002), 36–59; John L. Brooke, *The Refiner's Fire: The Making of Mormon Cosmology, 1608–1644* (Cambridge, UK, 1994), 184–208.

100. Robert Bruce Mullin, *Miracles and the Modern Religious Imagination* (New Haven, CT, 1996), 1–30; Alison Winter, *Mesmerized: Powers of Mind in Victorian Britain* (Chicago, 1998), 246–47.

101. On Parker and miracles, see Dean Grodzins, *American Heretic: Theodore Parker and Transcendentalism* (Chapel Hill, NC, 2002), 451–52. See also Theodore Parker, "A Sermon of the Spiritual Condition of Boston, Preached at the Melodeon, on Sunday, February 18, 1849," in *The Collected Works of Theodore Parker: Volume VII, Discourses on Social Science*, ed. Frances Power Cobbe (London, 1864), 149–50; Parker to Dr. John Ronge, Boston, May 19, 1854, in John Weiss, *Life and Correspondence of Theodore Parker* (New York, 1864), 1:376.

102. George B. Cheever, *Wanderings of a Pilgrim in the Shadow of Mont Blanc* (New York, 1846), 136.

103. Quoted in *Ellsworth Herald*, January 20, 1854.

104. Monsignor Gaume, *The Catechism of Perseverance; an Historical, Dogmatical, Moral, Liturgical, Apologetical, Philosophical, and Social Exposition of Religion from the Beginning of the World Down to Our Own Days* (Dublin, 1878), 1:307.

105. F. M. Nachon, S.J., to Mary A. Perry, December 18, 1866, typescript copy in Grand Couteau–Miracle file, ANPSJ.

106. On the eighteenth century, see Éric Suire, *Sainteté et Lumières: Hagiographie, Spiritualité et propagande religieuse dans la France du XVIIIe siècle* (Paris, 2011), 214, 314–17.

107. For the evidence in convincing detail, see Hubert Wolf, *The Nuns of Sant'Ambrogio: The True Story of a Convent in Scandal*, trans. Ruth Martin (New York, 2014), esp. 307.

108. Nicole Priesching, "Grundzüge ultramontaner Frömmigkeit am beispiel der 'stigmatisierten Jungrau' Maria von Mörl," in *Ultramontanismus: Tendenzen der Forschung*, ed. Gisela Fleckenstein and Joachim Schmiedl (Paderborn, Ger., 2005), 79; [Francis Weninger], "Maria von Mörl," *Catholic World* 7 (October 1868): 32–40.

109. Patrick J. Hayes, "Jesuit Saint Making: The Case of St. Peter Claver's Cause in Nineteenth-Century America," *American Catholic Studies* 117 (Winter 2006): 1–32.

110. Testimony of Mary Moran, [1886], in BCANNO; Cornelius Michael Buckley, S.J., *Stephen Larigaudelle Dubuisson, S.J. (1786–1864) and the Reform of the American Jesuits* (Lanham, MD, 2013), 190–92, 219; Robert Emmett Curran, *Shaping American Catholicism: Maryland and New York, 1805–1915* (Washington, DC, 2012), 69–91; Nancy Lusignan Schultz, *Fire and Roses: The Burning of the Charlestown Convent, 1834* (New York, 2000), 51.

111. Quoted in "Hidden Saints," *Catholic World* 51 (July 1890): 536.

112. Testimony of Mary Wilson, February 1867, transcript, in RSCJ.

113. "Ceremonies at the Roman College on the Beatification of the Blessed John Berchmans," *Messenger of the Sacred Heart* 1 (April 1866): 9; Christopher M. S. Johns, *The Visual Culture of Catholic Enlightenment* (University Park, PA, 2015), 77–78, 98.

114. Clemens Boulanger to French Jesuits, November 17, 1842, in *Liber Continens Epistolas Encyclicals Visitatorius et Provincialium Provinciae Franciae Societatits Jesu Tomus Primus, 1820–1886* (Paris, 1892), 189.

115. Giacomo Martina, *Storia della Compagnia di Gesù in Italia (1814–1983)* (Brescia, It., 2003), 161–62.

116. "Ceremonies at the Roman College on the Beatification of the Blessed John Berchmans," 9. See letters from Boero to Angelo Paresche, S.J., a Roman Jesuit exiled to the United States, in file 3, box 77, MP.

117. *The Life of St. John Berchmans, of the Society of Jesus* (Philadelphia, 1888), vii.

118. Entry of April 10, 1866, in Burtsell and Callahan, *The Diary of Richard L. Burtsell*, 256.

119. Fr. Guiseppe Boero, appendix [1865] to *The Life of St. John Berchmans, of the Society of Jesus*, 246, 280–303. See also P. Virgilio Cepari, *Vita del Beato Giovanni Berchmans Della Compagnia Di Gesù* (Rome 1865); Mother Victorine Martinez notes, August 9, 1867, 48, in Wilson compilation, RSCJ.

120. Ferdinand Coosemans to Peter Beckx, June 19, 1865, in Missouriana, box 1007, VII-1, ARSI; Lydia Salviucci Insolera, "L'Ultima Grande Vista Al Collegio Romano Di Pio IX: Documenti Inediti," *Archivum Historiae Pontificiae* 45 (2007): 46; J.F.X., OC, "The Home and Heart of a Saint," *Messenger of the Sacred Heart* 22 (1887): 359–61.

121. *Narrazione Di Alcuni Miracoli Operatie Da Dio In Varie Diocese Del Belgio Ad Intercessione Del. B. Giovanni Berchmans della Compagnia Di Gesu* (Rome, 1866). I surveyed the other miracle reports in the Berchmans file, #397, ADPSJ. See also "Miracle of Blessed John Berchmans," *Letters and Notices* 4 (1868): 309–10; "Miracles of Blessed John Berchmans," *Letters and Notices* 6 (1869): 53–60.

122. Beckx to Coosemans, March 25, 1866, in Prov. Missouri, April 27, 1853, to June 25, 1886, ARSI; Coosemans to Beckx, June 16, 1866, in Missouriana, box 1007, VII-1, ARSI; Eleanor C. Donnelly, *A Memoir of Father Felix Joseph Barbelin, S.J.* (Philadelphia, 1886), 262.

123. Fr. Felix Benausse, S.J., to Jean-Marie Odin, April 12, 1866, in VI-2-k; entry of April 27, 1866, Diarium Praefect scholae, 1838–1907, in GCJA.

124. Boland, "The Story of Mary Wilson," 8–9.

125. Felix Benausse to Archbishop Jean-Marie Odin, February 22, 1867, 117, in Wilson compilation, RSCJ.

126. Burnichon, *La Compagnie de Jésus en France*, 134, 169, 174–75, 275–78; Fr. Jean Jordan to Bishop Antoine Blanc, October 26, 1846, in V-5-f.

127. Walter H. Hill, S.J., *Historical Sketch of the St. Louis University* (Saint Louis, 1879), 74.

128. Khaled J. Bloom, *The Mississippi Valley's Great Yellow Fever Epidemic of 1878* (Baton Rouge, LA, 1993), 39; Henry M. McKiven Jr., "The Political Construction of a Natural Disaster: The Yellow Fever Epidemic of 1853," *Journal of American History* 94 (December 2007): 734–42; John Duffy, *Sword of Pestilence: The New Orleans Yellow Fever Epidemic of 1853* (Baton Rouge, LA, 1966), vii.

129. Rev. Albert Biever, S.J., *The Jesuits in New Orleans and the Mississippi Valley* (New Orleans, 1924), 93–95; Mr. John Sherry, S.J., "Our Southern Houses during the Yellow Fever," *WL* 27 (1898): 53–63.

130. Louise Callan, *The Society of the Sacred Heart in North America* (New York, 1937), 512.

131. Felix Benausse to Beckx, November 1, 1866, in Neo-Aurelianensia, box 1002, II-10, ARSI.

132. Benjamin H. Trask, *Fearful Ravages: Yellow Fever in New Orleans, 1796–1905* (Lafayette, LA, 2005), 68–69; Boland, "The Story of Mary Wilson," 8.

133. Julius Maitrugues, S.J., "St. Charles' College, Grand Couteau, La," *WL* 5 (1876): 24.

134. Entry of March 14, 1865, in MWd, RSCJ.

135. Testimony of Mary Moran, [1867], in BCANNO.

136. Michael Pasquier, "Our Lady of Prompt Succor: The Search for an American Marian Cult in New Orleans," in *Saints and Their Cults in the Atlantic World*, ed. Margaret Cormack (Columbia, MO, 2007), 128–49; Rodger Payne, "Image and Imagination in the Cult of St. Amico," in *Saints and Their Cults in the Atlantic World*, ed. Margaret Cormack (Columbia, MO, 2007), 52–67.

137. *St. Roch's Campo Santo and World-Famed Shrine* (New Orleans, 1925), esp. 14–16.

138. On Seelos, see *Novae Auerliae: Beatificationis et Canonizationis Servi Dei Francisci Xaverii Seelos: Position Super Vita, Virtutibus et Fama Sanctitatis, Volume II, Part 1* (Rome, 1998).

139. Michael J. Curley, C.S.S.R., *Cheerful Ascetic: The Life of Francis Xavier Seelos, C.S.S.R.* (New Orleans, 1969), 286–316; Joseph Helmpraecht, C.S.S.R., to Sister Romualda Seelos, October 17, 1867, in *Novae Aureliae: Beaticationis et Canonizationis Servi De Francis Xaverii Seelos Positio Super Vita Virtutibus et Fama Sanctitatis, Volume II, Part 2* (Rome, 1998), 1308.

140. Peter Brown, *Authority and the Sacred: Aspects of the Christianisation of the Roman World* (Cambridge, UK, 1995), 57–78.

141. Felix Benausse to Peter Beckx, January 20, 1867, in Neo-Aurelianensis, box 1002, II-10, ARSI; Nachon to Beckx, January 25, 1867, in Neo-Aurelianensis, box 1002, II-11, ARSI.

142. Felix Benausse to Peter Beckx, March 4, 1867, in Neo-Aurelianensis, box 1002, II-13, ARSI.

143. *Lettres annuelles de la Société du Sacré Coeur de Jésus 2nd Partie, 1863–1866* (Paris, 1866), 163.

144. Rev. Felix Benausse, S.J., "Extract of the Sermon Preached on the Occasion of the Taking of the Habit of Sr. Wilson," 102–3, in Wilson compilation, RCSJ.

145. Felix Benausse to Jean-Marie Odin, December 28, 1866, in VI-2-m; Rev. Edgar J. Bernard, S.J., *A Miracle on American Soil* (Grand Couteau, LA, 1938), 19.

146. Jean-Marie Odin to Mother Victoria Martinez, December 27, 1866, copy in RCSJ.

147. Mother Mary Moran testimony, [1886], in BCANNO.

148. Felix Benausse to Jean-Marie Odin, January 23, 1867, in VI-2-m.

149. Ibid., February 22, 1867, in VI-2-m.

150. Stanislaus Billand, [1886]; letter from Spring Hill, Alabama, n.d., in *Lettres de Fourvière* (1867); Mother Mary Moran testimony, [1886], in BCANNO.

151. Felix Benausse to Jean-Marie Odin, February 22, 1867, in VI-2-m.

152. Felix Benausse to Beckx, January 20, 1867, in box 1002, II-10, ARSI.

153. Benausse, *Account of the Cure of Miss Mary Wilson*, 4, 7, 9.

154. Felix Benausse to Jean-Marie Odin, January 1, 1867, in VI-2-m; Benausse to Beckx, March 4, 1867, in Neo-Aurelianensis, box 1002, II-13, ARSI.

155. *Morning Star and Catholic Messenger*, March 1, 1868; Benausse to Beckx, January 20, 1867, in Neo-Aurelianensis, box 1002, II-9, ARSI.

156. Fr. Kennelly to Fr. Desmoulins, [1867], in *Lettres de Fourvière* (1867).

157. Sister Pulcherie Poursuine comments, n.d., 73, in Wilson compilation, RSCJ; "Grand Couteau," in *Lettres Annuelles de la Sociéte du Sacré Coeur de Jésus* (1863–66).

158. Diary entry of July 26, 1867, 35, in Wilson compilation, RSCJ.

159. Wilson to Martinez, n.d., 32, in Wilson compilation, RSCJ.

160. Testimony of Camille Zeringue, [1886], in BCAANO.

161. Account of Mary Wilson, February 2, 1867, in Wilson compilation, RSCJ; testimony of Mother Mary Moran, [1886], in BCAANO.

162. Diary entry of August 11, 1866, 31, in Wilson compilation, RSCJ.

163. Account by Mary Wilson, February 2, 1867, 18–19, in Wilson compilation, RSCJ.

164. Testimony of Elizabeth Lascance, [1886], in BCAANO.

165. Martinez notes, August 7, 1867, 47, in Wilson compilation, RSCJ.

166. Relation de la Mort de M. Mary Wilson novice du G. Coteau (extrait d'une letter de sa Superior), [1867], in documents about Mary Wilson, dossier 2: Existent Houses, province of Saint Louis, Grand Couteau, RCSJ–Rome.

167. Diary entry of July 16, 1866, 25, in Wilson compilation, RSCJ.

168. Diary entry of July 26, 1866, 26, in Wilson compilation, RSCJ; diary entry of July 31, 1866, in Wilson compilation, RSCJ.

169. Diary entry of August 7, 1866, in Wilson compilation, RSCJ.

170. Martinez notes, July 31, 1867, 45, in Wilson compilation, RSCJ.

171. Ibid., August 10 and 12, 1867, 49, 53, in Wilson compilation, RSCJ.

172. Ibid., August 13, 1867, 53–55, in Wilson compilation, RSCJ.

173. Statement of Joseph Campbell, January 27, 1868, 87, in Wilson compilation, RSCJ.

174. Martinez notes, Augut 14, 1867, 66, in Wilson compilation, RSCJ.

175. Ibid., 67, in Wilson compilation, RSCJ.

176. Boland, "The Story of Mary Wilson," 14; "A Notice on the Life of Mary Wilson, Novice of the Sacred Heart," 70, copy in RSCJ.

177. Fr. Kennelly to Fr. Desmoulins, [1867], in *Lettres de Fourvière* (1867).

178. Boland, "The Story of Mary Wilson," 15.

179. Comments by C. Zeringue, [1867], 78, in Wilson compilation, RSCJ.

180. "Amérique—Etats Unis (Nouvelle Orlèans)," in *Lettres de Laval* (December 1867): 13–15; "Récit d'Une Guérison Obtenue a Grand-Couteau," in *Lettres d'Aix* (December 1877), 132–35; Varia, *Lettres d'Aix* (April 1878): 169.

181. "Grand Couteau," *Lettres Annuelles* (1867–68); Boland, "The Story of Mary Wilson," 16.

182. Quoted in *Grand Couteau House Journal*, August 30, 1868, copy in RCSJ.

183. Benausse to Beckx, April 20, 1868, in Neo-Aurelianesnia, box 1002, II-14, ARSI.

184. *Grand Couteau House Journal*, November 3, 1878, copy in RCSJ.

185. Nuns were disproportionately involved in miracle accounts. See Duffin, *Medical Miracles*, 54–58, 163.

186. Theobald Walter Butler, S.J., to unknown, January 8, 1886, copy in RSCJ.

187. Fr. John Montillot, S.J., to Fr. Torquatus Armellini, S.J., August 22, [1884?], copy in "A Notice on the Life of Sr. Mary Wilson," RCSJ.

188. Testimony of Mary Moran, [1886], in BCANNO.

189. Testimony of Mary Jane Miller, [1886], in BCANNO.

190. Fr. Theobald Butler, S.J., to Daniel Hudson, C.S.C., March 4, 1886, in X-3-b; *Romana Sue Mechlinnen. Canonizationis Beati Joannis Berchmans Scholastici e Societate Jesu Confessoris. Positio Super Miraculis* (Rome, 1886), copy in RP 3716, ASV; "Ex S. Rituum Congregatione," *Acta Sanctae Sedis* (Rome, 1887), 20:356–64.

191. Testimony of Mary Jane Miller, [1886], in BCANNO.

192. J. A. Conway, "Letter from Fr. Conway," *WL* (1887): 16.

193. "Ex S. Rituum Congregatione," 20:356–64.

194. "Our New Saints," *WL* 18 (1889): 80–82; Chandlery, "Biographical Sketch," *Letters and Notices* 30 (April 1908): 366; "A Letter of Our Very Rev. Father Anthony M. Anderledy to the Fathers and Brothers of the Society of Jesus on Frequently Renewing the Memory of the Glorious Deeds of Sts. Peter, John, and Alphonsus" [1890], in *Select Letters of Our Very Rev. Fathers General to the Fathers and Brothers of the Society of Jesus* (Woodstock, MD, 1900), 370; P.J.C., *Memoirs of San Girolamo, Fiesole, from 1873 to 1893* (Roehampton, UK, 1901), 83–84.

CHAPTER 5: PHILADELPHIA, PENNSYLVANIA: AMERICANS

1. Quoted in "New Church of the Gesu," *WL* 18 (1889): 98–99; "The Gesu Church," n.d., writings of Burchard Villiger file, history of Saint Joseph's College/Saint Joseph's University box, SJU, VSJP.

2. Fr. Benedict Guldner, S.J., Church of the Gesu, 1851–1914, in folder 2, history of Saint Joseph's College/Saint Joseph's University box, SJU.

3. Peter Beckx to Villiger, February 27, 1874, in letters from Father General file, SJU.

4. David R. Contosta, *Saint Joseph's, Philadelphia's Jesuit University: 150 Years* (Philadelphia, 2000), 48.

5. Announcements of February 6, 1881, and October 18, 1882, book of announcements, Church of the Gesu, copy in VSJP.

6. Fr. Edward Welch, S.J., to Fr. Daniel Hudson, C.S.C., March 18, 1886, in X-3-b.

7. Contosta, *Saint Joseph's, Philadelphia's Jesuit University*, 42; *Golden Jubilee, 1888–1938, Church of the Gesu, Philadelphia* (Philadelphia, 1938), 14; Eleventh Annual Report of the Solicitors: Gesu Church Debt Association, March 1, 1910, to March 1, 1911, copy in VSJP.

8. Fr. John Grassi, "The Catholic Religion in the United States in 1818" [1819], *WL* 11 (1882): 31.

9. Cornelius Michael Buckley, *Stephen Larigaudelle Dubuisson, S.J. (1786–1864) and the Reform of the American Jesuits* (Lanham, MD, 2013), 166.

10. "The Success of June," *Messenger of the Sacred Heart* 25 (1890): 553–55.

11. [Burchard Villiger], Account of Sacred Relics in Gesu Church, [ca. 1891], VSJP. See also Carmen Croce, *Memory and Devotion: The Relic Collection of Burchard Villiger, S.J.* (Philadelphia, 2012).

12. The extent to which the Gesù in Rome served as a model for Jesuit churches around the world is a long-running debate among architectural historians. The scholarly consensus registers the global influence of the Gesù, but not as part of a rigid "Jesuit style" now understood as more a creature of nineteenth-century anti-Jesuit polemics than a lived reality. See Evonne Levy, *Propaganda and the Jesuit Baroque* (Berkeley, CA, 2004). See also, for example, Ramòn Gutiérrez and Graciela María Viñuales, "The Artistic and Architectural Legacy of the Jesuits in Spanish America," in *The Jesuits and the Arts, 1540–1773*, ed. John O'Malley and Gauvin Alexander Bailey (Philadelphia, 2005), 271–310.

13. Rev. John J. Ryan, S.J., *Memoir of the Life of Rev. Burchard Villiger of the Society of Jesus* (Philadelphia, 1906), 238.

14. Quoted in *The Gesu Parish Centennial* (Philadelphia, 1968), 8.

15. On the Roman Gesù, see Gauvin Alexander Bailey, *Between Renaissance and Baroque: Jesuit Art in Rome, 1565–1610* (Toronto, 2003), 187–260.

16. Ryan K. Smith, *Gothic Arches, Latin Crosses: Anti-Catholicism and American Church Designs in the Nineteenth Century* (Chapel Hill, NC, 2006), 83–117.

17. Levy, *Propaganda and the Jesuit Baroque*, 16–17, 29–30.

18. James Whiteside, *Italy in the Nineteenth Century, Contrasted with Its Past Condition* (London, 1848), 2:91; William L. Vance, *America's Rome: Volume Two: Catholic and Contemporary Rome* (New Haven, CT, 1989), 95.

19. "Consecration of the Church of the Immaculate Conception, Boston, Mass," *WL* 6 (1877): 150–51. Ellen Skerrett, *Born in Chicago: A History of Chicago's Jesuit University* (Chicago, 2008), 14–44.

20. "New Church of the Gesù, Philadelphia, PA," *WL* 18 (1889), 99.

21. George B. Cheever, *The Pilgrim in the Shadow of the Jungfrau Alp* (New York, 1846), 153.

22. "Autobiography of Father Burchard Villiger," *WL* 32 (1903): 51–80; "Jubilee of St. Joseph's College Philadelphia," *WL* 31 (1902): 7.

23. Gerald McKevitt, *The University of Santa Clara: A History 1851–1977* (Stanford, CA, 1979).

24. R. Ollivier, S.J., to Fr. E. Chambellan, May 27, 1877, in box 56, FAM, AFPSJ.

25. Roger Geiger, "The Era of Multipurpose Colleges in American Higher Education," *History of Higher Education Annual* 15 (1995): 57.

26. *WL* 23 (1894): 470.

27. Lyman Beecher, *Plea for the West* (Cincinnati, 1835), 149; Harriet Beecher Stowe, "What Will the American People Do?" *New York Evangelist*, February 5, 1846.

28. *Chicago Tribune*, May 25, 1857, reproduced in Skerrett, *Born in Chicago*, 12.

29. Bernardin Wiget to Provincial, January 20, 1860, box 76, folder 30, MP.

30. Andrew Greeley, *The American Catholic: A Social Portrait* (New York, 1977), 46.

31. Kathleen Mahoney, *Catholic Higher Education in Protestant America: The Jesuits and Harvard in the Age of the University* (Baltimore, 2003), 127–28.

32. Francis X. Talbot, S.J., *Jesuit Education in Philadelphia: Saint Joseph's College, 1851–1926* (Philadelphia, 1927), 67.

33. On the early Saint Joseph's, see Raymond Noll, S.J., "A History of St. Joseph's College, Philadelphia, PA, before the Civil War" [1962], copy in SJU; Rev. Joseph Berg, *A Lecture Delivered in the Musical Fund Hall, on Monday Evening, December 23, 1850, on the Jesuits* (Philadelphia, 1850), 28.

34. Roothaan to Ignace Brocard, November 10, 1851, in Contosta, *Saint Joseph's, Philadelphia's Jesuit University*, 37.

35. Fr. Joseph Ashwanden to Roothaan, August 12, 1852, copy in Noll, "A History of St. Joseph's College," appendix.

36. Felix Barbelin to Peter Beckx, December 1854, copy in Noll, "A History of St. Joseph's College," III.7.

37. Talbot, *Jesuit Education in Philadelphia*, 78.

38. Gerald McKevitt, "Jesuit Higher Education in the United States," *Mid-America* 73 (1991): 213.

39. Quoted in ibid., 213–14.

40. Miguel Anselmo Bernad, "The Faculty of Arts in the Jesuit Colleges in the Eastern Part of the United States: Theory and Practice (1782–1923)" (PhD diss., Yale University, 1951), 129; Allan P. Farrell, trans., *The Jesuit Ratio Studiorum of 1599* (Washington, DC, 1970).

41. Quoted in *Church and College Society Bulletin* (February 1896): 21.

42. "The Woodstock Academy," *WL* 23 (1894): 322.

43. Roothaan to Bishop Antoine Blanc, January 15, 1840, in V-4-j. See also Cornelius M. Buckley, S.J., *Nicholas Point, S.J.: His Life and Northwest Indian Chronicles* (Chicago, 1989), 151–52.

44. Quoted in Contosta, *Saint Joseph's, Philadelphia's Jesuit University*, 56.

45. Quoted in *Church and College Society Bulletin* (February 1896): 21.

46. Charles H. A. Esling, "Reminiscences of St. Joseph's College Philadelphia, 1854–1863" [1901], history of Saint Joseph's College/Saint Joseph's University, fiftieth anniversary box, SJU.

47. Quoted in Contosta, *Saint Joseph's, Philadelphia's Jesuit University*, 53–54.

48. John Baptist Miège, S.J., to Urban Miège, September 1847, in Herman Muller, S.J., *Bishop East of the Rockies: The Life and Letters of John Baptist Miege, S.J.* (Chicago, 1994), 10.

49. Quoted in Mahoney, *Catholic Higher Education in Protestant America*, 35.

50. Charles W. Eliot, "Recent Changes in Secondary Education," *Atlantic Monthly* 84 (October 1899): 442–43.

51. Timothy Brosnahan, S.J., "President Eliot and Jesuit Colleges," reprinted in Mahoney, *Catholic Higher Education in Protestant America*, 257–70, quote on 268.

52. Quoted in Anthony J. Kuzniewski, S.J., *Thy Honored Name: A History of the College of the Holy Cross, 1843–1994* (Washington, DC, 1999), 183.

53. Read Mullan, S.J., to Charles Eliot, May 25, 1900, in Casey Christopher Beaumier, S.J., "For Richer, for Poorer: Jesuit Secondary Education in America and the Challenge of Elitism" (PhD diss., Boston College, 2013), 23.

54. Fr. John J. Ryan, S.J., "Reminiscences of Some Distinguished Men of Science Connected in the Past with Georgetown College," *WL* 30 (1901): 94–103; Robert Emmett Curran, *The Bicentennial History of Georgetown University* (Washington, DC, 1993), 152–53.

55. Joshua Wachuta, "Where Is Darwin in a Jesuit College Library?" paper presented at the conference Crossings and Dwellings: Restored Jesuits, Women Religious, American Experience, 1814–2014, Chicago, October 2014; Noll, "A History of St. Joseph's College," 18; Contosta, *Saint Joseph's, Philadelphia's Jesuit University*, 64.

56. Quoted in Allan P. Farrell, *The Jesuit Code of Liberal Education* (Milwaukee, 1938), 388–89.

57. Mahoney, *Catholic Higher Education in Protestant America*, 76.

58. Fr. Luis Martín, "On Some Dangers of Our Times" [1896], in *Select Letters of our Very Reverend Fathers General to the Fathers and Brothers of the Society of Jesus* (Woodstock, MD, 1900), 507.

59. Father Joseph Bayma, "Letter from California," *Letters and Notices* 7 (1871): 59.

60. Stonestreet to Blenkinsop, August 24, 1854, quoted in Walter Meagher, S.J., "The History of the College of the Holy Cross: 1843–1901" (PhD diss., Fordham University, 1943), 33. On Loyola, see Skerrett, *Born in Chicago*, 30. On Detroit, see JoEllen McNergney Vinyard, *For Faith and Fortune: The Education of Catholic Immigrants in Detroit, 1805–1925* (Urbana, IL, 1998), 199.

61. Roothan to Charles Stonestreet, October 4, 1852, in Gilbert J. Garraghan, S.J., *The Jesuits of the Middle United States: Volume I* (New York, 1938), 120.

62. Villiger, "On the Law of the Society of Jesus in General" [1894], file 2, box 102, MP.

63. Quoted in *Gesu Church Calendar* (August 1896): 15.

64. Felix Barbelin, S.J., to Beckx, August 16, 1853, copy in Noll, "A History of St. Joseph's College," III.3.

65. "Letter from Mr. Guldner," *WL* 1 (1872): 46; residence of the Gesu, [ca. 1888], file 2, box 81, MP.

66. Bapst to Charles Billet, March 5, 1873, in *WL* 20 (1891): 243.

67. W. G. Ritch, "Jesuitism in New Mexico" [1878], pamphlet in Huntington Digital Library; Dianna Everett, "The Public School Debate in New Mexico: 1850–1891," *Journal of the Southwest* 26 (Summer 1984): 107–34.

68. "Passage of the Blair Educational Bill—Mr. Blair's Attack on the Jesuits," *WL* 17: (1888): 128; Daniel W. Crofts, "The Blair Bill and the Elections Bill: The Congressional Aftermath to Reconstruction" (PhD diss., Yale University, 1968), 151–52, 200.

69. Christopher Clark, "From 1848 to Christian Democracy," in *Religion and the Political Imagination*, ed. Ira Katznelson and Gareth Stedman Jones (Cambridge, UK, 2010), 203.

70. John Ireland to Cardinal James Gibbons, December 1890, copy in Daniel F. Reilly, *The School Controversy (1891–1893)* (Washington, DC, 1943), 240.

71. John Ireland, "State Schools and Parish Schools" [1890], in John Ireland, *The Church and Modern Society: Lectures and Addresses* (Chicago, 1905), 202.

72. Ambrose Rubillon to James Perron, March, 1877, in John Louis Ciani, "Across a Wide Ocean: Salvatore Maria Brandi, S.J., and the 'Civilta Cattolica' from Americanism to Modernism, 1891–1914" (PhD diss., University of Virginia, 1992), 63.

73. Fr. Michael Accolti, S.J., to James McMaster, May 8, 1874, in I-2-a.

74. Letter from Fr. Aloys Bosch, [1896], in Karl Markus Kreis, ed., *Lakotas, Black Robes, and Holy Women: German Reports from the Indian Missions in South Dakota, 1886–1900* (Lincoln, NE, 2007), 220.

75. Thomas O'Neil, S.J., to Anthony Anderledy, S.J., January 15, 1892, copy in David P. Miros, "Rudolph J. Meyer and Saint Louis University: A Study of the Society of Jesus' Theological and Educational Enterprise at the Turn of the Century, 1885–1915" (PhD diss., Saint Louis University, 2005), 197–201.

76. Klaus Schatz, *Geschichte der deutschen Jesuiten, Vol. 2, 1872–1917* (Münster, Ger., 2014), 192–95; "De Americano Liberalismo" [1893], in Marylandiae, box 1010, III-13, ARSI.

77. Simmens to Brocard, June 30, 1850, in file 14, box 73, MP; Bapst to unknown, [1861], in folder 17307, ABPSJ.

78. [Matteo Liberatore], "Il liberalismo e gli Stati Uniti di America," *Civiltà Cattolica*, 4th ser., 6 (1876): 272–86, 529–40.

79. Rev. S. Brandi, S.J., *"The School Question in the United States: A Critical Examination of Dr. Bouquillon's 'Rejoinder to Critics,'" Originally Published in* Civiltà Cattolica, *March 5, 1892* (New York, 1892), 5, 8–9.

80. Salvatore Brandi to René Holaind, October 16, 1892, in Ciani, "Across a Wide Ocean," 168.

81. "Ripugnanza Del Concetto Di Cattolico Liberale," *Civiltà Cattolica*, 7th ser., 8 (1869): 18; Theodor Meyer in Klaus Schatz, *Geschichte Der Deutschen Jesuiten, Vol. 1, 1814–1872* (Münster, Ger., 2014), 230; [Matteo Liberatore], "Il liberalismo e gli Stati Uniti di America," *Civiltà Cattolica*, 9th ser., 6 (187): 272–86, 529–40.

82. Ciani, "Across a Wide Ocean," 93. On Mazzella, see John Ciani, S.J., "Cardinal Camillo Mazzella, S.J.," in *Varieties of Ultramontanism*, ed. Jeffrey von Arx, S.J. (Washington, DC, 1998), 103–17; P. Mazzela, letter of March 29, 1869, in *Lettres de Fourvière* (1869).

83. Ciani, "Across a Wide Ocean," 103–5; "The Grand Act," *WL* 20 (1891): 87–93.

84. Salvatore Brandi to Michael Corrigan, March 13, 1895, in I-l-I; Ciani, "Across a Wide Ocean," 206.

85. *Longinqua Oceani* [1895], in John Tracy Ellis, ed., *Documents of American Catholic History, Volume II* (Chicago, 1967), 502.

86. John Ireland sermon of 1889, reprinted in William Hughes, ed., *Three Great Events in the History of the Catholic Church in the United States* (Detroit, 1889), 17.

87. Theodore Roosevelt to Charles Henry Parkhurst, March 19, 1895, in Elting E. Morison, ed., *The Letters of Theodore Roosevelt, Volume 1, The Years of Preparation, 1868–1898* (Cambridge, MA, 1951), 954.

88. Mary Christine Athans, B.V.M., *"To Work for the Whole People": John Ireland's Seminary in St. Paul* (New York, 2002), 79; Gerald P. Fogarty, *The Vatican and the American Hierarchy from 1870 to 1965* (Collegeville, PA, 1985), 149.

89. Denis O'Connell to John Ireland, September 14, 1897, in Fogarty, *The Vatican and the American Hierarchy*, 158; Denis O'Connell to Sabine Parravicino, February 1, 1898, copy in microfilm reel #1, Americanist collection, AUND.

90. M. F. Brunetière to Mons. J. J. Keane, December 2, 1898, copy in Italian translation in Ornella Pellegrono Confessore, *L'Americanismo cattolico in Italia* (Rome, 1984), 199.

91. Edward Purbrick to Michael Corrigan, June 26, 1898, in Fogarty, *The Vatican and the American Hierarchy*, 168.

92. Schatz, *Geschichte der deutschen Jesuiten, Vol. 2*, 193–95; José Ramón Eguillor, Manuel Revuelta, and Rafael M. Sanz de Diego, eds., *Memorias Del P. Luis Martín General de la Compañía de Jesús (1846–1906), Vol. 2* (Madrid, 1988). The quotations are from unpublished section 2317. Some of Martín's memoir is as yet unpublished, and I am grateful to David Schultenover, S.J., for providing me with these copies of the Spanish-language originals housed in the Jesuit Aragón Province archives in Spain. On Martín, see David G. Schultenover, S.J., *A View from Rome: On the Eve of the Modernist Crisis* (Bronx, NY, 1993).

93. Brandi, quoted in Ciani, "Across a Wide Ocean," 151. Fr. Filippo Cardella, quoted in Gerald McKevitt, *Brokers of Culture: Italian Jesuits in the American West, 1848–1919* (Stanford, CA, 2007), 267. See also Fr. Filippo Cardella, S.J., "Las Misiones en la República de Nicaragua," copy in *Los Jesuitas En Nicaragua En El Siglo XIX* (San José, Costa Rica, 1984), 532–44.

94. Martín, *Memorias*, unpublished sections 2307–08, 2310 (copy in possession of author).

95. Ibid., 2309, 2311.

96. Brandi to Corrigan, October 12, 1898, in I-l-I; Brandi to Corrigan, January 2, 1899, in I-l-i.

97. Quoted in McKevitt, *Brokers of Culture*, 267.

98. *Testem Benevolentiae* [1899], in Ellis, *Documents of American Catholic History, Volume II*, 540; [Brandi], "Leone XIII e l'Americanismo," *Civiltà Cattolica*, 17th ser., 5 (March 18, 1899): 641, 647.

99. Martín, *Memorias*, sections 2312, 2317.

100. Villiger, "On the Law of the Society of Jesus in General" [1894], in file 2, box 102, MP.

101. Rev. John J. Ryan, S.J., *Memoir of the Life of Rev. Burchard Villiger of the Society of Jesus* (Philadelphia, 1906), 267.

102. Quoted in ibid., 172.

103. Varia, *WL* 23 (1894): 192.

104. Ryan, *Memoir of the Life of Rev. Burchard Villiger of the Society of Jesus*, 301.

105. "Prominent Jesuit Very Ill," *New York Times*, November 4, 1902, 1; Ryan, *Memoir of the Life of Rev. Burchard Villiger*, 306–8.

106. McKevitt, *Brokers of Culture*, 328.

107. Ibid., 272.

108. Thomas Gannon to Fr. Rudolph Meyer, August 1903, in Marylandiae, box 1013, II-19, ARSI, copy in APPSJ; McKevitt, *Brokers of Culture*, 294.

109. Thomas Gannon to Fr. Rudolph Meyer, August 1903, in Marylandiae, box 1013, II-19, ARSI, copy in APPSJ.

110. Rudolph J. Meyer, "Church and State," *American Catholic Quarterly Review* 22 (January 1897): 110–11.

111. Contosta, *Saint Joseph's, Philadelphia's Jesuit University*, 51.

112. Schatz, *Geschichte der deutschen Jesuiten, Vol. 1*, 222.

113. Fr. Matteo Liberatore, S.J., *Principles of Political Economy*, trans. Edward Heneage Dering (London, 1891), 194.

114. The manuscripts were first published in Giovanni Antonazzi and Gabriele de Rosa, eds., *L'enciclica Rerum Novarum e il suo temp* (Rome, [1957] 1991). I rely on the informative summary in John Moloney, "The Making of Rerum Novarum, April 1890–May 1891," in *The Church Faces the Modern World: Rerum Novarum and Its Impact*, ed. Paul Furlong and David Curtis (Stratford-upon-Avon, UK, 1994), 27–39.

115. Daniel T. Rodgers, *Atlantic Crossings: Social Politics in a Progressive Age* (Cambridge, MA, 1998), 76–119.

116. Rupert Ederer, trans., *Heinrich Pesch on Solidarist Economics: Excerpts from the Lehrbuch der Nationalökonomie* (Lanham, MD, 1998), 74. Pesch is also quoted in Joseph N. Moody, *Church and Society: Catholic Social and Political Thought and Movements, 1789–1950* (New York, 1953), 547.

117. John T. McGreevy, *Catholicism and American Freedom: A History* (New York, 2003); Contosta, *Saint Joseph's, Philadelphia's Jesuit University*, 74.

118. Franz Wernz to Joseph Hanselman, October 30, 1906, in folder 7, box 124, MP.

119. Ciani, "Across a Wide Ocean," 380. More generally, see Giovanni Sale, *'La Civilta Cattolica' Nella Crisi Modernista (1900–1907)* (Milan, 2001).

120. Manuel Revuelta Gonzàlez, S.J., *La Compañía de Jesús en la España Contemporánea Tomo I Supresión y reinstalación (1868–1883)* (Madrid, 1984), 670; Curran, *The Bicentennial History*, I: 65.

121. Contosta, *Saint Joseph's, Philadelphia's Jesuit University*, 50–51, 69. The pattern of accepting fees was similar in England and Ireland. See Bernard Basset, S.J., *The English Jesuits: From Campion to Martindale* (New York, 1968), 403; Louis McRedmond, *To the Greater Glory: A History of the Irish*

Jesuits (Dublin, 1991), 161–63. On the permission to accept fees, see General Congregation 22, decree 42 [1853], in John W. Padberg, S.J., Martín D. O'Keefe, S.J., and John L. McCarthy, S.J., eds., *For Matters of Greater Moment: The First Thirty Jesuit General Congregations. A Brief History and a Translation of the Decrees* (Saint Louis, 1994), 456.

122. K.M.T., "The Ratio Studiorum and the American College," *WL* 27 (1898): 182.

123. Broadly and brilliantly, with specific reference to the German Jesuit Hermann Muckermann and Austrian Jesuit Georg Bichlmair, see John Connelly, *From Enemy to Brother: The Revolution in Catholic Teaching on the Jews, 1933–1965* (Cambridge, MA, 2012), esp. 11–64. On *Civiltà Cattolica* especially, see David I. Kertzer, *The Popes against the Jews: The Vatican's Role in the Rise of Modern Anti-Semitism* (New York, 2001), 135–46; Ruggero Taradel and Barbara Raggi, *La segregazione amichevole: La Civiltà Cattolica e la questione ebraica, 1850–1945* (Rome, 2000); José David Lebovitch Dahl, "The Role of the Roman Catholic Church in the Formation of Modern Anti-Semitism: *La Civiltà Cattolica*, 1850–1879," *Modern Judaism* 23 (2003): 197. On Jesuit anti-Semitism in the United States, see Peter D'Agostino, *Rome in America: Transnational Catholic Ideology from the Risorgimento to Fascism* (Chapel Hill, NC, 2004), 87–88.

124. Countess De Courson, *The Jesuits and Their Centenary Celebration* (Dublin, 1914).

125. Gabriel Codina, S.J., "A Century of Jesuit Education, 1900–2000," in *Jesuits: A Yearbook of the Society of Jesus*, ed. Jose De Vera, S.J. (Rome, 1999), copy at http://www.bc.edu/offices/mission/ (accessed November 1, 2015).

126. José Ma. Brinsó, S.J., *El Primer Centenario del Restablecimiento de la Compañia de Jesús: 1814–1914* (Manila, 1914), 29.

127. Schatz, *Geschichte der deutschen Jesuiten, Vol. 1*, 257–59; Christian Rak, *Krieg, Nation und Konfession: Die Erfahrung des deutsch-französichen Krieges von 1870/71* (Paderborn, Ger., 2004), 384–98, esp. 394.

128. John Ireland, "Patriotism" [1894], in Ireland, *The Church and Modern Society*, 143; Schatz, *Geschichte der deutschen Jesuiten, Vol. 2*, 84–85.

129. Hew Strachan, *The First World War: Volume I: To Arms* (New York, 2001), 1117–19.

130. Schatz, *Geshichte der deutschen Jesuiten, Vol. 2*, 317–321; Róisín Healy, *The Jesuit Specter in Imperial Germany*, (Boston, 2003), 215–226; Giacoma Martina, *Storia della Compagnia di Gesù in Italia, (1814–1983)*, (Brescia, It., 2003), 178–79, 255–257.

131. Marie-Claude Flageat, *Les jésuites françaises dans la Grande Guerre: Témoins, victimes, héros, apotres* (Paris, 2008), 368–372.

132. Ibid.

133. Lucien Roure, "Patriotisme, Impérialisme, Militarisme," *Études* 142 (March 1915): 433–53, quotes on 436, 453.

134. Woodrow Wilson to Fr. Joseph Rockwell, August 6, 1916, in file 3, box 88, MP.

135. Francis X. Talbot, S.J., *Jesuit Education in Philadelphia: Saint Joseph's College, 1851–1926* (Philadelphia, 1927), 78.

136. "War Aims Course" [1918], I.A 3.3.c, box 2, WCA. More generally, see David M. Kennedy, *Over Here: The First World War and American Society* (New York, 1980), 57–59. French Jesuits made much the same argument. See Flageat, *Les jésuites français dans la Grande Guerre*, 410–11. On Kant, see Wlodimir Ledóchowki, S.J., "On Following the Doctrine of St. Thomas" [1917], in *Selected Writings of Father Ledóchowski* (Chicago, 1945), 491.

137. Joseph H. Rockwell, S.J., circular letter, December 14, 1918, in I.A 3.3.c, box 2, WCA.

138. Contosta, *Saint Joseph's, Philadelphia's Jesuit University*, 203–4. More generally, see Philip Gleason, *Contending with Modernity: Catholic Higher Education in the Twentieth Century* (New York, 1996), 62–80. On Latin, see Casey Christopher Beaumier, S.J., "For Richer, for Poorer: Jesuit Secondary Education in America and the Challenge of Elitism" (PhD diss., Boston College, 2013), 107–17.

139. "Our Country First and Always," *America* 17 (May 19, 1917): 140.

140. Circular letter from Anthony Maas, S.J., December 19, 1917, in IA 3.3b, box 1, WCA.

141. Varia, *WL* 46 (1917): 426–27.

142. "War Notes about Ours," *WL* 46 (1917): 393.

143. Quotes for the two paragraphs are from Unknown to Fr. Vachel Brown, April 19, 1918; D. Byrne Flynn to his mother, December 25, 1918; D. Byrne Flynn to his mother, January 21, 1919; Joseph Moran to Fr. Vachel Brown, April 5, 1919; Clare Finerty to Fr. Vachel Brown, September 16, 1918; Clare Finerty to Fr. Brown, Christmas, 1918, all in World War I letters file, SJU.

CHAPTER 6: MANILA, PHILIPPINES: EMPIRE

1. Quoted in Frank T. Reuter, *Catholic Influence on American Colonial Policies, 1898–1904* (Austin, TX, 1967), 8. More generally, see Matthew McCullough, *The Cross of War: Christian Nationalism and U.S. Expansion in the Spanish-American War* (Madison, WI, 2014); James Barrett, *The Irish Way: Becoming American in the Multiethnic American City* (New York, 2012), 244–48.

2. Henry Charles Lea, "The Decadence of Spain," *Atlantic Monthly* 82 (July 1898): 42. More generally, see Richard L. Kagan, "Prescott's Paradigm:

American Historical Scholarship and the Decline of Spain," in *Imagined Histories: American Historians Interpret the Past*, ed. Anthony Mohlo and Gordon S. Wood (Princeton, NJ, 1998), 324–48.

3. John Ireland to Denis O'Connell, May 2, 1898, copy in ADR.

4. Denis O'Connell to John Ireland, May 24, 1898, reprinted in Thomas McAvoy, *The Americanist Heresy in Roman Catholicism, 1895–1900* (Notre Dame, IN, 1963), 163–66.

5. Denis O'Connell to Sabine Parravicino, June 10, 1898, copy in microfilm reel #1, Americanist collection, AUND.

6. Father F. J. Gasson, S.J., in *Boston Herald*, June 20, 1898, quoted in John Bilski, "The Church and American Imperialism, 1800–1900," *Historical Records and Studies* 47 (1959): 147.

7. Andrew Preston, *Sword of the Spirit, Shield of Faith: Religion in American War and Diplomacy* (New York, 2012), 223; F. J. Gasson, quoted in *New York Freeman's Journal*, December 30, 1899.

8. Quoted in *Revista Católica*, June 19, 1898.

9. "Stati Uniti," *Civiltà Cattolica*, 17th ser., 5 (March 11, 1899): 749–55.

10. José Ramón Eguillor, Manuel Revuelta, and Rafael M. Sanz de Diego, eds., *Memorias Del P. Luis Martín General de la Compañía de Jesús (1846–1906)* (Madrid, 1988), 2:720–21.

11. Maunel Revuelta González, S.J., *La Compañia de Jesús en la España Contemporánea Supresión y reinstalación (1868–1883) Vol. 1* (Madrid, 1984), 1079; "Cronaca," *Civiltà Cattolica*, 8th ser., 5 (May 14, 1898): 493–94.

12. Quoted in Eguillor, Revuelta, and de Diego, *Memorias Del P. Luis Martín General de la Compañía de Jesús (1846–1906)*, 720–21.

13. Samy Zaka, "Education and Civilization in the Third Republic: The University Saint-Joseph, 1875–1914" (PhD diss., University of Notre Dame, 2006), 45.

14. "Fr. Beckx, on BB. Canisius and Berchmans" [1865], in *Renovation Reading* (Woodstock, MD, 1886), 353. More generally, see Duncan Bell, "Empire and Imperialism," in *The Cambridge History of Nineteenth-Century Political Thought*, ed. Gareth Stedman Jones and Gregory Claeys (Cambridge, UK, 2011), 864–92.

15. J. P. Daughton, *An Empire Divided: Religion, Republicanism, and the Making of French Colonialism, 1880–1914* (New York, 2006); Matthew Burrows, " 'Mission Civilisatrice': French Cultural Policy in the Middle East, 1860–1914," *Historical Journal* 29 (1986): 109–35. On Italy, see R.J.B. Bosworth, *Italy and the Wider World, 1860–1960* (London, 1996), 121.

16. Bapst to Joseph Duverney, June 10, 1850, in *WL* 17 (1888): 225.

17. L. B. Palladino, S.J., *Education for the Indian: Fancy and Reason on the Subject* (New York, 1892), 10.

18. Jeremiah Rossi, "The Rocky Mountains," *WL* 17 (1888): 73.

19. Walter L. Williams, "United States Indian Policy and the Debate over Philippine Annexation: Implications for the Origins of American Imperialism," *Journal of American History* 66 (March 1980): 810–31.

20. González, *La Compañia de Jesús en la España Contemporánea*, 228.

21. Salvador M. Viñas to Fr. Pio Pi, S.J., November 23, 1898, in José S. Arcilla, S.J., ed., *Jesuit Missionary Letters from Mindanao, Volume One: The Rio Grande Mission* (Quezon City, 1990), 478; Manuel Valles, S.J., to Fr. Pio Pi, S.J., October 25, 1898, in Jose S. Arcilla, ed. and trans., *Jesuit Missionary Letters from Mindanao, Volume Five: The Surigao Mission* (Quezon City, 1990), 577, 582; Jose S. Arcilla, S.J., "The Jesuits during the Philippine Revolution," *Philippine Studies* 35 (1987): 302; Miguel Saderra Masó, S.J., *Philippine Jesuits, 1581–1768 and 1859–1924*, trans. Leo Cullum (Manila, [1924] 1974), 69–122.

22. Manuel Valles to the mission superior, October 25, 1898, in Fr. Pio Pi, "Carta Prolongo," in P. Pablo Pastells, *Misión de la Compaña de Jesús de Filipinas en el siglo XIX* (Barcelona, 1917), 1:ii–iii.

23. For the most incisive study, and the one I have relied on throughout this chapter, see Antonio De Castro, S.J., "Jesuits in the Philippines: From the Revolution to the Transition from the Spanish Jesuits to the American Jesuits, 1898–1927" (PhD diss., Pontifical Gregorian University, 2000).

24. Fr. Pablo Pastells to José Rizal, October 12, 1892, in Raul J. Bonoan, S.J., ed., *The Rizal–Pastells Correspondence: The Hitherto Unpublished Letters of José Rizal and Portions of Fr. Pablo Pastells's Fourth Letter and Translation of the Correspondence, Together with a Historical Background and Theological Critique* (Manila, 1994), 126.

25. José Rizal to Ferdinand Blumentritt, February 2, 1890, in *The Rizal–Blumentritt Correspondence* (Manila, 1961), 328.

26. Rizal to Pastells, September 1, 1892, in Bonoan, *The Rizal–Pastells Correspondence*, 121.

27. Jose S. Arcilla, S.J., "Ateneo de Manila: Problems and Policies, 1859–1939," in *The Jesuit Educational Tradition: The Philippine Experience*, ed. Raul J. Boanoan, S.J., and James A. O'Donnell, S.J. (Manila, 1986), 37; P. Bertrán to Governor General Izquierdo, December 24, 1872, in John N. Schumacher, *Father Jose Burgos: Priest and Nationalist* (Manila, 1972), 265.

28. Francisco Foradada, S.J., *La soberanía de España en Filipinas* (Madrid, 1897), excerpted in John N. Schumacher, S.J., *Readings in Philippine Church History*, 2nd ed. (Quezon City, 1987), 268.

29. "Guidelines from the General," July 12, 1902, in III-6-112, APPSJ; Martín to Edward Purbrick, May 9, 1900, in box 124, folder 4, MPA.

30. Quoted in Eguillor, Revuelta, and de Diego, *Memorias Del P. Luis Martín General de la Compañía de Jesús (1846–1906)*, 751.

31. William J. Callahan, *The Catholic Church in Spain, 1875–1998* (Washington, DC, 1998), 52.

32. Edward Purbrick, S.J., to Fr. Daughterty, S.J., April 21, 1898, in letters of Prov. Purbrick, in 1897–1900 file, Prov. correspondence misc file, NYPSJ.

33. Pio Pi, S.J., to Luis Martín, S.J., May 24 1898, in Philippinae, box 1001, XIII-10, ARSI; Gaspar Colomer to mission superior, November 25, 1898, in José S. Arcilla, S.J., ed. and trans., *Jesuit Missionary Letters from Mindanao, Volume Two: The Zamboanga-Basilan-Joló Mission* (Quezon City, 1993), 556–57.

34. Pastells, *Misión de la Compaña de Jesús de Filipinas en el siglo XIX*, 424. On the number of Jesuits, see Manuel Revuelta González, "Las Misiones de los jesuitas espanoles en America y Filipinas durante el siglo XIX," *Miscellanea Comillas* 46 (1988): 386.

35. Fr. Francisco Sino to Fr. Martín, August 1, 1899, in Philippinae, box 1001, XIV-19, ARSI; Francisco Sino, S.J., to P. Luis Adroer [prov. of Aragon], July 8, 1900, in Philippinae, box 1002, I-3, ARSI.

36. The Aragón Province of the Jesuits averaged almost 40 percent of their men working outside Spain in the period before World War I, while the Maryland–New York Province averaged 2 percent outside the United States. See De Castro, "Jesuits in the Philippines," 684–85.

37. Robert Gannon to fathers and brothers of Maryland–New York Province, September 15, 1904, in III-6-115, APPSJ.

38. Ibid.

39. For superb analysis on the broad topic, see Katherine D. Moran, "The Devotion of Others: Secular American Attractions to Catholicism, 1870–1930" (PhD diss., Johns Hopkins University, 2009), 144–212; William Stanton to a friend, February 7, 1902, in William T. Kane, S.J., *A Memoir of William A. Stanton, S.J.* (Saint Louis, 1918), 105; Donna J. Amoroso, "Inheriting the 'Moro Problem': Muslim Authority and Colonial Rule in British Malaya and the Philippines," in *The American Colonial State in the Philippines: Global Perspectives*, ed. Julian Go and Anne L. Foster (Durham, NC, 2003), 122.

40. Thomas B. Cannon, "Jesuits in the Philippines, 1889–1934," *WL* 77 (1948): 302; William A. Stanton to a friend, February 7, 1902, in Kane, *A Memoir of William A. Stanton*, 105.

41. H. W. Brands, *Bound to Empire: The United States and the Philippines* (New York, 1992), 72.

42. Robert Gannon to fathers and brothers of Maryland–New York Province, September 15, 1904, in III-6-115, APPSJ; Cannon, "Jesuits in the Philippines," 302.

43. Kenton J. Clymer, *Protestant Missionaries in the Philippines, 1898–1916: An Inquiry into the American Colonial Mentality* (Urbana, IL 1986); Peter G. Gowing, "The Disentanglement of Church and State Early in the American

Regime in the Philippines," in *Studies in Philippine Church History*, ed. Gerald Anderson (Ithaca, NY, 1969), 219; First Special Synod, [1906], in Casimir J. Grotnik, ed., *The Polish National Catholic Church: Minutes of the First Eleven General Synods, 1904–1963*, trans. Theodore L. Zawistowski (Scranton, PA, 2002), 41–42; Fr. John Thompkins, "A Letter from Vigan," *WL* 43 (1914): 54.

44. "Miss Crabtree on the Filipinos," *America* 9 (1913): 425.

45. *Report of the Philippine Commission to the President, Vol. IV* (Washington, DC, 1901), 109–11.

46. Ibid.; Fr. Pio Pi to José de la Viña, November 27, 1898, in IV-251, APPSJ; Gowing, "The Disentanglement of Church and State," 205.

47. James Monaghan, S.J., "Memorandum on the Religious Situation in the Philippines" [September 27, 1908], in Philippinae, box 1002, VI-22, ARSI.

48. Horacio de la Costa, S.J., *Light Cavalry* (Manila, [1942] 1997), 434.

49. Clarence Edwards to Daniel Hudson, C.S.C., October 23, 1904, in x-4-3. More generally, see Sister Mary Dorita Clifford, B.V.M., "Religion and the Public Schools in the Philippines: 1899–1906," in *Studies in Philippine Church History*, ed. Clifford Anderson (Ithaca, NY, 1969), 301–24.

50. Roosevelt to Maria Longworth Storer, March 27, 1899, in Elting E. Morison, ed., *The Letters of Theodore Roosevelt, Volume 2: The Years of Preparation, 1898–1900* (Cambridge, MA, 1951), 972.

51. John W. Burgess, "The 'Cultureconflict' in Prussia," *Political Science Quarterly* 2 (June 1887): 317.

52. Woodstock House Diary, November 4, 1884, in box 3, WCA; John Louis Ciani, "Across a Wide Ocean: Salvatore Maria Brandi, S.J., and the 'Civilta Cattolica' from Americanism to Modernism, 1891–1914" (PhD diss., University of Virgina, 1992), 69; Charles A. Brady, *The First Hundred Years: Canisius College, 1870–1970* (Buffalo, NY, 1970), 52–53.

53. Ambrose Aguis to Fr. Rudolph Meyer, December 29, 1906, in Philippinae, box 1002, IV-14, ARSI; Fr. John J. Thompkins, S.J., "Work at Manila," *WL* 34 (1905): 159; Fr. John J. Thompkins, "Our Missionaries to the Philippines," *WL* 34 (1905): 391–94.

54. William Stanton to a friend, November 21, 1901, in Kane, *A Memoir of William A. Stanton*, 92.

55. Mrs. William Howard Taft, *Recollections of Full Years* (New York, 1914), 138.

56. Horacio de la Costa, *Light Cavalry* (Manila, [1942] 1997), 227.

57. José Algué to provincial, November 4, 1898, in Arcilla, "The Jesuits during the Philippine Revolution," 315. More generally, see James Francis Warren, "Scientific Superman: Father José Algué, Jesuit Meteorology, and the Philippines under American Rule, 1897–1924," in *Colonial Crucible: Empire*

in the Making of the Modern American State, ed. Alfred W. McCoy and Francisco Scarano (Madison, WI, 2009), 508–22.

58. Fr. José Algué, "Manilla: An Interview with Admiral Dewey," November 28, 1898, in *WL* 28 (1898): 116.

59. W. B. Rogers, S.J., to Mr. T. H. Pardo de Tavera, May 27, 1903, in x-4-3; Paul Kramer, *The Blood of Government: Race, Empire, the United States, and the Philippines* (Chapel Hill, NC, 2006), 212, 264.

60. Pastells, *Misión de la Compañia de Jesús De Filipinas en el siglo XIX*, 426.

61. John J. Thompkins, "Notes from Vigan," *WL* 36 (1907): 323.

62. "The Grand Act at St. Louis University," *WL* 32 (1903): 89.

63. Ibid., 82–93; Manuel Peypoch, S.J., "Acto General de Teología en la Universidad de San Luis, Missouri, Estados Unidos el Día 29 de Abril de 1903," *Cartas Edificantes de la Asistencia de España* 3 (1903): 244–62.

64. Gustavo Niederlin to Society of Jesus, November 1, 1904, IV-292, APPSJ.

65. C. R. Edwards to Dean C. Worcester, May 5, 1904, copy in in *Fifth Annual Report of the Philippine Commission, 1904* (Washington, DC, 1905), 559; José Algué, S.J., to C. R. Edwards, May 1, 1904, copy in *Fifth Annual Report of the Philippine Commission*, 559. For a detailed description, including copies of correspondence, see José Algué, "Viaje del P. José Algué à los Estados Unidos y su intervención en la Exposición Universal de San Luis," *Cartas Edificantes de la Asistencia de España* 4 (1904): 320–63, Taft reference on 344, text of Algué speech on 353–54; William Howard Taft, *The Church and Our Government in the Philippines* (Notre Dame, IN, 1904), 8.

66. William A. Stanton to a friend, November 21, 1901, in Kane, *A Memoir of William A. Stanton*, 97.

67. John N. Schumacher, S.J., *Growth and Decline: Essays on Philippine Church History* (Manila, 2009), 252.

68. Robert Brown, S.J., to Father General, [1908], in Philippinae, box 1002, VI-20, ARSI; J. N. Schumacher, "Filipinas," in *Diccionario histórico de la Compañía de Jesús*, ed. Charles E. O'Neill and Joaquín María Dominguez (Rome, 2001), 2:1427.

69. Fr. Manuel Sauras, S.J., to Fr. Pablo Pastells, S.J., September 30, 1916, in Antonio F. B. De Castro, S.J., "Jesuit Linguistic Battles, ca. 1898–1932: Language, Power, and the Filipino Soul," *Philippine Studies* 58 (2010): 135.

70. James Monaghan, S.J., "Memorandum on the Religious Situation in the Philippines" [September 27, 1908], in Philippinae, box 1002, VI-22, ARSI.

71. Ibid.

72. Archbishop Ambrose Agius to Fr. Francis X. Wernz, S.J., November 19, 1906, copy in Pedro S. De Achútegui, S.J., and Miguel A. Bernad, S.J., *Religious Revolution in the Philippines: The Life and Church of Gregorio Aglipay, 1860–1960, Volume I: 1860–1940* (Manila, 1960), 372–73.

73. William Cameron Forbes, *The Philippine Islands, Volume I* (Boston, 1928), 482.

74. Fr. John Thompkins to Fr. Hanselman, December 19, 1919, in Philippinae, box 1003, VI-16, ARSI.

75. Marcial Sola, S.J., to Rev. Anthony Maas, S.J., January 16, 1918, in Spanish asst. file, NYPSJ.

76. Manuel Peypoch, S.J., to Rev. Father José Barrachina, S.J., December 28, 1911, in Philippinae, box 1002, IX-15, ARSI; Norberto Torcal, "Spanish Politics and Bullfights," *America* 5 (September 2, 1911): 491–92.

77. James Monaghan, S.J., "Memorandum on the Religious Situation in the Philippines" [September 27, 1908], in Philippinae, box 1002, VI-22, ARSI.

78. Quoted in "Our Missionaries to the Philippines," *WL* 34 (1905): 391.

79. Quoted in "Manila's Young Men Becoming Fastidious," *New York Times*, June 3, 1912, 5.

80. Fr. Philip M. Finegan, Varia, *WL* 39 (1910): 270.

81. Fr. Philip M. Finegan, Varia, *WL* 36 (1907): 415. On American bishops, see Richard Lee Skolnik, "The Catholic Church and Independence, 1898–1916," *Philippine Historical Review* 6 (1973): 91–113.

82. Brands, *Bound to Empire*, 104.

83. P. J. Barrachina to Zamesa, February 15, 1912, in Philippinae, box 1002, X-8, ARSI; Fr. José Clos to Franz Wernz, S.J., July 24, 1913, in Philippinae, box 1002, XI-24, ARSI; "Fr. Philip M. Finegan, S.J.," *WL* 60 (1931): 297.

84. Thomas Becker to provincial, September 10, 1913, in V-2-047, APPSJ; Ledóchowski to Joseph Rockwell, March 4, 1921, in correspondence from the general file, NYPSJ.

85. Erez Manela, *The Wilsonian Moment: Self-Determination and the International Origins of Anticolonial Nationalism* (New York, 2007); Pankaj Mishra, *From the Ruins of Empire: The Revolt against the West and the Remaking of Asia* (London, 2012), 187–215; Francis Burton Harrison, *The Cornerstone of Philippine Independence: A Narrative of Seven Years* (New York, 1922), 182–91.

86. Brands, *Bound to Empire*, 122.

87. De Castro is the first to analyze this in detail. See his "Jesuits in the Philippines," 552. See also Carlos Suria, S.J., *History of the Catholic Church in Gujarat* (Gujarat, 1990), 214–24.

88. Ledóchowski to Joseph Rockwell, June 4, 1920, in letters from general file, NYPSJ.

89. Fr. Edward P. Duffy, S.J., to the provincial of Maryland–New York, May 12, 1921, copy in De Castro "Jesuits in the Philippines," 664–67; Ledóchowski to P. Juan Guim, March 4, 1921, copy in De Castro, "Jesuits in the Philippines," 651–52.

90. Fr. Edward P. Duffy, S.J., to the provincial of Maryland–New York, May 12, 1921, copy in De Castro "Jesuits in the Philippines," 664–67.

91. Joaquin Vilallonga to Laurence Kelly, November 8, 1924, in IV-37, APPSJ.

92. Rockwell circular, April 13, 1921, in I.A 3.3.c, box 2, WCA.

93. Diary of a voyage to the Philippines, no author, in III-33-035, APPSJ; entry of April 19, 1921, in Woodstock House diary, in box 3, WCA; Henry L. Irwin, "Diary of a Philippine Missionary," *WL* 50 (1921): 319–31; Henry L. Irwin, "Diary of a Philippine Missionary," *WL* 51 (1922): 398–99.

94. Vincent Kennally, S.J., to Francis Breen, December 23, 1922, in file 5, box 96, MP.

95. Byrne to provincial, August 13, 1921, in Philippinae, box 1003, VIII-35, ARSI; Patrick Rafferty, S.J., to Joseph Hanselman, December 22, 1921, in Philippinae, box 1003, VIII-61, ARSI.

96. For preceding paragraph as well, see Charles Connor to Father General Wlodomir Ledóchowski, December 13, 1921, in 1921 consultors' report file, Philippines box, NYPSJ; Charles Connor to Father General Wlodomir Ledóchowski, January 19, 1922, in 1921 consultors' report file, Philippines box, NYPSJ.

97. Arthur J. Hohman to Ledóchowski, December 15, 1921, Philippinae, box 1003, VIII-54, ARSI.

98. Charles Connor to Father General Wlodomir Ledóchowski, December 13, 1921, in 1921 consultors' report file, Philippines box, NYPSJ; Charles Connor to Father General Wlodomir Ledóchowski, January 19, 1922, in 1921 consultors' report file, Philippines box, NYPSJ; Hohman to Joseph Rockwell, December 18, 1921, in Philippinae, box 1003, VIII-53, ARSI; J. M. Prendergast to Joseph Hanselman, March 14, 1921, in Philippinae, box 1401, ARSI.

99. Burchard Villiger to Peter Beckx, July 28, 1858, copy in Noll, "A History of St. Joseph's College," appendix; Gerald L. McKevitt, "Italian Jesuits in Maryland: A Clash of Theological Cultures," *Studies in Jesuit Spirituality* 39 (Spring 2007): 15.

100. Vilallonga to Ledóchowski, October 31, 1921, in Philippinae, box 1003, VIII-46, ARSI.

101. Connor to Ledóchowski, January 19, 1922, in 1921 consultors' report file, in Philippines box, NYPSJ; Patrick Rafferty, S.J., to Joseph Hanselman, December 22, 1921, in Philippinae, box 1003, VIII 61, ARSI; Elliot Gorn, *The Manly Art: Bare-Knuckle Prize Fighting in America* (Ithaca, NY, 1986), 196–97.

102. Hohman to Joseph Hanselman, December 22, 1921, in PPSJ.

103. Charles Connor to Father General Wlodomir Ledóchowski, December 13, 1921, in 1921 consultors' report file, Philippines box, NYPSJ.; Charles

Connor to Father General Wlodomir Ledóchowski, January 19, 1922, in 1921 consultors' report file, Philippines box, NYPSJ.

104. Wlodimir Ledóchowski, S.J., "An Exhortation to Our Writers," in *Selected Writings of Father Ledóchowski* (Chicago, 1945), 815–16.

105. Meeting of provincials, April 20, 1921, in Marylandiae, box 1020, I-4, ARSI.

106. Ledóchowski to Joseph Rockwell, June 17, 1921, in letters from general file, NYPSJ.

107. Ledóchowski to Joseph Rockwell, October 22, 1921, in letters from general File, NYPSJ.

108. Ledóchowski to Fr. Charles Connor, March 30, 1922 in 1921 Consultors report file, Philippines box, NYPSJ.

109. Ledóchowski to Joseph Rockwell, June 17, 1921, in letters from general file, NYPSJ; Ledóchowski to Laurence Kelly, October 28, 1922, in letters from general file, NYPSJ.

110. Ledóchowski to Laurence Kelly, December 16, 1922, in letters from general file, NYPSJ.

111. Francis Byrne to Joseph Rockwell May 22, 1922, in V-2-102, APPSJ; Francis Byrne to Joseph Rockwell, March 29, 1922, Philippinae, box 1004, I-37, ARSI; Vilallonga to Ledóchowski, March 30, 1922, in Philippinae, box 1004, I-38, ARSI; Vilallonga to Rockwell, October 10, 1921, in PPSJ.

112. Ledóchowski to Joseph Rockwell, June 17, 1921, in correspondence from the general file, NYPSJ; Jose S. Arcilla, S.J., *150: The Ateneo Way* (Quezon City, 2009), 105.

113. Francis Byrne to Joseph Rockwell, August 13, 1921, in Philippinae, box 1003, VIII-15, ARSI.

114. Francis Byrne to Joseph Hanselman, January 4, 1922, in Philippinae, box 1004, I-9, ARSI.

115. Francis Bryne to Joseph Rockwell, June 23, 1921, in III-6-138, APPSJ.

116. Francis Byrne to Joseph Rockwell, August 13, 1921, in Philippinae, box 1003, VIII-15, ARSI; Francis Byrne to Joseph Hanselman, January 4, 1922, in Philippinae, box 1004, I-9, ARSI.

117. Review of the Ateneo Cadet Corps by His Excellency Governor General Leonard Wood, [1925], in V-2-221, APPSJ; Miguel Bernad, *Unusual and Ordinary: Biographical Sketches of Some Philippine Jesuits* (Quezon City, 2006), 54.

118. Byrne to Fr. Hanselman, January 9, 1922, in Philippinae, box 1004, I-9, ARSI; Brand, *Bound to Empire*, 129–37; "Pioneers in the Philippines," *WL* 71 (1942): 187.

119. Richard O'Brien to Ledóchowski, January 22, 1929, in PPSJ.

120. Thomas Shanahan, S.J., to Edward Philipps, S.J., April 6, 1930, in IV-427, APPSJ.

121. Richard A. O'Brien, S.J., to Ledochówski, January 22, 1929, in PPSJ.

122. Unknown to Ledóchowski, in Phillipinae, box 1004, I-7, ARSI; Vilallonga to Joseph Rockwell, October 10, 1921, in Phillipinae, box 1003, VIII-43, ARSI.

123. McKevitt, *Brokers of Culture*, 249–59; Nicholas Russo, S.J., "The Origins and Progress of Our Italian Mission in New York," *WL* 25 (1896): 35–43.

124. Robert Anthony Orsi, *The Madonna of 115th Street: Faith and Community in Italian Harlem, 1880–1950* (New Haven, CT, 1985). See also Timothy Matovina, *Latino Catholicism: Transformation in American's Largest Church* (Princeton, NJ, 2011), 42–43.

125. Joseph I. Stoffel, S.J., "Regency in the Philippines (1934–1937)," 42–43, 51, in box 92, WCA.

126. Notanda for 1932–33, St. Ignatius Church, May 14, 1932, in V-18-018, APPSJ; James Hayes, S.J., to Ledóchowski, July 12, 1932, in Philippinae, box 1005, VI-21, ARSI; Schumacher, *Growth and Decline*, 252–53.

127. Varia, *WL* 62 (1933): 275–76.

128. Richard O'Brien to Ledóchowski, January 17, 1928, in PPSJ.

129. William F. Jordan, S.J., to Father General, May 1, 1939, in Philippinae, box 1006, VI-36, ARSI; Henry C. Avery, S.J., to Father General, January 20, 1934, in Philippinae, box 1006, I-15, ARSI; Henry C. Avery, S.J., to Father General, July 22, 1935, in Philippinae, box 1006, II-35, ARSI; Richard O'Brien to Father General, January 17, 1928, in Philippinae, box 1005, II-8, ARSI.

CONCLUSION

1. John Courtney Murray, S.J., "Governmental Supervision of Schools in the Philippines," *WL* 58 (1929): 48–53.

2. John Courtney Murray, "The Construction of a Christian Culture" [1940], in *Bridging the Sacred and the Secular: Selected Writings of John Courtney Murray, S.J.*, ed. J. Leon Hooper, S.J. (Washington, DC, 1994), 101–24; John Courtney Murray, *We Hold These Truths: Catholic Reflections on the American Proposition* (New York, 1960), 12.

3. John Courtney Murray, S.J., "One Work of the One Church," *Catholic Mind* 48 (June 1950): 358–64.

4. Peter McDonough, *Men Astutely Trained: A History of the Jesuit in the American Century* (New York, 1992), 78–79, 81; Dominque Avon and Philippe Rocher, *Les jésuites et la sociéte française XIX–XX siècles* (Toulouse, Fr., 2001), 153–62.

5. Fr. Peter Beckx to provincials of the Society of Jesus, January 10, 1855, reprinted in Joseph Burnichon, S.J., *La Compagnie de Jésus en France Histoire d'un Siècle 1814–1914 Tome Troisième: 1860–1880* (Paris, 1922), 669.

6. Samuel Moyn, *Christian Human Rights* (Philadelphia, 2015), 1–4.

7. James J. Meany, S.J., "The Hartendorp Case" (history seminar paper), in III-6-217-b, APPSJ; James J. Meany, S.J., "The Hartendorf Case," *WL* 72 (1943): 203–22.

8. More generally, see Thomas Kselman and Joseph A. Buttigieg, eds., *European Christian Democracy: Historical Legacies and Comparative Perspectives* (Notre Dame, IN, 2003); sermon by Anthony Keane, S.J., February 25, 1945, in III-6-389, APPSJ; James B. Reuter, S.J., and James J. McMahon, S.J., et al., "Mindanao to Santo Tomas," *WL* 74 (1945): 231.

9. W. C. Repetti, S.J., "Experiences in the Philippines during WWII," *WL* 91 (1962): 235–38; John Courtney Murray, S.J., "Current Theology: Christian Co-operation," *Theological Studies* 3 (January 1942): 413–31. On the general topic, see Kevin M. Schultz, *Tri-Faith America: How Catholics and Jews Held Postwar America to Its Protestant Promise* (New York, 2011), 4–7, 43–67; Moyn, *Christian Human Rights*, 65–100; John T. McGreevy, *Catholicism and American Freedom: A History* (New York, 2003), 166–88, 208–15.

10. Leo Cullum, S.J., to Murray, October, 28, 1952, in folder 39, box 1, JCM; Murray to Leo Cullum, S.J., February 1, 1953, in folder 39, box 1, JCM; John Courtney Murray, "The Problem of Free Speech" [1953], in Hooper, *Bridging the Sacred and the Secular*, 54–70.

11. Henri de Lubac, S.J., "La Question des éveques sous l'occupation," *Revue des Deux Mondes* 58 ([1944] February 1992): 70; Karl Rahner, *I Remember*, trans. Harvey D. Egan, S.J. (New York, 1985), 87.

12. Peter R. D'Agostino, *Rome in America: Transnational Catholic Ideology from the Risorgimento to Fascism* (Chapel Hill, NC, 2004), 202–8.

13. Seán Faughnan, "The Jesuits and the Drafting of the Irish Constitution of 1937," *Irish Historical Studies* 26 (1988): 79–102, quote on 89; Guiliana Chamades, "The Vatican and the Reshaping of the European International Order after the First World War," *Historical Journal* 56 (2013): 955–76.

14. Anna Su, "Woodrow Wilson and the Origins of the International Law of Religious Freedom," *Journal of the History of International Law* 15 (2013): 235–67; David M. O'Brien and Yasuo Ohkoshki, *To Dream of Dreams: Religious Freedom and Constitutional Politics in Postwar Japan* (Honolulu, 1996).

15. "Reports of Trouble for the Church Developing in the Philippines under Japanese Domination," July 7, 1942, in II-3-4, APPSJ; Alfredo G. Parpan, S.J., "A Study of Church–State Relations during the Japanese Occupation: The Jesuits in the Philippines (1942–1945)" (MA thesis, University of the Phillipines, 1979), 103–7; Sheldon Garon, *Molding Japanese Minds: The State in Everyday Life* (Princeton, NJ, 1987), 84–87.

16. Joseph A. Komonchak, "The Silencing of John Courtney Murray," in *Cristianesimo nella storia: Saggi in onore di Giuseppe Alberigo*, ed. Albert Melloni et al. (Bologna, 1996), 659–702; Henri de Lubac, *At the Service of the Church:*

Henri de Lubac Reflects on the Circumstances That Occasioned His Writings, trans. Anne Elizabeth Englund (San Francisco, 1993), 60–79.

17. *Gaudium et Spes* [1965], para. 1.

18. Olivier Roy, *Secularism Confronts Islam*, trans. George Holoch (New York, 2007), 37–42.

19. Patrick Kerkstra, "Is St. Joe's Prep Still a Power Factory?" *Philadelphia Magazine* (February 2013), http://www.phillymag.com/articles/big-men -campus/ (accessed June 15, 2015).

20. John F. Hurley, S.J., *Wartime Superior in the Philippines*, ed. José S. Arcilla, S.J. (Manila, 2005), 122–37.

21. "Fr. Carmelus Polino," *WL* 17 (1888): 385–86. On the inability (or unwillingness) of Catholic missionaries to promote democracy in the nineteenth century, see Robert D. Woodberry, "The Missionary Roots of Liberal Democracy," *American Political Science Review* 106 (May 2012): 244–74.

22. Antonio F. B. De Castro, S.J., "Jesuits in the Philippines: From the Revolution to the Transition from the Spanish Jesuits to the American Jesuits, 1898–1927 (PhD diss., Pontifical Gregorian University, 2000), 684.

23. John T. McGreevy, *Parish Boundaries: The Catholic Encounter with Race in the Twentieth-Century Urban North* (Chicago, 1996), 249–64; John Connelly, *From Enemy to Brother: The Revolution in Catholic Teaching on the Jews* (Cambridge, MA, 2012), 50–55, 98–101, 117–21.

24. J. Franklin Ewing to John Hurley, April 17, 1941, in IV-1120, APPSJ; J. Franklin Ewing, S.J., "Local Social Custom and Christian Social Action," in *Social Action in Mission Lands: Proceedings of the Fordham University Conference of Mission Specialists*, ed. J. Franklin Ewing (New York, 1955), 38; An Vandenberghe, "Beyond Pierre Charles: The Emergence of Belgian Missiology Refined," in *Mission and Science: Missiology Revised, 1850–1940*, ed. Carine Dujardin and Claude Prudhomme (Leuven, Bel., 2015), 162–69; Edward Murphy, S.J., *Teach Ye All Nations: The Principles of Catholic Missionary Work* (New York, 1957).

25. Étienne Fouilloux, "L'Action populaire au temps de la reconstruction, 1946–1958," *Chrétiens et Sociétés XVIe–XXIe siècles* 11 (2004): 49–60; Jean-Yves Calvez, *Traversées Jesuites: Mémoires de France, de Rome, du monde, 1958–1988* (Paris, 2009), 21–23; Klaus Schatz, *Geschichte der deutschen Jesuiten, Vol. 4, 1945–1983* (Münster, Ger., 2014), 324–25.

26. General Congregation 29, decree 5, [1946], and General Congregation 30, decree 54, [1957], in John W. Padberg, S.J., et al., *For Matters of Greater Moment: The First Thirty Jesuit General Congregations: A Brief History and a Translation of the Decrees* (Saint Louis, 1994), 624, 675.

27. J. Masson, "L'Église ouverte sur le monde," *Nouvelle Revue Théologique* 84 (1962): 1032–43, esp 1038. The parallels with Protestant missionaries—also shaped by training in anthropology, and concerned about ties between

Christianity and colonialism—are striking. See David A. Hollinger, *After Cloven Tongues of Fire: Protestant Liberalism in Modern American History* (Princeton, NJ, 2013), 26.

28. Joseph Mulry to unknown, March 22, 1936, Jesuit seminary mission bureau records, NYPSJ; Ledóchowski to Joseph Rockwell, June 17, 1921, in correspondence from the general file, NYPSJ; Victor B. Ibabao, S.J., "Aspects of Catholic Social Action in the Philipppines Prior to World War II: The Contributions of Fr. Joseph A. Mulry, the Jesuits, and the Ateneo Alumni" (MA thesis, Ateneo de Manila, 1986).

29. Fr. Luis Pacquing to Rev. Laurence J. Kelly, January 22, 1927, in III-6-157, APPSJ; Peter Lutz to Laurence J. Kelly, January 23, 1927, in III-6-158, APPSJ; Thomas Shanahan to Father General Ledóchowski, September 25, 1930, in PPSJ.

30. Edward C. Philipps, S.J., to Henry Avery, S.J., November 20, 1933, in V-2 300, APPSJ.

31. Status Promulgandus, "Si et Quando" [1944], in IV-1191-2, APPSJ.

32. Horacio de la Costa, *The Jesuits in the Philippines, 1581–1768* (Cambridge, MA, 1961); Horacio de la Costa, S.J., "Riding the Whirlwind," *Social Order* 2 (1952): 247.

33. *Gaudium et Spes* [1965], para. 75, 84–85. See also Boris Vilallonga, "The Theoretical Origins of Catholic Nationalism in Nineteenth-Century Europe," *Modern Intellectual History* 11 (August 2014): 331.

34. Provincials of the Society of Jesus, "The Jesuits in Latin America" [1968], in Alfred T. Hennelly, ed., *Liberation Theology: A Documentary History* (Maryknoll, NY, 1990), 77–83; Horacio de la Costa, S.J., "The Missionary Apostolate in East and Southeast Asia" [1972], in Horacio de la Costa, S.J., *Selected Homilies and Religious Reflections*, ed. Robert M. Paterno (Manila, 2002), 252–71; Pedro Arrupe, "Talk to the Jesuits of the Philippines" [September 19, 1971], in Pedro Arrupe, *Jesuit General in the Philippines* (Manila, 1972), 142; "Report on the Dialogue with the Father General" [September 19, 1971], in Arrupe, *Jesuit General in the Philippines*, 153.

35. For this and the preceding two paragraphs, see Karl Rahner, S.J., "Towards a Fundamental Theological Interpretation of Vatican II," *Theological Studies* 40 (1979): 716–27.

36. Adolfo Nicolás, S.J., "Depth, Universality, and Learned Ministry: Challenges to Jesuit Higher Education Today," in *Shaping the Future: Networking Jesuit Higher Education for a Globalizing World: Report of the Mexico City Conference, April 2010*, ed. Frank Brennan, S.J. (Washington, DC, 2010), 15.

37. Austen Ivereigh, *The Great Reformer: Francis and the Making of a Radical Pope* (New York, 2014), 64, 183.

38. http://www.news.va/en/news/pope-jesuits-brave-and-expert-rowers-in -barque-of (accessed August 23, 2015); Pope Francis at Closing Mass of

the Eighth World Meeting of Families, September 27, 2015, https://w2
.vatican.va/content/francesco/en/homilies/2015/documents/papa-fran
cesco_20150927_usa-omelia-famiglie.html (accessed November 11, 2015);
Pope Francis speech at World Meeting of Popular Movements in Santa Cruz,
Bolivia, July 9, 2015, http://www.news.va/en/news/pope-francis-speech-at
-world-meeting-of-popular-mo (accessed July 11, 2015).

ACKNOWLEDGMENTS

I sometimes wondered if I was the only historian of the modern United States trying to decipher handwritten letters. In Latin.

For help with translations from not just Latin but also the many languages used by Jesuits, thanks to Jasmin Avila, Charlie Ducey, James Farris (who graciously allowed me to use his translation of Fr. Ferdinand Helias's Latin memoirs), Doris Jankovits, Hannah Mattis, Liz McCorry, and especially Adam Snyder. Adam served as a research assistant, as did, at various times, Michael Ginocchio, Joseph Henares, John Joseph Shanley, Jonathan Riddle, and Catherine Godfrey-Howell. Jeffrey Bain-Conkin designed the maps.

I am grateful for the care Jesuits and their colleagues take in preserving and writing the Society of Jesus's extraordinary history, staffing and organizing at their own expense archives and historical journals open to all. Steve Schloesser, S.J., invited me to lecture at Loyola University in Chicago, peppered me with excellent suggestions, and provided an exceptionally generous reading of the manuscript. He also curated, along with Ellen Skerrett, a terrific exhibit on the material culture of Jesuits and nineteenth-century religious women, Crossings and Dwellings, on display at the Loyola Museum of Art in Chicago in 2014. Kyle Roberts and his students, also at Loyola, put together a stimulating project on Jesuit libraries that will be of significant use to historians, with early results available at http://jesuitlibraries provenanceproject.com/.

I first met the world's leading historian of the Society, John O'Malley, S.J., many years ago at a memorable dinner in Fiesole and I have been grateful for his friendship ever since. As I completed this project, Tom Banchoff and José Casanova from the Berkley Center at Georgetown University invited me to join theirs on the Jesuits and globalization. I benefited from their orchestration of a stimulating set of conversations and essays, soon to be published as *The Jesuits and Globalization* from Georgetown University Press. Philip Endean, S.J., Sabine Pavone, and Antoni Ucerler, S.J., improved my contribution, which uses brief sections from this volume's introduction, first chapter, and conclusion. James O'Toole scrutinized an early version of chapter 2; Patricia Byrne, C.S.J., did the same for chapter 4. Mark Schwehn pushed me to sharpen the introduction.

A partial list of archivists who went beyond the call of duty begins with David Miros at the Jesuit Archives of the Central United States in Saint Louis; he answered my repeated requests with alacrity. The list also includes Peter Schineller, S.J., at the Jesuit archives in New York City, Margaret Phelan at the Sacred Heart Archives in Saint Louis and Rome, Lee Leumas at the Archives of the Archdiocese of New Orleans, and the entire staff at the Georgetown University Library's Special Collections Research Center and the University Archives at Notre Dame. Madz Tumbali, S.J., was exceptionally gracious to a Manila newcomer and is a knowledgeable steward of the rich tradition of scholarship on the history of the Society in the Philippines.

Jim Pratt, S.J., introduced me to the Jesuit archives in Rome, sent me a two euro coin in the mail with precise instructions on how to take a bus to the archives from Stazione Termini, and put me up for a week. Mauro Brunello was equally welcoming during subsequent visits. Bill Connor and Leo Vacarro started the Villiger archives at St. Joseph's Preparatory School in Philadelphia in their spare time even as they provided full-time inspiration to their lucky history students. I would say this even if they had not invited me to deliver a lecture from the pulpit used by Burchard Villiger in the Church of the Gesu. Chris Dixon and Carmen Croce helped out at Saint Joseph's University. The irrepressible Dan Joyce, S.J., hosted me more times in Philadelphia than now seems decent. My onetime Notre Dame colleague, Jerry Neyrey, S.J., arranged for me to tour Jesuit sites and examine materials in Grand Couteau, Louisiana. My current Notre Dame colleague

Tom Kselman escorted me to the Jesuit archives outside Paris and superb restaurants with equal enthusiasm.

I wrote this book while happily serving as dean of the College of Arts and Letters at Notre Dame. I say happily because of the shared purpose and camaraderie created by T. D. Ball, Rob Becht, Marie Blakey, Linda Brady, Jim Brockmole, Karin Dale, JoAnn Dellaneva, Diana Dickson, Maria Di Pasquale, Kathy Fischer, Matthew Fulcher, Kate Garry, Stuart Greene, Peter Holland, Kathy Knoll, Kristi Leininger, Mo Marnocha, Tom Merluzzi, Margaret Meserve, Dan Myers, Maura Ryan, Mark Schurr, and Dayle Seidenspinner-Núñez. Cindy Swonger and Matt Zyniewicz are especially deserving of thanks. All buoyed me during low moments, and tolerated my continued interest in teaching and research.

Provost Tom Burish allowed me to work on this project during part of spring semester 2014 and President John Jenkins, C.S.C., asked about my progress with unnerving yet helpful regularity. Our Arts and Letters Advisory Council members—led by chairpersons Jes Hagale, Bob Kill, Joe Loughery, and Patrick Rogers—inspired me with their passion for Notre Dame and the liberal arts. My agent, Geri Thoma, never wavered. Alane Mason offered characteristically shrewd editorial advice, as did Fred Appel, Karen Carter, Cindy Milstein, and their colleagues at Princeton University Press. Editor Paul Baumann and his colleagues at *Commonweal* magazine sharpened my prose and provided an opportunity to test run ideas.

Audiences at the Catholic University of America, the Gregorian University, Loyola University in Chicago, Northwestern University, the Institute for Advanced Catholic Studies at the University of Southern California, the Institute for Advanced Jesuit Studies at Boston College, the University of St. Thomas, Saint Joseph's University, Saint Louis University, the University of Pennsylvania, and the global history seminar in London asked more good questions than I could answer.

Not that I needed to leave town. Many Notre Dame colleagues—including Margaret Abruzzo, Kathy Cummings, Darren Dochuk,

Felipe Fernandez-Armesto, Brad Gregory, Tom Kselman, Tim Matovina, Rebecca McKenna, Mark Noll, Fr. Robert Sullivan, James Turner, and Tom Tweed—listened to talks, read draft chapters, or even fought their way through the manuscript. Kathy permitted me to hide out in the offices of the Cushwa Center for the Study of American Catholicism, and along with Matteo Sanfilippo of the University of Tuscia, Viterbo, organized a remarkable summer seminar on global Catholicism at Notre Dame's Rome Global Gateway in 2014. Scott Appleby read pieces of the manuscript, too, with his usual insight, but my fondest memory of our friendship during these years will be of late-night conversations gliding from history to the university and beyond.

The most vivid memories are the most intimate. Nora is now a college student; Margaret is not far behind. Patrick and Leo will soon enter high school. All this, as all parents know, in the blink of an eye.

Sharing this family adventure and these busy years with Jean remains my most enduring gift.

INDEX

Adams, John, 1–2
Adenauer, Konrad, 213
Aglipay, Gregorio, 188–89
Alacoque, Margaret Mary, 109
alcohol consumption: Bapst's efforts
    against, 36–37; Cheever's opposition
    to, 46; German radicals and, 83–84
Alembert, Jean-Baptiste d', 18
Algué, José, 192–93, 194
America (Jesuit journal of opinion), 172,
    177, 197
American and Foreign Christian Union,
    48, 49
Americanism, 164–66, 171, 180
American Party, 23; Louisiana Creoles
    in, 118; in Maine, 42, 57. *See also*
    Know-Nothing movement
Anderledy, Anthony, 19–20, 141
Angel Gabriel (John Orr), 42–43, 52, 57
anti-Catholicism: antislavery views com-
    bined with, 55–59, 78, 83, 88, 90; in
    colonial Maryland, 163; in Missouri,
    77–88; in New England, 41–55; in
    nineteenth-century America, 20, 22–23,
    24; in nineteenth-century novels,
    80–81. *See also* German revolutionaries,
    exiled; Know-Nothing movement
anticlericalism, European: Americanism
    and, 165; contrasted with Southern
    Protestants, 120; devotional style and,
    117; expulsion from Portugal in 1901
    and, 169; in France, late nineteenth-
    century, 119, 169, 183; of Gavazzi, 81;
    of German exiles in US, 78, 79, 100; in
    Italy, 169; Jesuit concerns about demo-
    cratic politics and, 176; Jesuit suspicion
    of state power based on, 160–61; of
    Kossuth, 81; reaction against, denounc-
    ing religious freedom, 215; in Spain
    after Spanish-American War, 186

anticlericalism, in Louisiana, 119, 133
anticlericalism, in Philippines, 184
anti-Communism, 213, 215
anti-Jesuit laws, German, repealed in 1917,
    174
anti-Semitism, Jesuit, 172
Anzeiger des Westens, 78–80, 82, 85, 102
Apostolate of Prayer, 112
apparitions, 122, 123, 124; of Berchmans
    to Mary Wilson, 106, 132–34, 137, 138,
    139–40; of Jesus to Sister Alacoque, 109
Aquinas, Saint Thomas, 16; Ireland's
    jab at, 164; Thomism at Woodstock
    theologate, 24
Aquino, Benigno, 217
Arboleda, Julio, 11
Arnoudt, Peter, 112
Arrupe, Pedro, 220
astronomy, 15, 25, 156, 192. *See also* obser-
    vatories, Jesuit-run
Ateneo de Manila: Adolfo Nicolás at,
    222; American and Spanish Jesuits
    often in conflict at, 195, 196–97, 201,
    202, 203, 205–6; becoming private
    Catholic school, 190; De La Costa as
    graduate of, 220; first American rectors
    of, 205–7; growth under American
    leadership, 207; Murray's teaching at,
    210; rebuilt after World War II, 217;
    significant graduates of, 217; Taft's
    recognition of, 192
Aubigne, Jean-Henri Merle d', 47
authoritarian governments, Catholic sym-
    pathy for, 211–12

Bacon, Leonard, 49
Balmes, Jaime, 18, 77
Bapst, John: appreciation for religious lib-
    erty in US, 52; becoming US citizen,
    55; Democrats allying themselves with,